# Contents

# Credits

The publisher would like to thank the following for their kind permission to reproduce their photographs:

(Key: b-bottom; c-centre; l-left; r-right; t-top)

**Alamy Images:** Bernadette Delaney 261, Blend Images 128, Catchlight Visual Services 60, Janine Wiedel Photolibrary 223, Justin Kase zsixz 206, Les Gibbon 263, Libby Welch 82, MBI 131, medicalpicture 320, Photofusion Picture Library 1, 5, 219, Photofusion Picture Library 1, 5, 219, Photofusion Picture Library 1, 5, 219, Radius Images 211, Sally and Richard Greenhill 6, Steve Skjold 87; **Digital Vision:** 123; **Getty Images:** 228, Digital Vision. 127, Martin Rogers 305; **Imagestate Media:** Bananastock. 46, 63, Bananastock. 46, 63; **iStockphoto:** David Parsons. 124, Kenneth C. Zirkel. 33, michellegibson. 86; **Pearson Education Ltd:** Gareth Boden 67, 293, Gareth Boden 67, 293, Jules Selmes 35, 51, 73, 189, Jules Selmes 35, 51, 73, 189, Jules Selmes 35, 51, 73, 189, Jules Selmes 35, 51, 73, 189, Lord and Leverett 99, 316, Lord and Leverett 99, 316, Mindstudio 9, Rob Judges 3, Studio 8. Clark Wiseman 109, 133, 285, Studio 8. Clark Wiseman 109, 133, 285, Studio 8. Clark Wiseman 109, 133, 285; **PhotoDisc:** Steve Cole 135; **Science Photo Library Ltd:** GREGORY DIMIJIAN 201, HATTIE YOUNG 209; **Shutterstock:** Adrio Communications Ltd . 196, bat-2. 113, carlosseller. 187, Christopher Futcher. 221, Diego Cervo. 112, Dmitry Naumov. 137, Elena Elisseeva. 107, Emiliano Rodriguez. 244, GWImages. 101, Hannamariah. 249, iDesign. 283, iofoto. 213, Jeff Banke. 230, jokerpro. 71, Kharidehal Abhirama Ashwin. 251, Konstantin Sutyagin. 192, 193, 195, 197, Monkey Business Images. 22, Rob Marmion. 212, Sarah Garner. 147, Sean Prior. 182, Supri Suharjoto. 145, Xsandra. 259; **TopFoto:** Topham Picturepoint 303

All other images © Pearson Education

We are grateful to the following for permission to reproduce copyright material:

**p.112, 140** The Stationery Office for an extract from *Independent inquiry into inequalities in health (The Acheson Report)* by Sir Donald Acheson, November 1998, © Crown copyright 1998; **p.112, 113, 131** Department of Health for extracts from *Choosing Health: Making healthy choices easier*, Public Health White Paper, November 2004; and *Tackling health inequalities: A Programme for Action*, July 2003, © Crown copyright 2003-2004; **p.129** Home Office for Table 12.5 'Summary of trends in last year drug use among 16- to 59-year-olds between 1996 and 2008/09', and annual costs, *British Crime Survey* (2008/9), © Crown Copyright 2009; **p.135** Office of Public Sector Information for extract from The Food Safety Act 1990, © Crown copyright 2002 – 2008; **p.227** National Statistics for Figure 19.1 "Population, Highlights" *Social Trends Archive*, February 2006, © Crown Copyright 2006;

**p.239** Mind for an extract from the Mind factsheet *Statistics 1: How common is mental distress*, www.mind.org.uk, copyright © Mind 2010; **p.270** Department for Children, Schools and Families for Figure 20.8 "The Five key areas for Every Child Matters", © Crown Copyright 2010; **p.297** Pearson Education, Inc. for Figure 29.3 'Maslow's hierarchy of needs' from *Motivation and Personality, 3rd edition* by Abraham H. Maslow, Robert D. Frager and James Fadiman, copyright © 1987, Prentice Hall. Reprinted with the permission of Pearson Education, Inc., Upper Saddle River, NJ; **p.303** Cengage Learning, Inc. for Table 29.5 'Stage theory of attachments' based on material in *Developmental Psychology, Childhood and Adolescence 6th ed* by D. R. Shaffer, 978-0534-572204, copyright © 2002, Wadsworth, a part of Cengage Learning, Inc. Reproduced by permission. www.cengage.com/permissions.

Every effort has been made to trace the copyright holders and we apologise in advance for any unintentional omissions. We would be pleased to insert the appropriate acknowledgement in any subsequent edition of this publication.

BTEC Level 3

edexcel
advancing learning, changing lives

# HEALTH & SOCIAL CARE

LEVEL 3

Book 2 BTEC National

Marilyn Billingham | Pamela Davenport | David Herne
Stuart McKie | Marjorie Snaith | Hilary Talman
Series editors: Beryl Stretch | Mary Whitehouse

A PEARSON COMPANY

Published by Pearson Education Limited, a company incorporated in England and Wales, having its registered office at Edinburgh Gate, Harlow, Essex, CM20 2JE. Registered company number: 872828

www.pearsonschoolsandfecolleges.co.uk

Edexcel is a registered trademark of Edexcel Limited

Text © Marilyn Bilingham, Pamela Davenport, David Herne, Stuart McKie, Marjorie Snaith, Beryl Stretch, Hilary Talman

First published 2010

13 12

10 9 8 7 6

British Library Cataloguing in Publication Data. A catalogue record for this book is available from the British Library.

ISBN 978 1 846907 47 0

## Copyright notice

Edited by Kelly Davis
Designed by Tony Richardson (Wooden Ark)
Typeset by Phoenix Photosetting, Chatham, Kent
Original illustrations © Pearson Education Limited 2010
Cover design by Visual Philosophy, created by eMC Design
Picture research by Pearson Education Limited
Cover images: *Front*: **Masterfile UK Ltd**; *Back*: **Imagestate Media**: Bananastock tr; **Pearson Education Ltd**: Mindstudio tl, Rob Judges ©
Printed in Spain by Grafos, S.A. Arte sobre papel

## Disclaimer

This material has been published on behalf of Edexcel and offers high-quality support for the delivery of Edexcel qualifications. This does not mean that the material is essential to achieve any Edexcel qualification, nor does it mean that it is the only suitable material available to support any Edexcel qualification. Edexcel material will not be used verbatim in setting any Edexcel examination or assessment. Any resource lists produced by Edexcel shall include this and other appropriate resources.

Copies of official specifications for all Edexcel qualifications may be found on the Edexcel website: www.edexcel.com

# About your BTEC Level 3 National Health and Social Care book

Choosing to study for a BTEC Level 3 National Health and Social Care qualification is a great decision to make for lots of reasons. It is an area to work in which gives many varied opportunities for you to make a difference to people's lives in a positive way. At the same time you are gaining skills that you can transfer to other professions later. Working in the health and social care professions can also take you to different parts of the country and overseas. The opportunities are endless.

Your BTEC Level 3 National in Health and Social Care is a **vocational** or **work-related** qualification. This doesn't mean that it will give you all the skills you need to do a job, but it does mean that you'll have the opportunity to gain specific knowledge, understanding and skills that are relevant to your chosen subject or area of work.

## What will you be doing?

The qualification is structured into **mandatory units** (ones that you must do) and **optional units** (ones that you can choose to do). How many units you do and which ones you cover depend on the type of qualification you are working towards.

| Qualifications | Credits from mandatory units | Credits from optional units | Total credits |
| --- | --- | --- | --- |
| Edexcel BTEC Level 3 Certificate in Health and Social Care | 10 | 10 specialist 10 optional | 30 |
| Edexcel BTEC Level 3 Subsidiary Diploma in Health and Social Care | 30 | 30 | 60 |
| Edexcel BTEC Level 3 Diploma in Health and Social Care | 80 | 40 | 120 |
| Edexcel BTEC Level 3 Diploma in Health and Social Care (Social Care) | 100 | 20 | 120 |
| Edexcel BTEC Level 3 Diploma in Health and Social Care (Health Sciences) | 100 | 20 | 120 |
| Edexcel BTEC Level 3 Diploma in Health and Social Care (Health Studies) | 100 | 20 | 120 |
| Edexcel BTEC Level 3 Extended Diploma in Health and Social Care | 80 | 100 | 180 |
| Edexcel BTEC Level 3 Extended Diploma in Health and Social Care (Social Care) | 110 | 70 | 180 |
| Edexcel BTEC Level 3 Extended Diploma in Health and Social Care (Health Studies) | 130 | 50 | 180 |
| Edexcel BTEC Level 3 Extended Diploma in Health and Social Care (Health Sciences) | 110 | 70 | 180 |

You may have chosen a general health and social care qualification or you may be following a more specialist route, and the units you study will reflect this. Whatever your choice, you will need to complete a mix of mandatory units and optional units.

The table below shows how each unit in the book fits into each qualification.

| Unit title | Mandatory | Optional |
| --- | --- | --- |
| Unit 9 Values and planning in social care | Diploma H&SC (SC) | Certificate H&SC<br>Subsidiary Diploma H&SC<br>Diploma H&SC |
| Unit 10 Caring for children and young people | Diploma H&SC (SC) | Certificate H&SC<br>Subsidiary Diploma H&SC<br>Diploma H&SC<br>Diploma H&SC (HSt)<br>Diploma H&SC (HSc) |
| Unit 11 Safeguarding adults and promoting independence | Diploma H&SC (SC) | Certificate H&SC<br>Subsidiary Diploma H&SC<br>Diploma H&SC<br>Diploma H&SC (HSt)<br>Diploma H&SC (HSc) |
| Unit 12 Public health | Diploma H&SC (HSt) | Certificate H&SC<br>Subsidiary Diploma H&SC<br>Diploma H&SC<br>Diploma H&SC (SC)<br>Diploma H&SC (HSc) |
| Unit 13 Physiology of fluid balance | Diploma H&SC (HSt)<br>Diploma H&SC (HSc) | |
| Unit 14 Physiological disorders | Diploma H&SC (HSt) | Certificate H&SC<br>Subsidiary Diploma H&SC<br>Diploma H&SC<br>Diploma H&SC (SC)<br>Diploma H&SC (HSc) |
| Unit 19 Applied sociological perspectives for health and social care | | Diploma H&SC<br>Diploma H&SC (SC)<br>Diploma H&SC (HSt)<br>Diploma H&SC (HSc) |
| Unit 20 Promoting health education | | Certificate H&SC<br>Subsidiary Diploma H&SC<br>Diploma H&SC<br>Diploma H&SC (SC)<br>Diploma H&SC (HSt)<br>Diploma H&SC (HSc) |
| Unit 29 Applied psychological perspectives | | Diploma H&SC<br>Diploma H&SC (SC)<br>Diploma H&SC (HSt)<br>Diploma H&SC (HSc) |

# How to use this book

This book is designed to help you through your BTEC Level 3 National Health and Social Care course. It is specifically designed to support you when you are studying for the BTEC Level 3 National qualifications. The book is divided into 9 units to reflect the units in the specification. To make your learning easier we have divided each unit into a series of topics each related to the learning outcomes and content of the qualification.

This book also contains many features that will help you use your skills and knowledge in work-related situations and assist you in getting the most from your course.

We also provide a second book (Book 1) which gives you an additional ten units for study and you will find details of this either from your tutor or at www.pearsonfe.co.uk/btecH&SC.

# Introduction

These introductions give you a snapshot of what to expect from each unit – and what you should be aiming for by the time you finish it!

# Assessment and grading criteria

This table explains what you must do to achieve each of the assessment criteria for each unit. For each assessment criterion, shown by the grade button **P**, there is an assessment activity.

# Assessment

Your tutor will set **assignments** throughout your course for you to complete. These may take the form of research, presentations, written work or research assignments. The important thing is that you evidence your skills and knowledge to date.

Stuck for ideas? Daunted by your first assignment? These learners have all been through it before…

Credit value: 10

## 12 Public health

Public health is concerned with improving the health of the population, as opposed to treating the diseases of individual patients. Public health professionals work in partnership with many other agencies to monitor the health status of the community; identify health needs; develop programmes to reduce risk; screen for early disease; control communicable disease; foster policies that promote health; plan and evaluate the provision of health care; and manage and implement change.

In this unit you will develop your understanding of the role of public health systems, their origin and development and the range of key groups that influence public health policy today. You will also learn about the key organisations that can influence and shape health policy locally, nationally and internationally. The unit sets out current patterns of ill health and considers the key factors that contribute to them. The unit also looks at how trends in health patterns are monitored, and where you can access information to look at changing patterns of ill health. The unit closes by looking at the different methods of promoting and protecting public health in terms of health education, health protection and environmental measures. You will find more information on the principles and practice of health education in Unit 20 (Health education).

### Learning outcomes

After completing this unit, you should:

1  know the origins of public health policy and current public health strategies
2  understand factors that affect health status and patterns of ill health
3  understand how public health is promoted and protected

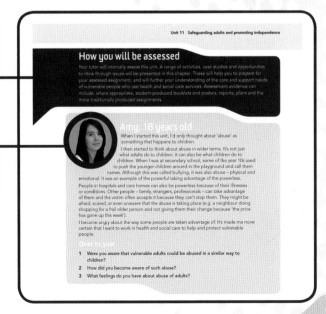

Unit 11  Safeguarding adults and promoting independence

### How you will be assessed

Your tutor will internally assess this unit. A range of activities, case studies and opportunities to think through issues will be presented in this chapter. These will help you to prepare for your assessed assignment, and will further your understanding of the care and support needs of vulnerable people who use health and social care services. Assessment evidence can include, where appropriate, student-produced booklets and posters, reports, plans and the more traditionally produced assignments.

**Amy, 18 years old**

When I started this unit, I'd only thought about 'abuse' as something that happens to children.

I then started to think about abuse in wider terms. It's not just what adults do to children; it can also be what children do to children. When I was at secondary school, some of the year 10s used to push the younger children around in the playground and call them names. Although this was called bullying, it was also abuse – physical and emotional. It was an example of the powerful taking advantage of the powerless.

People in hospitals and care homes can also be powerless because of their illnesses or conditions. Other people – family, strangers, professionals – can take advantage of them and the victim often accepts it because they can't stop them. They might be afraid, scared, or even unaware that the abuse is taking place (e.g. a neighbour doing shopping for a frail older person and not giving them their change because 'the price has gone up this week').

I became angry about the way some people are taken advantage of. It's made me more certain that I want to work in health and social care to help and protect vulnerable people.

**Over to you!**

1  Were you aware that vulnerable adults could be abused in a similar way to children?
2  How did you become aware of such abuse?
3  What feelings do you have about abuse of adults?

# Activities

There are different types of activities for you to do:
**Assessment activities** are suggestions for tasks that you might do as part of your assignment and will help you develop your knowledge, skills and understanding. **Grading tips** clearly explain what you need to do in order to achieve a pass, merit or distinction grade.

There are also suggestions for **activities** that will give you a broader grasp of the sector, stretch your imagination and deepen your skills.

## Assessment activity 9.1  P M D  BTEC

1 Using the example of one individual who uses services, write a description, in essay form, of how you would apply relevant principles and values when planning a package of holistic support for that person.

2 Extend your essay to include an analysis of the benefits to the individual, and also to the staff involved in delivery, of taking a holistic approach to planning.

3 Extend your essay to include a review of the reasons for working with professionals from more than one agency when planning support.

Identify how the key worker has assessed them and is meeting their holistic needs. Identify which professionals are involved in supporting the individual. Remember to ensure that confidentiality is maintained when undertaking this task.

**M** Interview the individual's key worker and find out the advantages for both the individual and key worker of working in a holistic way when planning support.

**D** When interviewing the key worker, ask 'what are the benefits of using different professionals in providing holistic care for your chosen individual?' Consider at least three reasons and justify each one.

### Grading tips

**P** For P1, you need to use your placement experience and produce a case study of an individual who is supported by the setting.

## Activity 9: Class debate

Identify and research some medical practices that provoke controversy and debate, such as informed consent in mental health, euthanasia, pain relief using cannabis, and organ transplantation.

You need to produce a list of arguments for and against your chosen topic and debate the issue with your group.

Think about the ethical principles you have covered in this section when putting your arguments together.

# Personal, learning and thinking skills

Throughout your BTEC Level 3 National Health and Social Care course, there are lots of opportunities to develop your personal, learning and thinking skills. Look out for these as you progress.

## PLTS

**Independent enquirer:** You will show your independent enquiry skills when relating principles and values to the support of individuals who use services.

# Functional skills

It's important that you have good English, maths and ICT skills – you never know when you'll need them, and employers will be looking for evidence that you've got these skills too.

## Functional skills

**ICT:** This task will enable you to use ICT systems and develop, present and communicate information via the information booklet you create.

# Key terms

Technical words and phrases are easy to spot, and definitions are included. The terms and definitions are also in the glossary at the back of the book.

## Key term

**Professional code of practice** – A set of guidelines and regulations, which explain the way members of a profession have to behave.

## WorkSpace

Case studies provide snapshots of real workplace issues, and show how the skills and knowledge you develop during your course can help you in your career.

There are also mini-case studies throughout the book to help you relate ideas and concepts to real life issues and situations.

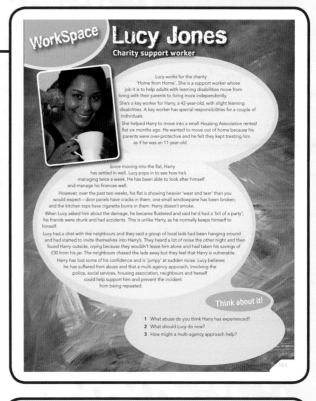

## Did you know?

Fascinating facts, figures and information are given, providing you with additional information relating to the ideas and concepts covered.

### Did you know?

The causes of anxiety in children may not always seem rational to an adult, as they are at different stages of development.

## Reflect

These are opportunities for individual reflection on, or group discussions about, your experiences in a health and social care context. They will widen your understanding and help you reflect on issues that impact on health and social care.

### Reflect

National research demonstrates that homophobia and bullying at school contribute significantly to the high suicide rate in young gay men. What negative comments or 'put downs' do people use that are about sexuality? If a gay person hears these comments, how do you think it might make them feel about themselves and the people around them?

## Further reading and resources

Recommended books, journals and websites to develop your knowledge on the subjects covered in each unit.

Unit 12 Public health

### Resources and further reading

Baird, G. et al. (2008) 'Travel time and cancer care: an example of the inverse care law?' in *Rural Remote Health* Oct–Dec; 8(4):1003. Epub 2008, Nov 13.
Baldock, J. & Ungerson, C. (1994) *Becoming Consumers of Community Care* York: Joseph Rowntree Foundation
Begg, N. (1998) 'Media dents confidence in MMR vaccine' *BMJ.* 1998;316:561
Benzeval, M., Judge, K. & Whitehead, M. (1995) *Tackling Inequalities in Health: An Agenda for Action* London: Kings Fund Publishing
Downie, R.S., Tannahill, C. & Tannahill, A. (1996) *Health Promotion Models and Values* Oxford: Oxford University Press
Draper, P. (1991) *Health Through Public Policy* London: Green Print
Ewles, L. & Simnett, I. (1999) *Promoting Health: A*

Jones, L. & Sidell, M. (1997) *The Challenge of Promoting Health: Exploration and Action* Buckingham: The Open University
Katz, J. & Peberdy, A. (1997) *Promoting Health: Knowledge and Practice* Buckingham: Macmillan/ OU Press
Naidoo, J. & Wills, J. (1996) *Health Promotion: Foundations for Practice* Edinburgh: Baillière Tindall
NHS, The Information Centre 'Statistics on Obesity, Physical Activity and Diet' (2006) England www.ic.nhs.uk/statistics-and-data-collections
Whitehead, M., Townsend, P., Davidson, N. & Davidsen, N. (1998) *Inequalities in Health: The Black Report and the Health Divide* Harmondsworth: Penguin Books

### Useful websites

British Heart Foundation www.bhf.org.uk/
Calculate your Body Mass Index

## Just checking

When you see this sort of activity, take stock! These quick activities and questions are there to check your knowledge. You can use them to see how much progress you've made or as a revision tool.

## Edexcel's assignment tips

At the end of each chapter, you'll find hints and tips to help you get the best mark you can, such as the best websites to go to, checklists to help you remember processes and really useful facts and figures.

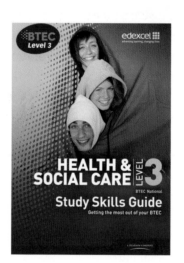

Have you read your **BTEC Level 3 National Study Skills Guide**? It's full of advice on study skills, putting your assignments together and making the most of being a BTEC Health and Social Care student.

Ask your tutor about extra materials to help you through your course. We also provide **Student Book 1** which gives you even more units for study. **The Teaching Resource Pack** which accompanies this book contains interesting videos, activities, presentations and information about the Health and Social Care sector.

Your book is just part of the exciting resources from Edexcel to help you succeed in your BTEC course.

Visit:

• www.edexcel.com/BTEC or
• www.pearsonfe.co.uk/BTEC2010

# 9 Values and planning in social care

This unit looks at how social care services need to acknowledge the uniqueness of each individual, and plan and deliver support services in a holistic way to ensure that all the individual's needs are met. By completing a range of activities you will develop an understanding of the diverse nature of the people who are receiving care and some of the ethical issues that can arise in health and social care settings. This will involve recognising the rights and responsibilities of both the individual and the social care practitioner. Sometimes these rights can appear to be in conflict. This unit enables you to explore the different issues and ethical dilemmas that could occur and discuss ways of resolving them.

By undertaking placements in care settings, you can link the theory you have been taught in the classroom to professional practice. As you progress through the unit, you will start to recognise good social care practice, develop your reflective practice skills and understand the importance of ensuring that you have professional boundaries in place. You will also gain an understanding of the importance of principles and values, which inform all health and social care practice. A vital part of principles and values is support planning, which means ensuring that individual needs are planned for and resources are put in place. As part of the support planning process, you will also gain an understanding of some of the ethical and legal boundaries that are involved when caring for vulnerable people.

## Learning outcomes

After completing this unit you should:

1 understand principles and values which underpin the planning of support for individuals

2 know processes involved in planning support for individuals

3 understand legislation, policies and codes of practice related to the planning of support for individuals

4 understand ethical principles in relation to providing support for individuals.

# Assessment and grading criteria

This table shows you what you must do in order to achieve a **pass**, **merit** or **distinction** grade, and where you can find activities in this book to help you.

| To achieve a **pass** grade, the evidence must show that you are able to: | To achieve a **merit** grade, the evidence must show that, in addition to the pass criteria, you are able to: | To achieve a **distinction** grade, the evidence must show that, in addition to the pass and merit criteria, you are able to: |
|---|---|---|
| **P1** Explain how the application of relevant principles and values will enable professionals to provide holistic support for individuals who use social services. **See Assessment activity 9.1, page 11** | **M1** Review the benefit to individuals and professional staff of taking a holistic approach to planning support. **See Assessment activity 9.1, page 11** | **D1** Analyse reasons for working with professionals from more than one agency when planning support for individuals. **See Assessment activity 9.1, page 11** |
| **P2** Identify the processes and assessment tools involved in planning support for individuals with different needs who use social services. **See Assessment activity 9.2, page 18** | **M2** Describe how three key professionals could be involved in planning support for individuals. **See Assessment activity 9.2, page 18** | **D2** Assess potential issues which could arise from the involvement of several professionals in the planning of support for individuals. **See Assessment activity 9.2, page 18** |
| **P3** Explain how one piece of legislation, one policy and one code of practice could be applied to planning support for individuals. **See Assessment activity 9.3, page 23** | | |
| **P4** Explain how to incorporate ethical principles into the provision of support for individuals. **See Assessment activity 9.4, page 30** | **M3** Justify how an ethical approach to providing support would benefit the individuals. **See Assessment activity 9.4, page 30** | |
| **P5** Explain why an ethical approach may provide workers with dilemmas. **See Assessment activity 9.4, page 30** | | |

# How you will be assessed

Your tutor will provide you with assignment briefs, which are designed to ensure that you meet the requirements of the grading criteria. You will find your placement experience very useful, as this will enable you to observe the way in which ethics, principles and values are incorporated into the practical delivery of support for individuals. You must complete all work set to a minimum of the pass criteria in order to pass this unit.

## Jessica, 17 years old

At first I found it a little difficult to understand what values and principles meant, and it was hard to see how they worked in practice. But then I went to my first placement at The Elizabethan Nursing Home and met Anna, the officer in charge, who explained the importance of policies and procedures and showed me the code of practice, which she has to follow to ensure that she can remain a registered nurse. Anna told me the importance of treating everyone with respect and making sure that they have privacy, even if they have little mobility or have difficulty talking. This was really useful for my first assignment, as I had to understand all the needs that people have, whatever age they are. My experience on placement also helped me to understand all the jobs there are in health and social care and how the different staff members have to work together to support each individual.

For my third assignment, I had to do some research on the law and how different pieces of legislation can support different people. Anna spent some time with me, explaining how this can make Mary and all the other residents safe and happy.

I found the last part of the unit challenging. We worked in groups to organise a class debate about ethical issues – this made me think about the importance of having control over my own life and what is involved when I am making decisions. I have enjoyed this unit and my placement experience and I am now determined to become a social worker.

## Over to you!

1   What qualities and skills do you think Jessica has that make her good at health and social care work?

2   Why is this unit so important?

3   What do you think you will find most interesting and most difficult in this unit?

# 1 Understand principles and values which underpin the planning of support for individuals

**Get started**

### Where do you stand?

Individually decide whether you agree or disagree with the following statements:

- Smacking children should be made illegal.
- Divorces should not be so easy.
- Gay men should be able to foster and adopt children.
- Murderers should be executed.
- Abortions should be banned.

Now get into groups of four and compare your individual responses. Were there any different opinions? Were you able to accept others' attitudes to these issues? Justify your own view to others and discuss the various views. How difficult was this for you personally? Were you able to change anyone's attitude?

## 1.1 Principles and values

When any discussion about **principles** and **values** takes place there can be a lot of disagreement, as our awareness of right and wrong is influenced by our upbringing. The influence of our parents or carers helps to form our attitudes to situations and scenarios at an early age and this process is known as **socialisation**. Values can be political, social, moral and spiritual; and the values derived from our individual experience affect our behaviour.

Individual attitudes are inextricably linked to values. Our personal attitudes affect the way in which we relate to others and our general behaviour towards them. Our attitudes are part of our individual identity but it is very important that it does not stop us accepting and valuing others. You probably find that you are most at ease with people who have similar attitudes to yours.

When people work together they may develop a group identity that involves shared values or norms. Norms are a general standard of expected behaviour, which is reflected in how social care settings set up their policies and procedures. By following policies and procedures correctly, social care workers can learn to work in a professional way to support individuals within their care.

It is very important that health and social care practitioners promote tolerance and understanding, and make sure that diversity is valued.

Sometimes your attitudes will be very obvious to those around you, even though you are not aware of it yourself. For instance, if you are not comfortable with someone you may show this through negative non-verbal communication (e.g. crossing your arms,

### Key terms

**Principles** – Based on values, principles are basic guidelines about the right way to behave, i.e. your own personal code of conduct. For example, you treat people with respect because you believe that is the right thing to do.

**Values** – Beliefs about what is important to you as an individual, and what you believe about what is morally right and wrong. Values are usually learned from your parents/carers and tend to change throughout your life.

**Socialisation** – The way in which an individual learns to conform to the accepted standards of behaviour within the culture/society in which they live. There are two forms of socialisation – primary and secondary. The primary process occurs when a child is influenced by primary carers' values attitudes and beliefs. The secondary process involves the way in which education, media, religion and legislation reinforce accepted modes of behaviour.

looking away or not smiling at him/her). Because of this, it will be difficult for you to establish a good relationship with that person; they will sense that you feel uncomfortable with them. However, you need to develop a non-judgemental attitude when working in a health or social care environment.

## Activity 1: Non-judgemental values and attitudes

Identify four ways of ensuring that as a social care practitioner you send positive signals to both children and adults that will make them feel welcome.

Now imagine that you are on a placement at a nursery and consider how you would deal with the following situations in a way that is fair, effective and non-judgemental:

- A mum who comes into the nursery is constantly late and always swears in front of her children.

- An extremely well dressed dad with a briefcase arrives to collect his son and completely ignores him, refusing to look at his paintings and craft activities, which he has produced for Diwali.

- A smartly dressed little girl comes to nursery, and makes fun of two little boys who are wearing hand-me-down clothes. You have heard her mother also making negative comments about the two little boys, calling them 'trouble-makers' and saying that they should not have a place in the nursery.

### PLTS

**Creative thinker:** This activity will enable you to demonstrate that you can recognise situations where an ethical approach to support may present workers with dilemmas.

A care practitioner working with children in an early years setting. Looking at this photo, how do you think the care worker relates to the children?

## Empowerment of individuals and the care value base

**Empowerment** means giving individuals enough information to enable them to make informed decisions and make choices about their life. It lies at the heart of the care value base, devised by the Care Sector Consortium in 1992 in order to provide a common set of ethical principles and values for health and social care workers. The care value base is now more commonly known as 'principles and

### Key term

**Empowerment** – Enabling individuals to take responsibility for their own lives by making informed decisions.

## Case study: Matt's placement experience

On his first placement, at a Sure Start Centre, Matt is faced with a series of challenges, which he finds difficult to deal with, as they are in conflict with his own attitudes and values. Although Matt is enjoying his placement experience he is becoming aware that not all children within the setting are valued and he is worried about the feelings of a four-year-old girl called Josie.

Josie comes from a travelling family. They have been in town for three weeks but the workers at the placement have not yet taken the opportunity to have a proper conversation with Josie's parents. When she starts talking about her caravan and horses, the staff do not really listen. Their attitude is that children should not be moved around all the time, and should not be living in a caravan.

1  Why do the staff treat Josie's parents differently?

2  How might this affect Josie?

3  If you were in Matt's position, what would you do?

values'. Principles and values describe the kind of attitude towards care you would appreciate if you were being cared for yourself. Creating a positive care environment requires health and social care workers to adopt principles and values, which become a 'way of being and working'. Principles and values include recognising and acknowledging the following points:

- empowerment of individuals
- promotion of choice
- promotion of **rights** (to dignity and privacy, safety and security)
- recognition of preferences
- involvement of individuals in planning their support
- respect for diversity, including individual identity, cultural beliefs, moral beliefs and values
- anti-discriminatory practice
- maintaining confidentiality.

## Key term

**Rights** – Things that everyone is entitled to receive. These are usually explained in legislation.

## Activity 2: Care values in practice

In small groups, research principles and values and design a role-play that incorporates all the care values. Perform your role-play to your teaching group and then produce a reflective account of the activity.

## Reflect

Think about an occasion or occasions when you felt completely disempowered, too frightened to speak up for yourself and had no control of the situation. How did you feel at the time? How did you feel after the event? If it happened again, what would you do differently?

## Promotion of choice

All individuals should be encouraged to exercise choice or control over their lives – for example, by choosing which activities they participate in when they are in a residential care setting. All individuals using social care services have a right to select,

either independently or with assistance, a range of options and activities which are specific to them. An advocate can help to ensure that choice is promoted by representing the individual and explaining what is important to them (not what other workers think is important). For instance, a young woman with learning disabilities might be prevented from having a boyfriend of her choice, as care workers may feel that they are protecting her, even though she is over eighteen and should be able to make the choice herself.

## Promotion of rights

All individuals in a health and social care environment have rights to confidentiality, choice and to have their individuality acknowledged and respected. In addition, they have a fundamental right not to be discriminated against, to practise their cultural and religious beliefs, and to receive equal and fair treatment at all times. All individuals have a right to voice their opinions and receive effective communication. They must have access to the policies and procedures of the organisation that is providing their care, and know how to make a complaint if they feel that their needs are not being met.

## Reflect

Think about any rights that you have at home, in college and in the workplace. Make a list of these rights and comment on how they are taken into account. Has there been an occasion when your rights have not been taken into account? If so, describe how you felt?

What rights do children have in care settings? Are these different to those of adults?

**Table 9.1:** Rights of children and adults in care settings

| Children in care settings | Adults in residential care, day care or nursing homes |
|---|---|
| Have the right to:<br>• be heard<br>• safety and security<br>• enjoy and achieve<br>• make a positive contribution<br>• have their wishes considered<br>• confidentiality<br>• be provided with stimulating activities. | Have the right to:<br>• choose own GP<br>• equal and fair treatment<br>• consultation<br>• protection<br>• make a complaint<br>• advocacy<br>• empowerment<br>• sense of identity. |

## Case study: Individual rights

Margaret has been diagnosed with the early symptoms of breast cancer. She has empowered herself and has found a revolutionary treatment, which she believes can give her a better prognosis. Margaret has approached her local primary care trust to request the treatment. After consideration, Margaret's request has been denied on the grounds that the treatment is still being tested and it is very expensive. Margaret has decided to take her battle to court to try to win the 'right' to treatment.

1  What conflicts of interest are there in this case?

2  What do you think the court ruling should be?

3  Why?

## Recognition of preferences

When providing social care support for vulnerable people, it is important to find out and recognise their preferences. This will ensure that they are able to live independently and allow them to stay in control of their daily lives. For example, individuals should be able to state their preference as to the type of support they wish to receive. For example, an older man being provided with care in the community might prefer to have a male social care worker to help with washing and dressing. If individual preferences are acknowledged it makes it easier to work effectively in partnership.

## Involvement of individuals in planning their support

Care should be person-centred, meaning that care is focused on the individual to ensure that independence and autonomy are promoted. When planning support the social care practitioner should use a variety of different methods to collect information about an individual's unique qualities, abilities, interests and preferences as well as their needs. This means asking the individual what support or service they would like to meet their needs. The social care worker should not make any decisions or start delivering a service without discussion and consultation with the individual involved.

## Respect for religious beliefs, moral beliefs, values and culture

Britain is a multicultural society and this has an impact on health and social care delivery. Not only do health and social care professionals come from a diverse range of backgrounds but so do the people who are receiving health and social care services. This means that there is a wide range of behaviours and beliefs which should be recognised and valued.

Living and working in a culturally and socially diverse society can provide experiences of a wide range of skills and expertise from different traditions and cultures. For those working in health and social care this can create exciting opportunities, such as new forms of treatment, different ways to deliver social care and, most importantly, learning opportunities for professional practitioners, individuals who are receiving care and individuals in the wider society.

The value of diversity should be obvious but, unfortunately, many people lack knowledge and understanding of different cultures, races or religions, and may therefore become fearful of something or someone who is different. This can be especially true of some people who are feeling vulnerable when they are in need of health or social care services. It is a legal requirement for all health and social care organisations to respect and value all individuals, irrespective of their religious or cultural beliefs or attitudes. Therefore, all health and social care organisations should recognise and value difference. A social care setting that embraces diversity demonstrates to care workers and individuals how valuing each other in our day-to-day behaviour can have a positive impact on working practices and the culture of the organisation. In practice, this means that that all organisations should have policies and resources that reflect our multicultural society.

## Anti-discriminatory practice

Essentially, discrimination is caused by **prejudice**, which in turn leads to negative behaviour. Giddens (2001) described discrimination as 'activities or actions that deny to the members of the group resources or rewards which can be obtained by others'.

Therefore, to **discriminate** is to distinguish between people on the basis of class or background without regard to individual merit. Examples include social, racial, religious, sexual, disability, ethnic, and age-related discrimination.

Discriminatory actions or behaviour can lead to some people not having their needs met. Negative behaviour can damage a person physically and psychologically and can cause stress. Discriminatory practice can prevent people gaining access to support services and the financial aid they need in order to maintain their health and well-being. In some cases this can lead to malpractice and abuse, putting individuals at risk of significant harm. Care workers need to understand the importance of avoiding discriminatory language and behaviour in order to employ anti-discriminatory practices in their own work. There is also a danger of **stereotyping** or making assumptions about people just because they are from a different background.

There are three main types of discrimination:

1 Direct discrimination (overt) is when individuals openly discriminate against others. Words or actions are used deliberately to disadvantage another person or group of people. For example, a social care practitioner may give preferential treatment to some of the people in their care, and withhold the treatment from some of the other individuals within the same care setting.

2 Indirect discrimination (covert) is when certain conditions are in place that show a preference for some people over others. For example, rules and regulations may make it impossible for a person belonging to a specific group to fully participate in society. This can be difficult to prove because it is not obvious that this is what is happening.

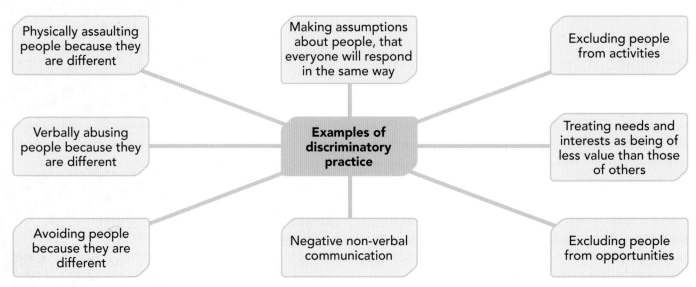

**Fig 9.1:** Some examples of discriminatory practice

**3** Institutional discrimination is where anti-discriminatory policies and procedures are not in place, and there is a lack of multiculturalism within the setting or no inclusive practice.

## Activity 3: Discriminatory practice

In groups, produce a social care scenario that includes examples of direct, indirect and institutional discrimination. Then discuss how an organisation can promote an anti-discriminatory culture.

## Holistic approach

All care work is about improving an individual's quality of life by taking a holistic approach to providing care. Holistic care means looking at all of a person's needs (physical, intellectual, emotional, social, cultural and spiritual) and providing opportunities for these needs to be met.

## Working in partnership

Since the introduction of the NHS Care and Community Act 1990 there has been an increased emphasis on different health and social care agencies working together in partnership. This includes sharing good practice and contributing to the support of vulnerable individuals. For example, when supporting children and families the social worker and the health visitor need to work together, using their different qualities and skills to develop a support plan.

## A multi-disciplinary/inter-agency approach

Multi-disciplinary working is about teams of workers from different specialist professions and services working together in order to prevent problems from occurring in the support planning process. Effective multi-disciplinary working can mean that the individual who is receiving care can get a better service and a better outcome from service providers. Working well with other agencies allows for all the different options to be considered and resources can be offered to be included in a support plan. In this way, realistic expectations and the limits of what can be offered can be discussed by all the different agencies, the support plan manager and the individual who is going to receive care services.

A well-organised multi-disciplinary team can help avoid duplication of roles and conflicts of responsibilities. However, working with different professionals and organisations can prove challenging, as each professional may have different priorities, which can involve allocation of financial and other resources. Key staff within the team may have different approaches to the targets and goals that have been set. For example, the community support worker could have a task-centred approach, just focusing on the specific task they have been asked to undertake and ignoring the wider picture. The social worker may have very different priorities, which could be linked to funding of services. The funding might not be adequate to meet all the needs of the individual named in the support plan. There could also be problems with acknowledging differences in opinions about how the rights and needs of the individual should be met, which could add to conflicts within the team.

It is extremely important for the service provider to be fully aware of the power they have in their professional capacity and not misuse this power. This means being aware of the conflicts that can emerge in relation to the individual's rights and needs. For example, if the social worker feels that regular respite care should be included in the support plan but the individual does not want this, the individual's wishes must be acknowledged in a supportive way. The relationship must be built on mutual trust and understanding. This is very important when difficult decisions are being

Why is a multi-disciplinary approach effective?

## Case study: Multi-disciplinary working with Jim

Jim was diagnosed with bipolar illness during his first year at university. Now in his mid-fifties, he has stayed with his parents in the same house all his life. Jim's parents have not had access to any support and they are increasingly worried about their ability to cope with Jim when he is at his most withdrawn and what will happen to him once they are no longer able to look after him. While they have tried to treat Jim as an adult, the reality is that he is the 'child' in the relationship. Jim's GP is well aware of this and she is concerned that Jim's parents are becoming increasingly frail and have difficulty in coping with Jim's mood changes and meeting his needs. Jim doesn't cook, clean or do his own laundry and his parents' friends are also his friends. After discussion with Jim and his parents, Jim's GP decides to refer him to the Community Psychiatric Team for a needs assessment. It is decided that Jim will move into supported tenancy and work with a support worker who will be his key worker.

There are several key people involved in supporting both Jim and his family. The first point of contact is the family's GP. A GP has extensive knowledge of

medical conditions and has skills to assess a problem and decide on a course of action, which can be a combination of treatment, prevention and education. In Jim's case his GP will monitor his condition and review his medication. Jim also has access to an approved social worker (ASW) who has completed additional specialised training regarding mental health issues/legislation. Jim's ASW will be able to assess whether Jim has the capacity to make his own decisions. If Jim is unable to make independent choices the social worker could act as his advocate or refer Jim to an advocacy service.

1 What is bipolar illness?
2 Identify the professionals who would be part of the multi-disciplinary and inter-agency team working with both Jim and his parents.
3 Devise a support plan that would support Jim in his transition.
4 Whose rights, wishes and needs must be paramount? How can the professionals in the multi-agency team ensure that both Jim's and his parents' rights are protected?

made, such as when an individual should move out of their home.

In the case study above, Jim's parents will also require support in their role as Jim's informal carers, which can be very tiring and emotionally taxing. There are carers' support groups in all local authorities, and voluntary organisations (such as Age Concern and the British Red Cross), which the social worker should refer them to, can also provide support. However, Jim's parents might prefer to empower themselves further by making use of online support, which they could access at their local library with the help of the librarian.

## Confidentiality

Individuals have a basic right to privacy and control over their personal details. Maintaining confidentiality has become a specific issue in principles and values. It is vital to successful care-giving to keep information provided by all individuals confidential. It is a legal and moral requirement and it also demonstrates that a trusting relationship has developed; it shows that the organisation values and respects the individuals who are receiving care. If in doubt a care worker should ask, 'How do I know it's confidential? Do I know the

information because of my professional role? Does the person I am supporting trust me to keep the information secret?'

However there may be times when this information has to be shared on a 'need to know' basis. For instance, there could be occasions when an individual discloses some information to a care worker and this information has to be passed on to another agency. The individual must be informed if any information is to be passed on.

## Fulfilling responsibilities

Health and social care workers have a clear responsibility to follow the policies and procedures of the organisation in which they are employed. These are outlined in a contract of employment and the professional code of practice. By following organisational policies, professional practitioners will ensure that they are safeguarding individuals within their care as well as being positive role models. In addition, practitioners have to meet the requirements of relevant legislation (such as The Health and Safety at Work Act), which is in place to protect individuals and care workers. Social care workers also have a duty to work with other professionals to ensure that a person-centred approach to the delivery of care is taken and monitored and is based on assessed needs.

Care workers have a responsibility to understand the importance of communication and handle all information in a sensitive and professional way.

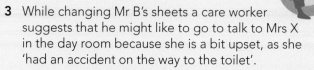

## Activity 4: Confidentiality dilemmas

Working in small groups, discuss the scenarios listed below and consider what you would do and what would be 'best practice'.

Think about how you would refer to the confidentiality care value guidelines to help you make a decision in the following situations:

1   You work with an older person, Mary, who tells you 'My son-in-law takes my pension every week, but don't tell anyone. He might stop my daughter from visiting me and I couldn't bear that.'

2   You are working in a children's centre and Jack, aged seven, discloses to you that Mum gets very angry with him, calls him names and quite often leaves him alone all weekend when she goes out with friends.

3   While changing Mr B's sheets a care worker suggests that he might like to go to talk to Mrs X in the day room because she is a bit upset, as she 'had an accident on the way to the toilet'.

4   Frank, a resident of a care home, tells his carer that he hasn't been taking his pills. He has pains but he 'doesn't want to go on'. He is saving them to take an overdose. He makes the carer promise not to tell.

5   You are updating computer records on screen. You receive a telephone call from a relative who asks about his aunt. The details are on the screen and clearly visible. However, you have not met the nephew, although he is named as his aunt's next of kin.

## Assessment activity 9.1

**P1  M1  D1**   BTEC

1   Using the example of one individual who uses social services, write a description, in essay form, of how you would apply relevant principles and values when planning a package of holistic support for that person.

2   Extend your essay to include a review of the benefits to the individual, and also to the staff involved in delivery of the care, of taking a holistic approach to planning.

3   Extend your essay to include an analysis of the reasons for working with professionals from more than one agency when planning support.

### Grading tips

**P1**  With appropriate consent, you could use your placement experience and produce a case study of an individual who is supported by

the setting. Identify how the key worker has assessed them and is meeting their holistic needs. Identify which professionals are involved in supporting the individual. Remember to ensure that confidentiality is maintained when undertaking this task.

**M1**  Interview the individual's key worker and find out the advantages for both the individual and key worker of working in a holistic way when planning support.

**D1**  When interviewing the key worker, ask 'what are the benefits of using different professionals in providing holistic care for your chosen individual?' Consider at least three reasons and justify each one.

## PLTS

**Independent enquirer:** You will show your independent enquiry skills when relating principles and values to the support of individuals who use services.

## Functional skills

**English:** When writing your essay you will show that you can communicate information, ideas and opinions.

# 2  Know processes involved in planning support for individuals

## 2.1 Processes

We all think about and plan our lives in different ways. Some people have very clear ideas about what they want and how to achieve it; others take opportunities as they arise. Some people dream and then see how they can match their dreams to reality. Sometimes it is useful to plan in a structured way and this is very important when recognising and planning care provision for vulnerable people.

Since the introduction of the NHS Care and Community Act 1990, all local authorities are required to carry out needs-led assessments, which should take into consideration individual preferences and choices. Needs-led assessments are person-centred; whereas resource-led assessments are driven by the availability of resources from a particular service or area. This is often referred to as a 'postcode lottery'. For example, an older person who has become frail and is losing their confidence might be offered a cheaper place in a day centre that would meet their social needs, but a sitting service might be more appropriate for both the individual and their informal carer.

When a support plan is produced for an individual they decide what is important to them and what they would like to change in their life. During the assessment process the social worker will discuss with the individual what is working and not working to ensure that they have a good quality of life. This will make it easier to identify what support or resources are needed to make their life easier. A support plan does not have to be complicated; it can be as detailed or as simple as required, as long as both carer and individual discuss, understand and agree the desired outcomes of the assessment.

## The cycle of assessment and planning

When producing a support plan it is very important to consider how to meet all of the individual's needs, while also considering the role of the informal carer. When the first assessment takes place the extent of all the individual's support needs might not be apparent. This makes it difficult to identify all the relevant support services that could be useful. Therefore it is important that dates are set for reviewing the plan with the person requiring care, their informal carer and any

relevant professionals, to see if all needs are being catered for. This process is often referred to as the support planning cycle.

The support planning and delivery process can be viewed as a cycle:

**Referral:** The first stage in the care planning cycle; it can be professional or self referral

**Holistic assessment:** Assessment of needs and preferences undertaken by the care plan manager using assessment tools, working closely with the individual

**Identifying current provision:** Care plan manager identifies the resources required to meet individual needs

**Care planning:** Care plan manager identifies realistic targets to be achieved and how this is to be done; appropriate care is organised; goals to be achieved by the individual, with support from professionals, are set

**Recording:** Care plan manager documents who is involved in care plan, including individual, family and neighbours, as well as other professionals

**Communicating:** Care plan manager ensures all those concerned receive copy of care plan and understand roles and responsibilities

**Implementation:** Date identified by care plan manager, in consultation with the individual, for when services are to be made available

**Monitoring:** Care plan manager discusses with individual and significant others what is working well and identifies anything which needs changing

**Reviewing:** Care plan manager reviews provision of care with individual and other professionals; identifies new goals and targets; alters the care plan

**Evaluating:** Care plan manager and individual decide a date to analyse and evaluate success of care plan, making any changes which have been identified

**Fig 9.2:** The sequence of steps in a support plan

| Person responsible for implementing, monitoring and reviewing care plan: | | Ms Eileen Walters: Community psychiatric nurse | | | |
|---|---|---|---|---|---|
| Today's date: | | 01.06.2010 | | | |
| Date of next review: | | 01.09.2010 | | | |
| | What is the problem? | How the problem is going to be solved? | Who is involved? | Time span? | Outcome? |
| Physical | To ensure Jim takes his medication. | Organise a medication routine.. | Community psychiatric nurse | Immediately and ongoing | To stabilise Jim's condition. |
| | To develop his self caring skills. | Establish a routine for daily living skills. | Key worker Jim | Ongoing | To establish independence. |
| | To improve his health and fitness. | To have a health and fitness plan. | A support group | Ongoing | To develop health and fitness. |
| Intellectual | Jim to be supported in joining the local library. | To provide intellectual stimulation. | Key worker and Jim | Ongoing | To develop intellectual skills. |
| | To enrol at local college, providing discrete courses for people who have mental health issues. | To provide a routine to encourage learning and intellectual development. | Key worker and Jim College tutor and Jim | Ongoing | To develop his life skills. |
| Emotional | Jim to be supported in his transition to supported tenancy. | To be provided with emotional support, leaving his parents home. | Community psychiatric nurse Key worker | Immediately | To deal with negative emotions linked to the transition. |
| | Jim to be supported with his mental health issues. | To be provided with psychological support. | Community psychiatric nurse | Ongoing | To stabilise his condition. |
| Social | Jim to develop a social network and widen his hobbies and interests. | To be supported in identifying support groups and individuals which are of interest him . | Key worker and Jim Librarian, college tutor and Jim | Ongoing | To develop Jim's communication and interpersonal skills. |
| Cultural Spiritual | Jim's cultural and spiritual needs to be identified. | To be supported in identifying his cultural and spiritual interests, could involve attending local church or Buddhist group. | Key worker and Jim | Ongoing | To ensure that Jim's holistic needs are met. |

**Fig 9.3:** A sample support plan. Can you think of anything to add or change?

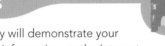

## Involvement of key professionals

Key professionals working with individuals in need and their families could include the following people.

### Social worker

The social worker's role is to ensure that the individual's rights are met. The social worker has a statutory responsibility to assess the level of support required to meet the needs of the individual and family they are working with. Social workers work with people to enable them to deal with or solve problems, such as child protection issues, gaining self-help skills or accessing various other support services.

### Health visitor

A health visitor is a qualified nurse who has undertaken additional training. The health visitor works closely with children and families, providing advice and guidance in relation to children's growth and development. The health visitor may also identify other health and/ or social care issues that the family is experiencing. Offering advice and guidance, they play a role in the areas of safeguarding and child protection.

### Family support worker

Family support workers work in partnership with the social worker. Once the social worker has completed the assessment of need, the family support worker will work closely with families, providing direct support with a variety of problems, which can include parenting skills, domestic skills and financial management.

### Probation officer

A probation officer is a qualified professional whose role is to supervise offenders within the community. (In Scotland they are referred to as criminal justice social workers.) The probation officer will operate within the statutory framework, ensuring that offenders are meeting the requirements of their court orders. The probation officer will work closely with the offender on behaviour issues, and work with other agencies to ensure that the rehabilitation process takes place.

### GP

A General Practitioner (GP) is a medical doctor with a general all-round knowledge of acute and chronic illnesses. The GP can provide preventative care and treatment for a wide variety of illnesses, and will refer the patient to a specialist if required.

### Involvement of family

Individuals needing support will often require the involvement of members of their wider family. The support that family members can provide varies according to both the needs of the individual and the capabilities of the family members.

## Advocates, interpreters and translators

Individuals who need support from health and social care services are not always able to state their needs clearly. There can be lots of reasons for this. It could be that they do not understand what their needs are, they could have an illness or condition that prevents them from expressing their needs, or they may have difficulties with their communication skills. It is very important that health and social care agencies provide a fair and effective service to people with whom they cannot communicate. Any barriers to communication can lead to the build-up of frustration, anger and misunderstanding. Misdiagnosis may occur and the individual's rights may be ignored.

### Advocates

An advocate could be a family member or someone from a statutory or voluntary organisation. An advocate's role is to speak on behalf of, not for, individuals. The advocate's main role is to empower and protect people by ensuring that their wishes are identified and met, where possible, and that their rights and entitlements are protected.

The importance of using an advocate was initially identified in Section 2 of the Bristol Inquiry report

(2001). Although primarily aimed at the NHS, this recommendation has effectively meant that health and social care providers should have links to advocacy services that represent the interests of care users. An advocacy service should provide:

- confidential guidance and support to individuals, their families and carers
- information on health and social care related issues
- confidential assistance in resolving problems and concerns
- opportunities to negotiate solutions, speak on behalf of, and express the wishes and choices of individuals who receive care services.

### Interpreters

Interpreters are professionals who communicate meaning from one language to another; this includes British Sign Language.

It is also important to train health and social care staff in how to work effectively with interpreters, as three-way communication can be extremely confusing. Other difficulties can arise when using an interpreter (such as social class, regional dialects, religion or geography), all of which may interrupt the process of interpreting and communication. It is therefore important to recognise that speaking the same language may not necessarily mean that the same understanding will follow.

Sometimes people are reluctant to use interpreters who are from the same community for fear that personal information will not be kept confidential, or that they will be judgemental. This is unlikely to happen with trained professional interpreters, who do not know the individual they are working with.

### Translators

Translators are people who change recorded material from one language to another.

It is important that health and social care organisations provide information in a range of languages to reflect the ethnic profile of the community. For example, leaflets and posters in hospitals or day centres should be printed in Urdu, Punjabi and Chinese as well as Braille. Organisations should also provide welcome signs in other languages, and translated signs. These help people from different ethnic groups find their way around buildings and help to provide a welcoming and reassuring environment. However, verbal messages need to be catered for (as well as written ones), and this can be provided through interpretation and translator services.

### Activity 6: Enabling communication

Produce a poster identifying reasons why a person may not be able to communicate their needs to a professional practitioner. Include the ways and type of resources that can be used to enable individuals to express themselves more clearly. You should explain the role of an advocate, interpreter and translator.

### Case study: Sylvia, the informal carer

Angela has been working with Les and Sylvia for several years; Les has advanced Alzheimer's disease (a degenerative form of dementia) and has become increasingly violent towards Sylvia. Sylvia has a hearing impairment and can only communicate by using sign language. Les has also lost the ability to distinguish between night and day and spends most nights awake and walking around the house. Angela, the care worker, has noticed that caring for Les is increasingly exhausting Sylvia, Les's informal carer. Angela discusses the situation with her manager and they decide to amend Les's support plan and recommend that Les has regular visits to the day centre and respite care to give Sylvia a break from her caring role. Sylvia is very upset when told of this and feels that she has not been consulted. She feels that she can no longer trust Angela and believes that she is undermining her role in caring for Les.

1. Think about principles and values and identify the issues that have arisen in this case.

2. What are the potential problems that may arise in Les, Sylvia and Angela's relationship and how can they be resolved?

3. Age UK could provide an advocacy service. What role could an advocate play in supporting Sylvia and Les?

## 2.2 Assessment

Assessment tools are resources that are used in the support planning process to help build up a holistic picture of an individual's needs and related circumstances. Once all the details are recorded, an assessment can be made, and suitable care and support can be identified.

**Table 9.2:** Examples of assessment tools

| Assessment tool | Description |
|---|---|
| Checklists | The social worker has a list of criteria, which is helpful during the initial assessment process to ensure that each criterion is covered. |
| Forms | It is essential that all relevant forms are completed to provide evidence of this information. |
| Diary of the professional | This should be used to record minutes of any meetings that take place, all the decisions that have been made, and who attended each meeting. |
| Diary of the individual using the service | By keeping a diary, the individual can express their choices and preferences and can also evaluate the social care that they are receiving. |
| Questions | At the initial meeting with the individual, it is important to ensure that the process is fully understood. This requires skilful use of questioning, including a combination of open and closed questions. The support plan manager must avoid using leading questions, as this could lead to a misuse of power. |
| Records of incidents and accidents | To make sure that monitoring and reviewing is undertaken, the key worker is advised to keep a record of incidents and accidents. This can indicate when support needs should be changed or adapted. |
| Observations | Observations can help to describe behaviour patterns, self-care skills or the medical situation of the individual. |
| Personal histories | A holistic view needs to be undertaken. This means making reference to previous medical history and personal status (i.e. relationships, carers, etc.), as this becomes central to their current assessed needs. |
| Flowcharts | A flowchart can be used to summarise other forms of assistance that may be appropriate to the individual. |
| Discussions | Effective communication and the sharing of information within a multi-agency team are very important when meeting individual needs. The assessment process relies on a series of discussions involving everyone in the support planning process. |

## Case study: Benjamin

Benjamin is 76 and moved to England from Jamaica in 1950. He lives alone in a housing association maisonette. He was referred to a charity for older people by the hospital social worker because of his increasingly frequent visits to the Accident and Emergency Department at his local hospital

Belinda, from Age UK, is dealing with his case. Belinda observed that Benjamin was looking neglected and he explained that his maisonette had cardboard at the windows, no hot water and poor heating. Benjamin misses his friends in his old community, which is 48 km (30 miles) away.

After taking details of his personal history Belinda arranged a series of meetings with Benjamin and other professionals and recorded a brief summary of each meeting. Belinda also arranged an appointment with Benjamin's doctor, who diagnosed gout in his feet and early signs of cataracts in both eyes. Next, Belinda asked Samuel, a volunteer from the local day centre, if he would support Benjamin, act as an advocate for him at meetings, and help him to deal with any forms and documents.

Belinda arranged a meeting with the social worker to discuss Benjamin's issues. She also produced a support plan, which would offer Benjamin holistic support. Belinda, Benjamin's GP, the manager of the housing association, Samuel and Benjamin attended a meeting. All the professionals brought their records with them, which recorded incidents that had involved Benjamin. During the meeting the professionals and Benjamin (with Samuel's help), discussed his needs, how they were to be met, each professional's role and responsibilities, and the outcomes they expected. Benjamin was happy with the outcome and Belinda explained that they would meet again to check progress in two months' time. In the meantime Samuel would continue to support Benjamin, arrange for him to attend the local day centre, and act as his advocate whenever necessary.

1 Identify which assessment tools Belinda used with Benjamin, and explain how useful each tool was.

2 Using the example of the support plan shown on page 13, produce a support plan for Benjamin.

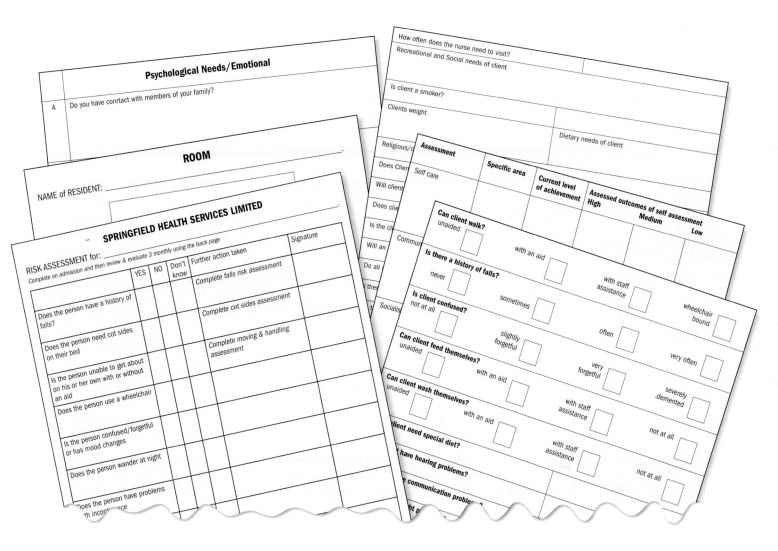

**Fig 9.4:** How would these different types of assessment tools be used?

# 2.3 Implementing support plans

Once a support plan has been produced, it should be viewed as a working document, which can be changed and adapted according to the changing needs of the individual. Careful thought is required as to how care is to be delivered.

## Approaches to implementing support plans

There are several different approaches that can be considered when implementing support plans, and the choice of approach partly depends on the particular goals that have been set. The key members of staff, who play a part in delivering care, will each have a different approach to implementing support plans, according to their role, responsibilities and skills.

### Behavioural

This approach involves identifying behaviour that needs to be changed and the desired behaviour that the individual is hoping to achieve. It is based on behavioural psychology (see Book 1, Unit 8) and will often involve praising or rewarding the individual for any behaviour that is in line with the desired outcome. This way the desired behaviour is reinforced and becomes a natural way of behaving for that individual.

### Task-centred

This approach involves identifying particular tasks or skills that the individual needs to achieve. The task-centred approach centres on supporting the individual to achieve the task for themselves and therefore develop independence in that particular area.

### Therapeutic groups

These are often used when a number of individuals require similar support in a particular area. Groups can be for general support (e.g. to improve self-confidence) or for more specific areas such as overcoming alcohol addiction or learning anger management skills.

Whatever approach is used, it is important for the individual to be involved in the decision-making process and not disempowered. Professional social carers can often unintentionally misuse their powers. For example, when caring for vulnerable people it is quite easy to speak or act for them, which would be a misuse of power. This not only disempowers the individual but also keeps them dependent on the worker and stops them developing autonomy.

## Activity 7: Implementing the support plan

Using the case study on page 16, consider which approach or approaches were being used to support Benjamin. Can you think of any other approaches that could be used to provide further support for Benjamin?

## Assessment activity 9.2

**P2** **M2** **D2** **BTEC**

Produce an information booklet for new social work assistants that:

1. identifies the processes and assessment tools that would be involved when planning support for individuals with contrasting needs
2. describes how three key professionals could be involved with planning support for individuals
3. assesses two potential issues that could arise from professionals working together.

### Grading tips

**P2** For this grade, you need to clearly identify the processes and assessment tools that would be involved. Include a range of assessment tools, stating how and when they would be used in each case.

**M2** Select three key professionals from health and social care and related services and describe the role they would play in the process of planning. You should also state how these professionals would work together to support individuals.

**D2** You should consider possible difficulties and then discuss these in relation to planning support for individuals.

## PLTS

**Creative thinker:** You can show your creative thinking skills by considering how processes and assessment tools are involved in the assessment of individuals and planning their support.

## Functional skills

**ICT:** This task will enable you to use ICT systems and develop, present and communicate information via the information booklet you create.

# 3 Understand legislation, policies and codes of practice related to the planning of support for individuals

## 3.1 Legislation

Legislation refers to the laws that Parliament makes; these laws reflect the statutory right of organisations, groups and individuals. All social care settings should understand the importance of adhering to legal guidance, as this can protect against poor practice. Legislation also ensures that everyone is clear about their rights and responsibilities within the care environment.

**Table 9.3:** Examples of laws affecting health and social care

| Legislation | Description |
|---|---|
| Care Standards Act 2000 | • Established a National Care Standards Commission (the NCSC no longer exists; its functions are now the responsibility of the Care Quality Commission).<br>• Ensures registration of health and social care establishments, including statutory, voluntary and private organisation.<br>• Established the General Social Care Council and the Care Council for Wales.<br>• Established Children's Commissioners for England and Wales.<br>• Safeguards children and vulnerable adults in a variety of health, social care and educational environments.<br>• Ensures that health and social care providers are legally and morally obliged to keep the details of all individuals using their care service confidential. |
| National Minimum Standards | • The principles of care are delivered through the National Minimum Standards.<br>• The Care Standards Act identified the minimum standards of social care practice for a range of social care services, which all organisations must meet.<br>• The standards cover issues like staff levels, different types of health and social care expertise, qualifications and licence to practice, and ensure that the right standards of care are met. |
| Disability Discrimination Act 1995; extended 2005 | • The Equality and Human Rights Commission assists individuals to uphold their rights as set out in the Disability Discrimination Act (DDA).<br>• The Act covers four main areas: employment, housing, transport and education.<br>• It is unlawful under the DDA for an employer to treat a person with disabilities less favourably than someone else because of a disability. |
| Data Protection Act 1998 | • Gives individuals certain rights regarding information held about them. (Personal information covers both facts and opinions about the individual.)<br>• Places obligations on those who process information while giving rights to those who are the subject of that data.<br>• Clearly states that each individual should have their wishes considered and that organisations have a duty to protect individuals from harm, including self-harm.<br>• Outlines when confidentiality can legitimately be breached, especially if it is in the public interest or if there is a risk, either to the individual or another person, or a court order has been issued.<br>• In such cases, the individual must be informed if information is being disclosed to a third party. It is also essential to follow principles and values procedures and the organisation's policies and procedures for reporting and reacting to confidential information. |
| Freedom of Information Act 2000 | • Gives the public a general right to request information held by public authorities.<br>• Also means that public authorities have to provide access to information that is held in the public's interest. |

*continued*

**Table 9.3:** *continued*

| Legislation | Description |
|---|---|
| Nursing and Residential Care Homes Regulations 2002 | • Introduced after the Care Standards Act.<br>• Regulations outline the statutory and regulatory requirements regarding roles and responsibilities in nursing and residential homes. |
| Race Relations Act 1976 | • Introduced to promote equality within society.<br>• However, failed to tackle the inequalities that existed within public organisations; intolerance and lack of understanding of cultural issues was very apparent.<br>• The 1999 Macpherson Inquiry into the death of Stephen Lawrence identified institutional racism within the London Metropolitan police force. The report highlighted the fact that policies and procedures within public organisations should not be used to discriminate against people of different races, cultures or religions. |
| Race Relations Amendment Act 2000 | • Macpherson Inquiry led to the Race Relations Amendment Act, which requires named public authorities to review their policies and procedures; to remove discrimination and the possibility of discrimination and to actively promote race equality.<br>• It amends the Race Relations Act 1976, which makes it unlawful to discriminate against anyone on grounds of race, colour, nationality (including citizenship), or ethnic or national origin.<br>• All public organisations have a legal responsibility to ensure that policies and procedures are in place to make sure that the organisation reflects inclusive practice.<br>• In addition all staff are required to be culturally competent, value diversity and promote tolerance and understanding. |

# 3.2 Policies

All health and social care settings should value the diversity of all individuals receiving care and those in the wider community.

## Organisational policies

Organisations should have policies and procedures that promote equal opportunities and reinforce the codes of practice of specific professional bodies. Organisational policies are the mechanism by which legislation is delivered and implemented. Policies in organisations are likely to include:

- Health and Safety
- Harm Minimisation
- Risk Assessment
- Equal Opportunities
- Confidentiality
- Bullying and Harassment
- Conflict of Interests.

**Reflect**

When on placement ask your supervisor for copies of the organisation's policies and procedures and produce a short reflective account, explaining how one of the policies is used to support the individuals in the setting.

# 3.3 Codes of practice

Since 2000, health and social care services have become strictly regulated and it has become essential for all settings to have a **professional code of practice**. Codes of practice are put in place in order to guide and inform practitioners of their rights and, most importantly, their responsibilities. All health and social care workers are expected to undertake an induction period, which includes the right training leading to relevant qualifications. This will enable them to perform their roles efficiently and professionally.

**Key term**

**Professional code of practice** – A set of guidelines and regulations, which explain the way members of a profession have to behave.

## General Social Care Council Codes of Practice

The General Social Care Council/Care Councils for England, Scotland, Wales and Northern Ireland all follow the same codes of practice. All four bodies were set up on 1 October 2001 under legislation to regulate the social care profession.

The General Social Care Council (GSCC) is responsible for increasing the protection of people who are receiving care, their carers and the general public by making sure that the social care workforce puts into practice codes of behaviour that meet professional codes of conduct. The codes of practice for everyone working within the social care sector include information on protecting the rights, and promoting the interests, of individuals who are receiving care and their professional carers. Most importantly, professional codes of practice are intended to raise standards of practice and to increase confidence in the social care sector.

## Organisational codes of practice and codes of practice specific to professional bodies

The Social Care Register was launched in April 2003, and all UK qualified social workers have to register and abide by the code of practice. When applying for registration, individuals have their qualifications, health and character checked, including an enhanced check by the Criminal Records Bureau. This will be changed in July 2010, when vetting and barring legislation will be introduced. Once this is completed, individuals will have a licence to practise. Social workers will have to renew their registration on a three-yearly basis, and this will be subject to proof of continuing professional development. In health, the Nursing and Midwifery Council is the regulatory body, and manages the registration and regulation of qualified nurses, midwives and health visitors. The GSCC code for social care has similar principles to the Nursing and Midwifery Council's code.

### The Vetting and Barring Scheme

In October 2009, the system for checking the suitability of potential employees and volunteers started to change. The new Vetting and Barring Scheme requires all paid employees and volunteers who work with children or vulnerable adults to be registered with the Independent Safeguarding Authority (ISA) before commencing work. From November 2010, it will be a legal requirement for individuals to register with the ISA if they intend to work, or currently work, with children and/or vulnerable adults in England, Wales and Northern Ireland.

### Activity 8: Evaluating codes of practice

Go to the websites of The General Social Care Council (www.gscc.org.uk) and The Nursing and Midwifery Council (www.nmc-uk.org/) and download copies of both codes of practice. Read through both codes of practice and produce a leaflet identifying any similarities and any differences between the two.

### Functional skills

**ICT:** This search will demonstrate your ability to access relevant websites, and use your ICT skills to present information.

## Case study: The importance of codes of practice

Geraint has arrived for his first day at Great Days Residential Centre, working with adults who have profound disabilities and complex needs. During his induction training, his manager, Kirsteen, introduces Geraint to the centre's code of practice, which he must follow. It states that Geraint must:

- respect the rights of all the residents, while making sure that their behaviour does not harm themselves or other people who are living in the residential setting
- make sure that he establishes and maintains the trust and confidence of everyone who is in his care
- be a positive role model, not only in the setting, but while on trips and visits out in the community
- know that when he is supporting Jack, he is a professional carer, not a 'friend'.

Geraint is introduced to Jack and Kirsteen explains to Geraint that he will be Jack's key worker and will be responsible for planning support for Jack, which includes social activities as well as his physical, intellectual and emotional support. Geraint reads through Jack's support plan and discovers that Jack likes to play wheelchair rugby, visit the local pub and go to watch his favourite football team. Geraint is delighted, as they support the same team and visit the same local pub on a regular basis. Geraint is looking forward to planning the trips with Jack.

1 Identify what Geraint should do before any outing with Jack is undertaken.

2 Can you think of any possible conflicts of interests with which Geraint might be faced?

3 How can a code of practice support Geraint's professional practice?

# Lizzy Spencer
## Rehabilitation unit manager

Lizzy Spencer has recently been appointed as a unit manager on a rehabilitation unit. She leads a team of 20 staff, which consists of both trained and untrained health and social care staff. Currently she is very concerned about the attitude of some of the staff members towards Mr Farooq, who came to the unit two weeks ago. Mr Farooq is a 64-year-old professional man who had a serious road accident. His acute injuries have been treated. However, he must now receive specialist care. Mr Farooq is a practising Muslim.

Ms Spencer has noted that some staff avoid chatting to Mr Farooq and has even noticed some staff ridiculing him when he asks for assistance to access the prayer room.

Ms Spencer has also noted that many of the other individuals in the unit object to Mr Farooq having a different choice of meals.

In an attempt to resolve some of the issues, Lizzy and her line manager rewrite the unit policies that relate to equal opportunities. All staff are given training to make sure they understand the new policies and are given a copy of the recent legislation and the UKCC Code of Conduct. The policies are also made available to everyone in the unit and their families. Ms Spencer also encourages all the untrained staff to begin training and asks their assessor to focus initially on the unit that tackles the principle of non-discriminatory practice.

As a result of the new policies, many day-to-day procedures are put into place. For example, each individual now has the same wide choice when ordering meals.

## Think about it!

1 Obtain a copy of the code of conduct of the General Social Care Council and explain how the code protects Mr Farooq's rights and interests.

2 Give two reasons to explain how the unit's new policies would be used to promote the rights of Mr Farooq and other individuals within the unit.

3 Analyse how Ms Spencer has supported the staff in promoting individuals' rights and how effective this is in supporting Mr Farooq's rights.

## Assessment activity 9.3

(P3)  BTEC

Based on a specific social care service, e.g. your placement, identify one piece of legislation, one code of practice and one policy. Explain how each could be applied to planning support for your individuals using the service.

### Grading tip

P3  Identify how the legislation, policy and code of practice influence the way each of your support plans is constructed and delivered by the setting.

### PLTS

**Creative thinker:** In identifying and describing how to apply legislation, policies and codes of practice to support plans, you will show creative thinking skills.

### Functional skills

**English:** Presenting and communicating information via support plans will demonstrate your writing skills.

# 4 Understand ethical principles in relation to providing support for individuals

## 4.1 Ethical principles

When working in a health or social care environment, professional practitioners are quite often faced with situations involving moral dilemmas. Therefore, it is very important for health and social care workers to have a clear understanding of **morality** and the meaning of moral decisions and how they are linked to health and social practice.

This section introduces some of the key **ethical principles** that influence health and social care practice.

Health and social care workers also need to have a good understanding of their legal position, and the morals and ethics that form the basis of their professional code of practice. This is very important when a person refuses medical treatment or decides to take a course of action that might not be in their best interests. In such situations legislation and professional codes of practice can provide valuable guidance for the health and social care worker.

The care worker also needs to consider the following ethical points when dealing with moral dilemmas:

## Duty

When working with vulnerable individuals, all health and social care practitioners have a duty of care to protect their rights. If a proposed course of action or a proposed treatment could be harmful to the individual, practitioners have to weigh up the advantages and disadvantages. For example, cancer patients are quite often advised to undergo a course of chemotherapy or radiotherapy. Both treatments involve some harmful side effects, but the benefits should outweigh the harm caused by the treatment.

## Safeguarding individuals

Social care providers should ensure that environments safeguard vulnerable individuals. This involves recruiting new staff and providing resources to ensure that individuals' needs are met. However, there are times when the behaviour or actions of one individual could harm other people within the organisation. This could be an individual with mental health problems who might become violent towards other people. If

this is the case then the social care professional must follow the organisation's policies and procedures and if the behaviour of an individual is likely to result in significant harm to themselves or other people then the individual has to be restrained. Section 5 of the Mental Capacity Act 2005 provides guidelines for the social care professional, relating to the degree of harm that is likely to be suffered by a person if he or she is not restrained.

## Beneficence

Beneficence refers to actions that promote the well-being of others. In the medical context, this means taking actions that serve the best interests of patients. Social care professionals have a duty to act in an individual's best interest at all times. This can involve balancing the benefits of medical treatment against the risks and costs. Health care professionals quite often have to weigh up arguments over cost, the effectiveness of treatment and the benefit that patients gain from the proposed course of action. For example, the cancer drug Herceptin could cost £30,000 for one person – would this money be better spent on saving multiple heart attack victims?

**Fig 9.5:** Think about these ethical principles, which lie at the heart of health and social care

## Social justice

All individuals should have equal access to medical treatment and be fully aware of their legal rights. Practitioners have to make sure that relevant legislation is put into practice. The Children Act 1989, for instance, states that local authorities must act in the 'best interests' of all children, and that each child has a fundamental right to housing, health care and education. However, there are times when social justice is not available to all individuals – for example, asylum seekers' children who are being detained at Yarl's Wood Detention Centre without access to adequate medical care.

## Empowerment and autonomy of the individual

Empowering an individual means ensuring that they know enough to make an informed choice about decisions that could affect the quality of their life. This helps individuals to have control over their own lives.

Vulnerable people who receive health and social care services rely on professional carers to ensure their independence. It is important that care workers empower individuals and don't use **benevolent oppression** to make decisions for individuals in their care, especially when it might seem that risky behaviour is involved. While staff might appear to be acting in 'the best interest' of individuals, they could in fact be denying a person's right to act as an independent individual and control their own life.

Examples of benevolent oppression include:

- not allowing relationships to develop between consenting adults
- limiting alcohol intake of individuals
- leaving the bathroom door open; not 'allowing' an individual to take a bath/shower in private
- preventing individuals with physical/learning disabilities from going out alone
- choosing activities that are thought to be suitable, but are not the choice of the individual
- not providing resources to encourage independence and autonomy.

## Promotion of dignity, independence and rights of the individual

It is very important when working with vulnerable people, especially when undertaking personal care activities, that dignity, independence and the rights of individuals are taken into consideration. For example, when supporting an older woman to bathe and dress, make sure that the task is undertaken in a way that protects her dignity. This involves letting her choose the toiletries she wants to use and providing ways in which her independence can be encouraged and her rights recognised.

## Moral status of the individual

When working in health and social care, professionals will meet a diverse range of people who hold a variety of different values and attitudes. These can quite often be in conflict with those of other people. For example, people hold very different views on abortion and euthanasia. Professional practitioners have to be sensitive to the moral status of the people they are working with, and not cause offence by making comments that undermine the views of other people.

All principles are equal – one is not more important than another. In recent years there has been a closer focus on individual autonomy and it has become essential to offer choice and empower individuals. However, does respect for autonomy mean that a patient can request treatment that a health care practitioner does not think is in his/her best interests, or that they think will not work? If this occurs, respect for autonomy can come into conflict with **nonmaleficence** or justice.

### Key terms

**Morality** – Refers to social conventions about the right and wrong behaviour expected of each individual. These rules are linked to the moral values of society.

**Ethical principles** – Guidelines for appropriate behaviour, focusing on actions, attitudes and values. The health and social care professional must always behave in an anti-discriminatory and anti-biased way.

**Benevolent oppression** – When well-meaning social carers make decisions on behalf of the individuals in their care, or prevent them from behaving in an apparently risky way, in the interests of their safety.

**Nonmaleficence** – To 'do no harm'.

## Activity 9: Class debate

Identify and research some medical practices that provoke controversy and debate, such as informed consent in mental health, euthanasia, pain relief using cannabis, and organ transplantation.

You need to produce a list of arguments for and against your chosen topic and debate the issue with your group.

Think about the ethical principles you have covered in this section when putting your arguments together.

## Functional skills

**English:** This activity will develop your speaking and listening skills. You will also improve your skills in presenting arguments and listening to others. Recording your conclusions will develop your written skills.

# 4.2 Ethical dilemmas

## Potential conflicts

When working with vulnerable groups of people in health and social care settings there are times when care workers are faced with a conflict of interests. Often ethical dilemmas will not have a 'correct' answer and will depend upon a number of considerations.

Nevertheless the care worker is faced with a dilemma and is expected to make a decision. Before making a decision, the care worker must consider:

1 What are the risks to the individual and any other people?

2 What are the professional and legal responsibilities?

3 What are the policies of the organisation?

4 Have I got all the facts of the case?

Examples of possible dilemmas include being asked to prescribe the contraceptive pill to under-16s without parental consent, having to involve social services when parents have drug addictions, having to decide on allocation of scarce resources, and deciding whether to pass information on to other agencies. One of the most controversial dilemmas involves the treatment of terminally ill patients, who are very close to death and may be in a great deal of pain. In such

cases, a doctor may not wish to prolong the situation and may therefore resort to withholding treatment, known as an **act of omission**.

## Rights, responsibilities and duties

Legislation, policies and codes of practice provide clear guidelines as to the rights and responsibilities of care workers and these should be adhered to at all times. The duties of the care worker are clearly laid out in such documents, as well as in their contract of employment. In most situations a care worker's duties are clear and there is no conflict of interest. However, at times there can be a conflict of rights and ethical principles to consider.

For example, the rights of one person may clash with the rights of others. For instance, in a supported housing project there may be a resident who likes to play music late into the evening, while another resident likes to retire early and get up early.

In other cases, one person may have two rights that conflict with each other. For example, in certain situations an individual's right to privacy and confidentiality may clash with the right to be protected from harm.

Cultural or religious values may also conflict with the right to be protected from harm. For example, a Jehovah's Witness (who does not agree with blood transfusions) may find themselves in hospital with a medical condition where a blood transfusion offers the only means of saving their life.

In these situations the rights and duties of the care workers may also conflict with those of the individual using the service, and a decision will have to be taken as to which is the best course of action.

## Key term

**Act of omission** – Failure to act in a way that a person would usually act. In health and social care, a professional may sometimes fail to provide care in order to save someone from the greater harm of a prolonged and painful death. In other words, in a medical context doctors cannot give lethal injections, but they can withhold treatment when someone is in the final stages of life.

## Activity 10: Conflicts of rights

Consider the following scenarios:

1 Fred has become increasingly confused and wanders at night, repeatedly waking his neighbours. The neighbours demand action. Social workers offer Fred residential care but the offer is refused. Whose rights should take precedence?

2 Sam discloses to his key worker that his father and older brother have been abusing him. Sam pleads with his key worker not to tell anyone else. The right of confidentiality conflicts with the right to be protected from harm. Which right is more important in this situation?

3 Mary and Jack are Jehovah's Witnesses and have refused permission for Jenny, their five-year-old daughter, to have a blood transfusion. Doctors would have to overrule the parent's right to choice and religious beliefs if they want to treat Jenny. Would it ever be acceptable to agree with Mary and Jack's wishes?

## PLTS

**Independent enquirer:** This activity will help you demonstrate that you can work out how to incorporate ethical principles into support for individuals.

## Balancing services and resources

There has been a lot of discussion about the way in which health and social care services should be provided, especially when there is limited funding and almost unlimited demand. Practical decisions on how resources should be allocated are often difficult to make. Should children and young people get priority, as they have their whole lives ahead of them? Or should consideration be given to the ageing population, as they have paid their national insurance contributions and taxes for longer? Should the focus be on people living in poverty or people who have disabilities?

For example, Mark is a critically ill child who needs very expensive surgical treatment and has low survival expectancy. Should the NHS do the operation or should the money be allocated to hundreds of tonsillectomy operations? Which is the most important?

## Conflicts of interest between individuals and organisations, individuals and relatives and groups of users of services

When working with vulnerable people who are receiving social care services, there can quite often be a conflict of interest between the individual and the organisation. For example, an older person who is a wheelchair user and is living in a residential home might be a smoker and be unable to give up his habit;

## Case study: Assisted suicide of a paralysed rugby player

Daniel James, a 23-year-old rugby player, was paralysed from the chest down during a training session. Daniel felt his body had 'become a prison' and he tried to commit suicide on several occasions. With his parents' support, Daniel travelled to the Dignitas Centre in Switzerland in April 2008, where he was assisted to end his life. Unlike other people who have travelled to the Dignitas Centre, Daniel was not terminally ill, and this case has led to debate about whether Daniel was right to take his own life or whether, with support, he could have come to terms with his disability and lived a fulfilling life.

Making reference to ethical principles, answer the following questions:

1 Did Mr and Mrs James have a moral and legal obligation to assist Daniel to commit suicide?

2 Was Daniel suitably empowered to take the decision to go to Switzerland?

3 What rights did Daniel have in making the decision to travel to Switzerland?

yet the legal requirements and policies and procedures of the organisation state that the environment does not permit smoking. Should the older person have to go outside the building or should the officer in charge provide a space for the person to smoke inside?

Other conflicts could involve the way in which an older person chooses to spend their money – for example, they may decide to leave money in their will to people other than their immediate family. For people with learning disabilities, the conflict of interests could be related to who they form close relationships with, which could include an intimate relationship. In situations like these, policies and procedures have to be followed closely and a risk assessment could be undertaken to assess the level of potential harm to the individual concerned and other people. It is important that the individual is able to express what they would like; in these situations an advocate is very useful.

## Choices with regard to support regimes

When providing social care support, it is very important to ensure that individuals are listened to and that their choices are acknowledged. In supported tenancy environments this could mean a choice of menu, choice of hobbies and interests and deciding who they would like as their key worker. The choice of support could also involve Direct Payments, which means that the individual who is receiving care in the community is enabled to arrange and pay for their own care and support services instead of receiving them directly from local authority social care services.

## Harm minimisation

One of the most important aspects of providing effective health and social care services is ensuring that the general environment is safe for individuals who are receiving a particular service. For example, within an early years setting, it is important to undertake a risk assessment of the environment and any set activities before children enter the setting. However, it is also important that, while playing, children learn to take responsibility and make independent decisions for themselves and learn how to avoid or deal with potential risks. By taking the appropriate action after completing a risk assessment, not only will the environment be safe and secure but harm minimisation will have been considered.

Individuals may sometimes take part in particular types of behaviour that can be viewed by professionals as harmful, but the individual is unable or unwilling to stop the particular behaviour. This is highlighted by social care services working with vulnerable young people who self-harm, perhaps through alcohol or drug misuse or having an eating disorder. Traditionally, any support offered would focus on interventions to stop people from harming themselves. These interventions usually focus on the habit and not the holistic needs of

## Case study: Conflict of interest

Will is a 28-year-old man with meningitis, who is brought into Accident and Emergency by his partner Patti. He is unconscious, has low blood pressure and there is evidence of renal failure. He is seriously ill and requires intensive care support to help him make a full recovery. The intensive care unit (ICU) is full, with some patients who are critically ill, but some are in a stable condition. There is evidence that moving a patient too soon out of ICU increases their chances of complications. There is an intensive care bed in another hospital 160 km (100 miles) away, but Will might not survive the journey. The consultant has to decide what to do.

**Consider the following points and discuss in groups your answers to the questions:**

1 Maximising benefit: what is the benefit to Will – he might not survive even with treatment? What would be the benefit of moving another patient out of the ICU?

2 Responding to need: Will is in urgent need of intensive care; does the hospital have a moral responsibility to respond to such an urgent need even if his chance of survival is small and it involves potential risks to other patients?

3 Respecting autonomy is an important ethical principle in health and social care: what about the wishes of the patients in the ICU? What about Will's wish to have appropriate care?

4 Duty of care: the health professionals in the ICU have a duty of care to all the patients in the unit. Does the intensive care team have a duty of care to other patients in other areas of the hospital?

## Case study: Alan and Jane

Alan and Jane both have learning disabilities and live in a supported tenancy in the community with eight other people. Both have their own rooms and during the past six months have become very close. They both enjoy music, going to the local pub for a drink and going to the cinema. They have started to spend more time alone in Jane's bedroom, listening to music.

Alan has revealed to Sam, his support worker, that while listening to music they both enjoy holding hands and 'giving each other a hug'. Even though Alan and Jane are in their mid-twenties, Sam is very concerned and discusses the situation with his supervisor Claire.

Without consulting Alan and Jane, Claire decides that they are not to be left alone and their outings are to be restricted. Alan becomes very angry and Jane begins to cry. When Jane's sister visits, Claire explains

that she is protecting Jane and Alan. But Jane's sister is concerned that Jane is not being allowed her independence, and her quality of life is being affected.

Claire's behaviour is an example of benevolent oppression, but she would argue that she has to consider the importance of Alan and Jane's needs and balance them with their rights. It is obvious that Claire and her staff need to be aware of the ethical principles to follow when faced with such dilemmas.

1   Identify the ethical dilemma that Claire and her team face.

2   How could Claire and Sam encourage Alan and Jane to become empowered and achieve autonomy?

the person. However, working in this way can be counter-productive, resulting in individuals ignoring the guidance and support that would enable them to stop self-harming. Effective social care practice now focuses on harm minimisation, which means accepting and respecting the individual's right to make decisions about their own health and well-being, which could include using food or alcohol to deal with emotional or psychological issues.

For example, in a hostel for young people with alcohol or drug misuse problems, there would be consideration of the environment, which should be organised to reduce opportunities for self-harm. This would include having a 'Harm Minimisation Policy', which included clear guidance about drugs and alcohol that would apply to everyone at the setting – staff and visitors, as well as the young people. The success of a risk recognition/minimisation policy is

likely to depend upon a consistent approach being taken to the management of the physical environment, the gathering and reviewing of information relating to who attends the setting, and individual risk assessments being applied to everyone within the setting.

It is very important that the setting provides good-quality service and the staff remain non-judgemental in their approach. This helps avoid reinforcing feelings of hopelessness and despair. Settings should also make provision for any relapse that could occur and make plans for how relapses can be prevented. These provisions could include one-to-one sessions with a key worker and the individual concerned and, after discussion, identifying a plan of action. In contrast, group work, relaxation sessions, counselling with trained staff and other useful strategies can ensure that harm is minimised.

## Activity 11: Ethical dilemmas

In small groups, read the following scenarios, and highlight the ethical dilemmas that are presented. Making reference to principles and values, explain what action the care worker should take in each case:

Rezwana is 15. She arrives at a young women's hostel bruised and tearful. She tells the staff that her father and brothers have arranged a marriage for her with a distant relative, aged 52, in Pakistan. She has been told that she will be 'forced' to marry if she does not obey her family. She begs the staff not to contact her family or her social worker Trisha, as she does not trust her – she believes that Trisha does not respect her wishes and breached her confidentiality. Rezwana disclosed to Trisha that her father and brothers were physically and emotionally abusing her. Trisha told the police, and Rezwana's father and brothers were arrested, then released without charges. This made Rezwana's home life very difficult.

Alfie is 12. He goes to the school nurse with bruising and panic attacks. He discloses to the nurse that he has got involved with some of his brother's 'friends', and that he is bringing drugs into school for 'customers' of his brother. He asks the nurse not to say anything.

Miriam has been married to Yosef for 12 months and has just given birth to her first son. Before she met Yosef, Miriam had a long-term relationship, which ended in pregnancy and a termination. She notices that a member of staff, Laura, was the nurse who cared for her during her last stay in hospital. Laura is also a member of the same synagogue as Miriam and Yosef. Miriam is worried that Laura will tell Yosef of her past.

Danny, aged 19, has been going to a counsellor, Amanda, for several months. On his last visit, Amanda asks Danny if he would like to go for a drink to celebrate the end of his therapy. Danny is flattered, as Amanda is an attractive 'older' woman and they get on well. While in the wine bar, Amanda's supervisor Jane, sees the couple together and is concerned that professional boundaries may have been crossed.

Points to consider:

1 The principle of respect for autonomy means that personal information should not be disclosed without consent. However, in some cases the autonomy of another person might be an issue.

2 Although keeping personal information confidential is important, there has to be a balancing of the benefits and harms of disclosure and non-disclosure.

3 What would the harm of non-disclosure be, compared to the harm that might result from disclosing information without consent, essentially a breach of confidentiality?

## Assessment activity 9.4

(P4) (P5) (M3) **BTEC**

1 Write an essay that explores ethical principles in relation to supporting individuals. The essay must explain

- how ethical principles are incorporated into provision of support for individuals

- why an ethical approach may provide health and social care workers with dilemmas when planning and providing support.

2 Incorporate into the essay a justification of how an ethical approach to providing support would benefit individuals.

### Grading tips

(P4) (P5) Use examples to illustrate the points you make in the essay. If the examples are from placements, you should seek permission and maintain confidentiality of both individuals and the placement setting.

You should provide reasons of how an ethical approach can benefit individuals.

(M3) Think about how an ethical approach would improve the support and services received by each of the individuals you described in the first part of the question.

## PLTS

**Creative thinker:** Recognising where an ethical approach to support may present workers with a dilemma shows creative thinking skills.

# Resources and further reading

Butt, J. & Mirza, K. (1996) *Social Care and Black Communities* London: HMSO

Cutherbert, S. & Qualington, I. (2006 Values for Social Care Practice) *Health and Social Care: Theory and Practice* Maidenhead: Open University

Giddens, A. (2001) Sociology, fourth ed, Oxford: Polity Press, John Wiley Ltd

Lloyd, M. (2010) *A Practical Guide to Support Planning in Health and Social Care* Maidenhead: Open University

Senior, M. & Viveash, B. (1998) *Health and Illness. Skills Based Sociology* London: Palgrave Macmillan

## Journals

*Community Care*

*Guardian* (Wednesday edition)

*Children and Young People Now*

# Useful websites

Age UK www.ageuk.org.uk

Children's Workforce Development Council www.cwdc.org.uk

Community Care Magazine www.communitycare.co.uk

Department of Health www.dh.gov.uk

Equality and Human Rights Commission www.equalityhumanrights.com

General Social Care Council www.gscc.org.uk

Public Guardian's Office www.publicguardian.gov.uk

Skills for Care and Development www.skillsforcareanddevelopment.org.uk

Guardian Newspaper www.guardian.co.uk/society

Independent Safeguarding Authority www.isa-gov.org

# Just checking

1 Explain what is involved in a holistic approach to care work.
2 Why is empowerment important when working with individuals in health and social care?
3 What does 'multi-disciplinary team working' mean?
4 Explain the different types of referral methods.
5 Identify the different types of tools that are used in the assessment process.
6 What is a code of practice?
7 Name two policies that are used in organisations.
8 What do ethical principles consist of?
9 Explain what an ethical dilemma is.

edexcel

# Assignment tips

1 When explaining how principles and values are applied by social care workers, it is important to consider how these professional values can at times conflict with the values of the individual who requires support. Therefore, you need to consider how practitioners can promote choice and rights, and recognise individual preferences, while respecting religious, cultural and moral beliefs.

2 It is important to understand the importance of working holistically to make sure that every individual has a good quality of life.

3 You may find examples from your vocational placement of the benefits for both individuals and professional staff of working in a multi-disciplinary way, ensuring that all needs are catered for. You might choose to interview your placement supervisor to help you with your research, which will help you to construct case studies.

4 It is important to maintain confidentiality if you are using specific examples. Always seek permission from your placement supervisor, avoid naming individuals and your placement and do not use photographic evidence.

5 Support plans are working documents, which contain private and confidential information; your supervisor will be a good source of information, and can explain how the referral assessment and planning process take place.

6 You may see an example of a blank support plan, which will give you some idea of who is involved in the assessment of individual needs and how support is identified.

7 Always remember to include individual choices and preferences when constructing a support plan, and identify realistic goals and tasks to be achieved.

8 Your placement experience will be extremely useful in terms of seeing how legislation impacts on the way policies and procedures and codes of professional practice are applied.

# 10 Caring for children and young people

Not all young people have the care and education they would wish for. There are various reasons for this, many of which are out of the hands of the young people themselves. This unit will explore the many reasons why children and young people may need to be looked after and examine the organisations that provide care for them. Some children will need to be looked after because their life circumstances have changed and their parents can no longer care for them in the family home. Others may have poor life experiences that mean they need to be looked after. We will also consider the roles of the staff who work within these organisations and those who open their homes to care for children in a family environment. In order to fully comprehend the issues involved, we will take a close look at the risks to children and young people caught up in abusive or exploitative situations.

If you are contemplating a career working with children and young people you need to be able to recognise the signs and symptoms when they are maltreated and know what to do if they disclose their history to you. You will also consider strategies that might be used to empower children and young people and safeguard them from a variety of abusive and exploitative situations. In addition, you will explore a range of support mechanisms that can be employed to assist children and young people in coping with their difficult life experiences.

## Learning outcomes

After completing this unit you should:

1 know why children and young people might need to be looked after
2 know how care is provided for looked after children and young people
3 understand the risks to children and young people of abusive and exploitative behaviour
4 understand the strategies used to safeguard children and young people from abusive and exploitative behaviour.

# Assessment and grading criteria

This table shows you what you must do in order to achieve a **pass**, **merit** or **distinction** grade, and where you can find activities in this book to help you.

| To achieve a **pass** grade, the evidence must show that you are able to: | To achieve a **merit** grade, the evidence must show that, in addition to the pass criteria, you are able to: | To achieve a **distinction** grade, the evidence must show that, in addition to the pass and merit criteria, you are able to: |
|---|---|---|
| **P1** Outline why children and young people may need to be looked after away from their families. **See Assessment Activity 10.1, page 40** | **M1** Discuss how policies and procedures help children, young people and their families whilst the child is being looked after. **See Assessment Activity 10.2, page 49** | |
| **P2** Outline the arrangements for providing quality care for looked after children and young people. **See Assessment Activity 10.2, page 49** | **M2** Explain the roles and responsibilities of two members of the children's workforce in relation to looked after children and young people. **See Assessment Activity 10.2, page 49** | **D1** Evaluate the regulation of care provision for looked after children and young people. **See Assessment Activity 10.2, page 49** |
| **P3** Explain the factors that would lead to the suspicion of child maltreatment or abuse. **See Assessment Activity 10.3, page 59** | | |
| **P4** Explain appropriate responses when child maltreatment or abuse is suspected. **See Assessment Activity 10.4, page 68** | | **D2** Justify responses where child maltreatment or abuse is suspected or confirmed, making reference to current legislation and policies. **See Assessment Activity 10.4, page 68** |
| **P5** Explain the strategies and methods that can be used to support children, young people and their families where abuse is suspected or confirmed. **See Assessment Activity 10.4, page 68** | **M3** Assess strategies and methods used to minimise the harm to children, young people and their families where abuse is confirmed. **See Assessment Activity 10.4, page 68** | |

# How you will be assessed

You will be assessed through a range of tasks or assignments and it will be explained carefully to you what needs to be done or produced in order to meet the grading criteria. For example, you may be asked to present your research to the class or produce a leaflet or write an essay. You will find some suggestions as you work through this chapter and the particular grading criteria being assessed will be identified at each stage.

## Marie, 18 years old

When I first thought about this course I was pleased at the range of units that I could study but I must admit that I had not realised how detailed the content was. My goal is to become a social worker and I would like to specialise in working with children and young people so this course is ideal to further my long-term aims. I have visited a variety of places and have had a work placement so I can link my college work to the practice in the workplace.

I am pleased that I have not been involved with anything to do with safeguarding children and young people but it is so important to be aware of the reasons why children are looked after and what can be done to help them in and through a range of different situations. I thought that this unit would not be as interesting as some of the others but it has proved to be very interesting and uplifting, as it enables you to understand how children and young people can be helped and supported through difficult times in their lives. This course has provided great experience and will certainly benefit me when I move on to university or into a career.

## Over to you!

1   Why do you think some children and young people are in care?
2   What are some of the major issues they face?
3   What do you think you will find most interesting and most difficult in this unit?

# 1 Know why children and young people might need to be looked after

### Mixed feelings

Were you ever in a situation as a child when you did not know what was happening? Adults might have been talking in a way that was designed to keep things from you and you were perhaps unsure how to behave or what to do. Maybe one of your parents was ill or had injured themselves, and other family members were trying to organise who was going to look after you.

* How did this make you feel?
* Do you think that children and young people should always be told what's happening? Give reasons for your answer.
* What other feelings might children and young people experience when they are separated from their parents?

## 1.1 Looked after children

There are a number of reasons why children may be looked after by people other than their own family. Those reasons may include family breakdown, bereavement, parental illness or incapacity of some kind. They may be linked to behavioural problems or even the child's own illness. These will be discussed in more detail later.

### Following the imposition of a care order

It is the duty of each local authority to consider the welfare of all children. The Children Acts of 1989 and 2004 try to ensure that children are supported and kept within the family home, if at all possible. However, if a child, for whatever reason, needs to live away from home and is cared for by a local authority, this child is known as being 'looked after'. Some children in this situation may have multiple behaviour problems and will often require individual support and care – some have been excluded from school and may have difficulty in developing relationships with other people. There are times when a care order needs to be imposed for the overall benefit of the child and their family. This means that social services, under the local authority, have the responsibility of caring for the child or young person and making decisions for them.

Each local authority will endeavour to ensure that an appropriate placement is found for the length of time that the child or young person will need to be looked after. The ultimate goal is that the child will eventually return to live with his or her own family. However, this may not always be possible. In many cases a substitute family is required, or the young person may have reached an age when they can live independently.

### With the agreement of parents

There are times when parents realise that they are struggling with their parental responsibilities and that the child would benefit from a period of time away from the family home. Once the situation has improved, the child often returns to the care of their parents.

## 1.2 Potential reasons why a child might be looked after

Sometimes a child or young person might need to leave their home because of problems that are related either to their family or to themselves. For example, the family may be unable to care for the child because of an accident, or the child may present such difficult behaviour patterns that the family is unable to cope.

Alternatively, the child or young person may be abused or exploited and might need to be cared for away from the family home for reasons of safety.

## Family-related reasons

These could include bereavement, parental illness or incapacity (such as mental health problems or substance misuse). We'll explore these in more detail below.

### Bereavement and upheaval

Looked after children are often very vulnerable, as they have faced a great deal of upheaval and disruption. They may have been affected by damaging experiences such as abuse and rejection. There may have been traumatic experiences in their lives such as family bereavement and they may have learned to internalise their turbulent emotions. As a result, many of them have great difficulty with their education and often fall behind the majority of children in their class. Their ability to concentrate is greatly reduced and they may display specific needs that must be addressed and met before progress can be made. However, school is often the only stable factor in the child's life – everything else except school may be in turmoil.

### Parental illness or incapacity

The reasons why children and young people find themselves being looked after are varied. Their parents may be temporarily unwell or unable to cope, in which case the child may return to the family home at some stage as this situation improves. Meanwhile, they may spend time with foster parents, in children's homes or in residential schools. The length of time they spend in this situation will vary according to circumstances. Family breakdown happens for many reasons, including bereavement, parental illness, incapacity, mental health problems or even substance abuse. The family unit may break down totally because of violence and discord and the child may require care that could be temporary or even permanent. A child who is being abused may need to be removed from that situation for their own safety and well-being. Such circumstances may result in their needing particularly sensitive care and they may require therapy later to help them come to terms with what has happened to them.

Fig 10.1: What is going to happen now?

## Case study: Unexpected events

Amy, aged five and Oliver, aged seven, together with their parents, have just moved to a new house, far away from their friends and other family members. They have settled into their new house and decided to have a special lunch at a nice restaurant. Mum, Dad and Oliver all ordered chicken and Amy asked for fish. They enjoyed the meal and then went to look around the area. They had a pleasant afternoon. However, after they arrived home, Oliver and his mum and dad began to feel ill. Amy was fine and was unsure what was happening.

The situation deteriorated and the on-call doctor called an ambulance, which took all members of the family to hospital. Amy was quite concerned and even started to feel frightened. The members of the family who were ill had to be kept in hospital and it turned out that they had serious food poisoning. This was attributed to the chicken, as Amy was the only one who did not display any symptoms.

1 How might Amy be feeling at this time?

2 How could she be looked after while her parents are in hospital?

3 How might the other members of her family be feeling at this time?

## Suspected or actual maltreatment

When a child is the victim of maltreatment it is important that they are removed from the situation to a safe place, which may be with another family. This might also happen if there is suspected abuse taking place. The safety of the child or young person is the most important factor while the allegations are being investigated.

## Child or young person-related reasons

A child or young person might need to leave their family home because of their own health problems, behavioural problems, learning difficulties or disability. It may also be because the child has committed an offence. Again, we'll explore these in more detail below.

## Health problems

A child or young person may have an illness or condition that makes it difficult for them to live in a family home and so alternative arrangements must be made for long- or short-term care. The **provision** required might be specific so that the child would benefit from the use of specialist resources, which may only be available outside the family home.

---

### Case study: Specialised provision

Adrian lives at home with his mother and two younger brothers, to whom he is very close. The house they live in is specially adapted, as Adrian is a wheelchair user. The adaptations help him to be independent, although his mother and brothers still need to help him with some everyday tasks. Recently, his mother has been feeling unwell and has found out that she needs an operation. She will have to be hospitalised for at least two weeks and then she will require some time to recuperate. Close relatives have made various suggestions for looking after the children while this takes place. Adrian's brothers can move in with their aunts but no one seems able to provide a suitable place for Adrian. Their houses are not adapted for wheelchair use and the family is concerned about how Adrian can be looked after during this time.

1 Make a list of suggestions for the three brothers.
2 Who else might be involved in this situation?
3 What might Adrian be feeling at this time?
4 What might his brothers be feeling?

---

## Behavioural problems

Some possible causes of changes in behaviour, which might lead to problems for children, young people and their families, are listed in Table 10.1.

## Learning difficulties

There are many families within the UK with children and young people who have learning difficulties. Some families are unable to cope with the challenges this presents, and may reject their child. In such cases, it can be helpful for the child to be looked after outside the family home. This may only be a temporary measure but, in many cases, if the child requires specialist assistance, it may become a more permanent arrangement. Alternatively, temporary **respite** care allows a family time to relax and deal with their own needs so that they are better equipped when their child returns to the family home.

## Disability

Children and young people with disabilities may be part of families with so many other demands on them that they find it difficult to cope. Short-term respite care may be a possibility or there may need to be longer-term provision. If the family home cannot provide for the specialised needs of the individual, alternative care may be sought, which primarily benefits the child or young person.

## A child who has committed an offence

There are some young people who, for a variety of reasons, get caught up in a cycle of offending and breaking the law. Their criminal activity may result in the young person being **remanded** or detained. In general, the number of children and young people who are in care because they have been remanded or detained make up less than two per cent of the total who are looked after. When a young person is remanded or detained it is usually as a result of criminal charges and a short-term care order may be made.

**Table 10.1:** Some reasons for behavioural change in children and young people

| Stress | Many children suffer from stress, leading to poor school performance, and emotional and behavioural problems. Stress may be the result of an unstable home life or feeling unloved. Their parents may not have the skills needed to bring up children, or the child may feel that unrealistic demands for achievement are being made on them. |
|---|---|
| Anxiety | Anxiety is quite common among children and young people. Chronic anxiety disorders require early diagnosis if they are to be treated in time. If they are left unrecognised, they may result in a disability, dysfunction and, in some cases, even suicide. |
| Depression | Childhood depression is a growing concern, has many different causes, and may even lead to suicide. The child or young person may become unresponsive, withdrawn and not seek the company of others. Without appropriate treatment, depression can have serious consequences. Finding the root cause of depression may be difficult and the young person may need counselling and therapy. |
| Obsessive–compulsive disorder (OCD) | Children with obsessive–compulsive disorder are growing in number. Relatively little is known about this disorder but early recognition and treatment can help to reduce the suffering it causes. |
| Phobias | Phobias often come under the heading of childhood anxiety disorders but they are now becoming so common that they may be dealt with as a separate issue. Panic disorders are also linked to phobias and these can have a devastating effect on a child. Once again, early recognition and treatment are essential. |

## Did you know?

The causes of anxiety in children may not always seem rational to an adult, as they are at different stages of development.

## Key terms

**Provision** – What is provided or put in place for the benefit and support of an individual. This may include specially built or adapted buildings, trained staff or specialist equipment that will assist individuals with a range of diverse conditions and situations.

**Respite** – A break or a time of relief from the demands of care.

**Remanded** – To be kept separate from society for a period of time in a young offenders' institution or a prison.

**Fig 10.2:** Young people might offend because they want attention. Can you think of other possible reasons?

## Activity 1: Support groups

Undertake an Internet search to obtain information on support groups for families with specific needs (e.g. a family with a child who has spina bifida). List three different groups and then discuss your findings with another person in your class so that ideally you will have a list of six support groups between you.

### PLTS

**Self-manager:** This activity will help you provide evidence of the self-management skills needed to do independent research.

## Assessment activity 10.1

P1 **BTEC**

Imagine that you are a researcher for a local radio station and you have been asked to put together a piece on looked after children and young people.

Carry out some independent research and use a report or presentation to outline why children and young people may need to be looked after.

### Grading tip

P1 You will need to consider a range of reasons why children and young people might need to be looked after and include both short- and long-term solutions. You must ensure that your sources are reliable and remember to avoid websites citing information from other countries, e.g. the USA or Australia.

# 2 Know how care is provided for looked after children and young people

## 2.1 Legislation/legal framework

It has long been recognised that children and young people are vulnerable and are therefore at great risk of being abused and exploited. There is now a comprehensive legal framework in place to protect them. This is constantly being reviewed, as the structure of society changes.

## Activity 2: Every Child Matters in action

In pairs, list the five main aims of *Every Child Matters* (see Table 10.2). Under each of the aims write down how you think this might impact on a child aged 12.

### Functional skills

**English:** This activity will help you provide evidence of being able to produce written work after participating in discussion.

**Table 10.2:** Legislation to protect children and young people

| Legislation | Main provisions |
| --- | --- |
| United Nations Convention on the Rights of the Child 1989 | • International agreement that considers the rights of all children and young people.<br>• Consists of 54 articles covering a range of rights, including the right to be free from violence, the right to play, the right to express themselves and have their views taken into account.<br>• Convention provides additional rights to ensure that children and young people living away from home, and those who have disabilities, are treated fairly and their specific needs are met. |
| *Every Child Matters: Change for Children* (2003) | • Considers the well-being of children and young people from birth to 19.<br>• Five principles at the heart of this legislation apply to every child, whatever their background or circumstances. All children should:<br>  1  be healthy<br>  2  stay safe<br>  3  enjoy and achieve<br>  4  make a positive contribution<br>  5  experience economic well-being.<br>• All organisations working with children and young people must work together to protect children from harm and help them achieve their goals. Information will be gathered concerning vulnerable groups so that support strategies can be put in place. Children and young people will be involved in decision-making processes. The first Children's Commissioner for England was appointed in 2005 to help give children and young people some input into government. |
| Children Act 1989, 2004 Children (Scotland) Act 1995 | • The Children Act 1989 was initially designed to ensure that all local authorities were making equal provision to support children, young people and their families.<br>• It includes the support of children with disabilities who, when they reach the age of 18, come under the NHS and Community Care Act 1990.<br>• In 1995, the Children Act was updated in Scotland, with the same view that 'the welfare of the child is paramount'. It updated the law of Scotland relating to looked after children and young people.<br>• The Children Act 2004 accompanies *Every Child Matters* (see above), which considered all aspects of children's services, including new statutory duties for local authorities. |
| The Report of the Child Protection Audit and Review (2002) (Scottish Executive) | • Highlighted joint responsibility for children's welfare. |
| The Education (Admissions of Looked After Children) (Wales) Regulation 2009 | • Provides guidance on how looked after children and young people should access education and how this might be prioritised. |
| Regulations and Guidance for Looked After Children: Towards a Stable Life and Brighter Future 2006 (Wales) | • Contains proposals to strengthen arrangements for the placement, health and well-being of looked after children and young people. |

*continued*

**Table 10.2:** *continued*

| Legislation | Main provisions |
|---|---|
| Human Rights Act 1998 | • Came into force in England and Wales in 2000 and incorporated the European Convention on Human Rights into the national legislative framework.<br>• Enables children, young people and adults to seek protection of their rights both nationally and internationally, through the European Court of Human Rights in Strasbourg. |
| Data Protection Act 1998 | • Prevents personal information from being misused, while protecting safe use of data for legitimate reasons. There are eight principles to ensure that personal information is:<br>1 fairly and lawfully processed<br>2 processed for limited purposes<br>3 adequate, relevant and not excessive<br>4 accurate<br>5 not kept longer than necessary<br>6 processed in accordance with a person's rights<br>7 kept secure<br>8 not transferred abroad without adequate protection. |
| Framework for the Assessment of Children in Need and their Families 2000 | • Introduced to secure the well-being of children and young people at vulnerable times during their lives.<br>• Provides a framework for assessment of children and their families.<br>• Many families require help to resolve their problems. The assessment will identify the needs of the child or young person and this may be the first stage of a much longer process of support and possible intervention. |
| Common Assessment Framework (England) | • Vital to providing integrated services that focus on the needs of the child or young person.<br>• Used for children with additional needs, who may require support to help them achieve the five outcomes of *Every Child Matters*.<br>• Provides a standardised way of considering a child's or young person's needs and deciding how they can best be met.<br>• Aims to identify the needs of the individual at an early stage and also considers the roles of the parents, others and a range of factors influencing their achievement.<br>• Consists of a pre-assessment checklist followed by a three-step process, which covers preparation, discussion and the delivery of services for the benefit of the child or young person. |
| Protecting Children and Young People: Framework for Standards (Scottish Executive 2004) | • Defines child abuse as a 'deliberate act of ill treatment that can harm or is likely to cause harm to a child's safety, wellbeing and development' (Scott 2008).<br>• Lays down guidelines to support children and advocates a multi-agency working framework to ensure that all those involved are kept informed. |
| Care Matters: Northern Ireland: A Bridge to a Better Future (Consultation Stage) | • Consultation document that seeks to outline ways of improving services for children and young people in a wide range of situations. |
| Children (Leaving Care) Act 2002 Northern Ireland | • Gives guidance about making provision for children and young people who are being or have been looked after. |

# 2.2 Care available for looked after children and young people

Several different care possibilities are available and some of these are listed in Table 10.3 below.

**Table 10.3:** Possible forms of care

| Type of care | Characteristics |
|---|---|
| Temporary/ permanent care | Temporary or permanent care can be arranged but a number of assessments and procedures have to be completed before the care of a child or young person becomes permanent. An example would be a child who has been in foster care for a considerable time and whose natural parents are deemed to be incapable of caring for a minor. |
| Foster care | Foster care is often short-term but can become long-term as circumstances change. Foster carers are checked by the local authority to ensure that they are suitable and competent to provide care in their own homes They need to be adaptable, as they may be caring for a baby one day and an eight-year-old a week later. Children and young people in foster care can sometimes present very complex problems. |
| Respite care | Respite care is usually decided in advance and is a short-term arrangement. Often the child or young person has learning difficulties and/or disabilities and the family need a break. Respite care consists of a child spending some time in a residential establishment that caters for their specific needs. |
| Residential care | Children and young people may be taken into residential care for various reasons – perhaps as respite for a family unit or as a temporary emergency situation in an abusive family situation. Residential childcare may be arranged for children and young people with behavioural difficulties so that specialised staff are available to interact with them. |
| Adoption | Adoption is a formal, legal process in which the child or young person becomes a permanent member of a family other than their natural birth family. Sometimes parents give up all responsibility for a child and offer that child or young person for adoption. Adoption can also follow the death of the child's natural parents. |

## Case study: Childminder's dilemma

Shama is two years old and lives with her mother, who works in a local shop. Shama spends most days with her childminder, Mary, who also cares for another child. Mary always knows what time Shama will be collected and her mother is very reliable.

Mary is aware that Shama's mother has been dealing with some personal and emotional issues and today she is expecting Shama to be collected at 4pm. When her mother does not arrive on time, Mary assumes that she has been slightly delayed and is not immediately worried.

However, as time passes, she starts to be concerned about Shama's mother. She tries to contact her by

telephone but there is no answer. She then contacts the shop but is informed that Shama's mother left at her usual time. She now tries the emergency contact number but again, there is no answer. Shama is totally unaware of what is happening and is playing quite happily.

1   In pairs, list three possible scenarios suggesting what might have happened to Shama's mother.

2   Discuss these scenarios, then write down the answers to the following questions:

- What should Mary do next?

- Who else might she contact?

## Planning for care in partnership with the child/young person, parents and other agencies

It is in the child's or young person's best interests that any care provisions are established and organised, whenever possible, in a mutually acceptable way. In some cases the family and parents have requested support and help, perhaps on a short-term basis. The chance of a successful outcome is greatly increased if all parties (including other agencies involved) can agree on the partnership arrangements for the mutual care and support for the child or young person.

### Fostering agencies

There are a number of fostering agencies and the British Association for Adoption and Fostering is often able to direct people to agencies in their area. All agencies focus on the **paramountcy principle**,

### Key term

**Paramountcy principle** – The Children Act 1989 states that 'the welfare of the child is paramount', meaning that it is of supreme importance or vital. All agencies focus on this point at all times.

detailed in the Children Act (1989), that, in all decisions relating to the health and welfare of a child or young person, the best interest of the child is paramount and of supreme importance.

## 2.3 Organisation of care provision

Care for children and young people is provided by the following agencies:

- central government
- local authorities
- third sector:
    1 the voluntary sector
    2 independent providers
    3 charitable organisations.

These are all explored below and cover the four countries of the United Kingdom.

### Central government

There are a number of relevant departments and services within central government as detailed in Table 10.4.

**Table 10.4:** Departments and services within central government

| Government department | Services |
|---|---|
| Department of Health | • Responsible for public health issues and monitoring and regulating the NHS.<br>• Aims to provide for public health and well-being with easily accessible services and highly qualified and dedicated staff. |
| National Health Service (NHS) | • Involved in all types of health care, including care of children and young people with learning difficulties or disabilities.<br>• Has a duty of care to provide the appropriate resources and assistance for the family.<br>• Staff will work very closely with other agencies and a multi-disciplinary team may be involved in the overall care plan for an individual. |
| National Service Framework for Children, Young People and Maternity Services | • Established in 2004 and set the standards for children's health, social services and other related services.<br>• Promotes an integrated approach to multi-agency working when supporting children, young people and their families.<br>• Death of eight-year-old Victoria Climbié in 2000 was one of the reasons why the National Framework came into being.<br>• These guidelines offer a more cohesive approach, especially when dealing with vulnerable children and young people. |

## Case study: Work is best

The Richardsons seem like a fairly typical family. Mr Richardson works varying shifts at a local factory and Mrs Richardson works behind the bar at a local pub so she works most evenings and some lunchtimes. They have three children: thirteen-year-old Sharon; Jack, who can be quite adventurous, is ten; and Amy, who is very quiet, is four years old.

In general the children are well cared for and the parents are able to provide adequately for the family. However, there are times when neither Mr nor Mrs Richardson are at home and the burden of care usually falls on Sharon. She finds it quite difficult at times and shouts at the two younger children when they do not do as she wishes. Amy has become extremely quiet recently and spends a lot of time sitting in a corner and hugging herself. Jack has responded by becoming more 'adventurous' and Sharon does not really know how to cope. She cannot ask her parents, as they have shouted at her before and told her that it is her job to look after the children.

The schools the children attend have noticed changes in their behaviour recently and have talked to the children about improving their work and trying to find out what the problems are. As a result, Sharon is very unhappy. Jack has decided that he would be better off living somewhere else and goes to a friend's house to 'live'. His friend's mother listens to Jack as he tells her about his life and she rings the police for advice.

Consider the family situation and make informed suggestions in response to the following questions, giving reasons for your answers.

1   What do you think might happen next?

2   Who else might be involved?

3   How might the family situation improve?

4   What emotions do you think each child is experiencing?

## Local authority services

Each local authority has a duty of care for children and young people and may become involved in all cases where they are at risk of not being cared for appropriately. They will provide help and assistance for families and in many cases will work in partnership, providing resources to keep the family together.

However, there are other times when the authority must intervene for the good of the child. This might mean providing temporary care until a parent recovers from an accident or illness or it may involve removing the child to a place of safety until a danger is reduced or eliminated.

**Table 10.5:** Services provided by local authorities

| Local authority services | Features of services |
|---|---|
| Integrated services | Integrated children's services plan to provide the best start in life for children. They draw together all the services, especially for those with special and specific needs. They will include education, health, social services and youth justice and will produce objectives for a more integrated approach. |
| Children's services Local Authority Children's Services in England (LACS) Local Councils in Scotland Health and Social Service Care Trust in Northern Ireland | The Children Act 2004 introduced legislation to protect children and young people to a greater degree. Children's services throughout the UK deal with education, health and social care issues related to children, young people and their families. They aim to provide an integrated approach and all the services provided are subject to inspection under the Children Act 2004. |
| Children's Trusts – England | Children's trusts bring together all the local children's and young people's services and assist with the improvement of these services to meet the outcomes of *Every Child Matters*. |

## Voluntary sector – pre-school provision

Pre-school provision covers a range of services, some provided by volunteers (e.g. carer and toddler groups and play provision in church halls or local community centres). The leaders of these groups may have some training but many have not and, as long as the parents or carers do not leave their children, then there is no legal requirement that they should.

### Reflect

Think back to your own primary school education and the people you had contact with at school. List two people who had a positive impact on you and explain why. Then list two people who had a negative impact on you and explain why.

### Independent providers and organisations

Private nurseries usually cater for children from birth up to the age of four (although many three- and four-year-olds attend local authority nurseries). Staff are trained in early years and there may be some members of staff who are working towards a recognised qualification. The arrangements for childcare are usually made on an individual basis between the nursery and the family, as the provision required will vary considerably. The family will pay a fee based on the number of hours or sessions the child attends.

Childminders are suitably qualified individuals, who use their own home as the setting for looking after children and young people. The venue and personnel involved

Early years provision covers children from birth to five years old

### Activity 3: Information sheet

Carry out research on the Internet and produce an A4 information sheet on one of the following;

- NSPCC
- Childline UK
- Barnardo's
- Kidscape
- National Children's Bureau

You can then present it to the rest of the group/class.

### Functional skills

**ICT:** This research activity will enable you to demonstrate your ability to select appropriate information from a range of Internet sites and present it in a word-processed document.

undergo rigorous inspections and they must be trained and registered as local authority childminders.

Organisations such as Barnardo's, the NSPCC and the British Association for Adoption and Fostering are nationally recognised for their work in caring for the needs of children and young people. They uphold the principle that the 'welfare of the child is paramount', and are actively involved in increasing positive support for children generally and particularly those who are being looked after.

## 2.4 Types of services

### Universal

These services are open to all children and young people and can be used by all those who need them.

### Specialist

These services are very specialised (e.g. for partially sighted or deaf people) and can be accessed by individuals who need the specific type of provision they offer.

### Targeted

These services are designed for specific groups of people. For example, youth work is targeted at a specific age group and provides specific types of activities for young people.

# 2.5 Job roles

Within the organisations mentioned there are various job roles. Some of these are listed below.

## Commissioning, directing and managing services

### Director of Children's Services

After the Children Act 2004, every local authority had to appoint a Director of Children's Services. This person is responsible for the delivery of education, health and social service programmes and duties within the authority. Additionally, they are responsible for developing a more integrated service.

## Directly working with children and young people

### Volunteers

Many people give up their time to work on a voluntary basis with children and young people in a range of settings. They are often highly trained and devote a great deal of time and energy to developing skills and knowledge to enable them to provide the best they can for children and young people in a variety of situations.

### Social workers

Trained and qualified social workers support families with children who present problems and difficulties in a wide range of areas. They often work as part of a **multi-disciplinary team** to provide a comprehensive support framework.

> ### Key term
>
> **Multi-disciplinary team** – A team of professionals drawn from a range of disciplines or services, e.g. health care, education and social services, all working together towards a common goal.

Senior social workers may be appointed as a 'guardian ad litem' by the Children and Family Court Advisory and Support Service (CAFCASS). They represent the child's interests in cases where the child's wishes may differ from those of the parents. CAFCASS is a service that safeguards and promotes the interests of the children involved in family court cases (not criminal) and seeks to ensure that the children are represented in cases such as adoption, separation/divorce, or when children are being removed from their parents' care because of safeguarding issues.

### Health visitors

Health visitors visit every family when a baby is born, once the specialist skills of the midwife are no longer required. The health visitor is a nurse with further qualifications in other aspects of childcare who visits the family to provide advice and support on a wide range of situations. Many families only require the support of a health visitor for a relatively short time after the birth of a baby, but an increasing number of families require additional support and advice for a longer period of time.

### Nursing/health care/social care assistants

This group includes people working towards a specific qualification, who are working as an assistant in their specialised area. They will work closely with the nursing/health care/social care staff to support children, young people and their families.

### Youth workers

Youth workers work with children and young people, usually between the ages of 13 and 19. They usually work in youth centres, clubs, schools, etc, and may work as part of a youth offending team. However, some work in less traditional ways, as detached youth workers, trying to engage with young people who might be more at risk in the community. They may be involved in delivering programmes, supporting young people, working with parents and community groups and undertaking other activities as and when required.

> ### Activity 4: Working with young people
>
> Youth work is a profession that appeals to a wide range of individuals. Working in small groups, gather information about as many types of youth work as you can. Produce an information sheet in which you itemise each one. (You could also illustrate it.)

### Tutors

Usually working in colleges or educational establishments, tutors provide help and support, both academic and pastoral. They often help young people develop their functional skills and personal skills.

### Educational psychologists

There are specialist psychology services that work with children and young people. This may be within the education system, where they will provide advice and support in the face of complex difficulties. Educational psychologists also work with parents and families and provide support for multi-agency working.

### Play workers

Qualified play workers can provide a range of play and leisure activities specifically designed for children and young people. The emphasis is on play and exploration for the individual child or young person.

### Foster parents

Foster parents accept children and young people into their homes and provide family care for the individual. The care offered may be emergency care, where immediate help is required. They work closely with social services to provide secure, reliable care.

## 2.6 Regulation of care provision

When children/young people are cared for by others in any capacity (e.g. school, nursery, foster care, childminder), certain regulations must be followed.

All individuals who have main contact with the child or young person will be screened by the Criminal Records Bureau (CRB) and the premises or setting will be inspected by the local authority and/or by the Office for Standards in Education (OFSTED).

### Criminal Records Bureau

The Criminal Records Bureau acts on behalf of Registered Bodies to check criminal records through a Disclosure service. For people working with or in close contact with children and young people, an Enhanced Disclosure is required. This requires a more detailed level of check than the Standard screening procedure and will include a check through local police records. From November 2010, those working with children and young people regularly will need to be registered with the Independent Safeguarding Agency (ISA).

### General Teaching Council for England

This is the professional regulatory body for teachers. There is a separate General Teaching Council for Scotland and Northern Ireland. They have a professional Code of Conduct and Practice for Registered Teachers, which sets standards by which all teaching staff should be measured.

### General Social Care Council (GSCC)

This is the professional regulatory body for social care workers, which has codes of practice that set clear guidelines for all those who work in social care. There is a register of those who are qualified to work in the sector. Just as doctors and nurses are on a register and can be 'struck off' if they contravene their professional code of practice, social workers who display serious misconduct can be removed from the GSCC register.

### Office for Standards in Education (OFSTED)

OFSTED is a government department that inspects and regulates any setting that provides care and education, including childminders, schools, nurseries, crèches, day care and out-of-school care.

## Case study: Who cares for the carer?

Mrs Wilson has been a widow for three years, and has two children. Emily is three and her son Jason is eleven. Jason misses his dad very much and there have been a lot of changes in the family.

Shortly after Emily was born, she was diagnosed with cerebral palsy. She has difficulty with mobility, speech and co-ordination. Intellectually she seems to be doing well but finds it difficult to communicate.

Mrs Wilson has found it hard to bond with Emily and largely blames this on her husband's death. She has started drinking a lot and Jason often looks after Emily. This was okay when Emily was very little and helpless. However, now Jason's mum is drinking more, Emily is more demanding, and he is struggling to cope.

The family have a social worker but they try to hide many of their problems, as they fear that they will be split up. Jason's schoolwork is suffering and he never plays with other children and so feels socially isolated. No one comes to his house, as his mother is usually drunk.

In pairs, discuss the situation and respond to the following questions.

1 List the issues for this family.

2 Who can help Mrs Wilson? Who can help Jason? Who can help Emily?

3 Do you think it is possible for the family to stay together? Give reasons for your answers.

## Assessment activity 10.2

(P2) (M1) (M2) (D1)   BTEC

Imagine that you are a young parent and have recently moved into a new area with your two young children, following separation from your partner who was drinking and abusive. You are worried about the behaviour of your children and are concerned about them being looked after. You carry out research to find out the support available in your local area and decide to organise the information into a resource pack you can refer to easily if necessary. The pack:

- outlines the arrangements for providing quality care for looked after children and young people

- examines how policies and procedures help children, young people and their families whilst the child is being looked after

- explains the roles and responsibilities of two members of the children's workforce in relation to looked after children and young people

- evaluates the regulation of care provision for children and young people.

### Grading tips

(P2) Public library and newspapers provide useful information. Make notes to outline the arrangements for providing quality of care for children and young people.

(M1) Add to your notes to discuss the role of policies and procedures in more detail.

(M2) In particular, focus on two individuals who you think will be most helpful if your children were to become looked after.

(D1) In order to judge the quality of the provision for looked after children research the role of regulators and use inspection reports for local providers to evaluate provision in the local area by comparing their strengths and weaknesses and use the comparison to explain your judgement.

# 3 Understand the risks to children and young people of abusive and exploitative behaviour

Child protection must always take priority for anyone who is working with children and young people. However, while considering this important aspect of child care, it must also be remembered that children do sustain bruises and minor injuries during the normal rough and tumble of play. It is important to listen to children and take note of their body language and general behaviour and appearance.

## 3.1 Types of maltreatment
### Physical abuse

Early years workers must be aware of the signs of physical abuse, which can include hitting, nipping, burning and inflicting physical harm of any kind.

**Table 10.6:** Physical signs of abuse

| Physical abuse | Indications |
| --- | --- |
| Bruising | Children who are systematically punched, beaten or hit will have multiple bruises, possibly fractures and tissue or organ damage and this can even lead to death. |
| Burns | Small round burns usually indicate marks made by a lit cigarette or similar item. Burns of all types are extremely painful and prone to infection. Hands or feet may be placed in hot liquid as a punishment and such injuries will require medical attention. |
| Unexplained injuries | Sometimes non-accidental injury occurs because of stresses and strains in the family situation. However, some children are systematically abused and ill-treated and it is vital to be alert to signs of unexplained injuries. |
| Soreness | Soreness might be a sign of bruising or an underlying fracture resulting from abuse. Most children experience tenderness and soreness at times, but when this occurs regularly or persists then the situation requires investigation. |
| Infections | A child who is continually ill or has regular infections may not be receiving the care and attention or nutrients they need to build up their immune system and this could be a physical sign of neglect. |
| Underweight | Children are weighed regularly throughout their lives. It is one of the first things that happens after birth, and continues with every medical check throughout childhood. If a child does not progress at the recognised rate then further tests may be carried out to see if there is an underlying cause. One such reason may be that the child is not receiving the right diet to grow at the established rate. |
| Poor personal hygiene | Neglect often leads to poor personal hygiene and the child may be wearing clothes that are dirty and too big or too small. There will be other signs and symptoms to alert carers to the situation. |
| Failure to thrive | Failure to thrive is an accumulation of the signs and symptoms that indicate child abuse. Further investigation is required if the child is failing to meet the accepted norms of development. |

Fig 10.3: Types of abuse

Children need time to experiment and grow up at their own pace!

## Sexual abuse

Sexual abuse can take a number of different forms.

Table 10.7: The different forms of sexual abuse

| Sexual abuse | Indications |
|---|---|
| Inappropriate touching | Adults will often hold a child's hand or cuddle them, especially when they are upset. The touching becomes inappropriate when it is unwanted or directed in a sexual way (e.g. touching the bottom or the genitals). |
| Inappropriate language | Children should never be subjected to language and conversation that is inappropriate or of a sexual nature. The innocence of childhood should be respected and protected at all times. |
| Inappropriate sexual advances | This may include inappropriate touching and kissing and speaking to children about intimate issues. |
| Looking at children in an inappropriate way | While many people enjoy watching children play in all innocence, some will watch children at play in parks and nursery gardens with malicious intent. |
| Showing children inappropriate pictures | This type of behaviour is designed to eventually engage children in sexual activity. |
| Talking to children in an inappropriate way | Engaging children in manipulative conversation may be designed to lull them into a sense of security, leading to a more intimate relationship. |

## Emotional abuse

**Table 10.8:** The different forms of emotional abuse

| Emotional abuse (including effects on intellectual development) | |
|---|---|
| Constant shouting | Shouting at children all the time will inevitably destroy their self-esteem and make them unwilling to participate in any conversation with their abuser. |
| Dominating adults | If the child is totally dominated then the developmental process can be impaired. For example, the child may be held back from developing normally, as they are not allowed to 'get dirty' or indulge in messy play. |
| Threatening behaviour | Children who are threatened in systematic ways will be withdrawn and lack confidence in their own abilities. If the threats start suddenly then the child's behaviour will change and the early years care and education worker should be aware of this. |
| Belittling and undermining | Systematic belittling will destroy a child's self-esteem and they will lack confidence, which will mean that they will be reluctant to attempt anything new. |
| Verbal abuse | This is often a mixture of belittling, undermining and shouting. It all has the effect of destroying the child's spirit and confidence. |

## Intellectual abuse

Intellectual abuse occurs when a child's cognitive development suffers. This might happen for a range of reasons. When a child is abused in other ways they may be unable to think or function intellectually. For example, they cannot think properly if they are emotionally abused, in pain or are hungry or in fear of their safety. Similarly, if they are deprived of time at school or of basic educational materials, or if their work is systematically destroyed, they are not going to be able to function effectively.

## Neglect

Signs of **neglect** may include:

- inappropriate clothing
- being dirty or smelly
- having an unkempt appearance
- being underweight – always hungry
- having skin irritations
- being withdrawn
- being isolated
- being dejected
- having low self-esteem
- being listless.

Be on the lookout for such children as, while the neglect may not be deliberate, the family will need help to develop the necessary skills to raise children effectively.

## Bullying and harassment

Young people often bully and harass other young people and children. However, adults can also bully children and young people in an exploitative manner. Bullying may take many forms and some of these are described in the case study on page 53.

Many children and young people hide the fact that they are being bullied. They may feel that they have somehow brought it upon themselves. They are often reluctant to tell other people, as they feel vulnerable and intimidated.

# 3.2 Risk of maltreatment

Abuse and **maltreatment** can happen to children both within and outside the family. It can also happen within a care setting. These issues are explored below.

### Key terms

**Neglect** – When a child does not have what they need to function effectively. They may be deprived of security, safety, shelter, warmth, food or love.

**Maltreatment** – Ill-treatment or abuse; when a child's rights are compromised and they are not cared for fairly.

## Case study: Horrible school days

Eleven-year-old Jamil has just started attending his local comprehensive school. He does not know many people there, as his family have recently moved into the area. He has tried to make friends but it is early days and the friendships have not become very strong yet.

Some older boys have been targeting Jamil, and they are making his time outside the classroom very difficult. They have taken his lunch money, torn his school blazer, verbally abused him, and on one occasion chased and hit him.

Jamil is reluctant to tell anyone about this, as he has been threatened with worse treatment if he does. But he does not want to go to school and is lying to his parents about what is happening. One of his new friends is worried about Jamil and tells his parents. They, in turn, tell Jamil's parents, who inform the school. The headteacher says that the school will deal with the situation.

In small groups respond to the following, giving reasons for your answers:

1 What do you think the head teacher should do?

2 List three strategies that the school might have in place to deal with bullying.

3 What other support might Jamil and/or his friends need?

Now share your group's thoughts with another group and note the similarities and differences in your answers.

### PLTS

**Team workers:** This activity will provide evidence as you work together in a team to collate information and viewpoints.

**Effective participators:** This activity will enable you to demonstrate your ability to participate in group activities.

## Abuse within the family

The majority of children are not at risk of abuse within their own family but there are situations that increase the risk. External stresses and strains on a family may cause one or both parents to react in anger and the child might suffer as a result. There are individuals who have volatile personalities and react adversely to the youngest or most vulnerable members of the family unit. There are instances of parents who lack the appropriate parenting skills and are unable to look after children who may be neglected and malnourished as a result. Instances of abuse within the family home can cover the whole range of abusive situations, for example, physical, emotional, sexual and neglect.

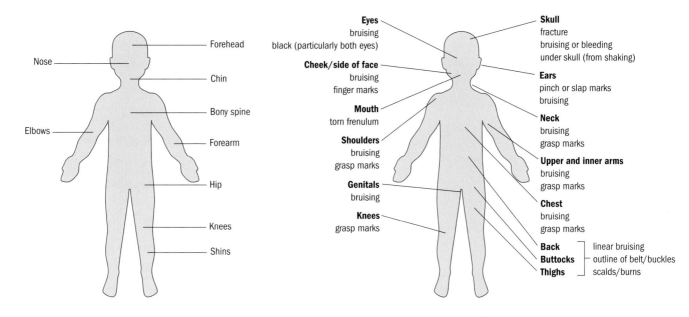

Common sites of accidental injuries

Non-accidental injuries

**Fig 10.4:** Accidental and non-accidental injuries

## Abuse outside the family

Child abuse occurs more commonly within the family home. However, it is important to keep in mind that other adults and relatives may be responsible for abusive situations, while other children or young people may carry out abuse through bullying or harassment.

## Abuse in a care setting

There have been a number of high-profile cases where child abuse has occurred within a care setting. Although these cases are relatively rare they make major headlines in the press. However, there are many other less-reported cases of abuse in these situations, especially instances of bullying and harassment.

## Strangers

Children often learn about 'Stranger Danger' at school, and it is important that they are aware of the issues surrounding strangers who seek out the company of children with intent to harm. Unfortunately children need to be warned that all strangers are potential threats to their well-being, as they do not have the skills to differentiate and many potential and actual abusers are very clever and cunning people. The more confident and outgoing children are less likely to be targeted by strangers and it is important that children's confidence and self-esteem is boosted whenever possible.

### Activity 5: All is not what it seems!

Imagine that you notice the following signs on a child in your placement and suggest possible causes for each, placing the most likely cause first:

- Bruised cheek
- Small round burn marks on the forearm
- Small bruises on front and back of upper arm
- Bruises on both shins
- Large graze on side of leg

Which of the above would you be most concerned about?

What would you do next?

# 3.3 Indicators of maltreatment

There are a variety of indicators that a child or young person may have been maltreated, some of which are listed below. Bear in mind that these may be indications of other issues in the individual's life and not always of abusive situations. However, they should never be ignored and always warrant investigation by appropriate personnel.

## Physical indicators

**Table 10.9:** Physical indicators and their causes

| Physical indicator | Possible cause/s |
|---|---|
| Bruising | <ul><li>Might be caused by gripping, nipping and hitting with a foreign object.</li><li>Finger marks, e.g. four small bruises on back of arm and one on front.</li><li>Bruising in unusual places, e.g. inner thighs, stomach, under hairline, inner buttocks.</li></ul> |
| Unexplained injuries | <ul><li>Injury might not match the explanation the child gives.</li><li>Burns and scalds, especially on buttocks and feet.</li><li>Cigarette burns – small round burns that are uniform in size.</li></ul> |
| Soreness | <ul><li>Genital or anal soreness – sexual abuse.</li><li>Soreness inside mouth – sexual abuse or physical violence.</li></ul> |
| Infections | <ul><li>Genital, urinary infections – sexual abuse.</li><li>General infections – weak immune system – neglect.</li></ul> |
| Underweight | <ul><li>Neglect – malnourishment.</li></ul> |
| Poor personal hygiene | <ul><li>Neglect – lack of parenting skills.</li></ul> |

## Behavioural indicators

All types of abuse will lead to a change in the child's behaviour, as they have been subjected to things that a young person should never have to experience. Each child copes with their trauma in their own way, as they feel that they are powerless to stop whatever is happening to them.

**Table 10.10:** Behavioural indicators and their signs

| Behavioural indicator | Signs |
|---|---|
| Withdrawal | A child who suddenly shows signs of withdrawal is displaying signs that something is bothering them and this could be an indicator of abuse or exploitative behaviour. |
| Aggression | Some children are more aggressive than others but if a child suddenly begins to display aggressive behaviour, when previously they did not, this may indicate that the child is disturbed about something. |
| Distress | When a child feels temporarily safe and secure they may let down their defences and become distressed over relatively stress-free situations. This often indicates that the child is under some degree of stress. |
| Rocking/head banging | This type of repetitive behaviour is an indication that the child is disturbed about issues that they feel unable to talk freely about. |
| Hunger | Some children appear to be extremely greedy when presented with food. This may indicate that the child is not receiving adequate nutrition at home. |
| Reluctance to go home | Children who are being abused in any way may show a reluctance to go home, especially if the abuser is in the house. The child may not put their fears into words but may try to find excuses to avoid the family home. |
| Low self-esteem | Low self-esteem can result in undesirable behaviour, which may manifest itself in emotional problems, unhappiness, depression, robbery or even violence. Whenever possible, adults should try to build a child's self-esteem. |
| Developmental delay | Children who are being abused or exploited are unhappy and will not be able to function on a higher intellectual plane, which may result in an apparent developmental delay. According to Maslow's Hierarchy of Needs, individuals cannot function at higher levels until their fundamental needs are met. |

# 3.4 Wider factors suggesting risk of maltreatment

A number of factors need to be considered when studying abusive behaviour, in relation to both the abuser and the abused. These predisposing factors may help explain why abuse occurs and alert carers to the possibility of abuse.

## Dysfunctional family relationships

Sometimes members of families do not seem to have the same values and the family breaks down into isolated groups. The family unit no longer functions as a whole but as individual members living in the same building. The family is deemed to be dysfunctional and is not supportive of its members.

## Child or young person acting out abuse

There have been several cases in the news about children or young people being the perpetrators of abuse. This is typically emotional abuse, as in cases of bullying, but in recent years there has been a greater incidence of physical abuse, even cases of torture leading to death. Occasionally animals are abused because the child or young person might transfer their abusive situation onto a defenceless creature. There have been instances when children from very stable, non-abusive backgrounds have carried out appalling acts of cruelty on animals. This should never be taken lightly and can escalate to injuring other children or young people.

## Family history link to abuse

If a parent abuses their children on a regular basis then the child may reach maturity thinking that this is the normal, accepted way to deal with children. In this way the abusive situation may continue and lead to an unbroken cycle of abuse from one generation to another.

## Poor or impaired parenting skills

If a child lives in a family where the parenting skills are so poor that the child is unlikely to be nurtured or adequately cared for, abuse may inadvertently occur in the form of neglect. When children are born into a family they are typically raised with the same values that their parents have. Some families today live on take-away meals and have limited social interaction at home. Children may spend lengthy periods watching television or playing solitary electronic games, which means that they are not developing social skills through meeting other families and friends.

## Lack of attachment

Some parents find it difficult to form close attachments with their child for a number of reasons. Some babies are not very easy to relate to and seem to cry a lot – a young mother may find this difficult to cope with. Occasionally the parents are not mature enough for the situation they find themselves in and pass the responsibility of the child to others, such as the child's grandparents. Separation and illness may also contribute to attachment difficulties.

## Risk of exploitation

There is a risk that children may be exploited via visual, written and electronic forms of communication and media. Nowadays more and more children are at risk of coming into contact with unsuitable forms of communication. This is largely because of advances in technology, which mean that children, young people and families have easier access to inappropriate materials. Parents have a responsibility to monitor the types of DVDs and Internet sites their children can access. However, some families allow children to watch films intended for a much older audience and many children are now very familiar with Internet chat rooms. They may not realise that other people may use these to groom children and young people for their own purposes.

## Substance abuse

A child's parent or carer may abuse a number of substances such as alcohol, prescribed drugs, illegal drugs and solvents. These may change the user's perceptions and lead to altered behaviour, which in turn can become abusive. If the individual has become dependent on substances, and the supply is stopped, then that can also have a detrimental effect on behaviour, resulting in violent emotional and/or physical outbursts.

**Fig 10.5:** Is she learning or being exploited?

### Activity 6: Parenting skills

In pairs discuss the following:

- How do most people learn about being a 'good' parent?
- Why are people reluctant to join a parenting class?
- Suggest three ways in which families can develop good parenting skills.

### Reflect

Spend an hour watching a mainstream commercial television station e.g. ITV sometime between 5pm and 8pm. Make a note of the advertisements and consider whether they are aimed at children or adults? Are they suitable for children? If not, why not?

# 3.5 Consequences of maltreatment

The consequences of abuse are far-reaching and have a long-term effect on the individual. Children and young people who have been abused may have difficulties with mental health, social behaviour, low self-esteem, forming relationships and in their general emotional development. Some children do go on to form meaningful relationships, but there is a risk that they may become abusers themselves.

Table 10.11: Effects of abuse and possible consequences

| Effects of abuse | Possible consequences |
|---|---|
| Emotional and psychological dysfunction affecting relationships | • Child may have extremely low self-esteem and could enter into further abusive situations in adulthood.<br>• May not reach their full potential, as they may have been belittled, making them feel unable to take on roles of responsibility.<br>• May have great difficulty forming meaningful relationships later in life and any relationships may be impaired by previous experiences.<br>• May be emotionally immature and display displaced anger.<br>• Some individuals self-harm and will require professional help to come to terms with their experiences.<br>• Occasionally, abused individuals may become abusers and form relationships based on their own background. |
| Intellectual | • May find it very difficult to concentrate on cognitive activities.<br>• The child's priorities of thought change dramatically and the focus is mainly on feelings and emotions.<br>• May suddenly fall behind their expected level at school, as brain development may be affected. This may be one of the first signs that the individual is having difficulties in their personal life. |
| Social inadequacy | • May have long-term effects in social relationships.<br>• Children who have been abused sexually may find it difficult to form any intimate relationships as they grow older. They may be unable to trust another person with their innermost thoughts and feelings. |
| Illness | • Effects of consistent physical abuse may last for the rest of a child's life.<br>• Children who have been punched or kicked violently may have sustained internal damage, which could affect normal bodily function or result in disability.<br>• Fractured bones that have not healed properly may result in a deformity or impaired use of a limb.<br>• May be problems with the immune system and the individual may be prone to auto-immune disorders or even psychosomatic illnesses.<br>• Other possible outcomes of abuse are unwanted pregnancy (together with the emotional burden that entails) and sexually transmitted disease and infections, which may affect the individual for many years. |
| Mental ill health | • Emotional effects of abuse can be catastrophic and the individual may experience a range of mental health issues.<br>• Attempted suicide is not uncommon as the person feels so unworthy and undervalued.<br>• There are also issues around substance abuse, which might be used as a coping strategy in some circumstances. However, instead of alleviating the problem it will only make it harder to deal with everyday life. |

## 3.6 Theories of maltreatment

Several theories of maltreatment or abuse have been put forward in an attempt to categorise and explain why abuse takes place. Each may explain some aspects of abuse but none seems to cover all the aspects. The main theories are listed below in Table 10.12.

### Activity 7: Theories of abuse

In August 2007, Baby Peter died at the age of 17 months. This shocked the nation, especially when it was revealed that he had sustained more than 50 injuries. In pairs, research the background to this and determine which theories of abuse might be applied or linked to this case. Give reasons for your choices.

## 3.7 Issues

### The changing face of the family

The concept of family life has changed considerably over the years. Family units can be made up in a number of different ways and the children will have various types of relationships within those units. As well as conventional two-parent families, children may live with one biological parent and have visitation rights with the other, and both parents may have other family units of their own. Some children will live with their mother and grandparents, while others are in a reconstituted family. Anyone working with children and young people needs to be aware of the background and culture of the individuals in their care.

### Social disadvantage

Many families are disadvantaged and this adds stresses and strains to the family unit, which may contribute to abusive or exploitative situations. Families in poor housing and on low incomes may find it difficult to buy nourishing food and the children may be in poor health and be very demanding. Children who are not well may be frustrated and want more attention. They may be unreasonable in their wants and their moods may vary considerably because they are generally feeling ill and unhappy.

### Different concepts of discipline

Discipline differs greatly from one family to the next and has close links with parenting styles. Some parents impose sanctions, while others resort to more physical forms of punishment.

### Cultural variations

There are cultural variations when it comes to bringing up children and you should note that these are not always linked to race. In some families, girls and boys are treated in different ways – for example, it may be 'a girl's place' to serve the other members of the family. In some cultures the female is not valued in the same way as the male and this can lead to bullying and harassment within the home.

**Table 10.12: Theories of abuse and their characteristics**

| Theory of abuse | Characteristics |
| --- | --- |
| Medical | There is a view that child abuse is a disease with specific signs and symptoms. According to this approach, child abuse can supposedly be treated and 'cured'. However, this simplistic approach does not take into account the complexities of many cases of abuse. |
| Sociological | This theory concentrates on our changing society and how these changes have affected family functioning. Unemployment, low wages, poor housing, disadvantage and poor health are all seen to contribute to abusive situations. However, statistics show that abuse also occurs in families with high income, good housing, etc. |
| Psychological | This theory focuses on family functioning and how people relate to each other within the family unit. It emphasises family breakdown and dysfunction as factors and suggests that the use of therapy can prevent or reduce abuse. |
| Feminist | This theory focuses on the power relationships between men and women within a family and asserts that most abusers are male. While this argument might be quite convincing in the case of sexual abuse, some 10 per cent of abusers are known to be female and the victims of abuse are both male and female. |

**Assessment activity 10.3**  (P3) BTEC

You are a support assistant for four unrelated children in a reception class and two of the children give you cause for concern that they may be experiencing some maltreatment or abuse. You find it helpful to explain the factors that could lead to the suspicion of child maltreatment or abuse in a report.

**Grading tip**

(P3) Review what has been observed about the children to explain your suspicions that abuse has taken place. Consider the possible type of maltreatment as evidenced from your observations of the children, review the possible risks of maltreatment for each child including wider factors relevant to each of them, potential consequences of any maltreatment as explained by theories of maltreatment and other relevant issues. You might find it helpful to put together a short pen portrait of each child to identify key features relating to the children before you start this activity.

# 4  Understand the strategies used to safeguard children and young people from abusive and exploitative behaviour

## 4.1 Strategies for working with children and young people

A number of strategies can help to protect children and young people from being abused or exploited and some of them are listed below. These strategies reduce the risks of abuse, and help children and young people realise that they have the right to be safe, secure and free from harm.

### Being respectful

Respect must be earned; it cannot be ordered or demanded and, once gained, it can easily be destroyed. Consideration should always be shown for other people's viewpoints and differing opinions need to be appreciated. Once respect is established, individuals may confide in you or inform you of changes or difficulties within the family unit. This information may explain changes in their behaviour and make it possible for you to help the child through a difficult experience.

### Child-centred approach

Remember that the child or young person is at the centre and that they are the people who need to be empowered and supported so they can take control of their lives. They should be encouraged to develop strategies that will enable them to avoid situations that put them at risk. They also need be helped to be strong enough to seek appropriate support and guidance if they find themselves in an adverse situation.

### Providing active support

Support needs to be readily available and practical when people are in need. It may be useful to have someone who will listen, but children also need someone who can provide the necessary support and be proactive in a practical way.

You should endeavour to increase the children's self-confidence and raise their self-esteem so that they are resilient and empowered. Children and young people who know they are valued and loved, and who are used to making decisions, are more likely to refuse unwanted advances and less likely to be drawn into exploitative situations.

### Empowering children and young people

Children need to understand that they have rights of their own. They rely on adults to nurture them and keep them safe but they need to be aware of what is right and what is wrong. If they do not feel they

Children need someone to confide in. Who did you confide in when you were a child?

you help me tidy up' may evoke a negative answer. If adults do not accept the child's answer then they are taking away their choice and disempowering them. In this situation, it may be better to say 'Come on, it's time to tidy up' instead of asking a question. However, assertiveness should be encouraged in context and children's rights taken into consideration at all times.

Self-confident, outgoing children are less likely to be targeted by a potential abuser and this is a fact that should always be kept in mind. Self-confident children, with high self-esteem and resilience, are usually talkative children, who are very open about what is happening in their lives and will speak out if they do not like something. The child with low self-esteem and lack of confidence tends to be less talkative and may feel that they cannot speak out, particularly if coerced. Accept the child as they are, and praise them at all times. Explain that what they are doing is good and worthy of praise, talk to them openly and give them the attention they deserve, as you encourage them to be more assertive and responsible.

are being treated fairly in any way they should be encouraged to tell someone about it. They should voice their concerns and opinions to adults they trust. If they are listened to and treated fairly all the time, they will feel empowered to react accordingly in any situation.

## Supporting assertiveness, self-confidence, self-esteem and resilience

Children need to be assertive at times and should be encouraged to do so. However, often adults like to be in charge and do not like being challenged, especially by children. When adults give children a choice they need to accept, for example, that the question 'Will

## Sharing information and not keeping secrets

Encourage children and young people to have open relationships with people so that they can share information. They also need to realise the difference between bad secrets and good secrets. Good secrets are usually only to be kept from one or two people (e.g. a present for someone's birthday or a surprise outing) but they can be shared with other people. Bad secrets are usually those which are to be kept from

## Case study: Difficult to comprehend

Simon is 14 and lives with his mother and grandmother. Both women have had very negative experiences in their relationships with men – and this may be one reason why they have both been involved in abusing Simon since his birth. This has never been noticed by anyone outside the family. The maltreatment is mainly physical and emotional abuse and he has never been allowed to socialise with friends from school.

Simon has always thought that this was the way families behaved. However, he has recently become friendly with a small group of people at school, who often talk about their home life and Simon is starting

to realise that his experiences are markedly different from theirs. He has decided to confide in one of the teachers that he likes, although he is afraid of the repercussions.

**Comment on the following and give reasons for your answers:**

1  What should the teacher do next?

2  Do you think that abuse by females is common or rare?

3  Why is it more difficult for society to come to terms with the concept of female abusers than male abusers?

everyone else except the people directly involved (e.g. inappropriate pictures, words or touching). Children need people to confide in so that they can express their concerns and fears.

## Giving children information according to their age, needs and abilities

Children and young people need to be aware of their bodies, how they function and how to respect them and keep them safe. As they grow older, they need to be aware of the emotions that might affect them as they mature. They should also be aware of the changes in their bodies and how these changes may affect other people. As children and young people mature, they are exposed to strong peer pressure and adult images in the media. They should be aware of the dangers of early or inappropriate relationships and understand how to ensure their own safety.

In some cases, children and young people may also need to be aware of infections and diseases associated with abusive and exploitative situations. This includes conditions affecting wounds and injuries but more often the transmission of diseases associated with sexual activity. There are a variety of sexually transmitted diseases including herpes, syphilis, gonorrhoea and chlamydia. These must be treated quickly, as they can otherwise have long-term effects leading to infertility and other conditions.

# 4.2 Strategies for working with parents and families

Whenever possible, it is important to work closely with the parents and families of children and young people. In this way a sense of trust and respect can be encouraged, together with a feeling that everyone is working together for the good of the child.

## Developing supportive partnership relationships with parents and families

When working with children and young people, it is essential to develop supportive relationships. Everyone involved needs to trust you, and be aware that you wish to establish good links with all involved. Parents and families may regard you as a role model and someone they can talk to regarding the child or young person. It is important that the child is at the centre and that everyone works together for the well-being of the child or young person.

## Involving parents in the assessment of children's needs

In many cases parents have vital information about the specific needs of their children and about any problems they may be trying to come to terms with. Assessment of a child's needs must involve their parents in order to gain an accurate overall picture.

### Activity 8: Role model

When you are working with children, it is important to remember that you are a role model for many of them.

In pairs discuss how a childcare/young person worker might be able to positively influence child/parent relationships.

Prioritise three main points and write them down. Share them with another group and discuss any similarities or differences in your list.

### Functional skills

**English:** Contributing to discussions, communicating ideas and opinions, participating in debate and presenting information to others will all allow you to demonstrate your speaking and writing skills.

Fig 10.6: Why do you think it is so important to develop good communication skills?

## Helping parents to recognise the significance and value of their contributions

Parents must be made aware of the importance of their contribution to the assessment process and they must feel valued. In some cases the parents share a responsibility for the situation but, if the family is to be supported as a whole, then all contributions must be valued and parents' feelings respected.

## Encouraging the development of parenting skills

Parenting skills do not always come naturally to people, especially if they were raised in a family situation where those skills were lacking. There are many courses available on developing parenting skills, but people do not like to admit that they need help in this area. Those working with children and young people can help parents to improve parenting skills informally by developing meaningful relationships with them and spending time talking about children and young people.

# 4.3 Procedures where maltreatment is considered, suspected, confirmed or excluded

## Policies of the setting

It is important that everyone working with children and young people in a care and education setting is aware of, and has read, the policies of the setting. These should be available and easily accessible and many settings ask individuals to sign to show that they have read the policies. This safeguards the organisation and the staff and ensures that a common practice is used in all cases.

### Reflect

You should have read the safeguarding policy from your placement. Take some time to reflect on it and consider whether you understand it clearly and know what your role would be if a child made a disclosure to you. If you are unsure about any point, now is the time to ask questions.

## Implementing safe working practices

Within any setting there will inevitably be a number of policies and procedures and staff need to be aware of these. They will include equal opportunities, health and safety, behaviour and child protection. There will be a number of other policies written to safeguard the children, young people, staff and visitors from danger and to ensure safe practice throughout the setting. It is important to be aware of the content of the policies and procedures so that everyone knows what to do in any situation.

## Whistleblowing

Many settings have now also adopted a whistleblowing policy so that if any inappropriate behaviour is observed among the staff it can be reported in an appropriate way, which will trigger an investigation. The person reporting the situation will be supported and protected but they must be aware that they may need to be interviewed by the police and other agencies, if necessary.

## Reporting arrangements

The policy of the setting will specify the lines of reporting in cases where abuse is suspected or confirmed. It is important that these procedures are strictly adhered to, or the case could be severely compromised. Within a care and education setting, the procedure is usually to report to the line manager or person in charge of the setting, who will then contact appropriate people in authority.

All information should be recorded factually, as this may be required as evidence later. Written reports should be re-read carefully to ensure there is no ambiguity and that all information is fully recorded, is accurate, factual and contains no speculation or judgemental phrases or statements.

## Security of records

All records must be safely and securely stored, and only accessible to those people who need to see them in a professional capacity and not accessible to those who are just curious. Confidentiality is paramount in these instances. Breaking confidentiality could, in severe cases, lead to police involvement and even prosecution, as these records may be used in court appearances if there are criminal proceedings.

## The sequence of events leading to registration on the child protection register

Cases of suspected or confirmed abuse should initially be reported to the line manager. Many establishments have a nominated child protection officer or manager and, wherever possible, cases of actual or suspected abuse or neglect will initially be referred to this person. They will in turn contact the area child protection team, who will initiate an investigation or, in cases where the child might be deemed to be in danger, involve social services or the police. The police have trained child protection officers who will help with the investigation. The child should never be left in a dangerous situation and may need to be removed to a place of safety.

After investigation a child protection conference will be convened, taking all the evidence into consideration, and a decision will be made as to whether the child needs to be recorded on a child protection register. In severe cases criminal charges may also be brought against the perpetrators of the abuse. The child protection register is confidential and only people officially working with children (e.g. in health, education or social services) have access to it. It contains the names of all children thought to be at risk of abuse and it alerts all agencies to work together for the safety and protection of those children and young people.

# 4.4 Roles and responsibilities

## Following the policies and procedures of the setting

Everyone involved in the care and education of children and young people has a responsibility to follow the policies and procedures of the setting. This is especially important in cases of abuse and neglect, as failure to do so may endanger the child further or may even be detrimental to the case against the perpetrators. For example, children who disclose should be supported but not questioned by untrained people, as this may negate the validity of any evidence gleaned.

## Observation

Systematic observation of children and young people within the setting is good practice, as it helps ensure that planning is linked to the needs of

the individual and that development is monitored and recorded. As a result of these observations, it may be noticed that a child's behaviour has altered or that there are unexplained marks on their body. Through observation, members of staff could therefore be alerted to a potentially abusive or exploitative situation, which warrants further investigation.

Observations should be kept confidential within the setting and access only given to those who have reason to need it (e.g. the line manager, educational psychologist, social services, the police, etc). All records and reports should contain facts and not uninformed judgements. These may be used in case conferences later so they should always be dated and signed.

Intelligent observation helps to keep a child safe

## Recognising maltreatment indicators

The signs and symptoms of abuse have been covered earlier in this unit but most care and education settings provide in-service training on child protection issues. Many local authorities also require employees to undertake appropriate training as part of a continuous professional development programme. It is essential that everyone is aware of the signs and symptoms of abuse so that immediate action can be taken to ensure the child's safety.

## Knowing how to respond if maltreatment is suspected

If a child discloses sensitive information, which raises concerns about their safety, then the policy of the setting should be followed immediately. The child should be believed and supported and the procedures implemented straight away. This is why it is so important to be aware of the content of policies and procedures because, while it may be rare to implement them, when it is required it is vitally important that they are followed to the letter.

## Knowing what action to take following disclosure

If a child discloses to you it is important to respond appropriately. Listen very carefully and do not make any judgements, as that can give the impression that you are blaming the child or young person. Avoid asking questions, as this may jeopardise any further actions that may be deemed necessary. Explain to the individual that they were correct to talk to you but that you will have to tell other people. You must ensure that the child is treated with respect and they know that you believe what they are telling you. There will be a designated safeguarding officer within the setting and you must report what has happened to this officer. They will then take over responsibility.

Your next task is to ensure that you record, in writing, everything that has occurred. Make sure that you only document facts and not impressions that you might have formed. This record must be dated and signed, as it may be used later as evidence, which is why it is vital that you write it as soon as possible after the disclosure has taken place. If too much time elapses then it will not be considered as reliable evidence so it must be done within 24 hours or sooner if at all possible.

## Maintaining confidentiality according to the policies of the setting

The policy of the setting will include information about the confidentiality code to be followed. There is a legal obligation to pass on information to the area child protection team and the police but all information should be kept confidential and not given to anyone without due cause. Passing information to other parties could jeopardise the safety of the child and any ensuing legal procedures.

# 4.5 Responding to direct or indirect disclosure

To disclose information is to tell another person about an incident or event. The word *disclosure* is usually linked to sensitive information, often connected to cases of abuse and exploitation.

- *Direct disclosure* occurs when the child or young person informs someone directly that they have been abused or exploited and it may begin as a comment that requires further investigation.
- *Indirect disclosure* often involves a third party, who may have information that, added to comments from the child, 'rings alarm bells'. Staff may observe behaviour that might indicate possible abuse or the child may be sexually aware and act in an inappropriate way. The child or young person may make a comment that alerts the listener to potential problems.

## Listening carefully and attentively

When a child or young person indicates that something is wrong, the adult must listen carefully and not interpret words incorrectly. Listening carefully shows that you are taking what the child or young person says seriously and that you are not shocked. It is important not to show disgust or shock, as the child will be more reluctant to disclose if you do.

## Communicating at the child/young person's own pace

The child or young person should be supported and there should be no pressure to hurry things along. It may have taken a great deal of courage to reach the point of disclosure and the child should be allowed to determine the pace of the proceedings. If they feel rushed they may also feel uncomfortable and as if they are being judged, so it is vital that they are able to control the situation. Remember, they may have been threatened with untold horrors if they tell anyone about their abuse and they will feel extremely vulnerable.

## Taking the child or young person seriously

The child or young person should be kept as calm as possible and it should be evident to them that they are being taken seriously. It may be extremely traumatic for a child to disclose sensitive information about themselves and they will obviously have put a great deal of trust in the person they are talking to. In the majority of cases children will not be able to make up the things they disclose and their word should always be treated with the utmost gravity.

## Reassuring and supporting the child/ young person

The child or young person should receive support and reassurance and will need to be assured that they are not to blame for anything that has happened.

## Unconditional acceptance

It is important that the child is accepted, no matter what they have said, as they will already feel that they are in some way to blame or have brought the situation upon themselves by their actions or behaviour. The term *unconditional acceptance* is used to convey a message that, whatever has happened, and in whatever way, that child or young person is a valued person without blame and will be supported and accepted.

## Boundaries of confidentiality

While confidentiality must be respected, in the case of abusive situations there is a legal responsibility to pass information to the authorities investigating the case. These authorities may include a number of different agencies (e.g. area child protection teams, police, social services, etc.).

## Following the correct procedures of the setting promptly

The procedures of the setting are in place to safeguard all involved and it is important that they are followed correctly and promptly. If the procedures are followed then no one can be blamed if the outcome is not as desired.

## Dealing with your own feelings and emotions

Once a care worker is involved in a child protection case, they will have their own feelings to deal with and these may be very strong. They may feel that they have begun proceedings that they no longer have any control over and they may have strong negative feelings towards members of the child's family. It is necessary for these feelings to be addressed and in some cases a debriefing exercise is beneficial. In others it may be deemed appropriate to undertake sessions with a counsellor who may help the individual rationalise and deal with their emotions.

# 4.6 Support for children/young people who disclose

## Provide access to professional support

Once a child has disclosed what is happening, there are authorities and agencies that can protect and support them. The truth needs to be told, which means the child must be sensitively encouraged to talk about what has been happening to them. The information then has to be passed on to the relevant authorities so that the allegations can be investigated. The Local Safeguarding Children's Board, as part of the local authority social services, will be involved, as will the police who will lead the investigation.

*Every Child Matters* was concerned with all agencies working together as a multi-disciplinary workforce for the well-being of children and young people and this became part of the legislation in the Children Act 2004. After the devastating revelations of the Victoria Climbié (2000–2001) case, it was felt to be vitally important that all agencies involved in cases such as this work together and keep each other informed. In this way it is hoped that the errors that occurred in that case will not be repeated. A wide range of professionals may be involved with children and young people who have been exploited or abused. Their roles have been mentioned previously in this unit and it is vital that everyone working with a child or young person does so with integrity and sensitivity.

## Case study: Internet grooming?

Kirsty (aged 14) loves to spend time in her bedroom, on her computer, and she and her friends communicate regularly and post photographs of recent events – it is great fun. While using one of the chat rooms she became friendly with Mark, who said he was a year older than her. They seemed to have a great deal in common and they 'chatted online' for weeks and became very close. They exchanged photographs and decided that it would be good to meet up, and a date, place and time were agreed.

Kirsty's parents don't really approve of her spending so much time on her computer so she decides that it might be best not to tell them. She is quite excited about meeting Mark and takes time getting ready, making herself look especially nice. She leaves the house at 6.30pm after telling her parents that she's going to a friend's house.

1 List at least three concerns you might have about this scenario.

2 What are the immediate dangers for Kirsty?

3 What could her parents have done to reduce the risk of this happening?

Give reasons for your answers.

## Unconditional acceptance for the child/young person

It is often extremely difficult for children to disclose information, as they may feel that no one will believe them. Again, it is essential that care workers believe what the child or young person is saying. It may be partial or full disclosure but the individual must never be made to feel insecure or that they are not believed. The child may feel dirty, useless and unloved and they must be shown unconditional acceptance, respect and love for them as an individual and for the courage they have demonstrated in disclosing.

## Empowering children and young people

Children and young people should be given strategies that will empower them in abusive and exploitative situations. Lessons or programmes, specifically and sensitively designed to address some of the issues related to abuse, are often used by settings and the individuals should be encouraged to understand that it is OK to say 'no' and to be aware of what is unacceptable or inappropriate behaviour by others.

## Awareness of the potential impact on the child/young person and other family members

There will always be some impact on the child and on other members of the family because of the very nature of the situation but this will be more traumatic if the abuser is a member of the nuclear (immediate) family. In cases where someone outside the nuclear family has abused the child or young person, then the family can be a source of strong and powerful support

for them. There are support mechanisms available that can help families come to terms with abusive and exploitative situations (e.g. individual or whole family counselling and play therapy for younger members).

## Counteracting possible stereotyping

It is important that people do not fall into the trap of stereotyping. A family may be poor but that does not mean that they will be neglectful. It is important that any stereotyping is counteracted immediately or it will prove detrimental for the family and for the child or young person involved.

# 4.7 Minimising the effects of abuse

## Encouraging expression of feeling

Children and young people who have suffered abuse may have had to suppress their natural feelings and keep their emotions blocked for a long time. They need the opportunity to express their feelings openly. They may feel a loss of control as some of the feelings which have been repressed are likely to be very strong and unusually powerful and, because of this, they will need a lot of support.

## Improving self-image

Children who have been abused will inevitably have a poor self-image and may need help in developing a more positive view of themselves. People often go through stages where they feel that they somehow deserve what has happened to them or that they have encouraged it or been at fault in some way. They will

# Shamia Khosani
## Play co-ordinator

Shamia works with children in an after-school club. Usually there are 12 to 15 children attending and they are involved in all types of activities and challenges. She is an after-school play co-ordinator, which involves planning and supervising activities for children after their normal school day finishes. She plans the activities and is involved with the children as and when appropriate. Shamia reports directly to her line manager, who has overall responsibility for the daily sessions. The children love attending and get on very well with each other, especially when there is such a large group. On a recent occasion Shamia noticed that Gemma was not her usual outgoing self and that she was very quiet and reticent.

Shamia found a quiet place to talk to Gemma to ask if she was feeling all right. Gemma said that she was OK but her Uncle Andy was visiting and she didn't like him and didn't want to be alone with him. Later, Gemma came to Shamia and said that Uncle Andy read her stories from books but she didn't want to listen to them because people were being naughty in them.

Gemma continued, during the session, to give little snippets of information to Shamia and it appeared that Uncle Andy was reading adult material to Gemma and showing her sexually explicit photographs. Gemma did not like being close to him but he insisted that she sit on his knee and cuddle in close.

He had volunteered to 'babysit' on the following evening and Gemma was becoming really upset about the situation. Shamia explained that she would have to tell other people about this, as they only wanted Gemma to be happy. Shamia spoke to her line manager who was also the Designated Safeguarding Officer for the setting and she then wrote down everything that had been said as she remembered it. Gemma said that she did not want to go home that evening and Shamia sat with her to talk to her and support her.

## Think about it!

**In pairs or small groups:**

1 Discuss these events and comment on Shamia's actions and the way she has dealt with the situation.
2 Reach a conclusion about what should happen next.
3 Was there anything else that should have been done?
4 What might be the conclusion of this scenario?

need to be reassured that this is not the case and be supported through the difficult times and encouraged when they are feeling more positive.

## Building self-esteem and confidence

Praise and encouragement are positive tools in the hands of dedicated people who work with children and young people. Children who have been through traumatic events need a great deal of positive reinforcement in order to rebuild their self-esteem and confidence. Many individuals feel used and unworthy of respect and it can take a long time to build up positive relationships and trust. Workers in this sector must have a sensitive and supportive nature as well as being calm and patient.

## Play therapy

Play therapy is used both to diagnose and treat children and young people who have been through traumatic experiences. Using play therapy, they can live out their fears and express emotions in safe and secure environments with staff who are highly trained and who can support them at times of need.

## Counselling

Counselling (as has been noted earlier in this unit) is an important service that is provided for everyone involved in cases of abuse. There are specially trained personnel who are equipped to offer counselling specifically for the young.

## The role of voluntary organisations

There are several charities and voluntary organisations that help children and young people at risk. These may be the first point of contact for anyone who suffers abuse or who is aware of abusive situations. Organisations such as the NSPCC have specific campaigns to involve members of the public in trying to stop child abuse. Other organisations, such as ChildLine, provide telephone contact for anyone seeking advice. They all have an important role to play in supporting the authorities and those in abusive situations. Community support networks have been set up to provide links with agencies, which can provide specific support for anyone with problems. They provide information about a wide range of services that may be beneficial for families with children and young people.

---

## Assessment activity 10.4    P4 P5 M3 D2  BTEC

Using the scenario described in Assessment activity 10.3:

- explain appropriate responses when child maltreatment or abuse is suspected
- explain the strategies and methods that can be used to support children, young people and their families where abuse is suspected or confirmed
- assess the strategies and methods used to minimise the harm to children young people and their families where abuse is confirmed
- justify responses where child maltreatment or abuse is suspected or confirmed, making reference to current legislation and policies.

### Grading tips

**P4** You would need to explain all the appropriate responses and order of events, initially from you as a support assistant and then how you

would report and document your suspicions of this maltreatment.

**P5** Here you will need to provide an explanation of a range of strategies and methods that might be used to support children and families where abuse is suspected or confirmed.

**M3** Once you have identified the strategies, you will need to assess them and consider strengths and weaknesses, as they will not all be suitable for every situation.

**D2** This is your opportunity to link the responses to the policies and procedures that are in place and how they comply with current legislation.

You might want to carry out some independent research into this section and produce a written report or make a presentation to other members of the group.

# Resources and further reading

Beckett, C. (2003) *Child Protection: an Introduction* London: Sage Publications

Boys, D. & Langridge, E. (2007) *BTEC National Health and Social Care Book 1* Cheltenham: Nelson Thornes

Bruce, T. & Meggitt, C. (2006) *Child Care and Education* London: Hodder Arnold

Cairns, K. & Stanaway, C. (2004) *Learn the Child: Helping Looked After Children to Learn: A Good Practice Guide* BAAT Publication

Cheminais, R. (2007) *How to Achieve the Every Child Matters Standards: A Practical Guide* London: Sage Publications

Dunnett, K. (ed) (2006) *Health of Looked After Children* Lyme Regis: Russell House Publishing

Ferguson, H. (2004) *Protecting Children in Time: Child Abuse, Child Protection and the Consequences of Modernity* Basingstoke: Palgrave Macmillan

Fowler, J. (2002) *A Practitioner's Tool for Child Protection and the Assessment of Parents* London: Jessica Kingsley Publishers

Gardner, R. (2005) *Supporting Families: Child Protection in the Community* Chichester: Wiley

Guishard-Pine, J., McCall, S. & Hamilton, L. (2007) *Understanding Looked After Children* London: Jessica Kingsley Publishers

Hughes, L. & Owen, H. (2009) *Good Practice in Safeguarding Children: Working Effectively in Child Protection* London: Jessica Kingsley Publishers

Lindon, J. (2008) *Safeguarding Children and Young People: Child Protection 0–18 years* London: Hodder Education

Nolan, Y. (2005) *S/NVQ Level 3 Health and Social Care Candidate Handbook* Oxford: Heinemann

Nolan, Y. (2006) *S/NVQ Level 3 Health and Social Care Candidate Book Options Plus* Oxford: Heinemann

Stretch, B. & Whitehouse, M. (2007) *BTEC National Health and Social Care Book 2* Oxford: Heinemann

Walker, S. (2006) *Safeguarding Children and Young People: A guide to integrated practice* Lyme Regis: Russell House Publishing

# Useful websites

British Association for Adoption and Fostering www.baaf.co.uk/

Children and Young People Now www.cypnow.co.uk/

Children in Wales www.childreninwales.org.uk/index.html

Children in Northern Ireland www.ci-ni.org.uk/

Every Child Matters – Youth www.dcsf.gov.uk/everychildmatters/Youth/

Every Child Matters resources www.dcsf.gov.uk/everychildmatters/resources-and-practice

4 Nations Child Policy Network – Scotland http://childpolicyinfo.childreninscotland.org.uk/

Fostering Network www.fostering.net

National Society for the Prevention of Cruelty to Children www.nspcc.org.uk/

National Children's Bureau www.ncb.org.uk/

The Tavistock and Portman – leaders in mental health care and education www.tavi-port.org

## Just checking

1   Why might a child or young person be looked after?
2   Why is it important to have a robust legislative framework for the care of children and young people?
3   What type of care for children and young people might be classed as temporary?
4   What is the role of local government in providing care for children and young people?
5   What is the role of a foster parent?
6   What are the signs and symptoms of physical abuse?
7   Give an example of peer abuse.
8   How might a child or young person be at risk of electronic exploitation?
9   Why is it important to follow the policies and procedures of the setting?
10  Why is it important to support and reassure the child or young person who discloses that they have been in an abusive situation?

edexcel

## Assignment tips

1   This unit deals with a very sensitive subject and you need to present a balanced view of the scope of care. You will need to discuss with your class teacher how you can present your information for the various assignments.

2   When taking on different roles for the assignments, remember the importance of not being judgemental.

3   Good sources of information for the assessment activities can be found on the DCFS website – www.dcfs.gov.uk. If you are searching for specific job roles, it is worth checking that they relate to your local area.

4   There may be opportunities to link your work in this unit with other units such as Unit 1 Developing effective communication and Unit 6 Personal and professional development.

5   If you are in a placement, it might be beneficial to talk to the staff who may have come across similar situations to the ones in your assignments. You must keep confidentiality in mind at all times.

6   You might find useful additional information about the services available for families, children and young people on local authority websites and it may be helpful to investigate this in your area.

# 11 Safeguarding adults and promoting independence

**The issue of abuse and mistreatment of vulnerable adults – those who are unable, for whatever reason, to look after themselves – is rather like an iceberg. There appear to be more cases hidden beneath the surface of the care system than rise to the surface and are reported in the media and the courts.**

In this unit, you will be introduced to issues relating to vulnerable people and their needs. Child protection, which raises similar issues, has had a high profile and a long history as a recognised area of concern. However, it is only since the 1980s that the protection of vulnerable adults has started to produce a similar level of concern and has attracted public attention.

This unit introduces you to the different types of abuse and the signs that it is occurring. It will help you to understand the underlying factors involved in such behaviour and the approaches used to overcome, or at least reduce, the risks of individuals being abused. The protection offered by legislation and regulations will be examined. The role of the professional supportive relationship will also be looked at. It is recommended that this unit is not tackled until later in your studies when you have gained a wider understanding of health and social care.

## Learning objectives

After completing this unit you should:

1 know types and indicators of abuse
2 understand factors which may lead to abusive situations
3 know legislation and regulations which govern the safeguarding of adults
4 know working strategies and procedures to reduce the risk of abuse of adults
5 understand the role of supportive relationships to promote the rights, independence and well-being of adults using health and social care services.

# Assessment and grading criteria

This table shows you what you must do in order to achieve a **pass**, **merit** or **distinction** grade, and where you can find activities in this book to help you.

| To achieve a **pass** grade, the evidence must show that you are able to: | To achieve a **merit** grade, the evidence must show that, in addition to the pass criteria, you are able to: | To achieve a **distinction** grade, the evidence must show that, in addition to the pass and merit criteria, you are able to: |
|---|---|---|
| **P1** Describe forms of abuse which may be experienced by adults. **See Assessment activity 11.1, page 83** | **M1** Assess the likely immediate effects of two different forms of abuse on the health and well-being of adults. **See Assessment activity 11.2, page 87** | **D1** Evaluate the potential long-term effects of these two types of abuse on the health and well-being of adults. **See Assessment activity 11.2, page 87** |
| **P2** Describe indicators that abuse may be happening to adults. **See Assessment activity 11.1, page 83** | | |
| **P3** Explain factors that may lead to abusive situations. **See Assessment activity 11.2, page 87** | | |
| **P4** Outline key legislation and regulations which govern safeguarding adult work. **See Assessment activity 11.3, page 90** | **M2** Describe legislation and regulations, working strategies and procedures in health and social care used to reduce the risk of two types of abuse. **See Assessment activity 11.4, page 96** | |
| **P5** Outline working strategies and procedures used in health and social care to reduce the risk of abuse. **See Assessment activity 11.4, page 96** | | |
| **P6** Explain the role of supportive relationships to reduce the risk of abuse and neglect. **See Assessment activity 11.5, page 104** | **M3** Discuss the role of supportive relationships in reducing the risk of abuse and neglect, using examples. **See Assessment activity 11.5, page 104** | **D2** Evaluate the role of multi-agency working to reduce the risk of abuse of adults, with reference to legal frameworks, regulations, working strategies and procedures. **See Assessment activity 11.5, page 104** |

# How you will be assessed

Your tutor will internally assess this unit. A range of activities, case studies and opportunities to think through issues will be presented in this chapter. These will help you to prepare for your assessed assignment, and will further your understanding of the care and support needs of vulnerable people who use health and social care services. Assessment evidence can include, where appropriate, student-produced booklets and posters, reports, plans and the more traditionally produced assignments.

## Amy, 18 years old

When I started this unit, I'd only thought about 'abuse' as something that happens to children.

I then started to think about abuse in wider terms. It's not just what adults do to children; it can also be what children do to children. When I was at secondary school, some of the year 10s used to push the younger children around in the playground and call them names. Although this was called bullying, it was also abuse – physical and emotional. It was an example of the powerful taking advantage of the powerless.

People in hospitals and care homes can also be powerless because of their illnesses or conditions. Other people – family, strangers, professionals – can take advantage of them and the victim often accepts it because they can't stop them. They might be afraid, scared, or even unaware that the abuse is taking place (e.g. a neighbour doing shopping for a frail older person and not giving them their change because 'the price has gone up this week').

I became angry about the way some people are taken advantage of. It's made me more certain that I want to work in health and social care to help and protect vulnerable people.

### Over to you!

1   Were you aware that vulnerable adults could be abused in a similar way to children?

2   How did you become aware of such abuse?

3   What feelings do you have about abuse of adults?

# 1 Know types and indicators of abuse

**Get started**

## Who might be vulnerable?

Discuss and mind-map groups of people who may be vulnerable because of their care needs. Having identified who might be vulnerable, develop your mind map further by jotting down a couple of reasons for their vulnerability. This can be taken further by identifying possible abusers.

Fig 11.1: Can you tell who is vulnerable?

## Making the links

This unit introduces you to an area of concern that the general public have only become aware of in the last 25 years. It links in with issues raised in other units such as Unit 2 (Equality, diversity and rights). It can also be linked with Unit 6 (Personal and professional development).

More importantly, it may link in with your own experiences of being vulnerable at various times in your life. If you find that some of the issues or situations in this chapter are upsetting or disturbing, for whatever reason, you should discuss them with your teacher, tutor, school nurse, counsellor or whoever you feel most comfortable with. It is important not to bottle up your feelings.

Traditionally, the term 'vulnerable adults' has been used when referring to frail older people or people with learning disabilities. However, anyone who may potentially be taken advantage of, falls into this category.

There are many examples of people who are vulnerable. Patients in hospital recovering from an operation, people with mental health problems living in a hostel, people with disabilities who have mobility problems and are living on their own, people with drug or alcohol addictions and teenagers who have had their drinks 'spiked' on a Saturday night out – they are all vulnerable. It is important to consider 'vulnerability' in the broadest terms.

## Activity 1: How vulnerability feels

Spend a few minutes thinking back to times when you felt vulnerable as a child, such as:

- walking home from school in the dark
- having people laugh at you when you didn't know what the joke was
- starting secondary school or college and not knowing what to expect.

Write down how you felt. Imagine feeling like that most of the time. This is what vulnerable people have to live with.

## PLTS

**Creative thinker:** This encourages you to demonstrate creative thinking by using your imagination and empathy skills.

## Functional skills

**English:** You will use English writing skills in this activity when writing down your feelings.

## Defining abuse

**Abuse** is a word that is commonly used. It is important to be clear as to the context and meaning of it in this chapter. Historically, the abuse of adults has tended to take place behind closed doors and was unreported. It happened in the family or in such institutions as the workhouse or long-stay hospitals.

The term 'elder abuse' was first used in the late 1970s and early 1980s. In 1995 the charity Action on Elder Abuse defined elder abuse as 'a single or repeated act or lack of appropriate action, occurring within any relationship where there is an expectation of trust, which causes harm or distress to an elder person.'

The focus was later widened, as abuse became more widely recognised in other vulnerable groups such as people with physical disabilities, mental health issues and sensory loss. People who were seen to be 'at risk' were known as 'vulnerable adults'.

### Key term

**Abuse** – This is defined by the Department of Health as 'a violation of an individual's human and civil rights by any other person or persons'.

## Did you know?

The term 'granny bashing' first appeared in newspaper headlines in the 1970s, as cases of physical abuse of older people became more widely reported.

# 1.1 Types of abuse

The more common types of abuse are:

- physical
- sexual
- psychological (previously known as emotional)
- neglect or acts of omission.

Other forms of abuse include:

- exploitation/financial
- discriminatory
- institutional
- bullying
- self-harm
- domestic violence/abuse.

## Activity 2: Examples of abuse

Collect reports of abuse from the media (using magazine, newspaper articles and the Internet). In groups, share and compare your examples.

Which forms of abuse are most commonly reported?

Tip – keep collecting these reports throughout your course, as you will be able to use these as case studies and examples in your work later, as well as in the Assessment activities.

## PLTS

**Independent enquirer:** This activity enables you to demonstrate your independent enquiry skills by researching, reviewing and selecting information on abuse.

## Functional skills

**ICT:** You will use ICT skills in this exercise to find and select appropriate media articles on abuse.

## Physical abuse

Any physical contact can potentially be seen as a form of physical abuse. It depends on the degree of force, or the nature of the contact, and the intention behind the action.

Clear cases of abuse would be classed as common assault and subject to criminal prosecution. This could include hitting, slapping, kicking and pushing – the sort of actions involved in bullying. These may be carried out by care workers who lose their temper with a person because they are being difficult or it may be in retaliation for being hit with a walking stick by a confused patient. Possible scenarios could be:

- Jane often refuses to open her mouth when offered food on a spoon – she has had a stroke and is unable to feed herself. This time, when the care worker tries to feed her, she spits out a mouthful of food into the worker's face. The worker loses her temper and slaps Jane 'to teach her a lesson'.

- John is angry at having to move to a care home when his wife is no longer able to look after him. He is becoming confused and shows his anger by lashing out with his stick at anyone who comes near. An agency worker has come in to cover for sickness and hasn't been told about him. As she bends down to pick something up, he hits her across her back. He is surprisingly strong. The worker instinctively lashes out in pain and hits John.

The more difficult-to-identify forms of physical abuse may occur within the context of 'caring'. Examples could be:

- A confused resident in a nursing home may be given extra medication to 'quieten her down' and make her less demanding, as there are staff shortages on the night shift.

- A boy in a children's home loses his temper and starts to attack other people. A staff member, who has not been trained in 'restraint', holds him down inappropriately and the boy ends up with a fractured arm.

In these situations physical abuse has taken place, although not all of the professionals intended to harm the individual. Some are as a result of inappropriate actions by the staff when they are in difficult circumstances.

It can be very difficult to control reflex behaviour, such as lashing out, pushing, hitting, if you are caught unawares, as this is an automatic reaction, carried out instinctively. Professionals need to guard against such responses, at all times.

### Case study: George

Sally is working as a support worker in a care home. Yesterday it was time for a meal and George was asleep in the chair, in the TV room. She went to wake him. He is hard of hearing and could not hear her calling. She needed to touch him in order to wake him. He woke with a start and lashed out with his hand as he had been in a deep sleep and had been dreaming about being captured in the war. He didn't mean to hurt her but he caught her on the nose, which really hurts, making her eyes water.

**Imagine yourself in a similar situation and answer the following questions:**

1 Can you be sure you wouldn't react instinctively in a physical way?

2 How could you guard against reacting in such a way, without it affecting the care you give?

## Sexual abuse

Such abuse may range from rape to inappropriate touching. All staff have a duty of care towards individuals. It is inappropriate and against professional guidelines (and, in some cases, illegal) for care workers to engage in a sexual relationship with someone who is in their care.

### Reflect

Why do you think it is wrong for care workers to have a sexual relationship with an individual they are caring for? In what caring situations might such behaviour take place?

There have been prosecutions of staff who have taken sexual advantage of patients who have been paralysed or sedated. Staff have been engaged in inappropriate relationships with people in their care who have learning disabilities. The individuals have not been able to give their full consent because of their limited understanding of the situation.

**Did you know?**

A newspaper reported the case of a young couple whose wedding was cancelled after the registrar received a letter of objection from the Local Authority. The woman had learning disabilities and social workers had intervened because they were of the opinion that she was not able to make an informed decision about getting married.

## Emotional or psychological abuse

A person who is being abused may also be threatened in order to keep them quiet. They might be told that it is 'our little secret' or that they will lose their accommodation if they tell anyone what has happened.

**Reflect**

Why do you think adults who are being abused often keep quiet about it rather than speak to another member of staff? Do you think that having a complaints procedure would make it any easier to speak out?

Continuous put-downs and name-calling in front of others causes humiliation and a loss of self-respect and pride. This can lead to a self-fulfilling prophecy. A negative prediction (e.g. 'you are no good and a bad mother') will lead to the person believing that she is a bad mother and a lack of confidence that may be reflected in her mothering skills.

Just as bullying at school can lead to the bullied being driven to take extreme action (such as committing suicide), the same can happen to vulnerable adults. This can be the case if they have difficulty in getting away from the bully – for example, in a care home or closed psychiatric ward or if they have a mobility restriction.

**Case study: Rhea**

Rhea is on work experience in a nursing home. Last week she saw an older resident drop a cup of tea that the care worker had just handed to her. The worker shouted at the older lady, saying she should be more careful. The older lady cried and said she was very sorry. After that, the older lady never asked for a cup of tea from that worker again – she seemed afraid of her.

1 How should the care worker have reacted?

2 If you were a care worker and you saw what happened, what would you do?

Although the focus so far has been on staff as the abusers, other individuals can also carry out abuse. Examples have included:

- people being assaulted by other residents in care homes
- patients in mixed psychiatric wards raping or sexually assaulting other patients
- groups of established tenants in sheltered accommodation picking on new tenants when they use communal lounges and facilities.

## Neglect or acts of omission

**Neglect** can be said to take place when there is a failure to provide proper care and attention. In children, there is usually clear evidence of a failure to thrive and grow. Neglected children do not have regular meals or clean clothes that are appropriate for the time of year. Their personal hygiene can be poor.

For vulnerable adults, neglect may be self-imposed because of mental health problems. The individual may be suffering from depression. They may be unable to motivate themselves to do anything (e.g. prepare and eat food or wash their clothes) and may have poor hygiene levels.

Neglect, as a form of abuse, would result from another person's inaction or failure to meet the individual's needs. Neglect has taken place in care homes and hospitals where individuals, who have not been able to feed themselves, have not been fed by carers. Meals have been taken away untouched, on the assumption that the person 'did not feel hungry'. As staff change three times a day, if accurate records are not kept, the patient's lack of food intake is overlooked. Patients have been admitted to hospital, from care homes, suffering from malnutrition. These are acts of **omission**. Although the meal is supplied, staff omit to check why people are not eating. It may be because they are sick and choose not to eat or because they are unable to feed themselves. What would you do? Reports of this happening appear in the media from time to time.

**Key terms**

**Neglect** – A failure to provide, to give proper care and attention; ignoring someone.

**Omission** – Leaving something out or failing to do something.

Other needs can be neglected, as shown in the table below.

Table 11.1: Examples of needs and how they can be neglected

| Needs | Examples of neglect |
| --- | --- |
| Physical | Developing bedsores because of a lack of medical care and not being turned in bed often enough |
| Intellectual | Not having the opportunity to read your favourite books and newspapers because the staff keep forgetting to take your broken reading glasses to be repaired |
| Emotional | A lack of bonding and emotional care from staff because of their aloofness and 'must get the job done' attitude |
| Social | Living at home but being unable to get out; becoming socially isolated – not having your social needs taken into account in your support plan |
| Cultural | Not being provided with the opportunity to mix with people of your own culture |
| Spiritual | Being a devout Muslim with disabilities but not being taken to the mosque to worship |

## Other forms of abuse

### Exploitation

Vulnerable adults are open to **exploitation** in many ways. One of the main forms of exploitation relates to financial matters.

Financial abuse might happen when a person receives home care and support. They might be used to leaving their purse on the sideboard and then they think they are becoming forgetful because they don't seem to have as much money as they thought. They might not be able to find a piece of jewellery they have not worn for some time and assume they have misplaced it or lent it to someone in their family. Sadly, it might be a support worker who is stealing from them.

The individual may have mobility restrictions and they perhaps ask a neighbour to collect their weekly pension from the Post Office and do 'a bit of shopping' for them. The neighbour might ask if they could buy a few items for themselves and will pay back the money when their giro comes through. This happens every week and the borrowed money is never forthcoming. The pensioner does not like to say anything because there is no one else available to collect their pension.

### Activity 3: Forms of exploitation

Working in small groups or by yourself, produce a thought shower of the different ways that vulnerable people, in care settings, can be exploited. If someone is being cared for in their own home, this counts as a care setting.

You should be able to come up with at least six examples.

### PLTS

**Independent enquirer:** For this activity, you can show your independent enquiry skills by researching 'exploitation in care settings' and applying it to home care.

### Functional skills

**English:** This activity encourages speaking and listening skills through discussion.

### Reflect

How would you feel if you were the pensioner in that situation? How would it affect you to feel that you could not trust anyone, especially the person who is providing your care?

### Discriminatory abuse

**Discriminatory** abuse tends to overlap with other forms of abuse but it relates to people who are discriminated against because of their:

- ethnicity
- gender
- age
- disability
- sexuality
- health status
- religion.

**Fig 11.2:** Financial abuse can happen when an individual receives home care and support

For example, a person may be assaulted because of the colour of their skin. Such abuse is not only a criminal assault but is illegal under the Race Relations Act. You may have have looked at this in Unit 2 Equality, diversity and rights.

### Institutional abuse

People's rights can be abused by the practices and **procedures** of the organisation that cares for them. For instance, it used to be common practice in care homes and hospital wards to start waking people from 5.30 a.m. onwards to enable the night staff to wash everyone and give them breakfast before the day staff came on duty. This was for the benefit of the organisation and not the patients.

Home-based users of services who need help in going to bed and getting up in the morning may be put to bed at 8 p.m. and have to wait until 8 a.m. (or later) before the carer returns. Their choice as to when to go to bed is overruled by the organisation's need to 'get around' a number of clients, using a limited number of staff.

In the past, care organisations have tied confused people to chairs to stop them wandering and harming themselves. This form of abuse could well be accepted as common practice across an organisation. New members of staff can be introduced to poor, and potentially abusive, care practices by staff telling them 'this is the way we do things here'. This can include:

- leaving toilet doors open so people can be checked on
- having some residents as their 'favourites' and ignoring the quieter ones
- making fun of people's bodies when bathing them
- spooning food into people's mouths before they have finished their previous mouthful, to hurry them up.

## Key terms

**Exploitation** – Taking advantage of someone for your own selfish purposes.

**Discriminatory** – Denying one individual or a group the same rights as another individual or group.

**Procedure** – A way of going about something; to act in a certain defined manner; to follow guidelines.

## Activity 4: Guidelines for good practice

You are a member of a senior management group in a care organisation. You are required to produce a policy on how people should be treated and what staff should do if they become aware of abusive practice. Working in a small group, identify the main points you would wish to include in the policy document. Hint – 'principles and values' would be a good starting point.

## Functional skills

**ICT:** This activity will allow you to demonstrate computer skills for research and word processing of the policy document.

### Bullying

This type of abuse can take many forms and may occur on different levels. Not only can it be a case of staff picking on and intimidating people, it can also apply to staff bullying other staff members, users of services bullying staff members, and users of services bullying each other. For example:

- The manager of a private care home may bully staff into working long or extra hours with the threat that, if they do not, they will lose their job.

- Residents in a Supportive Housing Project may demand that a new resident moves out because they have heard he is HIV-positive.

- New residents may be bullied by cliques, or closed groups, of long-established residents, leading to psychological abuse and distress.

## Case study: 'Mabel's chair'

When Pete was on work experience in a care home, he saw a new resident being shouted at by a group, in the TV room, because he had sat in the 'wrong' chair. The new resident was told that Mabel always sat in that chair. He was a timid person and seemed shaken by the experience. Pete did not see him go into the TV room again, while he was there. People can be nasty to each other.

**Imagine you are the new resident. How would you feel?**

Residential care may have systems that are abusive to the rights of individuals. Residents may be 'put to bed' early to allow night staff to get on with the laundry, ironing and cleaning. In theory, they may have a choice about bedtime but, in practice, they may be bullied into going early as staff start cleaning around them and ask very pointedly 'Isn't it time you went to bed?' People are often over-compliant and accept whatever is happening to them. They may find it difficult to put up any resistance because of their low self-esteem.

**Fig 11.3:** Which seat would you use?

### Self-harm

Self-harm or self-abuse can take the form of self-inflicted wounds such as cuts to the arms and wrists, burns with lighters and cigarettes, and piercing of the skin with pins or sharp objects. These forms of abuse can be used to detract from, or replace, the psychological and emotional pain being felt by the individual. It can also be a reaction to feeling trapped in a situation from which there does not appear to be any escape. An example of this could be when someone is being sexually abused by a member of staff in a care home and feels unable to complain or move. The fear and frustration can lead to self-harm as a cry for help.

Abuse through overuse of drugs, alcohol and prescribed medication can be another form of self-harm used to deaden psychological and emotional pain, while creating a temporary sense of well-being. This can occur in all age groups and care situations.

### Domestic violence/abuse

Recent legislation and policy relating to vulnerable adults (e.g. 'No Secrets' 2000) makes no reference to domestic violence as a form of abuse but it clearly fits in with the definitions of abuse.

If there has been domestic violence within a partnership or family before an individual became a user of services, it may continue even after the person moves into supported accommodation or a care home. Domestic violence covers physical, sexual and psychological abuse but other forms, such as financial abuse, may also exist.

As can be seen in the case study below, it is not always easy to identify when abuse is taking place. Vulnerable adults can be frail, afraid, prone to accidents, forgetful and 'not wanting to cause any bother'. It is therefore important for professionals to be alert for indicators of abuse and self-harm to enable early intervention.

A point to remember: abuse is not always carried out with the intention of doing harm – it might be the result of bad practice. However, the result is still the same.

# 1.2 Indicators of abuse and self-harm

## Disclosure

Abuse, real or suspected, may be revealed in a number of different ways. For example:

- You may find that someone wants to tell you about it because they trust you.
- It might be from someone who has observed the abuse taking place, e.g. a resident seeing a care worker shaking another resident because they were too slow getting dressed.
- A doctor, when giving a person with learning disabilities their annual health check, might come across unexplained bruising on their back and find out that a neighbour, when drunk, hits the patient.

The abuse is **disclosed** to the professional, sometimes with a request for confidentiality. Confidentiality is also covered later in this unit and in Unit 9 Values and planning in social care.

### Key term

**Disclose** – Reveal information to another person.

## Case study: Mavis

Mavis is 80 and lives in her own house. Her partner died some years ago and, when she started to have difficulty in moving around and looking after herself, her 50-year-old son offered to move in and help.

He has always had a short temper and shouts at her when she is slow to do things. He has been known to push her out of the way when he is in a rush. Once when this happened, she slipped and fractured her wrist. She told the hospital she had slipped on the stairs. He also 'charges' her for the care he provides.

He has taken control of her pension book and gives her 'pocket money'.

1 What forms of abuse are taking place?

2 What difficulties might social services have in investigating suspected abuse?

3 Identify other situations in which domestic violence/abuse may take place. What forms might it take?

## Unexplained injuries

Medical opinion is often required to identify when an injury is non-accidental and even then the conclusion may not be clear. For example, an injury may result from a fall but it may not be clear whether the fall was the result of a push or an accidental trip. However, there are some clear indicators (such as fingermark bruises on the upper arm) that show the person has been grabbed and may have been shaken. Bruising around the mouth may be as a result of forced feeding. Burns from cigarettes and scalding, as a result of being placed in a bath with water that is too hot, are more obvious. Unexplained cuts or scar tissue in unexpected places, or forming patterns, may indicate either abuse by others or self-harm as a reaction against being abused.

**Malnourishment** in an individual who has been in a 24-hour care environment, like a care home or hospital, shows itself in terms of unexplained weight loss and dehydration and is a clear indicator of neglect. This may be as a result of poor care and attention.

### Did you know?

The recommended daily calorie intake for a male is 2550 calories and 1940 calories for a female.

## Poor hygiene

Poor personal hygiene in someone who is unable to look after themselves and requires assistance in day-to-day tasks (e.g. bathing, changing and washing clothes, etc.) can fall into the same category. However, this may also indicate someone who is suffering from depression.

## Changes in behaviour

It is important for care workers to be aware of, and investigate, any changes in behaviour that appear to be out of character for the individual.

Examples of this may be:

- low self-esteem – no longer valuing themselves and lacking any motivation to bring about change in their lives
- mood swings – going from being a cheerful individual to one who is socially withdrawn and depressed

- willing to accept any suggestions from others without question and acting in a **submissive** manner. They often make little eye contact and individuals who previously held a range of strong views may become **passive**.

Vulnerable adults may subconsciously signal that all is not well by use of attention-seeking behaviour. Having minor accidents; soiling themselves; becoming argumentative may also be indicators of abuse.

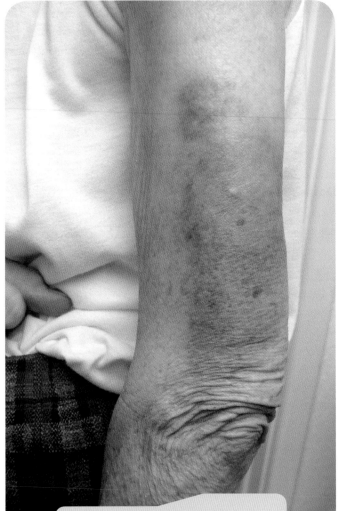

What other injuries might be clear indicators of abuse?

## Key terms

**Malnourishment** – The result of receiving inadequate nutrition.

**Submissive** – Doing what others want; being unusually compliant.

**Passive** – Not playing an active part; not reacting.

## Case study: Regina

Regina, aged 18, used to be the life and soul of the party. Then she was involved in a car accident. She lives at home and is cared for by her parents. She is unable to walk and has limited use of her hands. Her parents provide for most of her care needs, e.g. bathing, feeding, going out in the wheelchair. They are very strict and domineering. Regina had planned, before the accident, to move out. She now feels very vulnerable and powerless because she relies on them. She says very little apart from 'please' and 'thank you'. She keeps quiet and goes along with what they want because she is afraid of being shouted at. They constantly remind her of how little she can do and how much they do for her. She sees no way out of the situation.

1   Put yourself in Regina's position – and write down how you feel.

2   How might this situation affect your health, both in the short and long term?

Talking about suicide and having suicidal thoughts can also reveal feelings of helplessness and being trapped with no way out.

It is important to look for patterns of behavioural change rather than focus on one incident. For example, does a resident's behaviour become more withdrawn when a particular member of staff is on duty?

## Financial difficulties

Other indicators may include unexplained withdrawals from bank accounts (without any obvious benefit to the individual in terms of new clothes or furniture, etc.). This can lead to shortage of food in the house and reluctance to use the heating, even when it is cold, and it may indicate that someone else is enjoying the financial benefits. Sometimes it can be difficult to determine whether the money was given or taken, for instance, by a family member.

## Stress and related health problems

The stress caused by abuse may show itself through associated health problems. Stress affects our cardiac, neurological, respiratory, gastro-intestinal and muscular systems.

## Activity 5: Stress

Working in small groups, separately research the above systems and produce examples of short- and long-term symptoms likely to be shown by people suffering from stress.

People who are under stress for any length of time may experience some of the following symptoms: panic attacks, palpitations, headaches, breathing difficulties, ulcers, loss of appetite, tension, bowel problems and sleep difficulties. Which of these relate to the previously mentioned systems? Which are likely to occur fairly immediately and which over the longer term?

Finally, a reluctance to be touched or to undress for medical examination or be bathed by staff may indicate sexual abuse, while physically flinching when a voice is raised may indicate psychological and/or physical abuse.

## Assessment activity 11.1

 P1 P2    BTEC

You are a member of a social services training team whose role is to encourage good practice among staff working in care homes for adults.

Your team decides to establish a file on abuse to be used as a resource by the trainees preparing for their assessment. In small groups, gather a range of information about abuse and share this across your group.

Using this resource and other sources if necessary, individually produce a leaflet which describes different forms of abuse that may be experienced by adults and include descriptions of the indicators that the abuse may be happening to adults.

### Grading tips

P1 Support your work with examples of forms of abuse to demonstrate your understanding.

P2 Remember to give examples of indicators of abuse to demonstrate your understanding.

# 2 Understand factors which may lead to abusive situations

## 2.1 Adults most at risk

There are certain groups of people who appear to be more vulnerable to, or at risk of, abuse than others. These tend to be people with physical or learning disabilities and/or mental health problems. They also include older people and those suffering from dementia and other confusional states, as well as those with a previous history of being abused.

People in these groups tend to be over-compliant and accepting of whatever happens to them. This may be partly due to the medication they are taking. They often have low self-expectations and low self-esteem. Their illness, condition or age tends to make them isolated, with limited social networks. As a result, they become dependent on their abusers, or potential abusers, for help, services and social interaction. Being vulnerable increases the fear of retaliation from the abuser. Individuals can blame themselves for their abuse by feeling 'it's all their fault'. The abuser can reinforce this, as in the case of Regina, seen earlier.

Individuals, such as those with learning or physical disabilities, may be naive and have limited sexual knowledge, which leaves them more open to being taken advantage of. There is evidence that adults can be groomed in the same way as children can be.

People with a previous history of being abused may come to see it as a continuation, in different circumstances and a different setting, of the 'norm'. They feel disempowered and unable to resist.

### Activity 6: Who is at risk?

1  Jot down, in your own words, which groups of people are likely to be most at risk and why.

2  Identify other groups of adults who may be at risk.

You may have identified:

- people with **aphasia**
- people with sensory impairment
- people who are **comatose** or semi-comatose.

## Why might these groups of people be seen as vulnerable?

If people are unable to communicate verbally, they may have difficulty letting others know about their abuse. For instance, there have been reported cases where carers have taken sexual advantage of patients who have been unconscious.

## 2.2 Environments

Care is provided in a range of different environments and each can hold the potential for abuse.

### Activity 7: Care environments

For each of the different care environments identified below, provide an example of the type of abusive behaviour that could take place there:

- own home
- community care
- day care
- hospitals
- residential care
- independent living
- health services.

## 2.3 Contexts

### People who are dependent on others for personal care

Living alone, and depending on others, can be isolating for people with limited social networks. They

### Key terms

**Aphasia** – A difficulty in either producing or understanding speech.

**Comatose** – Being in a coma, a deeply unconscious state.

may find their main social contact is with their carers. Such isolation and dependency can increase the vulnerability of an individual who is confused, frail or has a learning disability.

People who live with their families may be subject to abuse by one or more family members. While not living in an isolated situation, they may be subject to a lack of privacy and financial abuse – for example, their mail might be opened and their benefits taken from them. They may suffer psychological abuse through name-calling and being the family scapegoat (being blamed whenever anything goes wrong).

In both situations, vulnerability is increased because the abuse takes place within the family and is more difficult to identify and resolve.

> ## Reflect
>
> Think about the advantages and disadvantages, for vulnerable people, of living at home, either by themselves or with their family.

## People who lack mental capacity to give consent

Individuals who do not have the mental capacity to consent to sexual relationships are vulnerable to exploitation. They are likely to be unaware of the consequences of their actions (e.g. pregnancy, risk of sexually transmitted disease or being taken advantage of emotionally) and are therefore unable to give informed consent.

## Adults who may not have the social awareness that abuse has taken place

People with learning disabilities may live in the community, in supported houses, that are not staffed at night. They can become prey to local teenagers and young adults who take advantage of their open, trusting nature and use their accommodation as a 'drop-in' and a place to have drinking parties, etc. The individual finds they are swept up in the activities and are unable to control the situation. Neighbours may also act as informal carers and develop an abusive relationship because of the imbalance of power in the relationship.

## Adults who feel shame or fear of reporting

Adults may allow abuse to continue because they feel ashamed of what is happening and they do not want to make it public by reporting it. For example, Jonas (in the case study below) might believe he will have to give up his flat and move back into the supported hostel he used to live in. He doesn't want to do that so has kept quiet about what has been happening to him.

## Communication difficulties

People with learning disabilities might have difficulty finding the words to explain what has happened. In the past, the police have often viewed them as unreliable witnesses because of communication difficulties and their statements lacking clarity about what took place.

Residential care has the potential for abuse on various levels. In addition to abuse by carers and invasion of privacy, there is the possibility of abuse by other residents and discriminatory practice by the organisation.

## Case study: Jonas

Jonas has a mild learning disability and lives in a housing association flat. His neighbours have offered to make his lunch and evening meal in return for half his money. He has agreed to this but finds the food is often cold and served in small portions. He is hungry most of the time and is having to spend his remaining money on snacks and chips. He feels unable to tackle them about this, as he is afraid of losing their friendship. He does not know anyone else on the estate and he does not want any trouble.

1 As his social worker, what help could you offer?

2 Jonas is offered another flat, in a different area, for his own well-being and is happy to take it. He has a support worker, for two months, to help him settle in. What role and help could the support worker offer?

## Bullying within care services

Bullying of new residents by cliques, or closed groups, of long-established residents is not uncommon, leading to psychological abuse and distress. Remember the case study 'Mabel's chair' earlier in the chapter? What do you think might be the short- and long-term effects of such bullying on a new resident?

## Discriminatory practice

Residential care homes may have systems that are discriminatory and abusive to the rights of residents. They may be 'helped to bed' or pressured – 'Isn't it time you went to bed?' – to allow night staff to get on with their duties, e.g. cleaning.

## Invasion of privacy

Discriminatory practice may involve walking into a resident's room without knocking or asking their permission to enter. It may also involve visiting family members picking up and reading a person's post, without permission.

## Relationships involving power

Traditionally, in the health service in particular, and the care sector in general, medical professionals have been seen as the experts, whose role is to heal and cure. The patients' role in the process has been one of compliance – the experts knew what was best for them and the patients trustingly placed themselves in their hands. This has sometimes led to an unequal relationship between carer and cared for. It has also increased the vulnerability of some groups.

## Social isolation

When people have little social contact with others (e.g. no friends, unable to get out of the house because of a disability, withdrawn into themselves because of depression, and so on), they become socially isolated. This may happen in a care home because a person has an aggressive personality and other residents keep away from them, or it can happen in a person's

own home because of mobility restrictions. Such individuals do not have a social network of friends and acquaintances in whom they can confide, if they are being abused. They are also vulnerable to 'grooming' – being unknowingly prepared for abuse by the potential abuser through compliments and offers of help, support and friendship.

Depression can be both a cause and a symptom of social isolation

## 2.4 People who may abuse

Abuse may be carried out by: health or care professionals; other people using services; paid carers; partners and relatives; friends; volunteers and strangers.

The potential for abuse lies in the nature of the interaction and the powerlessness of the individual. The individual's need for help with personal care increases the opportunity for abuse and can make it harder to be sure if it has actually taken place. It is an intimate and personal relationship that takes place behind closed doors or hospital screens and it is therefore difficult to monitor.

## Assessment activity 11.2

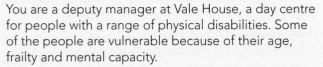

**P3** **M1** **D1** BTEC

You are a deputy manager at Vale House, a day centre for people with a range of physical disabilities. Some of the people are vulnerable because of their age, frailty and mental capacity.

You have responsibility for the training of new staff. They pick the people up, by coach, in the morning and have close links with families and carers so they have an important monitoring role. They need to be aware of the factors that may lead to the abuse of some of the people attending the centre. They also need to be aware of the likely short-term and long-term effects such abuse may have on the individual.

Produce a staff training pack, in which you:

- identify and explain the range of factors that might lead to abusive situations
- examine the potential short-term effects of two forms of abuse that you have identified
- evaluate the potential long-term effects of the two forms of abuse that you have identified.

Remember to include specific examples to illustrate the points you make in the pack.

### Grading tips

**P3** Consider the people who are at greatest risk of being abused, the environments they are likely to be in, possible contexts in which abuse might occur and the people who might abuse.

As part of the training pack, include a section in which you discuss the likely immediate, short-term effects of two different forms of abuse.

**M1** The examination of the short-term effects would be helped by in-depth exploration of two different 'abusive' case studies.

**D1** Consider the effects that loss of self-confidence and self-esteem would have on you, in the long term, in similar circumstances. Apply your projected experience to the two case studies used in M1.

# 3 Know legislation and regulations which govern the safeguarding of adults

## 3.1 Relevant legislation and regulations

A **law** has to be passed by an authority, such as Parliament. The vulnerable individual has the benefit of additional **legislation** and policies that apply to them specifically.

The European Convention on Human Rights and Fundamental Freedoms 1950 and the Human Rights Act 1998 spelt out the basic rights of all humans, regardless of their condition or situation. This includes the right not to be abused, which is incorporated into various other acts.

The anti-discrimination acts – Equal Pay Act, Sex Discrimination Act, Race Relations Act, Disability Discrimination Act and the Age Discrimination Act – all tackle the abuse that occurs as a result of discrimination.

The law exists to protect the individual

### Key terms

**Law** – A rule that has been established by an authority, e.g. Parliament, Assembly or a Local Authority.

**Legislation** – A term used for a set or group of laws.

## Activity 8: Law and legislation

There is often some confusion over what is meant by 'law' and 'legislation'.

Research both terms and identify clearly what each refers to.

## Did you know?

To understand a law, you only need to read a summary of it, which is easily found on the Internet. You don't have to read the law itself.

Since 1999, the Scottish Parliament and the Welsh and Northern Ireland Assemblies have had the power, to varying degrees, to create their own internal laws. The following legislation tends to be applied to England, Wales and Northern Ireland. Scottish legislation has been identified in the table and generally follows the spirit of the law but there are some differences. This can be identified by researching www.scotland.gov.uk and using the legislation search box.

The following table identifies the main laws and regulations that govern the safeguarding of vulnerable adults. It should not be seen as an authoritative statement on the law but more of a brief summary of the main points of related legislation and regulation.

**Table 11.2:** Main points of safeguarding-related legislation

| Legislation | Main points | Application |
|---|---|---|
| Safeguarding Vulnerable Groups Act 2006<br><br>Protection of Vulnerable Groups (Scotland) Act 2007<br><br>Protecting Vulnerable Groups (PVG) Scheme, which has similarities to the Vetting and Barring Scheme, will be introduced in Scotland towards the end of 2010 | • Requires people who work with children and vulnerable adults to be registered<br>• The Independent Safeguarding Authority (ISA) to be responsible for deciding who should be barred from working with the vulnerable<br>• The Vetting and Barring Scheme (as part of the ISA) will help employers to check on individuals' suitability to work with vulnerable people | • Applies to employed people and volunteers alike<br>• There are separate but linked Barred lists for those working with children and adults<br>• Checks must take place before an individual can work with the vulnerable |
| The Rehabilitation of Offenders Act 1974 | • Enables some convictions to be 'spent' or ignored after a period of rehabilitation or non-offending | • All heath and care employment is normally exempt from this Act and requires full disclosure of previous offences |
| The Police Act 1997 | • Criminal Record Bureau (CRB) checks, under this Act, are the norm in health and care organisations | • The CRB will work closely with ISA to ensure that a more detailed check is carried out |
| The Sexual Offences Act 1976 | • Created the Sex Offenders Register for identification and tracking purposes | • Enables sex offenders to be monitored and vulnerable people to be protected |
| Care Standards Act 2000<br><br>Scottish legislation<br><br>Regulation of Care (Scotland) Act 2001<br><br>The Adults with Incapacity (Scotland) Act 2000 | • Set **national minimum standards** for accommodation, services and good workplace practice in the care and protection of vulnerable people | • Established the Protection of Vulnerable Adults (POVA) Scheme that checked suitability of care workers. It identified professionals who had harmed individuals using services. It has been replaced by the ISA's Barred list |

**Table 11.2:** *continued*

| Legislation | Main points | Application |
|---|---|---|
| Care Homes for Older People: National Minimum Standards and the Care Homes Regulations 2003 | • Identified the minimum levels of care a vulnerable adult should receive in care homes | • Set the national minimum standards that all older people in care homes were entitled to expect |
| The Care Homes (Adult Placement) (Amendment) Regulations 2003 | • Required Adult Placement Schemes (foster care for vulnerable adults) to be registered and inspected | • Applied similar national care standards to these schemes as were set for care homes |
| Mental Health Act 1983 Mental Health (Care and Treatment) (Scotland) Act 2003 | • Created to balance the right of the individual against the need to protect them and others because of their behaviour and illness | • Allows for compulsory detention and treatment of people with mental illnesses<br>• Has procedures to ensure their rights are not being abused |
| Mental Capacity Act 2005 | • Established the Independent Mental Capacity Advocates Service (IMCAS) | • Aims to help vulnerable people who lack the capacity to make important decisions for themselves |
| Disability Discrimination Act 1995 (amended 2005 and by Disability Equality Act 2006) | • Defined disability and required 'reasonable adjustments' to be made, in varous areas, so that disabled people are not discriminated against | • Covers mental illness as well as physical conditions |
| Race Relations Act 1976, amended 2000 and 2003 | • Made discrimination on grounds of race, colour, nationality, ethnic or national origin unlawful | • People should not receive less of a service because of the colour of their skin or where they are from |
| Human Rights Act 1998 | • Gave people the power to challenge perceived discrimination by public bodies | • Vulnerable people, being cared for, have the right to privacy and protection |
| Data Protection Act 1998 | • Requires personal details and information to be kept secure and confidential | • From 2000, covers health and social care records – both computerised and written |

## Key term

**National minimum standards** – The minimum level and quality of care that people should expect to receive, regardless of where they are in the country.

## Case study: Mrs Shundell

Mrs Shundell is 80, frail and lives in sheltered accommodation, where there is a live-in warden. A support worker visits her three times a week.

• Describe how the legislation and regulation in the above table would help to reduce her risk of physical abuse from a member of staff.

## Assessment activity 11.3

You are in charge of a charity that runs a small care home and an adult placement scheme for people with mental health problems. A committee of volunteers oversees the charity's work.

A new member has been elected to the committee and has a meeting with you to find out more about the home and fostering scheme and how they are run.

Produce a brief summary that identifies and describes the key legislation and regulations that relate to your work and govern safeguarding vulnerable adults.

### Grading tip

(P4) You are required to produce an outline so you are not expected to produce a detailed piece of work but it should be contextualised to the small care home.

### PLTS

**Creative thinker:** This assignment encourages you to demonstrate creative thinking by summarising your findings.

# 4 Know working strategies and procedures to reduce the risk of abuse of adults

The main aim of the new Independent Safeguarding Authority (ISA), established under the Safeguarding Vulnerable Groups Act (2006), is to protect children and vulnerable adults from those who might seek to abuse them. Its **strategy** to achieve this is through monitoring people who seek access to them through their work, paid, unpaid and voluntary. They will have to register under the Vetting and Barring Scheme and will be checked against one of two 'barred lists' – one for those wishing to work with children and one for those who want to work with vulnerable adults. These lists have been operated by the ISA since October 2009.

## 4.1 Recruitment of staff

### Adults Barred List

This list replaced the POVA list (see Care Standards Act 2000) that had previously been in place since

2004. It lists people who are barred from working with vulnerable adults. It subdivides them into two categories – those people who are automatically barred because they offer a 'risk of threat' and those who offer a 'very probable risk of harm'. This discretionary barring process gathers information from various sources: police (Criminal Records Bureau, see below), health and social services, and employers. It looks at previous offences and/or evidence of inappropriate harmful, or potentially harmful, behaviour before a barring decision is made.

The Care Standards Tribunal hears appeals against such automatic bans but it can only consider points of law or findings of fact.

Employers and providers of services must check a person's status before employing them. Such checks will involve the Adult Barred List, Criminal Records Bureau (CRB) checks and the good practice of taking appropriate references from previous employers. It has been an offence, since October 2009, for an employer to employ someone they know has been barred by the ISA.

### Key term

**Strategy** – A long-term plan; a way of working.

## Case study: Working in care

Jordan, Sarah and Becca have all applied for a job as a support worker with an organisation that visits people, with learning disabilities, in their own homes.

Jordan is 18 and has a clean police record; Sarah is 20 and was given a police caution, when she was 14, because she allowed herself to be 'carried' in a stolen car; and Becca, aged 20, was found guilty of assault last year after a fight broke out in a nightclub.

* Which behaviour might be considered relevant for barring someone from working with vulnerable adults?

All staff who work with vulnerable adults have been required to register under the Vetting and Barring Scheme since July 2010.

## The role of the Criminal Records Bureau

People applying for employment that involves the care of vulnerable adults will continue to require a CRB check. However, since October 2009, they are required to have an Enhanced (in-depth) check, rather than the Standard (more general) check.

As can be seen, a more stringent approach to the safeguarding of vulnerable adults is being taken. The overall strategy has been one of closer monitoring and checking, as a means of offering greater protection to vulnerable people.

## 4.2 Sector guidance

There have been various guidelines drawn up to reduce the risk of abuse of vulnerable adults and give **guidance** to employers.

### Key term

**Guidance** – Giving direction; indicating how something should be done.

**Table 11.3:** Main points of safeguarding-related guidance

| Guidance | What does it cover? | Comment |
|---|---|---|
| The Protection of Vulnerable Adults Scheme for adult placement schemes 2004 Domiciliary Care Agencies and Care Homes 2006 (updated in 2009) | Required staff who work in care homes, provide personal care in adults own homes, or provide foster care for adults to be checked against the POVA list of banned professionals | Superseded by the ISA Vetting and Barred Scheme from October 2009 |
| No Secrets – Department of Health Guidelines 2000 | Identified who is at risk and why this might be. Set out a multi-agency framework to encourage different agencies to work closer together | Social Services to take lead role; involved council departments, local NHS bodies, police; required them to develop multi-agency codes of practice and ways of working together |
| Review of No Secrets guidance 2008 | National consultation exercise to review how it could be made better | Report on consultation exercise published in July 2009 – Government response awaited |
| Safeguarding Adults – A National Framework for Good Practice and Outcomes in Adult Protection Work 2005 | Set national standards, defined service models, or ways of delivering services and ways of working, at a local level; established ways of measuring achievement of the standards and introduced support programmes to assist in the process | Aimed at ensuring a nation-wide approach to protection of adults and closer multi-agency working |

*continued*

**Table 11.3:** *continued*

| Guidance | What does it cover? | Comment |
|---|---|---|
| Dignity in Care Initiative 2006 | Campaign to end toleration of indignity in health and social care services through raising awareness and encouraging people to challenge poor service and lack of respect | Continued to be developed; established 'Dignity Champions' to make a difference locally |
| Human Rights in Healthcare – A Framework for Local Action 2007/08 | Framework to assist local NHS Trusts to develop and apply human rights approaches in the design and delivery of their services | Services to focus on use of FREDA values – Fairness, Respect, Equality, Dignity, Autonomy |

These guidelines are aimed at producing clear working practices within and between various organisations to prevent poor practice and the gaps in service and communication that have led to a number of deaths of abused children and adults.

### Activity 9: Reviewing sector guidance

Study Table 11.3 above and sum up what the guidance has been trying to achieve since the year 2000.

## Organisational policies

Guidelines provide the basis on which organisations can develop their own policies. 'No Secrets' identified the importance of having local and regional frameworks within which policies, strategies and procedures can be developed between agencies, for the protection of vulnerable adults. Regardless of the size of organisation, be it a small charity running a drop-in afternoon club for older people or a county-wide private organisation offering residential nursing care through its twenty nursing homes, all must have policies and guidelines on expected behaviour from staff, good practice in the delivery of care and the support of individuals.

It was suggested that a multi-agency management committee could oversee the development and implementation of such an approach, and set out procedures to be followed when investigating allegations of abuse. 'No Secrets' also noted that abusers might be vulnerable adults who would need help, support and protection, in the form of an 'appropriate adult' throughout such an investigation.

Not only does this provide staff with a structure within which to work but it also enables individuals using the services to know what is acceptable and unacceptable, in terms of their treatment and care.

## Codes of practice for nursing and social work

In addition to organisational guidance, professional codes of practice require professionals to work to high standards, respect people using services as individuals and minimise risk to them. The Nursing and Midwifery Council and the British Association of Social Workers produce such codes for their members, as does the regulatory body – the General Social Care Council.

### Activity 10: Codes of practice

List up to ten things that you think should be in a code of practice for a nurse or a social worker. For example, what behaviour would you expect? Think back to when you might have been in hospital or seeing a nurse at school, or visiting a health centre or dentist.

Now look up the code and look for similarities and differences.

## 4.3 Strategies

In the past, there has been rivalry between agencies and professionals over funding and arguments over 'who does what', which has obstructed closer professional working. A number of strategies have now been developed that focus on improving co-operation for the benefit of those using services.

## Multi-agency working

The **support planning** process and **single assessment** process have encouraged greater inter-agency co-operation, with the individual's needs being central to the process. Rather than working separately, with each agency providing their own service without reference to each other, joint working encourages a sharing of information, a co-ordination of approach and less duplication of services.

Multi-agency working produces a multi-disciplinary approach. This is where professionals from different agencies combine their skills and expertise to meet the holistic needs of the individual. For this to work well, good communication and an understanding of the way in which other agencies work are essential. It also requires a 'lead' or co-ordinating professional to ensure that the needs of the individual are being met. This has not always happened and agencies have assumed others were taking care of the individual, when they were not. This has led to the death of a number of children and vulnerable adults through abuse or neglect.

The government's guidance paper 'No Secrets' (a separate guidance 'In Safe Hands' applies to Wales) details how this type of multi-agency co-ordination should happen.

### Key terms

**Support planning** – The joint planning of an individual's treatment and/or care that involves all concerned.

**Single assessment** – The assessment of an individual's needs is carried out by one professional/co-ordinator on behalf of a multi-disciplinary/agency team.

## Working in partnership with adults using services, families and informal carers

This encourages greater trust and empowerment of people using services. In turn, they are likely to feel more confident in talking about their worries, fears and possible abuse. The equality that is part of partnership working should encourage the growth of self-esteem, self-confidence and the strength to stop accepting abusive situations and behaviour as the norm. It also ensures an agreed approach that all involved, including families and informal carers, are aware of and can monitor. Protection is provided by the clarity of the situation.

## Closer working between professionals and within organisations

This enables better communication and information-sharing to take place. This may take the form of discussions between staff, team meetings, communication via emails and the use of written records such as a daily logbook. In a care home, or similar 24-hour caring context, there may be three shifts of different staff members providing continual care. A daily log enables staff coming on shift to be aware of what has happened since they were last on duty. This could be a couple of weeks ago if they have been on holiday or off sick. A sharing of concerns can result in early preventive action being taken. Patterns of behaviour can also be identified – for example, if a resident's behaviour seems to change when a particular member of staff is on duty or when a certain relative visits.

Fig 11.4: Having the opportunity to speak out

## Decision-making processes and forums

If decision-making is kept transparent and clear, everyone understands what is happening. There is also less likelihood that a culture of secrecy will develop in which abuse could take place. The use of forums (e.g. a monthly meeting of residents in a care home) encourages a sharing of ideas and exchange of opinions, and provides an opportunity for individuals to gain confidence in speaking out. They also have greater ownership of the decisions that affect their lives, such as being involved in interviewing new care workers. In addition, it provides an opportunity for procedures and guidelines to be explained, for rights to be emphasised, and for individuals to increase their expectations of the care they receive.

## Organisational policies and staff training

Clear guidelines about expected behaviour from professionals are important, not only to guide the professionals, but also so that individuals know what is acceptable and what is not. Complaints procedures need to be clearly understood and accessible to individuals, together with independent support when making a complaint. This could take the form of an advocate from outside the organisation.

Training needs to be provided when new procedures and policies are put into place so that everyone understands what is required. New staff need a formal induction period, during which all policies and procedures are explained. This provides the foundation for, and expectation of, future behaviour and practice in the organisation. It sets the tone for the future.

Abuse is often the result of poor practice and a lack of understanding about the consequences of certain actions. Training is an important counter to this. The inclusion of role-play and individuals talking about their experiences can give an insight into what it is like to be on the receiving end of care.

## The role of the Care Quality Commission

To ensure that organisations are working in the best interests of individuals and following the rules and regulations that apply to them, an independent regulator of health and social care services has been established. The Care Quality Commission took over the responsibilities previously held by the Commission for Social Care Inspection, the Healthcare Commission and the Mental Health Commission in April 2009. In addition to its regulatory role, it is also responsible for protecting the rights of people detained under the Mental Health Act.

# 4.4 Procedures for protection

The procedures to be followed, in cases of alleged or suspected abuse, are those laid down by the organisation in conjunction with the multi-agency framework. They consist of six stages as shown in the flowchart on the next page.

## 'Whistleblowing'

Since the Public Interest Disclosure Act of 1998, staff have had the right not to suffer detrimentally, or be dismissed, as a result of disclosing certain information to an employer or a regulator. This applies if a member of staff sees another member of staff verbally abusing an individual. In the past, some staff have been aware of abuse being carried out but have said nothing for fear of being called a 'grass'.

## Reflect

At school, college and in the community, people are called names and are open to being abused if they are seen to 'tell' on someone. Young people grow up in a culture of 'not telling'.

If you were working in a day centre and a person with learning disabilities told you that a member of staff had pushed them and helped themselves to their cigarettes, what would you do? If you mentioned it to your line manager, would this be 'telling'?

## Case study: Christine

Christine is 25. She had a motorcycle accident and suffered brain damage. She has the mental age of an eight-year-old and is very trusting. She attends a day centre for people with learning disabilities five days a week and lives at home with her parents.

- **Describe how the strategies and procedures used in health and social care are intended to reduce the risk of her being taken advantage of, financially or sexually, while attending the centre.**

**1 Alert**

- Concerns are raised through an allegation, suspicion or complaint.
- This information is passed on to the nominated person in the organisation, who has the responsibility of dealing with it.
- The priority is to safeguard and protect the vulnerable person/s. Staff have a supportive role.

**2 Referral**

- Allegation to be passed to police for possible criminal investigation and to social services for supervision of adult protection procedures.
- Staff must not 'contaminate evidence', e.g. asking leading questions or suggesting a quick shower.

**3 Decision-making**

- Feedback meeting to consider results of investigation and the lead body (usually social services) to decide if further action needed. Accurate record-keeping throughout is essential.
- Adult Protection Case Conference will then share results of investigation with vulnerable adult and family – needs assessment to be carried out.
- A protection plan will be incorporated into individual's care plan – agencies to be responsible for implementation of plan.

**4 Assessment**

- An assessment of the nature and urgency of the alleged abuse may be carried out within 24 hours of referral. No action will be taken, at this stage, unless urgent and agreed upon.
- A strategy meeting of all involved agencies will be held to identify investigating officer and consider action to be followed.
- Feedback meeting to be arranged.

**5 Review**

- The Protection Plan to be reviewed, on a regular basis, to check it is still meeting individual's needs. If not, new assessment needed.

**6 Monitoring and recording**

- The process is monitored and recorded throughout to ensure compliance with procedures and to identify areas for improvement.

**Fig 11.5:** The six-stage protection procedure

## Complaint procedures

An important element in protecting vulnerable adults is having an effective complaints procedure in place, which people are encouraged to use. The culture in the organisation should see complaints not as 'she's moaning again' but as a way to improve services and quality of life for individuals. Culturally, as a nation, we tend to put up with things rather than complain. It is also difficult for someone who lives alone and is being financially abused by their carer (e.g. having small amounts of money taken out of their purse), to complain. People need to feel they will be protected, and not victimised, if they make a complaint.

## Assessment activity 11.4   P5 M2   BTEC

You have recently been appointed as manager of a purpose-built residential unit for people with learning difficulties. The aim is to prepare people to live independently in their own flats. Support workers will soon be employed to help the tenants develop the appropriate life skills. The unit is due to take its first tenants next month.

Outline the working strategies that will need to be in place for the residential unit. You should consider strategies and procedures relating to

- the recruitment and training of staff
- individuals including assessment, decision-making, keeping records
- working in partnership to include informal carers, other professionals, inter-agency working, decision-making forums, quality standards
- procedures to reduce the risk of abuse such as whistleblowing, complaints, recording and monitoring, referral.

Describe how the strategies and procedures suggested for the residential unit and legislation and regulations could help reduce the risk of two types of abuse.

### Grading tips

**P5** For P5, you need to outline strategies and procedures you will use to safeguard the vulnerable individuals who will be living in the unit and reduce the risk of abuse. These need to cover such issues as vetting and recruitment of staff together with the relevant codes of practice, safeguarding individuals, working with others (individuals and agencies), and protection procedures.

**M2** Creating two case studies, based on individuals with learning difficulties, could help give your answer focus.

# 5 Understand the role of supportive relationships to promote the rights, independence and well-being of adults using health and social care services

As someone who is thinking of a career in health or social care, it is important that you develop the skills needed to form professional supportive relationships with individuals and their families. You need a basic understanding of the elements that make up such a relationship. It is from this understanding that skills can grow.

## Activity 11: Principles into action

Produce your own examples of the core principles in terms of how you would wish to be treated when seeing your GP or dentist.

## 5.1 Core principles of care

In the 1990s, a basic set of standards for care was identified. It was originally known as the Care Value Base but is now more commonly called 'principles and values'. They are a set of principles, values and guidelines to be followed by all providing health and care services.

These principles are:

- to foster equality and diversity of people
- to foster people's rights and responsibilities
- to maintain confidentiality of information.

These principles identify the very essence (or core) of care and should set the minimum standards for service providers to work to. They can be summed up in five words – dignity, respect, equality, fairness and privacy.

Vulnerable people, along with other individuals, should expect to be treated with

- dignity and respect
- equality, in terms of the quality of care provided, but differently, in terms of the quantity of care, depending on their individual needs
- fairness, in terms of retaining their rights and responsibilities as citizens, regardless of the support they need
- privacy, in terms of confidentiality and having their own private space.

Principles and values are covered in more depth in various units, including Unit 9 Values and planning in social care and Unit 29 Applied psychological perspectives for health and social care.

## 5.2 Building effective relationships

### Adult at centre of planning

A professional relationship differs from a personal friendship in a number of ways.

Neil Moonie (2005) suggests that this difference is because:

- professionals work within a framework of values
- professional work always involves a duty of care for the welfare of individuals
- professional relationships involve establishing appropriate boundaries.

It is the professional's responsibility to ensure that a relationship stays within the boundaries laid down in legislation and by professional bodies. Although the relationship should be seen as one of 'equals' in terms of being supportive, empowering and between two people, it is still a relationship between someone who needs help and a professional in a helping role.

Many professional codes of practice now encourage a person-centred approach, which places the vulnerable adult at the very centre of the interaction. However, this has not always been the accepted view.

In the past, many professionals believed that they knew what was best for people who needed help and did not involve them in decisions. For example, in Canada, up until the early 1970s, women and young girls with learning disabilities were sterilised, without their informed permission, to stop them having 'unwanted babies'.

DENTAL TREATMENT ROOM

You don't necessarily choose to enter into a professional relationship – sometimes it is thrust upon you!

### Reflect

Imagine finding out, twenty to thirty years later, that the minor operation you were told you needed, but wasn't fully explained, sterilised you. You married ten years ago and have been trying to have a baby ever since.

How would you feel? In what way might this affect your future relationship with health or care professionals?

The development of trust between two people is an indication of the forming of an effective relationship.

## Methods of communication and listening

The individual's preferred method of communication should be used whenever possible. This might involve a signer for communicating with a deaf person, an interpreter for someone who does not have English as their first language, or use of Makaton for people with learning and communication difficulties.

It is important to listen carefully to what people are saying and use active listening skills (e.g. focusing on body language, gestures, eye contact, and so on) as well as the words they use. The more comfortable they are when communicating, the more effective the communication will be.

## Respect for culture, beliefs and lifestyle

An effective relationship involves respecting the person for who they are, their culture, beliefs, lifestyle and the choices they have made. These may be different from those of the professional but, by accepting the individual as a unique individual, you are accepting their right to be different. For example, you need to be aware of the individual's preferences, such as not wishing to be treated by a member of the opposite sex.

## Recognition of needs and preferences

With effective relationships come knowledge and understanding, enabling you to identify the individual's needs and preferences. People's needs differ from their wants, which are the first things they ask for. The role of the professional is often to help the individual to decide what their needs are.

It also enables you to become aware of small changes in their behaviour that could indicate that abuse is taking place, e.g. withdrawing into themselves when a certain member of staff comes on duty.

## Confidentiality

As part of the relationship, a clear understanding needs to be established as to what is meant by confidentiality. Professionals cannot offer 100 per cent confidentiality to individuals because information needs to be shared with other professionals, to meet the individual's care needs.

## Case study: Andrew

Ali, a care worker, is helping Andrew, who has had a stroke, to get dressed. He notices bruises, in the shape of fingerprints, on his arms. Andrew says that Jane, another care worker, shakes him if he is too slow when she helps him. He doesn't want anyone told about this, although it happens on a frequent basis.

Ali says he must tell his line manager. Does he have any choice in this?

# 5.3 Working practices

The way professionals work can minimise the risk of abuse. This can be done by making sure that their care practice stays focused on the needs of the individual and by making use of the Care Value Base. Clear and appropriate forms of communication should also be used.

The following table summarises examples of good working practice that offer ways of minimising the risk of abuse.

**Table 11.4:** Examples of good working practice that reduce the risk of abuse. The individual being cared for, Josie, lives at home by herself and has, for the past twelve months, been receiving a range of services from Social Services (Social Worker), the Health Centre (GP), Helping Hands (a private care agency) and Age UK (a volunteer visiting service). She is happy about the help she receives.

| Work practice | Purpose | Example |
|---|---|---|
| Needs assessment | Identifies individual's needs (with their involvement), and informs the support plan and other professionals involved. | Josie is involved in identifying her needs and feels empowered by being included in the process, rather than being ignored or marginalised. |
| Support planning cycle | A plan that sets out how needs are to be met, in detail, and by whom – all involved understand their responsibilities and the co-ordinator monitors its implementation and review. | The support plan enables Josie to know which professionals (e.g. support worker, community nurse, etc.) will be visiting her and when; and what they will be doing. She feels secure, as she knows the co-ordinator will be checking that everything is working as planned. |
| Person-centred practices | The individual is central to the care process and services/professionals should be working to meet the person's needs – the individual should feel a partner in the process. | Josie feels her needs are being taken into account and she is part of a process that treats her with respect and dignity. She doesn't feel isolated or ignored – she is encouraged to speak out about her feelings. |

*continued*

Being listened to

**Table 11.4:** *continued*

| Work practice | Purpose | Example |
|---|---|---|
| Record and method of communication | Communication between services, professionals, individuals and their families is clearly recorded so that everyone is aware of what is happening – the better the communication, the more those who are involved are kept informed. The language used is understood by all. | By keeping up-to-date records, there is clarity in the process and individuals may check if they are unsure of what is happening – openness protects against abuse. Josie feels confident, as all involved are kept fully informed. |
| Anti-oppressive practice | Adopting the person-centred approach ensures the focus is on the needs of the individual, and agencies or professionals are not forcing their ideas or agenda on the individual. | In the past, Josie had felt under pressure to move into a care home, as it was cheaper than community-based care. However, an advocate argued against this, as it was not in her best interests. |
| Anti-discriminatory practice | Services aim to meet the diverse needs of the individual and ensure they do not receive a lesser service than others who are in a similar position (which would be a form of abuse). | Whenever Josie sees her GP, she feels listened to and her pain is fully investigated – it is never dismissed (e.g. 'as you get older, you have to expect these things'). |

## Inclusive practice

The above table provides a range of examples of inclusive practice where the individual is fully involved in the decision-making process relating to their life. Such practice is based on an effective relationship that offers respect, trust and dignity.

## Protocols for sharing information

Good work practice dictates that there should be clear protocols or understandings within organisations about confidentiality and the sharing of information. This should be kept to a 'need to know' basis when dealing with personal information. For example, it is important for the cook in a day centre to know that a certain individual has a wheat allergy. However, there is no reason for them to be told about the person's financial status.

## Providing a safe and secure environment/ duty of care

Health and social care organisations have a legal responsibility to provide a safe and secure environment for staff and individuals using the services. This includes not only the physical but also the psychological environment. They also have a 'duty of care' towards both people using the service and staff. Neither group should be put at risk because of organisational shortcomings. Sufficient staff members need to be on duty to ensure that adequate care and protection are offered at all times.

## Advocacy and confidentiality

Advocates, from an external body such as Age UK or Mind, should be available to support individuals with any complaint they may wish to make. The names and telephone numbers of advocates should be made easily and freely available – for example, next to a public phone. This phone should be in a private zone to give the user some privacy. It should be a confidential process.

## Access to information

Individuals have the right to see their own records, under the Data Protection Act, Access to Personal Files Act and Access to Medical Records Act, for whatever reason, although a doctor has the right to deny such access if it is thought not to be in the patient's best interest.

Such working practices encourage a positive, open, person-centred environment in which the individual feels valued, supported and respected and able to make choices relating to their lives.

# Lucy Jones
## Charity support worker

Lucy works for the charity 'Home from Home'. She is a support worker whose job it is to help adults with learning disabilities move from living with their parents to living more independently.

She's a key worker for Harry, a 42-year-old, with slight learning disabilities. A key worker has special responsibilities for a couple of individuals.

She helped Harry to move into a small Housing Association rented flat six months ago. He wanted to move out of home because his parents were over-protective and he felt they kept treating him as if he was an 11-year-old.

Since moving into the flat, Harry has settled in well. Lucy pops in to see how he's managing twice a week. He has been able to look after himself and manage his finances well.

However, over the past two weeks, his flat is showing heavier 'wear and tear' than you would expect – door panels have cracks in them; one small windowpane has been broken; and the kitchen tops have cigarette burns in them. Harry doesn't smoke.

When Lucy asked him about the damage, he became flustered and said he'd had a 'bit of a party'; his friends were drunk and had accidents. This is unlike Harry, as he normally keeps himself to himself.

Lucy had a chat with the neighbours and they said a group of local lads had been hanging around and had started to invite themselves into Harry's. They heard a lot of noise the other night and then found Harry outside, crying because they wouldn't leave him alone and had taken his savings of £30 from his jar. The neighbours chased the lads away but they feel that Harry is vulnerable.

Harry has lost some of his confidence and is 'jumpy' at sudden noise. Lucy believes he has suffered from abuse and that a multi-agency approach, involving the police, social services, housing association, neighbours and herself could help support him and prevent the incident from being repeated.

## Think about it!

1  What abuse do you think Harry has experienced?
2  What should Lucy do now?
3  How might a multi-agency approach help?

# 5.4 Supportive practice
## The humanistic approach

The **humanistic approach** (see Unit 8, Psychological perspectives) focuses on treating people with dignity, respect and as unique individuals, with **diverse** needs. This approach, used by professionals to support people, emphasises the importance of the individual in terms of their uniqueness and value.

### Reflect

Consider how the humanistic approach runs through Section 5 of this unit.

Identify how, and where, it is embedded in the core principles of care and the importance of building effective relationships.

Carl Rogers identified the **core conditions** that should be present, in professionals' relationships, as being:

- **empathy** – the ability to 'see' and understand the situation through the eyes of the person who is experiencing it
- **congruence** – to be genuine, transparent and real; not acting as the expert but as an individual, working in partnership with the person
- **unconditional positive regard** – valuing, respecting and being non-judgemental towards the individual and appreciating them as a person.

### Activity 12: Core conditions

Consider a close relationship you have with a friend. In what way do the three core conditions exist in the relationship? Give examples of each. If these conditions did not exist, how would the relationship be affected?

## Key terms

**Humanistic approach** – This focuses on treating people with dignity, respect and as unique individuals with individual needs.

**Diverse** – Differing.

**Core conditions** – The essential ingredients/requirements for a person-centred approach.

**Empathy** – Trying to understand things from another person's viewpoint.

Supportive professional relationships with adult individuals should include the elements shown in the following table.

**Table 11.5:** Elements within a supportive professional relationship

| Element | Example |
|---------|---------|
| Helping | Willingness to assist: collecting a prescription from the doctor |
| Enabling | Removing an obstacle: moving chairs out of the way so that a wheelchair user can propel themselves to a table |
| Empowering | Giving the power to make decisions relating to own life: individual involved in the planning of their care package |
| Making choices | Being able to exercise own preferences from a range of options: doctor explaining the different types of treatment available so patient can decide on their treatment of choice |
| Maintaining privacy | Ensuring an individual has their own space regardless of circumstances: making sure the screens are securely around a patient's bed when carrying out a medical examination in hospital |
| Confidentiality | Protecting information that has been given on trust: not leaving files around for residents to read |
| Advocacy | Speaking on behalf of someone who cannot do so for themselves: making a complaint on behalf of an older person who is confused |
| Promoting rights | Ensuring an individual's rights are not compromised because of their support needs: people with learning disabilities have the right to make choices, as do others |
| Non-judgemental | Having an open mind about an individual: not stereotyping people based on what others have told you |
| Using preferred methods of communication | Communicating in the way that the individual wants, e.g. using a professional interpreter if English is not their first language and they have difficulty in understanding spoken English |

## Case study: Nancy

Nancy is 78 and has just moved into a care home. She needs help with day-to-day activities (e.g. washing, toileting, getting dressed).

She feels her family rushed into making the decision about moving. She's quiet and finds the staff often ignore her. When she is taken to the toilet the door is left open so they can check that 'everything is all right'. She is a vegetarian and, at mealtimes, is given the same as everyone else. She is told to eat the vegetables and leave the meat. One member of staff discussed her occasional incontinence with her in the TV lounge, while others were within hearing.

She is unhappy about the way she has been treated.

1   Identify which elements of a supportive relationship are not being applied and the likely effects on Nancy.

2   Explain what should happen so that she feels respected and supported.

## Meeting the individual's needs

Individuals may offer what is known as 'the presenting problem or need'. This is usually the one they feel comfortable discussing. However, it often leads on to identifying needs that are less visible.

We all have a range of needs:

- physical
- intellectual
- emotional
- social
- cultural
- spiritual.

When doing a needs assessment, all aspects should be explored with the individual's consent. Being responsive to their needs and concerns ensures that a person-centred approach is taken. Flexibility is the key to responding positively to the individual and their needs.

In the past, procedures were often rigid and for the benefit of the organisation and the staff (e.g. putting residents to bed early so that cleaning could be carried out). The focus now is on the individual.

If an individual makes a complaint, the complaints procedure should be user-friendly. The process needs to be fully explained and support offered, through the organisation or an independent advocate.

Supportive practice encompasses not only the individual but also their family and carers. However, the individual's wishes need to be taken into account, and confidentiality observed, at all times. The individual may not wish his family to know that he has suffered abuse at the hands of a care worker. This must be respected.

## Assessment activity 11.5

P6 M3 D2 · BTEC

Carla is 75 and lives by herself. She has had a stroke and needs help to get washed and dressed, cook a meal, and get ready for bed. She has no friends or family nearby and relies on Cherrelle, her support worker, to come in three times a day to help her. Cherrelle is usually the only person she has to talk to. A neighbour used to do shopping for her but never returned the change. This was stopped once Carla felt confident enough to tell Cherrelle about it.

Denzil is 20 and has recently moved into a hostel after having served 12 months for drug dealing. He does not want to return to a life of crime and has daily support sessions with Dave, a hostel worker. These have helped him regain his self-esteem. He feels strong enough to stay away from his old friends, who 'bullied' him into dealing.

Rafeyia is 30 and has learning disabilities. She attends a day centre four times a week and is always bright and cheerful. Recently, Clare, her support worker at the centre, has noticed that she has become quiet and withdrawn. It is suspected that a male individual may be bothering her. Clare is going to have a chat with her and believes their relationship will enable Rafeyia to tell her why she has changed.

1   Using the case studies above, produce a guide for new care workers that explains how supportive relationships with adults helps reduce the risk of abuse and neglect. You should discuss in some detail how supportive relationships would help reduce the risk of abuse and neglect for Carla, Denzil and Rafeyia.

John lives in a supported house, run by a private organisation, for people with learning disabilities. He attends college three days a week and a day centre for two days. He has a good relationship with a volunteer who visits him at weekends and takes him out on trips.

A friend from college has started to turn up at the day centre and at home. John seems reluctant to see him at times but will not say why. He has started to spend more money than usual on CDs and electrical gadgets, which he then gives to his friend as gifts. He is not his normal cheerful self. The volunteer feels that John is being taken advantage of and that financial and verbal abuse (threats) may be taking place.

2   Evaluate how multi-agency working can investigate John's case to minimise the suspected abuse. Include consideration of the contribution made by legal frameworks, regulations, working strategies and procedures in protecting John from abuse.

### Grading tips

P6 Remember that individuals do not lose any of their rights because they need help. They retain the basic right to be treated with respect and dignity and be supported in meeting their needs.

M3 The extent to which an individual is supported and empowered will enhance their experience. The relationship should be person-centred.

D2 Identify the agencies relevant to John's situation before you start so you have a clear picture of who is involved. Remember that the focus should be on multi-agency working and legal frameworks, regulations, working strategies and procedures.

# Resources and further reading

Brown, K. (ed) (2006) *Vulnerable Adults and Community Care* Exeter: Learning Matters Ltd

Crawford, K. & Walker, J. (2004) *Social Work with Older People* Exeter: Learning Matters Ltd

Criminal Justice Performance, Justice, Victims & Witnesses Unit (2003) *Speaking up for Justice* London: Home Office

Department of Health (2000) *No Secrets: Guidance on Developing and Implementing Multi-agency Policies and Procedures to Protect Vulnerable Adults from Abuse* London: HMSO

Fisher, A. (2006) *OCR National Level 3 Health, Social Care & Early Years* Oxford: Heinemann

Fisher, A. *et al* (2006) *Applied AS Health and Social Care* Dunstable: Folens

Johns, R. (2005) *Using the Law in Social Work*, second ed, Exeter: Learning Matters Ltd

Moonie, N. (ed) (2005) *GCE AS Level Health and Social Care* Oxford: Heinemann

Pritchard, J. (ed) (2001) *Good Practice with Vulnerable Adults* London: Jessica Kingsley Publishers

# Useful websites

Action on Elder Abuse www.elderabuse.org

Age UK www.ageuk.org.uk

British Association of Social Workers www.basw.co.uk

Care Quality Commission www.cqc.org.uk

Department of Health www.dh.gov.uk

Department of Health Social Care Bulletin www.careandhealth.co.uk

General Medical Council www.GMC-uk.org

Home Office www.homeoffice.gov.uk

International Network for the Prevention of Elder Abuse www.inpea.net

Legislation and explanatory notes www.legislation.hmso.gov.uk/acts

Information on the Court of Protection www.publicguardian.gov.uk/about/court-of-protection.htm

Nursing and Midwifery Council www.nmc-uk.org

Office of Public Sector Information www.opsi.gov

Scottish Parliament www.scotland.gov.uk

UK government (legislation and policies) www.direct.gov.uk

# Just checking

Martin is 25 and lived with his father who recently died. He has a mild learning disability and is able to look after himself, with a little support. He has decided to stay in the family home and social services have assessed him as needing ten hours a week social support. This will involve helping him with his shopping, budgeting, cooking and reminding him about such things as laundry, cleaning, etc.

You have been appointed as his support worker.

1  Helping, enabling and empowering are important elements in developing a supportive professional relationship. How would you use them in developing a relationship with Martin?
2  What are the differences between a friendship and a supportive professional relationship?
3  Name four behaviours that individuals, living in a care home, have the right to expect from professional workers.
4  In your own words, explain what is meant by the term 'vulnerable person'.
5  Give examples of physical abuse that might be experienced by adults receiving medical care.
6  What indicators of physical abuse should you be alert for?
7  What are the benefits for individuals of 'multi-agency working'?
8  Give a brief overview of the guidance offered in the policy document 'No Secrets'.

edexcel

# Assignment tips

1  Focus on the initial verbs in each grading criterion. 'Describe' means 'give an account of...'; 'explain' means 'make clear by going into depth; 'outline' means 'give the main features or general idea of...'; and 'evaluate' means 'judge/assess...'.

2  Read through the unit specification, either online or as hard copy, to gain an overview, before you start. Read through it when you are halfway through the unit, as it will make more sense as your understanding of the terminology develops, and again at the end to check that you have covered everything you need to.

3  When carrying out your research, keep a note of new terminology you need to look up or ask your tutor to explain. Once you understand it, use it – you will demonstrate knowledge and understanding of the unit.

4  Cross-references to other units that have been identified in the text will help you fit the pieces together, just like a jigsaw, to get the overall picture.

5  Don't get 'bogged down' in the legislation by using primary sources. Instead, read the summaries/ explanations supplied by the government, NHS, charity and local authority websites. See the 'Resources and further reading' section, on the previous page.

# 12 Public health

**Public health is concerned with improving the health of the population, as opposed to treating the diseases of individual patients. Public health professionals work in partnership with many other agencies to monitor the health status of the community; identify health needs; develop programmes to reduce risk; screen for early disease; control communicable disease; foster policies that promote health; plan and evaluate the provision of health care; and manage and implement change.**

In this unit you will develop your understanding of the role of public health systems, their origin and development and the range of key groups that influence public health policy today. You will also learn about the key organisations that can influence and shape health policy locally, nationally and internationally. The unit sets out current patterns of ill health and considers the key factors that contribute to them. The unit also looks at how trends in health patterns are monitored, and where you can access information to look at changing patterns of ill health. The unit closes by looking at the different methods of promoting and protecting public health in terms of health education, health protection and environmental measures. You will find more information on the principles and practice of health education in Unit 20 (Promoting health education).

## Learning outcomes

After completing this unit, you should:

1   know the origins of public health policy and current public health strategies
2   understand factors that affect health status and patterns of ill health
3   understand how public health is promoted and protected.

# Assessment and grading criteria

This table shows you what you must do in order to achieve a **pass**, **merit** or **distinction** grade, and where you can find activities in this book to help you.

| To achieve a **pass** grade, the evidence must show that you are able to: | To achieve a **merit** grade, the evidence must show that, in addition to the pass criteria, you are able to: | To achieve a **distinction** grade, the evidence must show that, in addition to the pass and merit criteria, you are able to: |
|---|---|---|
| **P1** Describe key aspects of public health strategies. **See Assessment activity 12.1, page 118** | **M1** Compare historical and current features of public health. **See Assessment activity 12.1, page 118** | |
| **P2** Describe the origins of public health policy in the UK from the 19th century to the present day. **See Assessment activity 12.1, page 118** | | |
| **P3** Describe current patterns of ill-health and how they are monitored. **See Assessment activity 12.2, page 130** | | |
| **P4** Explain the main factors affecting current patterns of health in the UK. **See Assessment activity 12.2, page 130** | **M2** Discuss the factors likely to influence current and future patterns of health in the UK. **See Assessment activity 12.2, page 130** | **D1** Evaluate the influence of government on factors that contribute to the current patterns of health AND illness in the UK. **See Assessment activity 12.2, page 130** |
| **P5** Explain health promotion and health protection. **See Assessment activity 12.3, page 142** | **M3** Assess the different methods that can be used for promoting and protecting public health. **See Assessment activity 12.3, page 142** | |
| **P6** Explain appropriate methods of prevention/control for a named communicable disease and a named non-communicable disease. **See Assessment activity 12.3, page 142** | | **D2** Evaluate the effectiveness of methods used to promote and protect public health for the two named diseases. **See Assessment activity 12.3, page 142** |

# How you will be assessed

This unit will be internally assessed by your tutor. Various exercises and activities have been provided to help you understand all aspects of public health and prepare for the assessment. These include writing reports, preparing a presentation and researching information from different sources. You will also have the opportunity to work on some case studies to further your understanding.

## Alfie, 18 years old

This unit really made me think about health quite differently. I did the 'Get started' stimulus exercise and at first I was thinking about advances in healthcare and how important they must be in improving health. However, after reading the first section and understanding the history of public health work, I began to realise what a big role welfare and environment play in health.

I found the story of John Snow quite fascinating, almost like a detective novel. It made me think about modern-day stories about new outbreaks of disease and how scientists try to work out the causes and how to contain them.

There were lots of different practical tasks and activities within the unit, which helped me to understand how I would be evaluated against the assessment criteria.

The main take-home point for me was a growing understanding of what a big role government plays in protecting health, not just in curing it through the health service. This was particularly true when it came to government strategies and the role the government has in providing safe, green and clean environments, clean water and a whole host of other things that I hadn't really thought about as health measures.

### Over to you!

1   What do you think is the most important aspect of public health?
2   What are you looking forward to finding out about in this unit?
3   What do you think you will find most difficult?

# 1 Know the origins of public health policy and current public health strategies

**Public health advances**

If you were asked to name the most important medical advance in the past 150 years, what would you suggest?

If you were asked to name the advance that has been most important to the public's health in that time, what would you say?

- Are they the same thing?
- If not, why not?
- Which do you think may have affected the greatest number of people?
- What does this tell you about the possible difference between medicine and public health?
- What might the major public health challenges of today be?

## 1.1 Historical perspectives on public health systems

### The nineteenth century

#### The Poor Law of 1834

Public health provision, as we know it today, originated with the nineteenth-century Poor Law system and the Victorian sanitary reform movement. The Poor Law was amended in response to the 1832 Royal Commission of Inquiry into the Operation of the Poor Laws. In their report, the Commission made several recommendations to Parliament. As a result, the Poor Law Amendment Act 1834 was passed, which stated that no able-bodied person was to receive money or other help from the Poor Law authorities except in a workhouse. Conditions in workhouses were to be made very harsh to discourage people from wanting to receive help. Despite its harshness, the Act did ensure that the poor were housed, clothed and fed and that children who entered the workhouse would receive some schooling. In return for this care, all workhouse paupers had to work for several hours a day.

#### The first national Public Health Act 1848

Industrialisation and the rapid growth of cities during the nineteenth century led to concerns about environmental problems such as poor housing, unclean water supplies, 'bad air' and the impact that these had on the health of the working population. Edwin Chadwick, a founding member of the sanitary movement, was an active campaigner on several public health issues including poor housing and working conditions and sanitary reform. Chadwick's *Report on an inquiry into the sanitary conditions of the labouring population of Great Britain, 1842* contained a mass of evidence linking environmental factors, poverty and ill health. It recommended the establishment of a single local authority, supported by expert medical and civil engineering advice, to administer all sanitary matters. Six years later, the national Public Health Act (1848) was passed and the first Board of Health was established.

#### John Snow and the Broad Street pump

In 1854, John Snow was interested in the role of drinking water in the spread of cholera and had observed that people who had drunk water provided by one water company were more likely to contract the disease than those who had not. By plotting the cases of cholera on a map, Snow established that all those falling ill were getting their water from a single pump, which drew its supplies from the sewage-contaminated

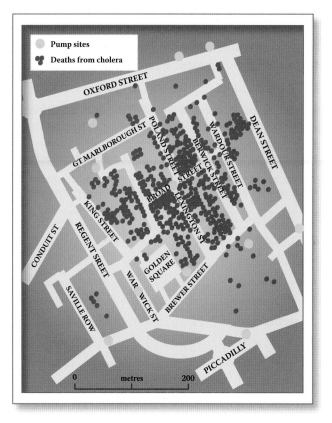

**Fig 12.1:** How did Snow's map help him to find the cause of the cholera outbreak?

River Thames. People using nearby wells to obtain their water had escaped infection. The connection between cholera and contaminated water was therefore established, before bacteriology was able to identify the causative organism.

Having identified the source of the infection as polluted water, he went on to remove the handle of the Broad Street water pump and halted the outbreak of cholera in Soho, London.

### John Simon and the 1866 Sanitary Act

John Simon was the third 'founding father' of public health. He succeeded Edwin Chadwick in his role in public health administration. He was instrumental in helping several towns install their first sewage systems throughout the 1850s and 1860s. In 1866 the Sanitary Act placed a duty of inspection on local authorities and extended their range of sanitary powers.

Even today the work of these three public health campaigners is held in the highest regard. In a recent poll by the *British Medical Journal* (January 2007), sanitation, and the efforts of Snow and Chadwick in particular, were rated the greatest medical advances of the last 150 years.

## The twentieth century

### The Beveridge Report, 1942

Following the Second World War, there was a strong feeling that the British people should be rewarded for their sacrifice and resolution. The government promised reforms that would create a more equal society, asking Sir William Beveridge to write a report on the best ways of helping people on low incomes. In December 1942, Beveridge published a report proposing that all people of working age should pay a weekly contribution. In return, benefits would be paid to people who were sick, unemployed, retired or widowed.

### The National Health Service (NHS)

In the aftermath of the Second World War, Clement Attlee's Labour government created the NHS, based on the proposals of the Beveridge Report. A 1944 white paper was followed by considerable debate, with resistance organised by the **British Medical Association (BMA)**. However, the structure of the NHS in England and Wales was established by the National Health Service Act 1946 and the new arrangements were launched on 5 July 1948. This was under health and housing minister Aneurin Bevan. Contrary to popular belief, the founding principles of the NHS called for it to be funded out of general taxation, not through national insurance. NHS services were provided by the same doctors and the same hospitals but:

- services were provided free at the point of use
- services were financed from central taxation
- everyone was eligible for care (even people temporarily resident or visiting the country).

### Key term

**British Medical Association (BMA)** – This is the professional body for the medical profession. It represents their interests at a national level, e.g. in negotiations with the government over changes in management of the medical profession.

The original structure of the NHS had three arms:

1 hospital services
2 primary care (i.e. family doctor services)
3 community services such as maternity and child welfare clinics, health visitors, midwives, health education, vaccination and immunisation and ambulance services.

### *Acheson Report* into inequalities in health, 1998

In July 1997, Donald Acheson was asked to review inequalities in health in England and to identify priority areas for the development of policies to reduce them. This followed two famous earlier reports in this field – the report of Sir Douglas Black in 1980 and the updated version from 1987, *The Health Divide*. Both these reports had been kept rather quiet because of the bleak picture they painted of widening health inequality in such a developed country and the implications for the government of the day.

Donald Acheson concluded his report with a list of 39 recommendations for addressing health inequality, 'judged on the scale of their potential impact on health inequalities and the weight of evidence'. The three areas identified as crucial to this process are:

1 all policies likely to have an impact on health should be evaluated in terms of their impact on health inequality

2 a high priority should be given to the health of families with children

3 further steps should be taken to reduce income inequalities and improve the living standards of poor households.

### *Saving Lives: Our Healthier Nation*, 1999

This was the health strategy released by the Labour government shortly after it came to power in 1997. It had clear links with the *Acheson Report*, proposing to tackle the root causes of ill health, including air pollution, unemployment, low wages, crime and disorder and poor housing. It focused on prevention of the main killers, including cancer, coronary heart disease and stroke, accidents and mental illness.

Local authorities are building over 11,260 km (7000 miles) of new cycle lanes with the help of Sustrans

## The twenty-first century

### The public health white paper – *Choosing Health: Making Healthy Choices Easier*, 2004

This white paper recognised that interest in health was increasing and recommended a new approach to public health, reflecting our rapidly changing and increasingly technological society. The paper acknowledged the government's role in promoting social justice and tackling wider causes of ill health and inequality, as well as recognising the need to empower individuals to change their own lives.

The strategy set out in the document had three underpinning principles:

1 informed choice: although with two important qualifications: **i** protect children and **ii** do not allow one person's choice to adversely affect another (e.g. passive smoking)

2 personalisation: support tailored to the needs of individuals

3 working together: real progress depends on effective partnerships across communities.

Its main priorities were to:

- reduce the number of people who smoke
- reduce obesity and improve diet and nutrition
- increase exercise
- encourage and support sensible drinking
- improve sexual health
- improve mental health.

The public health paper set out these areas for action:

1 Children and young people – by 2010, all schools in England should have active travel plans (a plan put together by the school showing how it will encourage active forms of transport like cycling, as opposed to travel by car).

2 Communities leading for health – local authorities, working with the national transport charity Sustrans, are to build over 11,260 km (7000 miles) of new cycle lanes and tracks.

3 Health as a way of life – NHS health trainers will help people to make healthy choices and stick to them. This will be a new kind of personal health resource.

4 A health-promoting NHS – all NHS staff will be trained to deliver key health messages effectively as part of their day-to-day work with patients.

5 Work and health – the NHS will become a model employer.

## Activity 1: Comparing public health strategies

Public health white papers usually acknowledge inequalities across social groups and the impact of the so called 'big killers' (i.e. the diseases that lead to the highest mortality rates). Look through the three key reports, *The Acheson Report*, *Our Healthier Nation* and *Choosing Health*, and answer the following questions:

- What are the main diseases that all three prioritise for action?

- What similarities can you find between the actions proposed in all three reports?

- What do all these reports have to say about levels of health inequalities in the UK?

What does this suggest about the actions taken from 1998 to 2004 to address health inequalities?

The role of the HPA is to reduce the impact of infectious diseases, chemical and radiation hazards and major emergencies

## Functional skills

**English:** This activity will help you demonstrate skill in comparing and understanding texts, using them to gather information, ideas, arguments and opinions.

### The Health Protection Agency (HPA)

The Health Protection Agency is an independent organisation dedicated to protecting people's health in the UK. It does this by providing impartial advice and authoritative information on **health protection** issues to the public, professionals and the government. It combines public health and scientific expertise, research and emergency planning within one organisation. It works at international, national, regional and local levels and has links with many other organisations around the world.

## Key term

**Health protection** – The measures taken to safeguard a population's health, e.g. through legislation, financial or social means. This might include laws governing health and safety at work, or food hygiene, and using taxation policy to reduce smoking levels by raising the price of cigarettes.

**National Institute for Health and Clinical Excellence (NICE)** – The independent organisation responsible for providing national guidance on the promotion of good health and the prevention and treatment of ill health.

The HPA:

- provides impartial expert advice on health protection and providing specialist health protection services

- identifies and responds to health hazards and emergencies caused by infectious disease, hazardous chemicals, poisons or radiation

- anticipates and prepares for emerging or future threats

- supports and advises other organisations with a health protection role

- improves knowledge about health protection through research and development, education and training.

### The National Institute for Health and Clinical Excellence (NICE)

**The National Institute for Health and Clinical Excellence (NICE)** is the independent organisation responsible for providing national guidance on the promotion of good health and the prevention and treatment of ill health. The Department of Health commissions NICE to develop guidance to inform practice in:

- clinical practice – the appropriate treatment and care of people with specific diseases and conditions within the NHS

## Case study: Jean

Jean is a public health nurse from the local health protection unit. Recently she has been working with the local hospital, which has a major outbreak of Norovirus (often called winter vomiting disease) on three wards. This is a relatively minor infection of the gut that usually causes unpleasant but mild symptoms of vomiting and diarrhoea for two to three days. However on a hospital ward with elderly and infirm patients, this can be potentially life threatening.

Jean's role is to trace the pattern of the infection from ward to ward, and ensure that the hospital is taking all the precautions needed to limit further spread. Her colleagues in the public health laboratory system will help by analysing samples from the patients to make sure that the infections are caused by the same organism, rather than two or three different ones.

1 Have you seen or heard about a similar outbreak in any of your local hospitals?

2 Managing the publicity around an outbreak can be tricky – how are they usually reported in the media?

3 What challenges would this present for hospital management in terms of balancing advice to the public but retaining public confidence in the hospital?

4 What steps should the hospital be taking to manage the outbreak? What might it be asking visitors to do as part of the management approach?

- public health – the promotion of good health and the prevention of ill health for those working in the NHS, local authorities and the wider public and **voluntary sector**
- health technologies – the use of new and existing medicines, treatments and procedures within the NHS.

## 1.2 Public health strategies

The official definition of public health is 'the science and art of preventing disease, prolonging life, and promoting health through the organised efforts of society'.

This definition, coined in 1988 in a report by Sir Donald Acheson (*Public Health in England*), reflects the central focus of modern public health strategy, which focuses on collective responsibility for health and on prevention. It relies on a multi-disciplinary approach that emphasises partnership with the people who are being served.

### Key aspects of public health strategy

The Faculty of Public Health defines good practice for public health as:

- being population based
- emphasising collective responsibility for health protection and disease prevention

- recognising the key role of the state, linked to a concern for the underlying socio-economic and wider determinants of health, as well as disease
- emphasising partnerships with all those who contribute to the health of the population.

Table 12.1 on the next page sets out the key aspects of public health practice in more detail with examples.

## 1.3 Sources of information for determining patterns of health and ill health

**Epidemiology** is the study of the spread of infectious diseases and how they can lead to epidemics. Epidemiologists examine the factors that influence the number of cases of a disease at any one time, its distribution and how to control it. This approach most clearly applies to infectious diseases such as influenza or HIV but is equally applicable to common diseases

### Key terms

**Voluntary sector** – Agencies that obtain their funding from charitable giving, specific funding from public sector organisations such as PCTs or through the National Lottery.

**Epidemiology** – The study of diseases in human populations.

**Table 12.1:** The key roles within public health practice

| Role | Explanation | Example |
|---|---|---|
| Monitoring the health status of the population | Tracking changes in the health of the population and alerting people to potential problems. | For example, the rising levels of **obesity** within the population. |
| Identifying the health needs of the population | Once trends and patterns are established, the likely implications for services can be identified. | In relation to obesity, this means assessing the likely increase in the need for diabetes support services. |
| Developing programmes to reduce risk and screen for disease early on | Attempting to reduce the levels of ill health by introducing new programmes that identify people as being 'at risk' of a condition and engaging them in preventative programmes. | For example, a doctor identifying that someone is at risk of developing diabetes because of their obesity and referring them to a weight management programme for support in losing weight. |
| Controlling communicable disease | Reducing the impact of infectious diseases through immunisation and other control measures. | While there are obvious examples such as measles, mumps and rubella, this might also include food hygiene measures in restaurants and take-aways to control the spread of food poisoning. |
| Promoting the health of the population | Health-promoting activities to reduce ill health in the population. | For obesity, this might include campaigns encouraging people to be more active or eat more fruit and vegetables. |
| Planning and evaluating the provision of health and social care | Assessing the provision of relevant health services and whether or not they are having sufficient impact on the problem. | In the case of obesity this might include assessing whether or not: <br>• local services can meet the demand for weight management advice <br>• there is sufficient 'capacity' (i.e. service provision) to meet the rising demand for obesity-related services <br>• the existing model of services is managing to help people to reduce their weight and sustain that change. |
| Target setting | Defining targets for a locality, region or country that might lead to disease reduction, improved vaccination rates, etc. | A national government target is to halt the rising rates of obesity in children under the age of 11 by 2010. A relevant local target might be based on weighing and measuring reception and Year 6 children. This data could be used to track progress against the national target. |

in the Western world such as coronary heart disease and cancer. Epidemiological data is essential in order to identify the health problems that are occurring in a population and target the relevant health promotion activity to address those problems. Data about illness and death is routinely collected and interpreted by a range of organisations including:

- the **World Health Organization**, which collects information about national and international health and can make comparisons between countries

- the government, which collects information to inform policies (e.g. information about substance

### Key terms

**Obesity** – When a person is carrying too much body fat for their height and sex. In the UK, people with a body mass index (see page 126) above 30 are categorised as obese.

**World Health Organization (WHO)** – Established on 7 April 1948, in response to an international desire for a world free from disease. Since then, 7 April has been celebrated each year as World Health Day.

use can inform national drugs policy, and information about rising rates of obesity can influence policy on nutrition)

- regional statistics and reports – this is a key role for public health observatories, which produce regional information about population health

- local reports and statistics – we will see later how the report from the local director of public health should inform local health planning

- epidemiological studies – occasionally specific studies are necessary to highlight topics (e.g. trends in cancers were highlighted in the *Cancer Atlas* published by the **National Statistics Office** in 2005)

- public health observatories that provide regional data about health for local planners to use (e.g. profiles of alcohol-related harm, which compare local authority areas against national rates, can be found on the North West Observatory website)

- the **Health Protection Agency**, which routinely produces reports on communicable disease rates and specific outbreaks or events.

One example of information that can be collected and used at all these levels is demographic data (or information about the population). For example, researchers might need to know the numbers of males and females, the numbers of people by age range 0–4, 5–9, 10–14, etc, the numbers from minority ethnic communities, etc. This is important information, which helps people to plan services. For instance, one current challenge is how to deal with an ageing population.

# 1.4 Key groups in setting and influencing public health policy

## Government and government agencies

- Government policy can have a major impact on health (e.g. the July 2007 ban on smoking in public places triggered the biggest fall in smoking ever seen in England; around 400,000 people gave up smoking in the year following the ban, which should prevent 40,000 deaths over the following 10 years). Source: Department of Health statistics, 2009

- However, as can be seen here and in Unit 20, health largely depends on other factors (e.g. education, employment, housing status and early years

---

### Key terms

**National Statistics Office (NSO)** – The national body that compiles information on the UK population and which is responsible for carrying out the census every 10 years.

**Health Protection Agency (HPA)** – An independent organisation dedicated to protecting people's health in the UK.

---

provision), which are all outside the control of the Department of Health.

- Reducing health inequalities is heavily dependent upon cross-governmental action, as stated in each of the health inequalities reviews, including those by Black (1980), Acheson (1998) and Marmot (2009).

## Pressure groups

Collections of people who hold similar beliefs based on ethnicity, religion, political philosophy or a common goal. Based on these beliefs, they take action to promote change and further their goals.

### Greenpeace

A worldwide non-profit organisation that campaigns to stop climate change, protect ancient forests, save the oceans, stop whaling and stop the nuclear threat.

### Friends of the Earth

- Another environmental pressure group that seeks to influence policy and practice. They campaign to fight climate change, challenge the influence of the global free trade system, expose poor business practice, work to reduce the impact on the environment of the movement of people and goods, and protect wildlife habitats.

- Their health role is more specifically illustrated by their work on greener farming, and campaigning for increased recycling and reduction of waste.

## International agencies

Organisations operating at this level include a range of charities such as Christian Aid, Oxfam and Save the Children, as well as pressure groups such as Greenpeace and key statutory organisations like the United Nations, European Commission, World Health Organization and UNICEF.

### The World Health Organization (WHO)

The World Health Organization came into being on 7 April 1948, following a proposal to establish a new and autonomous international health organisation. The WHO's constitution defines it as 'a directing and co-ordinating authority on international health work,' its aim being 'the attainment by all peoples of the highest possible level of health'. The following are listed among its responsibilities:

- strengthening health services
- information, advice and assistance in the field of health
- improved nutrition, housing, sanitation, working conditions and other aspects of environmental hygiene
- international conventions and agreements on health matters
- research in the field of health
- international standards for food, biological and pharmaceutical products.

### The United Nations (UN)

The United Nations is central to global efforts to solve problems that challenge humanity. Co-operating in this effort are more than 30 affiliated organisations, known together as the UN system. The UN and its family of organisations work constantly to promote respect for human rights, protect the environment, fight disease and reduce poverty. UN agencies define the standards for safe and efficient air travel and help improve telecommunications and enhance consumer protection. The UN leads the international campaigns against drug trafficking and terrorism. Throughout the world, the UN and its agencies assist refugees, set up programmes to clear landmines, help expand food production and lead the fight against AIDS.

## National agencies

### The Health Protection Agency

The HPA's role in the UK in managing communicable disease and preparing for emergency situations has already been mentioned. To illustrate their role in determining national policy, here are a few examples of areas where the HPA provided national information and guidance in 2005/6:

- The HPA published guidance on the management of Norovirus in cruise ships.

- An HPA report showed that homelessness increases the risk of infection for injecting drug users; three-quarters of injecting drug users have been homeless at some point; and those who have been homeless have higher levels of injecting risk and associated infections, primarily through the sharing of needles.

- A two-year study shows that the majority of patients dying following MRSA infection had significant underlying chronic medical conditions and short life expectancies, irrespective of their MRSA infection.

- An estimated 73,000 adults are now living with HIV in the UK, according to the HPA's report on the UK's sexual health, which also warned of a continuing HIV and STI epidemic in gay men.

### Cancer Research UK

Cancer Research UK is the world's leading independent organisation dedicated to cancer research. The charity supports research on all aspects of cancer through the work of more than 3000 scientists, doctors and nurses. Cancer Research UK is also the European leader in the development of new anti-cancer treatments.

### NICE

NICE guidance provides recommendations on promoting good health and preventing ill health. The guidance is for people working in the NHS, local authorities, and the wider public, and private and voluntary sectors.

There are two types of NICE public health guidance:

1 public health intervention guidance – recommendations on clear types of activity ('interventions'), provided by local organisations, which help to reduce people's risk of developing a disease or condition, or help to promote or maintain a healthy lifestyle

2 public health programme guidance – broader action to promote good health and prevent ill health; focuses on a topic (e.g. smoking), or on a particular population (e.g. young people), or on a particular setting (e.g. the workplace).

## Activity 2: Promoting active transport

NICE supports the use of congestion charging by local transport authorities to reduce the levels of obesity in the population. It would do this by encouraging active forms of transport, i.e. walking and cycling, as alternatives to using the car. However, in 2009 Manchester consulted on the introduction of a congestion charge and the proposal was rejected by the public. Research this on the Internet and answer the following questions:

1  What was the result of the Manchester vote?

2  Were you surprised by the strength of feeling against the congestion charge?

3  Why might congestion charges be unpopular? Try to find three reasons for and against the introduction of a congestion charge in a major city like Manchester.

4  In areas like inner-city London, where congestion charging has been introduced, what investments have been made to encourage other forms of transport?

5  If the town where you live had been improved in this way, would you be more active? For example, would you walk and cycle instead of using the car or bus? If not, why not?

## Assessment activity 12.1: What is public health?    P1 P2 M1  BTEC

You are a health correspondent for a major national newspaper and you have been asked to write a feature describing public health practice today and how it has evolved from its roots in the nineteenth century.

1  In the text of the article you should describe the key features of public health strategies as they relate to current times.

2  As an illustration feature for your article, develop a timeline which identifies key events, people, reports and policies which have influenced current public health policy and use text boxes to add notes that describe the contribution made by each of the items identified on the timeline.

3  Add further text to the article that compares current features of public health with public health measures used in the past, drawing attention to the way in which the strategies are similar and differ.

### Grading tips

**P1** You should carry out your own research but ensure that you include each of the key strategies, using a couple of examples to show how these apply in practice.

**P2** You should include examples of each of the following: influential events, the contributions made by individuals and important reports and policies in the timeline and the notes you add must be sufficient to describe the contribution each of the examples have made to public health.

**M1** The comparison could consider differences in the challenges faced, their relative importance, how some challenges remain and the new ones that are emerging today compared with the past.

## Functional skills

**English:** This exercise will help you demonstrate your writing skills in preparing complex documents, showing that you can communicate information and opinions clearly.

## PLTS

**Independent enquirer:** This activity will also help demonstrate your independent enquiry skills as you consider the key points in the history of public health, their relative importance and how modern-day and previous public health practices can be compared and contrasted.

# 2  Understand the factors that affect health status and patterns of ill health

## 2.1 Patterns of ill health

Generally people are living longer than ever before. Boys born in 2008 can expect to live to 77, compared with age 45 in 1900; and girls can expect to live to nearly 82, compared with age 50 in 1900. 'A child born today is likely to live nine and a half years longer than a child born when the NHS was established in 1948.' While the threat of childhood death from illness is falling and the infectious diseases of the last century have been eradicated or largely controlled, 'the relative proportion of deaths from cancers, coronary heart disease and stroke has risen. They now account for around two-thirds of all deaths'. Cancer, stroke and heart disease not only kill but are also major causes of ill health.

Source: Quoted sections from the 2004 white paper *Choosing Health: Making Healthy Choices Easier* (see page 25).

Although on average we are living healthier and longer lives, health and life expectancy are not shared equally across the population. In the early 1970s death rates among men of working age were almost twice as high for unskilled groups as they were for professional groups. By the early 1990s, death rates were almost three times higher among unskilled groups. There are regional differences too. In the 2008 Manchester Public Health Report the Director identifies that: 'Nationally, men in the local authority with the highest life expectancy (Kensington and Chelsea, 83.7 years) can expect to live 10 years longer than men in Manchester. Male life expectancy in Manchester is 73.4 years and female life expectancy 78.9 years.'

Table 12.2 lists some of the landmark reports that document these differences and the factors contributing to these inequalities.

## 2.2 Factors affecting health
### Socio-economic factors affecting health

By now you will have begun to recognise the range of factors that together impact on someone's health. We will explore some of these in more detail below.

### Key terms

**Mortality** – Deaths due to a particular condition.

**Morbidity** – This refers to the number of people who have a particular illness during a given period, normally a year.

Table 12.2: The key reports and their findings and proposals

| Key reports | Findings and proposals |
| --- | --- |
| *The Black Report*, 1980 | • Major finding was that large differentials in **mortality** and **morbidity** favoured the higher social classes and that these were not being adequately addressed by health or social services.<br>• Report presented a number of costed policy suggestions and concluded: 'Above all, we consider that the abolition of child poverty should be adopted as a national goal for the 1980s.' |
| *The Acheson Report*, 1998 | • Called for an increase in benefit levels for women of childbearing age, expectant mothers, young children and older people.<br>• Proposed more funding for schools in deprived areas, better nutrition in schools and promoting health through the curriculum (e.g. by teaching children not just about cooking but also about budgeting for food).<br>• Called for restrictions on smoking in public places, a ban on tobacco advertising and promotion, mass educational initiatives, increases in the price of tobacco and the prescribing of nicotine replacement therapy on the NHS. |

*continued*

**Table 12.2** *continued*

| Key reports | Findings and proposals |
|---|---|
| *Saving Lives: Our Healthier Nation*, 1999 | Included specific health targets in key disease areas:<br>• cancer – to reduce the death rate in under-75s by at least 20 per cent<br>• coronary heart disease and stroke – to reduce the death rate in under-75s by at least 40 per cent<br>• accidents – to reduce the death rate by at least 20 per cent and serious injury by at least 10 per cent<br>• mental illness – to reduce the death rate from suicide and undetermined injury by at least 20 per cent. |
| *Tackling Health Inequalities: A Programme for Action*, 2003 | • Set out plans to tackle health inequalities over the following three years.<br>• Established the foundations required to achieve the two national health inequalities targets, one relating to infant mortality and the other to life expectancy, complementing a range of other targets in the areas of smoking and teenage pregnancy.<br>• Starting with children under one year, aimed by 2010 to reduce by at least 10 per cent the gap in mortality between manual groups and the population as a whole.<br>• Starting with health authorities, aimed by 2010 to reduce by at least 10 per cent the gap between the 20 per cent of areas with the lowest life expectancy at birth and the population as a whole. |
| *Choosing Health: Making Healthy Choices Easier*, 2004 | • Recognised that interest in health was increasing and recommended a new approach to public health, with a strong emphasis on engaging local communities, thereby acknowledging the local inequalities that have become heavily entrenched in some localities. |

## Social class

Since the Black Report of 1980, it has been acknowledged that those from the lowest social groupings experience the poorest health in society. Current research suggests the countries with the smallest income *differences* have the best health status (rather than the richest countries). Where income differences remain great, as in the UK, health inequalities will persist. For example:

- children in the lowest social class are five times more likely to die from an accident than those in the top social class
- someone in social class five is four times more likely to experience a stroke than someone in class one
- infant mortality rates are highest among the lowest social groups.

One key influence on health inequalities, which is rooted in social class, is the difference in how people access health services. In 1994, Baldock and Ungerson tried to explain these differences by categorising people's attitudes to community care services using a simple model that described four roles people can adopt (see Table 12.3).

### Case study: Mary

Mary is 76 and has been a smoker since the age of 16. She has recently developed a recurrent chest problem. Her GP has examined her but he thought this infection was probably just a result of her poor physical health due to a recent hip operation. He has prescribed her two courses of antibiotics recently but hasn't seen her for a couple of weeks.

Mary is a classic clientist. She has accepted the GP's prescription and diagnosis without question, having been brought up to respect professionals and not question them. Martin is Mary's son. He is less confident and is worried that the GP might have missed something, particularly in the light of her long-term smoking habit.

1 What problems might Martin face in challenging the GP's diagnosis?

2 If the GP is Martin's doctor, how might this affect their relationship in the longer term?

3 What does this tell you about the power balance between doctor and patient and how prepared people might be to challenge decisions about their treatment?

**Table 12.3:** People's roles in relation to community care services

| Consumers | • expect nothing from the state |
| | • set out to arrange the necessary care by buying it themselves |
| | • believe that using the market gives them control and autonomy, much like buying a car |
| | • know about services but prefer to purchase their own care. |
| **Privatists** | • have learned to manage alone |
| | • find it hard to come to terms with increased dependency in later life |
| | • find it hard to ask for help |
| | • can become isolated and fail to access the necessary health care |
| | • generally do least well of the four in accessing services. |
| **Welfarists** | • believe in the welfare state and their right to use it |
| | • expect and demand rights to access the relevant services |
| | • have both the understanding and the know-how to make sure they get the most from the system |
| | • use it effectively to access both public and voluntary provision. |
| **Clientists** | • accept passively what they are offered without demanding or expecting more |
| | • don't expect services to be flexible in responding to their specific needs |
| | • commonly seen in older people and low-income groups |
| | • explains why people in disadvantaged communities often accept the poor state of their local health services and don't demand better provision. |

People may move between such roles depending on their circumstances. This model can explain why people will have different experiences of using the same health services and how this can contribute to local health inequalities.

## Age

As people get older, they are more likely to experience a wide range of illnesses. The health inequalities mentioned earlier remain present in the older generations and are often compounded by the loss of income that comes with retirement. This significantly increases the proportion of the population who are living on benefits, as compared to other age groups in the population. Another factor is the longer lifespan of women, which means that there are often higher rates of illnesses specifically associated with women.

## Gender

Men and women have widely differing patterns of ill health. Essentially, men suffer a higher rate of early mortality (death), while women experience higher rates of morbidity (illness). These differences are linked to physiological, psychological and other gender characteristics influenced by the differing roles that society at large expects the two genders to adopt. Typically, men are less likely to access routine **screening** and other forms of health service, while women (who are viewed as carers in the family) are

more likely to access health services and may therefore identify potential health problems earlier. The results can be seen in the following patterns.

- Under the age of 65, men are 3.5 times more likely to die of coronary heart disease than women.
- Suicide is twice as common in men as in women.
- Women experience more accidents in the home or garden, while men experience more accidents in the workplace or while doing sports.

## Key term

**Screening** – Identifying a disease or defect in an individual by means of tests, examinations and other procedures that can be rapidly applied. Screening identifies apparently well people who may have an underlying disease.

## Income and expenditure

Disposable income has a clear link to health status. The poorest people in England are over ten times more likely to die in their fifties than richer people, despite receiving similar healthcare. Obesity and smoking, two of the leading causes of preventable death, are more common in lower socio-economic groups. A person is more likely to smoke if they:

- have no educational qualifications
- live in rented accommodation

- do not have a car and/or phone
- live in a household where the adults are traditionally involved in manual labour
- live on means-tested benefits.

### Did you know?

According to information from the 2004 *Choosing Health* white paper (see pages 13 and 24), two-thirds of respondents agreed that tackling poverty would be the most effective means of preventing disease and improving health. Not surprisingly, people in the lowest socio-economic groups (67 per cent) and the socially excluded (71 per cent) are more likely to agree than people in the higher socio-economic groups.

## Employment status

For the vast majority of people, being unemployed leads to significantly poorer health. The unemployed have higher levels of depression, suicide and self-harm and a significantly increased risk of morbidity and mortality across all causes of death and illness. Men unemployed at both census dates in 1971 and 1981 had mortality rates that were twice those of other men in the same age range.

## Housing

Public health campaigners have been advocating improvements in housing to better the public's health since the middle of the nineteenth century. As we have seen, Edwin Chadwick's *Report on an inquiry into the sanitary conditions of the labouring population of Great Britain* (1842) resulted in the first national Public Health Act in 1848.

The link between housing and health holds true to this day: the Office for National Statistics Longitudinal Study shows that, between 1971 and 1981, age-standardised mortality rates for social tenants (those in rented accommodation) were 25 per cent higher than for owner-occupiers. Although general death rates have declined since that time, the gap between these groups has widened.

## Discrimination

Prejudice and discrimination can lead to worse health. For example, black and minority ethnic (BME) groups experience higher mortality from a range of diseases such as diabetes, liver cancer, tuberculosis, stroke and heart disease. Establishing the cause of these variations has proved difficult: while interventions have tended to concentrate on cultural practices, this has ignored the compounding factors of poverty and low employment levels in these groups. *Saving Lives: Our Healthier Nation* identified that people from ethnic minorities are more likely to live in poor/disadvantaged communities. The only possible explanation for this situation is that discrimination (in this case **racism**) must also be a factor, leading to a higher than average incidence of poverty and unemployment in these groups and contributing to their poorer health status.

### Key term

**Racism** – Discrimination against a person on the basis of their race background, usually based on the belief that some races are inherently superior to others.

## Education

It is now well established that educational success is associated with better health. There are a number of possible explanations for this link.

Educational success is linked to higher earnings, higher socio-economic status and lower rates of unemployment. Higher income tends to allow for a healthier lifestyle through being able to afford more nutritious but more expensive food, as well as better housing and holidays, etc.

Studies suggest that people with more years of education and higher-level qualifications tend to exercise more, eat more nutritious and healthy diets and smoke less, etc.

Education enables individuals to learn problem-solving skills. It gives them a sense of purpose and this, together with social competence, instills in them a greater belief in their ability to cope with adversity.

In general, children from low-income households leave full-time education much earlier and with fewer formal qualifications than their more affluent counterparts. Of all children born in 1970, for example, some 24 per cent failed to achieve any O-levels (like GCSEs) or equivalent by the age of 30, while 23 per cent went on to get a degree. Among children from low-income households, however, 38 per cent achieved no formal qualifications, and only 11 per cent went on to get a degree.

## Activity 3: Working on the frontline

Imagine you are a practitioner working in a public health role in a deprived local neighbourhood. You can see the injustice of these situations.

1 What challenges might that present for you personally and professionally, in managing your sense of injustice?

2 Are there any issues that might particularly relate to your own personal experience?

## Reflect

Most people think being healthy is just a matter of not smoking, not drinking too much alcohol, being active and eating the right things. However, you should be beginning to recognise the complex web of issues that together determine how healthy someone might be. How has this section made you re-appraise your own views about health inequalities and the challenges these issues can present to health and social care workers? Which issues have surprised you most and why?

# Environmental factors affecting health

The impact of the environment on health can be seen from two perspectives:

1 its capacity to benefit our health, e.g. parks and recreational spaces can encourage us to participate in regular exercise or even just allow us the opportunity to experience time away from the stresses and strains of everyday life

2 its capacity to do harm, e.g. through pollution or poor housing.

## Urban

It is almost a universal truth that people living in the major urban centres experience the poorest health. There can be no better illustration of this than Manchester, which has one of the worst health profiles in England and Wales:

- Men can expect to live 72.3 years in Manchester and women 77.9 years. This is the lowest life expectancy for men and the second lowest for women in England.

- Deaths from heart disease and stroke, smoking and cancer are the second highest in England.

## Rural

By contrast, rural areas appear idyllic, with their wide-open green spaces. A rural environment should, by definition, be beneficial to health. However, these areas also have their own, very specific set of health problems. For example:

- Road traffic accident (RTA) rates are higher in rural areas; in 2007, 69 per cent of car crash fatalities took place on a rural road (Dept of Transport 2007).

- Isolation, occupational stress, economic crises and unforeseen events (such as crop failure due to bad weather) can all contribute to mental health problems.

- Suicides are higher in rural areas, particularly farm suicides.

## Waste management

In the UK we have a very high level of unsustainable waste disposal, specifically in landfill, where nearly 80 per cent of the 28 million tonnes of municipal waste is disposed of each year. This is significantly higher than France (49 per cent), Austria (35 per cent) and the Netherlands (12 per cent). Historically, this has been a cheap option economically but it is environmentally costly. It contributes:

- 25 per cent of the UK's methane (a powerful greenhouse gas)

- nothing to sustainable development (all waste disposed of in this way is simply lost)

- significantly to our individual ecological footprint.

In the UK we have a very high level of waste disposal in landfill

## Water supply

As we saw earlier, the link between contaminated water and disease was clearly established in the nineteenth century by John Snow. Contaminants that may be in untreated water include micro-organisms such as viruses and bacteria; inorganic contaminants such as salts and metals; pesticides and herbicides; organic chemical contaminants from industrial processes and petroleum use; and radioactive contaminants. In the developing world today, poor access to safe water and adequate sanitation continues to threaten human health. In 2003, 1.6 million deaths were estimated to be attributable to unsafe water and sanitation, including lack of hygiene.

## Housing

The link between housing and health status is probably best explained as housing being an indicator for income deprivation, or social class. Those on low incomes are more likely to be experiencing overcrowding, poor washing and cooking facilities, damp and disrepair. Children who live in houses with damp are known to have higher than usual rates of respiratory conditions like asthma and other communicable infections, which are transmitted more easily in overcrowded conditions. Childhood accident rates are also highest in areas of high-density housing, where play facilities are limited and it is difficult for parents to supervise children at play outside.

## Pollution

Pollution occurs when the environment is negatively affected in some way. Pollution comes in many forms, including land, air, water and aesthetic pollution (visual). Many of these forms of pollution can potentially bring about long-term damage both to the environment and to human health and well-being on a global and national scale. Many people argue that pollution should be monitored and measured so that action can be taken to reduce it.

## Access to health and social care services

The ways in which people engage with services may influence their treatment outcomes but the physical location of services is just as important. For example, in one study the researchers found that the type of hospital to which a cancer patient was admitted and the duration of admission varied with travel distance from a patient's home. All patients travelling more than one hour had lower admission rates to a specialist cancer centre. Those travelling more than three hours were not always admitted to the facility nearest their home address and were admitted for significantly fewer days than all other groups.

Source: Baird, G. et al. (2008) 'Travel Time and cancer care: an example of the inverse care law?' in *Rural Remote Health* Oct–Dec; 8(4):1003. Epub 2008, Nov 13.

# Genetic factors affecting health

For some conditions, the key influencing factor is the presence or absence of a specific gene or gene combination. Specific examples are explored below.

## Sickle-cell anaemia

People with sickle-cell anaemia have haemoglobin (which carries oxygen from the lungs to all parts of the body) that is different from most people's haemoglobin. Normal red blood cells can bend and flex easily, but when sickle haemoglobin gives up its oxygen to the tissues, it sticks together to form long rods inside the red blood cells, making these cells rigid and sickle-shaped. Because of their shape, sickled red blood cells can't squeeze through small blood vessels as easily as the normal cells. The small blood vessels therefore become blocked, which stops the oxygen getting through to where it is needed. This, in turn, can lead to severe pain (called crises) and damage to organs such as the liver, kidney, lungs, heart and spleen.

Everyone has two copies of the gene for haemoglobin – one from their mother and one from their father. A person has the sickle-cell trait when one of these genes carries the instructions for sickle haemoglobin (HbS) and the other for normal haemoglobin (HbA).

How could the pollution caused by vehicle exhaust emissions be reduced?

This person is a carrier of the sickle haemoglobin gene but has enough normal haemoglobin in their red blood cells to keep them flexible and they don't display symptoms. If both copies of the haemoglobin gene carry instructions to make sickle haemoglobin then sickled cells can occur.

### Thalassaemia

This condition requires intensive medical care including monthly blood transfusions and a continuous injection for 8–12 hours each night at home. Beta thalassaemia major has a serious impact, not just on the quality of life of the sufferer and their family, but also on the NHS, as treatment for one person up to the age of 30 costs about £1 million.

- Up to 23 births of babies with beta thalassaemia major occur each year in the UK. Of these births, 79 per cent are to Asian parents.

- Beta thalassaemia major can be prevented by diagnosing and screening potential at-risk couples and offering them counselling both before and during pregnancy.

### Cystic fibrosis

Cystic fibrosis affects over 7500 people in the UK and over 2 million people in the UK carry the gene that causes it. It affects the internal organs, especially the lungs and digestive system, by clogging them with thick sticky mucus. This makes it hard to breathe and digest food. Average life expectancy is around 31 years, although improvements in treatment mean a baby born today could expect to live for longer. Cystic fibrosis is increasingly being diagnosed through screening but some babies and older children (and even adults) are diagnosed following unexplained illness.

### Disease susceptibility

In many cases, a single defective gene is not sufficient to cause a disorder. However, many of the common diseases of adult life, such as diabetes mellitus, hypertension, schizophrenia and most common congenital malformations (such as cleft lip, cleft palate and neural tube defects), have a strong genetic component. In these examples it is thought that a large number of genes each act in a small but significant manner to predispose an individual to the genetic condition. This can result in a disease caused by the interaction between multiple genes and environmental factors.

Scientists have been able to separate the random from the genetic by inspecting the occurrence of disorders in identical and non-identical twins because identical twins are genetically identical and non-identical twins are not.

Table 12.4: Genetic influence in common disorders

| Disease | Chances of both twins being affected (percentage) | |
|---|---|---|
| | Identical twins | Non-identical twins |
| Diabetes (mellitus) | 50 | 10 |
| Hypertension | 30 | 10 |
| Manic depression | 80 | 10 |
| Multiple sclerosis | 20 | 5 |

In many conditions, the chance of both identical twins being affected by the same disorder is much higher than non-identical. This implies that a strong 'non-random' or genetic component is influencing the chance of having these conditions.

### Sexuality

Sexuality is a central aspect of being human; it includes what sex we are, the gender identities and roles we adopt, sexual orientation (gay, straight, bisexual), eroticism and pleasure, intimacy and, fundamentally, the need to reproduce. It would be easy to see a person's sexuality as being a biological function but it is more complex than that, having psychological, social, economic, political, religious and many other influences. Sexuality has a major impact on health. For example, young gay men have the highest rate of suicide of all groups, and this is directly related to prejudice and discrimination due to their sexuality.

### Reflect

National research demonstrates that homophobia and bullying at school contribute significantly to the high suicide rate in young gay men. What negative comments or 'put downs' do people use that are about sexuality? If a gay person hears these comments, how do you think it might make them feel about themselves and the people around them?

## Lifestyle factors affecting health

### Culture

Culture is one of the most powerful influences on our health. Culture can mean many things, including our ethnicity, the region we live in, religious beliefs, and so on, but probably the most important cultural influence is our family, which can play a significant part in determining our health status through its key role in our socialisation, i.e. the types of behaviours we are raised to accept as normal. The health behaviours of adults in key positions in the family can have a major impact on the health of young people.

**Fig 12.2:** We are all raised to accept different types of health behaviours. How much exercise do you usually take?

### Diet

Nutrition has recently become a high-profile health issue, not least because obesity has risen up the health agenda (as illustrated by its prominence in *Choosing Health*). This is particularly because of startling recent trends in young children, which show a 60 per cent increase in the prevalence of being overweight among 3–4-year-olds and a 70 per cent increase in obesity rates, while most adults in England are now overweight and one in five (around 8 million) are obese (with a body mass index in excess of 30). Some 30,000 deaths a year are linked to obesity, at an estimated cost to the NHS of £500 million.

Source: NHS, The Information Centre 'Statistics on Obesity, Physical Activity and Diet' (2006) England www.ic.nhs.uk/statistics-and-data-collections

Obesity is a major public health concern contributing substantially to:

- type 2 diabetes
- coronary heart disease
- hypertension
- depression
- cancers
- high blood pressure
- stroke.

### Activity 4: Calculate your own BMI

Body mass index (BMI) is a reliable indicator of total body fat, which is related to the risk of disease and death. BMI can be calculated using this equation:

$$\frac{\text{weight in kilograms}}{(\text{Height in metres})^2}$$

- Now calculate your own BMI using the above formula.
- Are you within the normal range, 18.5–24.9?
- If not, what lifestyle changes might you need to consider?

### Functional skills

**Mathematics:** This activity will help demonstrate your mathematical skills when calculating your own BMI.

Diet also plays a major part in relation to the current trends in cancers. Over the past 25 years, the **incidence** of all cancers has risen by 8 per cent in men and 17 per cent in women. Up to 80 per cent of bowel and breast cancer may be preventable by means of dietary change.

### Peer pressure

You will read more about peer pressure in Unit 20, which deals with health promotion, but it is important to recognise that peer pressure (and peer preference) has an important role to play in influencing people's health.

### Mass media

The role of the media in influencing health patterns has been most graphically illustrated through coverage of concerns about the safety of the measles, mumps and rubella vaccine, also known as the **MMR vaccine**. A 1998 research paper by Andrew Wakefield, suggesting that the MMR vaccination in young children might be linked to autism, sparked a media frenzy, which gave considerable coverage to his viewpoint, despite reports from many other researchers that found no link between the MMR vaccine and autism.

A survey of mothers with children aged 0–2 years old found that 8 per cent considered the MMR vaccine a greater risk than the diseases it protects against, and that 20 per cent considered the vaccine to have a moderate or high risk of side effects. Worryingly, the survey also showed that 67 per cent of people knew that some scientists had linked the MMR vaccine with autism and they also thought that the evidence in favour of such a link was evenly balanced, or that the evidence even favoured a link. The long-term media coverage of controversy over the vaccine appears to have led the public to associate MMR and autism, despite the overwhelming evidence to the contrary.

### Access to leisure and recreational facilities

How we use our spare time in terms of recreation can have a significant influence on our health. Recreational pursuits can contribute to a wide range of health benefits such as physically active lifestyles, weight management, stress release and a sense of well-being that leads to improved mental health.

In 2004, the **Health Development Agency (HDA)** published a review of how people use their leisure time. It found that:

- those who participate in sporting activities are also more likely to participate in cultural activities, and vice versa
- for both sport and culture, the majority of people tended to do very little of anything
- higher levels of household income, education and social class were usually associated with higher rates of participation in most cultural and sporting activities
- after accounting for household income and social class, not having access to a vehicle was important in determining the amount of sporting and cultural activity that individuals were able to participate in.

### Smoking

The link between smoking and ill health is now well documented. 'Smoking is the single most important modifiable risk factor for coronary heart disease in young and old.' (*Saving Lives: Our Healthier Nation*, 1994 section 6.5). A lifetime non-smoker is 60 per cent less likely to have coronary heart disease (CHD) and 30 per cent less likely to have a stroke than a smoker. In general:

- tobacco smoking causes most lung cancers
- smoking is implicated in a wide range of other cancers, including those of the nose and throat and also cervical cancer
- overall about one-third of cancer deaths can be attributed to smoking
- smoking also contributes to CHD and stroke rates.

Obesity is a major public health concern today

### Key terms

**Incidence** – The rate of a disease at a given point in time.

**MMR vaccine** – A vaccination against measles, mumps and rubella.

**Health Development Agency (HDA)** – A national health agency set up in 2000 to provide information about what works in terms of health promotion activity. This in turn supports evidence-based practice in health promotion. Its role has subsequently been taken up by NICE.

Smoking mirrors other patterns of ill health, in that the highest levels are in the lowest social groups. Although the proportion of young people who smoke is similar across all social groups, by their mid-thirties, 50 per cent of young people from higher social classes have stopped, as opposed to only 25 per cent from the lowest income groups. This means that about one-third of the smokers in the UK population are concentrated in the lowest 10 per cent of earners.

## Activity 5: Reviewing media coverage

Working as a group, monitor the media for a seven-day period. When a health story is reported, look for it in print media, on news websites, radio and TV, podcasts, etc.

Now answer the following questions:

- What is the story about?
- Summarise the key features and main factual points.
- What new information is being described here?
- What was the source for the new information?
- Is the information contested, i.e. are there opposing views about the information?
- What differences in reporting on the main facts are apparent between the different sources?
- What might be the reasons for the differences in reporting?

## PLTS

**Independent enquirer:** This activity will help you demonstrate your independent enquiry skills as you analyse the media content, assess the differences between the reports and attempt to explain why there may be differences in the interpretation of the information.

Who can parents trust to give them the right information to help them make the right choice for their child?

### Recreational drug use

There has been growing public concern over the levels of drug use among young people. Expert opinion can frequently appear divided on the relative harm caused by illicit substances such as ecstasy and cannabis. Whereas licensed drugs are manufactured under strict controls, ensuring their side effects are well documented and their quality and purity are accurately controlled, the same cannot be said for illicit substances. According to the Home Office (2008/9), rates of use have been rising consistently over several decades but are now stabilising. Information from the British Crime Survey (2008/9) shows that in 16- to 59-year-olds regular use is actually a lot less frequent than people might expect:

- around one in three reported ever having used illicit drugs, one in ten had used drugs in the *last year* and around one in 20 had done so in the *last month*
- 15.6 per cent had used a class A drug at least once in their *lifetime*, 3.7 per cent having done so in the *last year* and 1.8 per cent in the *last month*
- cannabis is the type of drug most likely to be used
- use of any illicit drug in the *last year* has shown an overall decrease from 11.1 per cent in 1996 to 10.1 per cent in 2008/09.

**Table 12.5:** Summary of trends in last year drug use among 16- to 59-year-olds between 1996 and 2008/09

| Increase | Decrease | Stable |
|----------|----------|--------|
| • Overall class A drug use<br>• Cocaine<br>• Tranquillisers | • All reported drug use<br>• Hallucinogens<br>• LSD<br>• Amphetamines<br>• Anabolic steroids<br>• Cannabis | • Any stimulant drug<br>• Opiates<br>• Crack cocaine<br>• Ecstasy<br>• Magic mushrooms<br>• Heroin<br>• Glue |

Source: Home Office Statistical Bulletin, 2009

### Alcohol

The Government Strategy Unit's 2003 needs analysis report estimated the total cost of alcohol misuse in the UK at around £20 billion a year. This figure covered the cost of alcohol-related health disorders and disease, crime and anti-social behaviour, loss of productivity in the workplace, and problems for those who misuse alcohol and their families, including domestic violence. According to the report, the annual costs included:

- 1.2 million violent incidents (around half of all violent crimes)

- 360,000 incidents of domestic violence (around a third of the total)

- increased anti-social behaviour and fear of crime – 61 per cent of the population perceive alcohol-related violence as worsening

- £95 million on specialist alcohol treatment

- over 30,000 hospital admissions for alcohol dependence syndrome

- up to 22,000 premature deaths per year

- at peak times, up to 70 per cent of all admissions to accident and emergency departments

- up to 1000 suicides

- up to 17 million working days lost per year through alcohol-related absence

- between 780,000 and 1.3 million children affected by parental alcohol problems

- increased divorce – marriages where there are alcohol problems are twice as likely to end in divorce.

## Activity 6: Analyse the cost of illicit drug use in the UK

You are a drug policy researcher who has been asked to brief a government minister about the costs to society of drug use. Key information you have been asked for includes:

- the average weekly spend on drugs by a user

- what this adds up to nationally as a total spend on drug use

- what proportion of this spend is paid for by crime

- the types of crime that are usually involved to pay for drugs

- the average cost of each drug-related crime dealt with by the criminal justice system

- the number of drug-related deaths each year

- the total numbers of people in drug treatment each year

- the cost to the NHS of this treatment.

## Functional skills

**ICT:** This activity will help you demonstrate your ICT skills in finding and selecting information on the Internet.

## Assessment activity 12.2: Factors affecting the health of the public

(P3) (P4) (M2) (D1)    BTEC

Your editor was so impressed with your recent article on public health origins and practice that she has asked you to prepare a second article, a study on the health and well-being of two regional populations within the UK. The editor has suggested that you contrast the North West and the South West of England. She has asked for your report to include:

1   A description of ways in which the health of the public is monitored and provide an overview of the main patterns of health in the UK as whole, and select examples that are particularly relevant to the two regions selected for the newspaper article.

2   An explanation of the main factors that influence patterns of health in different parts of the UK, focusing particularly on those found in the selected regions. You should also discuss the factors likely to influence current and future patterns of health in the UK. The newspaper report should consider socio-economic, environmental, genetic and lifestyle factors and consider issues relating to these in some detail.

3   The newspaper is particularly interested in the factors that contribute to current patterns of health and illness in the UK and the editor asks you to evaluate the influence of government on these factors.

### Grading tips

For this assignment, you need to describe how patterns of health are monitored and the purpose of this, and explain the probable causes of the current patterns of ill health and inequality in the UK.

(P3) Look for examples of public health reports (both regional and national), which will give you the necessary public health information. You will probably find these on the Department of Health website, National Statistics Online

and regional government offices. Describe the purpose of public health reports, the role of the organisations that produce them and how the reports may be used both nationally and locally.

(P4) First of all, identify patterns in relation to at least three different aspects of public health, using national reports and regional statistics to help you. Then using the examples for each of the four types of factor, you will need to explain how they affect patterns of health.

(M2) Discuss each factor so that you explain the way in which it influences the pattern of health, the number of people involved and possible ways in which the influence of the factor could be managed to encourage better health. Try to support your comments with relevant statistics, remembering to acknowledge the sources of these by keeping a record of the website link and the date it was accessed. You can list these in a reference list at the end of your article.' Find data which shows predicted patterns of health over the future 2–3 decades and again, discuss the predicted trends.

(D1) You will first need to identify the ways in which government is influencing patterns in health and illness and then make judgements, supported by evidence eg from statistical data, of how effective government and its policies have been in reducing ill-health and encouraging better health. Select 2–3 examples and explore these in depth so you can judge the extent to which government policies are or are not effective in reducing ill health. You should also make a reasoned judgement about other ways in which public health in the UK could be improved.

# 3 Understand how public health is promoted and protected

## 3.1 Aims
### Improving health

Perhaps the best summary of governmental aspirations in this area can be found in the introduction to the 2004 white paper *Choosing Health: Making Healthy Choices Easier*:

> 'There have been big improvements in health and life expectancy over the last century … Future progress on this dramatic scale cannot be taken for granted … the relative proportion of deaths from cancers, coronary heart disease (CHD) and stroke has risen. They now account for around two-thirds of all deaths.'

Clearly the government has recognised that, while we now live longer, and the major causes of premature death of the last century are largely under control, the same cannot be said for today's main killers.

### Reducing health inequalities

The government's *Tackling Health Inequalities: a Programme for Action* set (for the first time) national targets for reducing the levels of health inequalities by 2010. It suggested a number of specific interventions among disadvantaged groups, which included:

- reducing smoking in manual social groups
- preventing and managing other risks for coronary heart disease and cancer (e.g. poor diet and obesity, physical inactivity and hypertension) through effective primary care and public health interventions – especially targeting the over-fifties
- improving housing quality by tackling cold and dampness and reducing accidents at home and on the road
- improving the quality and accessibility of antenatal care and early years support in disadvantaged areas
- reducing smoking and improving nutrition in pregnancy and early years
- preventing teenage pregnancy and supporting teenage parents
- improving housing conditions for children in disadvantaged areas.

It is a sad fact that the targets set in *Tackling Health Inequalities* remain unmet and these recommendations are therefore still just as relevant. This demonstrates the huge challenge of trying to reduce health inequalities.

## 3.2 Health education
### Activities

**Healthy eating campaigns**

You will read more about the government's current campaign 'Change 4 life' in Unit 20. Here we consider its forerunner, the '5 a day' campaign. Current recommendations are that everyone should eat at least five portions of a variety of fruit and vegetables each day, to reduce the risks of cancer and coronary heart disease and many other chronic diseases. Yet average fruit and vegetable consumption in England is currently less than three portions a day.

How could cookery lessons at school help children to learn about healthy eating? How could parents back up the message taught in these lessons?

The government-led '5 a day' programme has five strands, underpinned by an evaluation and monitoring programme:

- National School Fruit Scheme
- local '5 a day' initiatives
- national/local partners – government health consumer groups
- communications programme, including '5 a day' logo
- work with industry, including producers, caterers and retailers.

### Standards for school lunches

The School Food Trust (SFT) was commissioned in 2005 to advise ministers on standards for food in schools. These standards will apply to school lunches and other food provided in all local authority maintained schools in England. There are two sets of standards for school lunches:

- food-based, which will define the types of food that children and young people should be offered in a school lunch and the frequency with which they are offered
- nutrient-based, which will set out the proportions of nutrients that children and young people should receive from a school lunch.

The government has also decided that similar standards should apply to all school food other than lunches, as recommended by the SFT. This means that:

- no confectionery will be sold in schools
- no bagged savoury snacks other than nuts and seeds (without added salt or sugar) will be sold in schools
- a variety of fruit and vegetables should be available in all school food outlets (this can include fresh, dried, frozen, canned or juiced varieties)
- children and young people must have easy access at all times to free, fresh drinking water in schools.

### National No Smoking Day

No Smoking Day was established as a national event on Ash Wednesday in 1984. The campaign has always been aimed at encouraging smokers who want to stop smoking and has helped over 1.5 million to do so since then. The success of the day is largely due to the commitment of local organisers throughout the UK. The No Smoking Day campaign has become one

of the best-known awareness days in the UK and 1.2 million people took part in 2008. Each year, around 70 per cent of the population are aware that it is No Smoking Day. Smokers are using the day more than ever as their day to try to stop smoking.

**Fig 12.3:** Do you know anyone who smokes? If so, what might encourage them to give up? Find out more at www.nosmokingday.org.uk

### Health trainers

In 2004 *Choosing Health*, the public health white paper, committed the government to establishing a programme of health trainers from 2006. These people would provide advice, motivation and practical support on key lifestyle health issues to individuals in their local communities, particularly those at greater risk of poor health. The idea behind health trainers was that people tend to respond best to 'people like us'; therefore health trainers often come from, or are knowledgeable about, the communities they work with. In most cases, health trainers work from locally based services, which offer outreach support from local community venues. Health trainers work with clients on a one-to-one basis, assessing their health and lifestyle risks, helping them change their unhealthy behaviours, and providing motivation and practical support.

# Maggi White
## Health trainer

Maggi lives on a large estate in Newcastle. It's in the worst 20 per cent of neighbourhoods nationally for income deprivation. She gave up work in 1995 because of ill health; this led to debt problems, which eventually contributed to her losing her house. She now lives in a housing association-managed house on the same estate as the one she owned. For many years, Maggi has been claiming incapacity benefit.

Her slow recovery from depression brought her into contact with the Samaritans, where one of the workers encouraged her to volunteer. She was trained as a counsellor and started doing occasional evenings on the switchboard. She enjoyed doing something worthwhile, so she started to work part-time as an adviser for the local Citizens Advice Bureau. Her supervisor there recognised her helping skills and encouraged to apply to her local PCT to be a health trainer.

Maggi was appointed as a health trainer on her local estate, working with people in her own community, supporting them to give up smoking, improve their diets and become more active. She visits them in their homes, talks to them and encourages them, offering practical tips on how to maintain a healthier lifestyle. She knows what opportunities are available locally and can put people in touch with local community groups, e.g. walking, gardening or cooking groups.

She has been looking for other jobs in the caring profession and is starting to consider training (e.g. doing a health or social care course). These are all things she wouldn't have considered a year ago.

## Think about it!

1 What type of support do health trainers offer?
2 Where are health trainers recruited?
3 What are the key skills and competencies that you might need to be a health trainer?
4 How does the work of health trainers illustrate aspects of community development?

## 3.3 Protection

**Table 12.6:** Specific types of protection against disease

| Immunisation | • Process or procedure that protects the body against an infectious disease.<br>• Creates what is known as 'herd immunity' (i.e. if enough people within the population are immunised, the likelihood of any epidemic is greatly reduced).<br>• Government sets immunisation targets for local health services; any regular fall below these levels signals a potential epidemic. |
|---|---|
| Disease surveillance | • Key infections are under constant surveillance in order to detect significant trends, to evaluate prevention and control measures, and to alert appropriate organisations to infectious disease threats.<br>• Certain diseases (e.g. some classes of food poisoning, sexually transmitted infections and other communicable diseases such as TB) have to be reported to the HPA to enable these trends to be monitored. |
| Screening | • Defined as 'the identification of unrecognised disease or defect by the application of tests, examinations and other procedures which can be applied rapidly'.<br>• However, the majority of people screened will not be ill with the condition screened for. This begs the question: are we right to be treating a well population in this way? |
| Genetic screening | • Now widely available to help detect inherited conditions like cystic fibrosis in would-be parents who are unwittingly carrying the disease.<br>• However, the increasing ability to identify embryos with specific traits before they are implanted in the woman's womb have led to concerns about so-called 'designer babies'. |

## 3.4 Environmental protection

**Table 12.7:** Specific types of protection against environmental hazards

| Waste disposal/ treatment | Local authorities have responded to government recycling targets by running kerbside collections for recycling glass, paper, plastics, etc, with the following results:<br>• There was an increase in the national household recycling rate, from 34.5 per cent in 2007/8 to 37.6 per cent in 2008/9.<br>• Less municipal waste was sent to landfill, decreasing from 15.5 in 2007/8 to 13.8 million tonnes, or 50.3 per cent of total municipal waste, in 2008/9.<br>• The average residual household waste per head decreased from 324 kg per head in 2007/8 to 295 kg per head in 2008/9. |
|---|---|
| Supply of safe water | • Drinking water quality in England and Wales is regulated by the government through the Drinking Water Inspectorate (DWI), which checks that water meets the standards set in Water Quality (Water Supply) Regulations, based on European law and World Health Organisation guidelines. To achieve this, DWI staff carry out technical audits of each water company.<br>• UK regulations include additional standards to safeguard the already high quality of water in England and Wales; standards generally include wide safety margins. |
| Pollution control | • The Pollution Prevention and Control (England and Wales) Regulations 2000 (the PPC Regulations) control pollution from certain industrial activities. The PPC has introduced the concept of Best Available Techniques (BAT); operators must demonstrate the use of BAT to control pollution from their industrial activities in order to gain a permit.<br>• Operators of certain industrial and other installations (e.g. landfill sites, bleachworks, chemical plants, etc.) have to obtain a permit to operate. The permit will include conditions aimed at preventing pollution or reducing it to acceptable levels. |

The PPC regulations control pollution from certain industrial activities

## Food preparation, storage and sale

Consumers must have confidence that the food they buy and eat will be what they expect, will do them no harm and that they are protected from fraud. This is managed through the Food Safety Act 1990. Although food safety legislation affects everyone in the country, it is particularly relevant to anyone working in the production, processing, storage, distribution and sale of food. The Act sets out the following main responsibilities for all retailers:

- to ensure they do not include anything in food, remove anything from food or treat food in any way that means it would be damaging to the health of people eating it

- to ensure that the food they serve or sell is of the nature, substance or quality that consumers would expect

- to ensure that the food is labelled, advertised and presented in a way that is not false or misleading.

The Act is enforced by the Environmental Health and Trading Standards Departments of the local councils, who regularly visit those who produce, process, store, distribute and sell food. They have powers to close businesses temporarily and permanently under the Act in cases where they identify significant risks to the public health.

## Climate change

Climate change is already impacting on us. We have seen more extreme weather events such as dangerous heat waves, floods and coastal erosion, storms, wildfires, droughts, and severe declines in species biodiversity. Almost all scientists agree that these types of effects will become more frequent and have a greater impact unless action is taken to reduce $CO_2$ emissions.

The United Kingdom Climate Projections, published in June 2009, show that in the UK we face warmer, wetter winters and hotter, drier summers, with more drought, more intense heat waves, flooding and sea level rises. In future, rainfall could significantly decrease in the summer (particularly in the South-East) and significantly increase in the winter (particularly in the North-West). Heavier winter rainfall is expected to become more frequent, potentially causing more flooding.

The sea-level rise across the UK is projected to be between 200 mm and 800 mm by 2100. In the worst-case scenario, rises of up to 1.9 m are possible (albeit highly unlikely). The summer heat wave experienced in 2003 (which resulted in over 2000 extra deaths in the UK and over 35,000 extra deaths across Europe) is likely to become a normal event by the 2040s or the 2050s. By the 2060s or 2070s, the intense temperatures of 2003 could become the average temperatures experienced throughout much of Europe. The government is working to reduce the impact of climate change in five main areas, as shown in the following diagram.

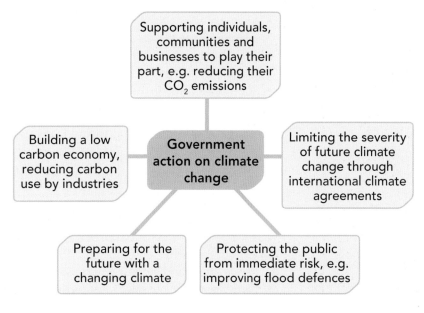

**Figure 12.4:** Reducing the impacts of climate change. Which area do you think should take priority?

# 3.5 Disease prevention

## Communicable diseases

Some communicable diseases are are routinely monitored to observe trends. This statutory requirement came into being in 1891.

**Table 12.8:** Key communicable diseases

| Tuberculosis (TB) | • Caused by the bacterium *Mycobacterium tuberculosis*, most commonly spread in droplets that are coughed or sneezed into the air.<br>• Usually affects the lungs but can affect other parts of the body (e.g. the lymph nodes, bones, joints and kidneys) and can cause meningitis.<br>• Full recovery possible with effective treatment, using a combination of 3–4 antibiotics for a period of six months or more.<br>• Prevention is through the use of the BCG vaccine, which uses a strain of *Mycobacterium bovis*, the organism that causes TB in cattle; organism has been modified in the vaccine so that it produces immunity against TB without causing the disease. Vaccine gives 70–80 per cent protection. |
|---|---|
| Sexually transmitted infections (STIs) | • *The Health of the Nation* (1992) focused on reducing rates of gonorrhoea and in the rate of conceptions among the under-16s by 50 per cent by 2000.<br>• Driven by steady rise in rates of gonorrhoea and chlamydia between 1995 and 1997, the government has invested in a national chlamydia screening programme to screen and treat, where necessary, at least 15 per cent of under-25s (the most sexually active and promiscuous age group).<br>• One likely spin-off will be an increase in diagnosis and treatment of other STIs as services actively seek out young people to test. |
| Meningitis | • Results from a bacterial infection caused by the organism *Neisseria meningitides* and causes an inflammation of the lining of the brain.<br>• Usually spread in droplets being coughed or sneezed into the air, or more directly through kissing.<br>• Highest risk group is the under-1s, followed by the 1–5 age group, and then young people aged 15–19 years.<br>• Immunisation with MenC vaccine became part of the routine childhood immunisation programme in the UK in November 1999.<br>• All babies to receive three doses of MenC vaccine by injection as part of their primary immunisation course at 2, 3 and 4 months of age.<br>• Top-up vaccination for under-25s who were not vaccinated before introduction of MenC vaccine. |
| Salmonella | • Common type of food poisoning that can be caught by eating food contaminated with the bacterium, e.g. unpasteurised milk, raw meat, undercooked poultry and eggs, etc.<br>• Usually causes diarrhoea, stomach ache, sickness, tiredness and fever.<br>• Advice routinely given to commercial food premises by environmental health officers to prevent its spread: uncooked food and cooked food must not be kept together in a fridge or on work surfaces; always ensure raw food is never stored above cooked food in the fridge; all food should be well cooked, especially eggs and chicken; wash hands after handling raw chicken.<br>• If you have an illness with diarrhoea and sickness, you must stay away from work. |

**Table 12.8** *continued*

| Methicillin-resistant *Staphylococcus aureus* (MRSA) | • *Staphylococcus aureus* is a very common bacterium that around 30 per cent of the population carry on their skin or in their nose without knowing it.<br>• Commonly causes bacterial infections such as boils, carbuncles and infected wounds.<br>• Some strains have developed some resistance to the more commonly used antibiotics (e.g. penicillin) and are called MRSA.<br>• People can carry MRSA in the same way as the usual *Staphylococcus aureus* without causing harm to themselves or others.<br>• Although first identified in hospitals, it is now found in the community and care homes.<br>• MRSA can be spread by hands so hand washing is the most important way to stop it spreading, particularly: between caring for clients/patients; after using the toilet; before eating/preparing food; after handling soiled linen/bedding/nappies; after touching animals; when hands appear dirty.<br>• Healthcare workers can use an alcohol hand rub to help to ensure that their hands are properly clean. |
|---|---|
| Poliomyelitis | • An infectious disease that used to be the most common cause of paralysis in young people, known as infantile paralysis.<br>• Once a common cause of death but widespread vaccination has greatly reduced it, and better hygiene and sanitation have also helped.<br>• Polio is prevented by the Hib vaccine (five-in-one), introduced in the UK in 2004 and given during childhood, which gives immunity to polio, as well as diphtheria, tetanus, pertussis and Hib. |
| Measles | • Highly infectious viral disease that causes symptoms including fever and distinctive red-brown spots.<br>• Most people recover within 7–10 days but there can be serious complications, some of which can be fatal.<br>• The mumps, measles and rubella vaccination (MMR) has made measles quite rare in the UK.<br>• First MMR vaccination should be given to all children at around 13 months old, with a booster dose before they start school (3–5 years old).<br>• 5–10 per cent of children are not fully immune after the first dose, so the booster jab helps to increase protection, leaving less than 1 per cent at risk. |

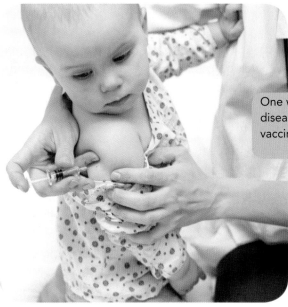

One way of trying to prevent the spread of diseases like measles and meningitis is to vaccinate children from a young age.

## Non-communicable diseases

### Skin cancer

The major cause of malignant melanoma (skin cancer) is exposure to the sun, which explains both the regional and social variations. Skin cancer is distributed in the reverse pattern to other forms of cancer, i.e. it is most common in the South-West and South-East and in social classes 1 and 2. In the North there are likely to be far fewer sunny days than in the South. The variations by social class are most usually explained by the use of tanning facilities and holidaying abroad, which those with greater disposable income can afford. Since the advent of the cheap package holiday, this gap has narrowed as more people gain greater access to holidays in hotter countries with stronger sunlight levels.

SunSmart is the national skin cancer prevention campaign run by Cancer Research UK. The campaign is funded mainly by UK health departments and is supported and guided by the UV Health Promotion Group.

### Activity 7: Sun safety

The current sun safety messages are

- **S**eek the shade – especially at midday
- **H**ats on – use a wide-brimmed hat
- **A**pply sunscreen of at least sun protection factor (SPF) 15
- **D**on't burn – it won't improve your tan
- **E**xercise care – always protect the very young

1  How often do you see people following this advice?

2  Why might people choose not to follow this advice?

3  What wider principle does this illustrate?

### PLTS

**Creative thinker:** This activity will help you demonstrate your creative thinking skills by questioning your own views about sun safety.

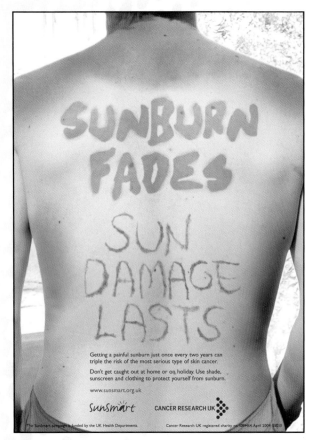

**SUNBURN FADES**

**SUN DAMAGE LASTS**

Getting a painful sunburn just once every two years can triple the risk of the most serious type of skin cancer.

Don't get caught out at home or on holiday. Use shade, sunscreen and clothing to protect yourself from sunburn.

www.sunsmart.org.uk

sunsmart          CANCER RESEARCH UK

The SunSmart campaign is funded by the UK Health Departments.          Cancer Research UK registered charity no. 1089464 April 2009. S5013

**Fig 12.4:** Do you know anyone who uses sun beds? If so, what might encourage them to stop? For more information visit www.sunsmart.org.uk. Courtesy of Cancer Research UK.

### Lung cancer

The link between smoking and ill health is now well documented. According to *Saving Lives: Our Healthier Nation*, 1999 section 6.5, 'Smoking is the single most important modifiable risk factor for coronary heart disease (CHD) in young and old.'

As we have already seen, a lifetime non-smoker is 60 per cent less likely to have CHD and 30 per cent less likely to have a stroke than a smoker. We also know that

- smoking is implicated in a wide range of other cancers including those of the nose and throat but also cervical cancer
- about one-third of all cancer deaths can be attributed to smoking
- smoking also contributes to coronary heart disease and stroke deaths.

## Activity 8: 'Stop smoking' services

Following on from the commitment to reduce smoking-related deaths in the NHS plan, the government set up a comprehensive NHS 'stop smoking' service, providing counselling and support to smokers who want to quit.

1 Find out how to access your local 'stop smoking' service.

2 What types of support does it offer people who are trying to stop smoking?

3 How many people did they help to quit last financial year (i.e. April to March)?

4 What is nicotine replacement therapy (NRT)?

5 Does including NRT improve the success rate for those wanting to give up smoking?

6 What did the Department of Health-funded evaluation of the NHS 'stop smoking' services programme, carried out by Glasgow University, say about:

- the national 'stop smoking' service
- the service's contribution to reducing health inequalities
- long-term quit rates for people attending the services?

### PLTS

**Independent enquirer:** This activity will help you demonstrate your independent enquiry skills through the additional research that is required.

### Functional skills

**ICT:** You can show your ICT skills by searching out and utilising information from the Internet.

### Bowel cancer

About one in 20 people in the UK will develop bowel cancer during their lifetime. It is the second leading cause of cancer deaths, with over 16,000 people dying from it each year. Regular bowel cancer screening reduces the risk of dying from bowel cancer by 16 per cent. Bowel cancer screening aims to detect bowel cancer at an early stage (in people with no symptoms), when treatment is more likely to be effective.

The NHS Bowel Cancer Screening Programme offers screening every two years to all men and women aged 60 to 69, while people over 70 can request a screening kit.

### Coronary heart disease

In most advanced industrial societies the death rates from coronary heart disease (CHD) have fallen by 30–70 per cent over the last two decades. The risk factors for CHD have been well known for many years and we can now also say that changing these risk factors has a clear effect on the incidence of CHD. These risk factors can be reduced by:

- primary prevention activity (e.g. changing behaviours such as smoking, diet and exercise)
- drug therapy for people with raised blood lipids using a class of drug called statins; recently, the Health Development Agency suggested that if 80 per cent of eligible patients received statins, this would result in approximately 20,000 fewer deaths each year
- reducing average cholesterol levels in the UK to levels similar to those in Sweden, Finland, the US and Australia; this would prevent approximately 25,000 deaths each year
- reducing smoking prevalence to American levels; this would result in 17,000 fewer deaths annually.

Together with a small reduction in average blood pressure, over 50,000 CHD deaths could be prevented annually, halving current mortality rates in England and Wales. This underlines the potential impact of health promotion (see also Unit 20).

### Stroke

Stroke (also known as cerebrovascular accident or CVA) occurs when the blood supply to a part of the brain is interrupted. The part of the brain with disturbed blood supply no longer receives adequate oxygen and the result can be brain cell death or damage, impairing local brain function. Stroke can cause permanent damage or even death if not promptly diagnosed and treated. Strokes are the third most important cause of death and adult disability, affecting around 200 per 100,000 population in the UK each year. The incidence rises with age but about 30 per cent of stroke occurs under the age of 65.

The risk factors are very similar to CHD and include advanced age, hypertension (high blood pressure), diabetes, high cholesterol and cigarette smoking.

Therefore many of the same interventions work for both.

### Diabetes

In 2006, according to the World Health Organization, at least 171 million people worldwide suffered from diabetes. Its incidence is increasing rapidly and it is estimated that by the year 2030 this number will double. Diabetes mellitus occurs throughout the world but is more common (especially Type 2) in the more developed countries. Type 2 diabetes can be prevented in many cases by making changes in diet and increasing physical activity.

## 3.6 Socio-economic support and protection

The importance of socio-economic support for the least well off in society is clearly described in *The Acheson Report* (1998):

'Policies which increase the income of the poorest are likely to improve their living standards, such as nutrition and heating and so lead to improvements in health. This can be done by improving social security benefits, specifically for families with young children and pensioners, by increasing employment opportunities and through changes in the tax system… At a population level, improvements in income and living standards are clearly associated with improvements in health and life expectancy.'

Therefore the benefits system, which provides support for some of the most vulnerable in society, has a key part to play in protecting health and reducing inequalities. Examples of a few key benefits and concessions are set out below.

### Welfare benefits

#### Child Tax Credit (CTC)

This is for families who are responsible for at least one child or qualifying young person. Child Tax Credit is paid direct to the person who mainly cares for the child or children, reflecting concerns that in some cases money might be retained by a parent who does little of the caring and used inappropriately. This benefit includes:

- a family element (the basic element for families responsible for one or more children)
- a higher rate of family element, often known as the 'baby element', paid to families with one or more

children under one year old; there is only one family element for each family, regardless of how many children are in the family

- a child element, one for each child within the family
- a disability element, paid for each child who is receiving Disability Living Allowance, or if the child is registered blind or has been taken off the blind register in the 28 weeks before the form is completed.

### Pensions

A pension is a way to save for retirement. People can start receiving their pension from age 50 (increasing to 55 by 2010). However, few people will risk this because their contributions paid up to this point are unlikely to be sufficient to maintain a good standard of living for the rest of their lives. There are currently three main types of pension:

1 The state pension – payable by the government from state pension age. The amount of basic state pension people receive depends on the amount they have paid in the form of national insurance contributions during their working life.

2 Company pensions – set up by employers to provide pensions for their employees on retirement and payable as well as the state pension.

3 Personal pensions – available from banks, building societies and life insurance companies, who invest people's savings on their behalf.

### Child benefit

Child benefit is a tax-free payment that people can claim for their child. The payment can be claimed by anyone who qualifies, whatever their income or savings, i.e. it is not means tested. A person may be eligible for child benefit if their child is:

- under 16
- over 16 and in education or training that qualifies for child benefit
- 16 or 17, has left education or training that qualifies for child benefit and is registered for work, education or training with an approved body.

People can claim child benefit even if their child doesn't live with them, reflecting the fact that many families are now based across two or more households as parents separate or divorce. However, if the child lives with someone else, people can only get child benefit if they:

- pay towards the upkeep of the child
- pay at least the same as the amount of child benefit they get for their child
- the person bringing up the child is not getting child benefit for them – i.e. if two people both claim child benefit for the same child, only one of them can get it.

## Free school meals

Parents do not have to pay for school lunches if they receive any of the following:

- income support
- income-based jobseeker's allowance
- income-related employment and support allowance
- support under Part VI of the Immigration and Asylum Act 1999
- the guarantee element of state pension credit
- child tax credit, provided they are not entitled to working tax credit and have an annual income that does not exceed £16,040
- working tax credit during the four-week period immediately after their employment finishes or after they start to work less than 16 hours per week.

Children who receive income support or income-based jobseeker's allowance in their own right qualify as well. All pupils who do not qualify for free school lunches must be charged the same amount for the same quantity of the same item.

## Housing support

People on a low income who need help to pay all or part of their rent may be entitled to housing benefit. The most housing benefit people can get is the same as the 'eligible' rent, which may not be the same as the full rent. Eligible rent includes:

- rent for the accommodation
- charges for some services, e.g. lifts, communal laundry facilities and play areas.

## Fare concessions

The government also provides a range of concessionary fares for vulnerable groups, which give them access to information, travel and care services.

Table 12.9: Other benefits available for older people

| | |
|---|---|
| **Bus passes and free travel for over-60s** | Off-peak local bus travel is free for anyone aged 60 or over in England. |
| **Senior Railcard** | People aged 60 or over can save a third on most standard and first-class rail fares throughout Britain. |
| **Free TV licences** | People aged 75 or over are entitled to a free television licence. |
| **Independent Living Fund** | People under 66 years old who are severely disabled may be entitled to money to help pay for personal and domestic care. |
| **Medical checks and support** | Some health services (e.g. sight tests, dental care, prescriptions and immunisations) are available free to those aged 60 and over. |

## Assessment activity 12.3

Jean (from the case study on page 114) is a health promotion nurse and you are a student on placement with her. Jean is due to apply to the local Primary Care Trust (PCT) for funding for her public health work but knows that funding for this is limited. She decides to make her case to the PCT funding committee using a short presentation and a written report. She asks you to help her in preparing the slides for the presentation and the written report and gives you clear guidance as to what she requires:

**Slides** – no more than five, to explain the terms health promotion and health protection, each to be appropriately clear but with the speaker's notes included on the notes pages. Jean wants you to provide her with a few extra bits of information she can use during the presentation so the slides are appropriately clear and straightforward. She asks you to provide the additional notes for each slide using the notes pages from the presentation software.

**Report Part 1** – is to explain the different methods for promoting and protecting public health before examining the methods in more detail, looking in general at their advantages and disadvantages in relation to promoting health and health protection.

**Report Part 2** – a section on the methods for prevention/control used for two specific types of disease, one communicable and one non-communicable Jean has requested should be

- either MRSA or TB (communicable)

and

- either diabetes or coronary heart disease (non-communicable).

Jean asks you to explain for each disease what methods of prevention/control would be appropriate, giving clear reasons, wants you to include statistics and to provide a list of sources of information used in writing the report.

**Report Part 3** – Jean thinks the PCT will be more likely to fund her public health projects if she indicates what methods would be most effective in controlling/promoting the two diseases. She asks you to consider the strengths and weaknesses of each of the methods and then to evaluate how effective each is in controlling the two named diseases and to include appropriate statistical information to support the claims made in the evaluation.

### Grading tips

**P5** Use the slides themselves to define the two terms 'health promotion' and 'health protection' and identify the different interventions for each. Use the notes pages to explain the health promotion or health protection effects of each intervention.

**P6** You will need to consider how the health promotion and health protection methods limit the number of people affected by each disease and reduces the severity of the ill-effects if people are affected. For each disease, you will need to explain how and why each method is effective in controlling it.

**M3** You will need to assess the possible methods/interventions in some detail and include an explanation as to how each is effective, i.e. what it does to prevent ill health.

**D2** The evaluation will require you to make a judgement about the effectiveness of the different methods in controlling each disease and to explain why. You should also make recommendations at the end of the report as to the which methods would be best/most effective for promoting and protecting public health for the two named diseases.

# Resources and further reading

Baird, G. et al. (2008) 'Travel time and cancer care: an example of the inverse care law?' in *Rural Remote Health* Oct–Dec; 8(4):1003. Epub 2008, Nov 13.

Baldock, J. & Ungerson, C. (1994) *Becoming Consumers of Community Care* York: Joseph Rowntree Foundation

Begg, N. (1998) 'Media dents confidence in MMR vaccine' *BMJ*. 1998;316:561

Benzeval, M., Judge, K. & Whitehead, M. (1995) *Tackling Inequalities in Health: An Agenda for Action* London: Kings Fund Publishing

Downie, R.S., Tannahill, C. & Tannahill, A. (1996) *Health Promotion Models and Values* Oxford: Oxford University Press

Draper, P. (1991) *Health Through Public Policy* London: Green Print

Ewles, L. & Simnett, I. (1999) *Promoting Health: A Practical Guide* Edinburgh: Baillière Tindall

Hall, D. (1996) *Health for all Children* Oxford: Oxford University Press

HM Government (2004) *At Least Five a Week: Evidence on the Impact of Physical Activity and its Relationship to Health* London: HMSO

HM Government (2004) *Choosing Health: Making Healthy Choices Easier* London: HMSO

HM Government (1992) *The Health Of the Nation* London: HMSO

HM Government (1992) *Immunisation Against Infectious Disease* London: HMSO

HM Government (1998) *The Independent Inquiry into Inequalities in Health* London: HMSO

HM Government (2001) *The National Strategy for HIV and Sexual Health* London: HMSO

HM Government (1997) *The New NHS: Modern, Dependable* London: HMSO

HM Government (1999) *Saving Lives: Our Healthier Nation* London: HMSO

HM Government (2003) *Tackling Health Inequalities: A Programme for Action* London: HMSO

Jones, L. & Sidell, M. (1997) *The Challenge of Promoting Health: Exploration and Action* Buckingham: The Open University

Katz, J. & Peberdy, A. (1997) *Promoting Health: Knowledge and Practice* Buckingham: Macmillan/OU Press

Naidoo, J. & Wills, J. (1996) *Health Promotion: Foundations for Practice* Edingurgh: Baillière Tindall

NHS, The Information Centre 'Statistics on Obesity, Physical Activity and Diet' (2006) England www.ic.nhs.uk/statistics-and-data-collections

Whitehead, M., Townsend, P., Davidson, N. & Davidsen, N. (1998) *Inequalities in Health: The Black Report and the Health Divide* Harmondsworth: Penguin Books

# Useful websites

British Heart Foundation www.bhf.org.uk/

Calculate your Body Mass Index www.nhlbisupport.com/bmi/bmicalc.htm

Cancer Research UK www.cancerresearchuk.org/

Department of Health www.doh.gov.uk

Drinking Water Inspectorate www.dwi.gov.uk

Gateway for Our Healthier Nation www.ohn.gov.uk

Give up smoking www.givingup-smoking.co.uk

Health Protection Agency www.hpa.org.uk

Home Office www.homeoffice.gov.uk

Information about immunisation programmes www.immunisation.org.uk

NHS cancer screening programmes www.cancerscreening.nhs.uk/

NHS in England www.nhs.uk/nhsengland

NHS immunisation information www.immunisation.nhs.uk

National Institute for Health and Clinical Excellence (NICE) www.nice.org.uk

No Smoking Day www.nosmokingday.org.uk

Office for National Statistics www.statistics.gov.uk

World Health Organization www.who.int/en/

## Just checking

1   What are the main roles within public health practice? How might each of these apply to a specific situation such as an outbreak of E. coli food poisoning?
2   Name three founding fathers of public health. What did they each contribute to improving public health?
3   Define *pressure group*. Give an example to explain how pressure groups influence public policy.
4   Give three examples of socio-economic factors that influence health and explain how each one impacts on health.
5   Briefly compare and contrast the differences in health issues in rural and urban communities.
6   What influences whether or not a person has sickle-cell anaemia? What are its effects and how can it be prevented?
7   Select three health-promoting activities and explain how each contributes to improvement of health.
8   Whose role is it to monitor the supply of safe water and how do they ensure the water we drink is safe?
9   Identify three communicable diseases. Explain how they are spread and how best to control them.
10  What is the impact of lung cancer on the nation's health? What steps are the government taking to reduce it?

**edexcel**

## Assignment tips

1   The key websites to use will be:

   • National Statistics Online, which carries a wealth of national data on health and social determinants (education, employment, housing, etc)

   • the public health observatories (particularly the North West Observatory, which is one of the easiest to navigate) for publications and information on specific regional and topic information

   • and the Department of Health website for policy and guidance documents as well as public health information reports.

2   This unit has clear links to Unit 20. Promoting health is included *within* the ten areas of competence for public health practice so expect to find lots of overlaps and links, e.g. key policy drivers.

3   You will have to handle a lot of data in some of the assignments so it's important to understand that data is best managed and marshalled in data tables and charts and then commented on in the text. Leaving lots of numbers in the text can make it difficult for the reader to follow the thread of the discussion.

4   Several of the assignments require a factual report writing style. Public health is a very politicised area of work. This means many of the arguments about public health action can be quite emotionally charged. However, you can only win the argument if your approach is cool, calm and based on facts rather than opinions. It's therefore very important to recognise your own feelings and put these to one side in your reports to ensure that they are effectively written.

# 13 Physiology of fluid balance

Water is essential for the maintenance of life; and keeping the volumes of body fluids in balance is vital when caring for individuals. This unit explains the underlying scientific principles of fluid balance, and will help you to appreciate more advanced studies in health-related science. You achieved a basic knowledge of homeostasis in Book 1, Unit 5 (Fundamental anatomy and physiology for health and social care) and in this unit you will extend your learning to include the control of water.

Unit 13 builds on the basic knowledge of the cells introduced in Unit 5 (in which the microstructure of cells and the contribution made by cell organelles to the overall functioning of cells was explored). The movement of materials into and out of cells is now considered, as well as the distribution of fluids and the role of water and dissolved substances in the body. You will also learn about the renal system and its very important role in homeostasis and fluid balance. This unit will be useful to anyone intending to work in the health or social care sectors, and to anyone wishing to progress to further or higher science studies.

## Learning outcomes

After completing this unit you should:

1   know the microstructure and function of a typical animal cell
2   know the movement of materials into and out of cells
3   know the distribution and constituents of fluids in the body
4   understand homeostatic processes in relation to water balance.

# Assessment and grading criteria

This table shows you what you must do in order to achieve a **pass**, **merit** or **distinction** grade, and where you can find activities in this book to help you.

| To achieve a **pass** grade, the evidence must show that you are able to: | To achieve a **merit** grade, the evidence must show that, in addition to the pass criteria, you are able to: | To achieve a **distinction** grade, the evidence must show that, in addition to the pass and merit criteria, you are able to: |
|---|---|---|
| **P1** Describe the microstructure of a typical animal cell and the functions of the main cell components.<br>**See Assessment activity 13.1, page 156** | | |
| **P2** Describe the ways in which materials move in and out of cells.<br>**See Assessment activity 13.2, page 165** | **M1** Explain the factors that influence the movement of materials in and out of cells.<br>**See Assessment activity 13.2, page 165** | **D1** Analyse the role of the phospholipid bilayer in terms of the movement of materials in and out of cells.<br>**See Assessment activity 13.2, page 165** |
| **P3** Describe the distribution and constituents of body fluids.<br>**See Assessment activity 13.3, page 172** | **M2** Explain the functions of the constituents of body fluids.<br>**See Assessment activity 13.3, page 172** | |
| **P4** Explain the role of the kidney in the homeostatic control of water balance.<br>**See Assessment activity 13.4, page 184** | | |
| **P5** Explain dysfunction in relation to water balance and their possible treatments.<br>**See Assessment activity 13.4, page 184** | **M3** Discuss dysfunction in relation to water balance and its possible treatments.<br>**See Assessment activity 13.4, page 184** | **D2** Analyse the impact on the human body of the dysfunction in relation to water balance.<br>**See Assessment activity 13.4, page 184** |

# How you will be assessed

This unit will be internally assessed by your tutors and will probably consist of four assignments.

You need to demonstrate that you meet all the learning outcomes for the unit. The criteria for a pass grade set the level of achievement to pass the unit. To achieve a merit, you must also meet the merit learning outcomes and, to achieve a distinction, every pass, merit and distinction learning outcome must be demonstrated in your unit evidence.

## Mike, 18 years old

My mother has always said that her brother Stu's illness made me want to go into nursing. He got some infection when he was only 25 and his kidneys stopped working. He used to go to hospital three or four times a week for treatment and was attached to a kidney machine for hours. During this time he had a special diet and had to measure his fluid intake and wee into a measuring jug. All this had to be put on a chart and sometimes he made me add it all up. My mum always worried about him because he never seemed very well.

After a few years of being on the machine, he went for an operation and, although he took a lot of tablets still, he was much better and didn't have to go to hospital very often. He even played some footie with me again. Ten years on, he started to become ill again and went back on the machine. He is now waiting to see if he can have another operation and is on a long waiting list. My mother went for some tests to see if she could help him have the operation but it wasn't any good. She won't let me try because of studying but I might when I am older.

Doing this unit helped me to understand some of Stu's problems and I got really stuck into the assessment part. It was quite hard, but I knew that I could do it.

### Over to you!

1   What did the machine do for Stu?
2   Why did he have to measure his fluid intake and output?
3   What type of operation did Stu have?
4   Why did he need to take tablets after it?

# 1 Know the microstructure and function of a typical animal cell

**How much do you know about cells?**

Using creative thinking and previous knowledge, get into a small group and carry out a thought shower to suggest answers to these questions:

1 How does a cell in the pancreas know that its job is to produce the hormone insulin, when cells in other places (such as skin and muscle) cannot make insulin?

2 There is a myth that we are all renewed every seven years, but in, truth, different cells are renewed at different intervals. What happens to all the old cells?

3 We take water into our bodies in enormously varied amounts every day, yet our bodies don't swell up when we take in a lot or shrink on days when we don't take in much – how is this monitored?

Despite the name of this learning outcome, you must understand that there is no such thing as a typical animal cell. This is a theoretical concept to help you learn about cell structure and physiology and apply this knowledge and understanding to particular cells such as liver or hepatic cells, white blood cells, red blood cells, etc. All these different cell types have different roles to play in the body, as well as having different shapes, sizes, functions and sometimes cell parts.

## 1.1 Cell structure

Human body cells are so small that they are invisible to the naked eye and for approximately 300 years they were viewed under light microscopes. Early light microscopes consisted of crude lenses used with daylight and very little could be seen through them.

### As seen under the light and the electron microscope

The light microscope gradually became more sophisticated, lenses became stronger and bright electric lamps were incorporated – but still, knowledge of cell structure advanced very little. This was mainly due to limits to the **resolution** of light with optical lenses. Special dyes were invented to stain particular structures to make them stand out more easily. A central **nucleus** (or several nuclei) readily took up stains and sometimes darker spots inside the nucleus were

visible – the **nucleoli**. The nucleus was surrounded by a shapeless blob of jelly called the **cytoplasm** (or cytosol), bounded by a cell or plasma membrane. The cytoplasm showed dark granules and fluid-filled 'cysts' scattered around. This was generally thought to be some kind of organic jelly.

In the 1950s, another type of microscope was developed, which avoided the use of light. It substituted a beam of electrons to produce an enormously enlarged image of a very small object.

This eventually opened up a whole new 'world' – the interior of a cell. The organic jelly of the cytoplasm was seen to be complex and structured. A new branch of science was born – **cytology**, or the study of cells.

You learned some of the difficult terms in cytology in Book 1, Unit 5. You will now take this basic understanding further.

### Nuclear and cell membranes (as a phospholipid bilayer)

Cells are bounded by their cell or plasma membranes, and nuclei are bound by nuclear membranes. These membranes have the same biochemical structure. The membranes are composed of a double layer of **phospholipid** molecules, proteins, cholesterol and, sometimes, sugars (see Figure 13.3, on page 150).

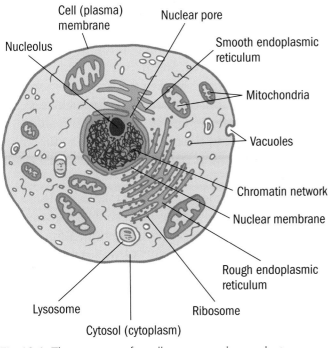

**Fig 13.1:** The structure of a cell as seen under an electron microscope

## Did you know?

The inside and outside of the cell membrane is aqueous. Tissue fluid bathes the outside of cells and is mainly water. Cytoplasm (inside the cell) is also a watery gel. This is why the lipid parts of the membrane are tucked inside, and the polar heads face the tissue fluid and cytosol.

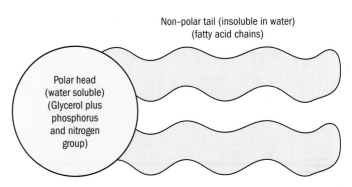

**Fig 13.2:** The structure of a phospholipid

The double layer (which has a sandwich-like appearance) is often called a bilayer, as the molecules are arranged in a special way. A phospholipid molecule looks rather like an old-fashioned clothes peg (see Figure 13.2). The 'head' is made of **glycerol** and a group of phosphorus and nitrogen atoms; and the 'legs' are made of chains of fatty acids.

The head is electrically charged and is often referred to as the **polar** head. It is said to be **hydrophilic** because it is able to exist against water molecules. The fatty acid chains do not carry charges and (like most fats or lipids) 'dislike' water and are called **hydrophobic**.

In the cell membrane the polar heads face both outwards and inwards, while the fatty acids face each other, like the meat in a sandwich (see Figure 13.3, on the next page).

**Cholesterol** molecules are inserted into the bilayer at intervals and these tend to help stabilise the freely moving bilayer, which acts rather like a fluid itself. The original model of the cell membrane was called 'the Fluid Mosaic model'. The phospholipid bilayer is dynamic but also flexible; its action can be likened to what happens when you place a spoon in a cup of tea,

to stir it, and lift it out – there is no 'hole' or space left behind with either action.

Also present are protein molecules: some lie only on the inner surface, others only on the outer surface, and still others pass all the way through the membranes

## Key terms

**Resolution** – The capability of making individual parts or closely adjacent images distinguishable. (In the absence of good resolution, stronger lenses make images blurred.)

**Nucleus** – Membrane-surrounded organelle, containing genetic material.

**Nucleoli** – Dark spots inside the nucleus, probably the site of ribosome synthesis.

**Cytoplasm** – Also known as cytosol; jelly-like material found between the cell membrane and the nucleus.

**Cytology** – The study of cell structure.

**Phospholipid** – A molecule consisting of glycerol, phosphate and lipid chains.

**Glycerol** – A sugary alcohol.

**Polar** – Carrying an electric charge, positive or negative.

**Hydrophilic** – Having an affinity for water.

**Hydrophobic** – Lacking an affinity for water.

**Cholesterol** – A type of fatty steroid present in cells.

and act as pores or channels for substances moving into and out of the cell. Various sugar chains may add to phospholipids (**glycolipids**) or proteins (**glycoproteins**) and appear to form a 'sugar coating' on the outside of a cell. Proteins, glycolipids and glycoproteins may enable cells to stick together to form tissues and act as identity markers or receptor sites for hormones, enzymes, etc.

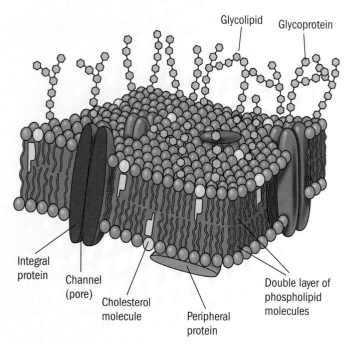

**Fig 13.3:** The structure of the cell membrane

## Key terms

**Glycolipid** – Phospholipid with a sugar chain attached.

**Glycoprotein** – Cell protein with a sugar chain attached.

**Nuclear pore** – A gap in the nuclear membrane.

**Nucleoplasm** – Soft, featureless material contained in the nucleus.

**Chromatin** – A complex of DNA and protein that forms chromosomes during cell division.

**DNA** – Short for deoxyribonucleic acid, which is responsible for transmitting inherited characteristics.

**Chromosomes** – Thread-like structures, composed of DNA and proteins, seen during cell division.

**RNA** – Short for ribonucleic acid, associated with controlling the chemical activities within the cell.

**Nucleotide** – Structural unit of DNA and RNA, consisting of a base, sugar and phosphate grouping.

**Base** – Chemically a purine or pyrimidine structure such as adenine, guanine, thymine, cytosine and uracil; a substance that accepts hydrogen ions.

## Nucleus and chromosomes

The nucleus is limited by the nuclear membrane, which is a phospholipid bilayer interrupted at intervals, known as **nuclear pores**. These 'gaps' provide direct communication between the cytoplasm and the nucleus. The soft material inside the nucleus is called **nucleoplasm** and it has no particular features. Embedded in the nucleoplasm is the **chromatin** network, composed of **DNA** and proteins. When a cell is dividing, the chromatin network condenses to form distinct **chromosomes** carrying genetic units. There are 23 pairs of chromosomes in humans. Other species have different numbers of chromosomes.

Another type of nucleic acid is also found in the nucleus and this is **RNA**. It is linked with controlling certain chemical activities taking place inside the cell. Lastly, there is the nucleolus or several nucleoli and these are believed to be the site for the production of RNA.

## DNA

DNA is made up of units called **nucleotides** and these repeat along the length of the molecule. A nucleotide consists of a **base**, sugar and phosphate grouping. There are four different bases in DNA: adenine, guanine, cytosine and thymine, often referred to by their initial letters for simplicity. Using a sophisticated form of X-rays and chemical analyses, teams of scientists were able to propose a model for the structure of DNA and later work has proved this to be true.

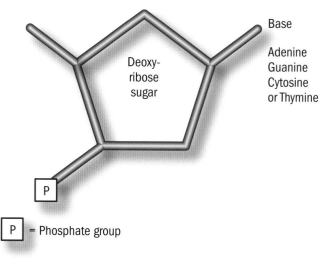

**Fig 13.4:** A nucleotide

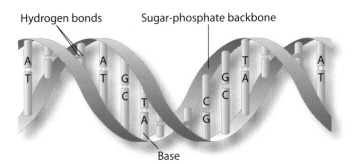

Hydrogen bonds    Sugar-phosphate backbone

Base

**Fig 13.5:** The structure of DNA

The bases always combine in the same way, adenine and thymine together and guanine and cytosine. So A and T and G and C form chemical 'rungs', with the sugar and phosphate molecules forming the sides of the ladder. The pairs of bases are held together by hydrogen bonds. However, the ladder looks as if it has been in a tornado, as it is twisted into a spiral shape known as a double helix (a helix is a spiral shape).

The DNA must unwind and split at the hydrogen bonds so that each strand can form a new strand, using raw materials in the cytoplasm. Enzymes assist in the process.

Thus two new DNA strands are formed, still in the nucleus, using the 'old' one as a pattern or template. Each has one 'old' strand and one new strand (made from raw materials) and is an exact copy of the original.

If the DNA is in the nucleus and the raw materials are in the cytoplasm, how do you think they get together? The answer is that the nuclear membrane contains pores (or gaps) and the raw materials enter the nucleus through the pores.

A sequence of bases on a section of DNA forms a code, or set of instructions, for cell metabolism. A particular pattern of bases will form a gene or unit of inheritance.

Metabolism is governed by enzymes, which catalyse all reactions. Enzymes are proteins and the sequence of bases on a particular stretch of DNA forms the code for production of enzymes and other proteins. Proteins are made up of amino acids, and the bases control which amino acids are linked together to form the specific protein.

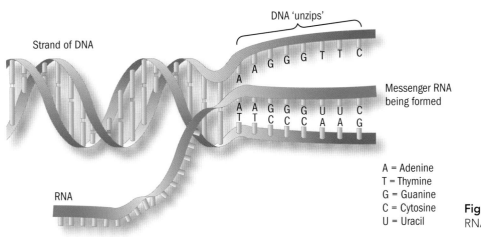

DNA 'unzips'

Strand of DNA

A A G G G T T C

Messenger RNA being formed

A A G G G U U C
T T C C C A A G

A = Adenine
T = Thymine
G = Guanine
C = Cytosine
U = Uracil

RNA

**Fig 13.6:** Transcription of messenger RNA (mRNA) from a section of DNA

DNA never leaves the nucleus under normal circumstances, and proteins are made in ribosomes on the rough endoplasmic reticulum in the cell, so clearly an intermediary must carry this code of bases from DNA in the nucleus to the ribosomes in the cell. This is the function of a type of RNA called messenger RNA, written briefly as **mRNA**.

## Activity 2: When mutations are caused

When DNA is not faithfully copied, this is called a mutation and it might have serious consequences for the health of an individual. However, not all mutations are harmful. In small groups answer the following questions:

1 Can you think of two inherited conditions arising from mutations?
2 Explain how the metabolism of the body might be altered if an enzyme is not copied faithfully.
3 Suggest why treatment for inherited diseases is difficult to achieve.
4 Could a disease caused by a mutation be passed on to offspring?

### PLTS

**Independent enquirer:** Analysing and evaluating information on cell mutation will enable you to show your independent enquiry skills.

In RNA, which exists mainly as a single strand, the sugar structure is slightly different (ribose instead of deoxyribose) and thymine is replaced by another base called uracil (U).

## mRNA

This type of RNA is made when a particular protein is needed, rather like a special order, but it is made in exactly the same way as DNA replicates itself. A section of DNA unwinds and splits and this time only one strand acts as the template. Using enzymes and raw materials, the mRNA is made up on the template strand, sometimes called the coding strand.

The section of mRNA that has formed detaches itself from the DNA, which 'zips' back up into its double helix. Newly formed mRNA moves through the nuclear pores to the ribosomes. The process of making mRNA on the DNA template is called **transcription**.

## Activity 3: Messenger RNA

Messenger RNA (mRNA) consists of the same bases as DNA except that uracil replaces thymine. It is made opposite a coding strand of DNA. Using your knowledge from this section and your own research, try to answer the following questions:

1 What would be the sequence of bases on mRNA made opposite a section of DNA coded as TCCGACT?
2 Try another one – CCTCATGAG.
3 Where in a cell is mRNA found and what is its task?

There are special gene regulatory proteins that tailor the number of transcribed copies to be made, according to cell needs.

Genes can code for similar proteins, and the mRNA can be cut and spliced to make different proteins. The parts of the mRNA that have been copied and removed from the gene are called introns and those that have been kept are called exons.

**Ribosomes** are made of another type of RNA, called ribosomal RNA (or **rRNA** for short). Ribosomes become attached to the mRNA strand and the process of converting the code into a sequence of amino acids begins. This process is known as **translation**.

Three bases on the mRNA correspond to one amino acid and this is known as a **codon**. There are many more codons than amino acids, so several codons can form one particular amino acid. There are 20 known amino acids. The sequence of bases for all amino acids has long been known. Three amino acids and their codons are given below as an example:

| Phenylalanine | UUC and UUU |
| Glutamine | CAA and CAG |
| Valine | GUA, GUC, GUG and GUU. |

A small molecule of yet another type of RNA carries the amino acids to the ribosome, to be formed into a protein chain – this is known as transfer RNA (or **tRNA**).

## tRNA

Two tRNA molecules with their amino acids can attach to a ribosome at the same time and a **peptide bond** will form between them; the ribosome then rolls on the mRNA and third and fourth amino acids are added, each forming a peptide bond with the next in the chain, and so on.

All types of RNA are made by transcription of a relevant section (gene) of DNA in the nucleus.

## Activity 4: Reviewing proteins

In Book 1, Unit 5, you learned about the digestion of proteins in the diet and that the end-products of protease digestion were amino acids. Use the Internet to research your answers to the following questions if you are uncertain:

1  What is the chemical structure of a protein?

2  How are proteins manufactured and broken down during digestion?

3  What happens to the parts of a protein after it is broken down?

## Functional skills

**ICT:** If you use the Internet to research information for this activity, you will be using ICT skills by searching, selecting and assessing the relevance of the information you find.

## PLTS

**Self-manager:** Researching and completing the answers to these questions within a specified time will demonstrate your self-management skills.

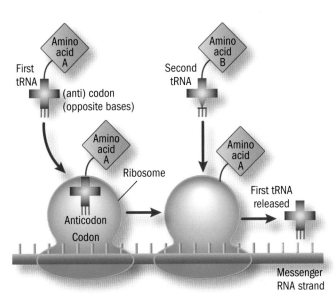

There are at least 20 different tRNA molecules coding for different amino acids

**Fig 13.7:** How mRNA translates into protein synthesis at a ribosome

## Endoplasmic reticulum (ER)

This is a system of flattened membranous sacs that fills the cytoplasmic part of the cell. It is continuous with the plasma membrane and the nuclear pores. Much of the ER has a rough appearance because it is studded with tiny black bodies known as ribosomes – this is known as **rough ER**. Some parts of the membranous sacs do not carry ribosomes and this is known as **smooth ER**.

## Ribosomes

You have already learned the location of most ribosomes as small spherical bodies on the ER. However, some also exist freely in the cytoplasm. They consist of 65 per cent rRNA and 35 per cent protein and exist in very large numbers, particularly in cells producing proteins for export (e.g. certain cells in the pancreas that manufacture insulin, a protein hormone). Ribosomal RNA is closely associated with the nucleoli, which are believed to be the site of synthesis. Structurally, ribosomes consist of two sub-units, one large and one small, each composed of protein and rRNA.

## Key terms

**mRNA** – Messenger RNA; carries the code for the synthesis of a protein and acts as a template for its formation.

**Transcription** – The process of forming mRNA from a template of DNA.

**Ribosome** – A tiny cell organelle responsible for protein synthesis.

**rRNA** – Ribosomal RNA; the type of RNA found in the ribosomes.

**Translation** – The process of forming a protein molecule in the ribosomes from an mRNA template.

**Codon** – A sequence of bases on mRNA that correspond to a particular amino acid.

**tRNA** – A small molecule of RNA, which carries amino acids to the ribosome to be made into protein.

**Peptide bond** – A chemical bond formed between the amine and carboxyl groups of two amino acids by the removal of the elements of water.

**Rough ER** – Endoplasmic reticulum studded with ribosomes.

**Smooth ER** – Endoplasmic reticulum without ribosomes.

## Golgi body

The **Golgi body** has also been called the Golgi complex or apparatus. It appears as a stack of flattened membranes with numerous **vesicles** pinched off the ends. These are termed Golgi vesicles. Some scientists believe that it is a specialised part of the smooth ER.

## Mitochondria

Mitochondria (the singular is mitochondrion) are round or sausage-shaped bodies found in large numbers (1000 plus) in the cytoplasm. Each is double-layered and the inner layer is folded to form internal 'shelves' called **cristae**. Enzymes that catalyse the breakdown of glucose are dissolved in the internal fluid, while enzymes associated with the formation of **ATP** lie in order on the cristae. Strangely, mitochondria have their own ribosomes and DNA, and some believe that they are the remnants of simple bacteria that became trapped inside cells millions of years ago.

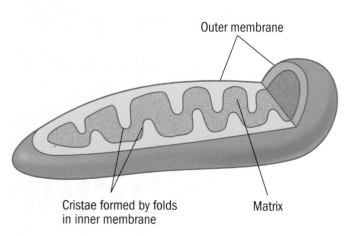

Outer membrane

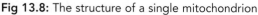

Cristae formed by folds in inner membrane

Matrix

**Fig 13.8:** The structure of a single mitochondrion

## Lysosomes

Scattered throughout the cell are vesicles of digestive-type enzymes known as **lysosomes**. They are the 'cleaners' or recyclers of the cell, clearing up debris, digesting old unwanted organelles and infectious agents like bacteria. Unwanted material, usually membrane-bound, fuses with one or more lysosomes and the digestive enzymes break the material down into raw materials. Whole, damaged or old cells can also be destroyed in this way, a process called **autolysis**. Some scientists think that cancer-causing agents, infectious organisms and poisons may act by damaging the membranes of lysosomes, thus causing cell damage or even mutations of genetic material.

## Other microstructures

Certain other microscopic structures, including centrioles and cilia, exist in some cells or in most cells at particular times.

### Centrioles

These are two tiny hollow cylinders that exist in a darkly staining part of the cytoplasm called the centrosome, close to the nucleus. Each contains a complex system of microtubules (nine groups of three, called triplets) that are capable of replicating themselves. They do this at the beginning of cell division, migrating to opposite ends of a cell. A spindle of microtubules is formed between them, and these control the separation of the chromosomes to form two new cells.

### Cilia

These are microscopic filaments that protrude from the free surface of a cell and in humans they are usually found adjacent to mucus-secreting cells. They 'beat' rhythmically to effect transport of mucus and other materials (such as debris in the respiratory passages and ova in the reproductive tract). The base of a cilium has the same microtubular structure as the centrioles and is believed to be formed from them.

# 1.2 Functions

You have already learned many functions of the parts of the cell (organelles), as you explored their structure and also when you studied them in Book 1, Unit 5. The following table will serve as both revision and supplementary information.

---

## Key terms

**Golgi body** – A series or pile of flattened membranes that lie close to the nucleus.

**Vesicles** – These can also be called cysts, vacuoles, etc, which usually mean fluid-filled sacs or pouches.

**Cristae** – Internal folds or shelves of mitochondria, holding an orderly arrangement of enzymes for ATP production.

**ATP** – Adenosine triphosphate; a chemical whose role in the cell is to store energy and release it for use when necessary.

**Lysosomes** – Membranous vesicles filled with digestive enzymes.

**Autolysis** – Self-destruction of the cell by lysosomes.

**Table 13.1:** Organelle functions

| Organelle | Functions |
| --- | --- |
| Cell membrane | • Acts as a selective barrier to substances entering and leaving the cell.<br>• Holds certain receptor sites to which other molecules, such as hormones, can attach.<br>• Contributes to the immunological identity of the cell.<br>• Interacts with the surrounding environment.<br>• Interacts with adjacent cells.<br>• Due to the fluid-like behaviour of the membrane, 'holes' or damage can be repaired almost instantaneously. |
| Nuclear membrane | • Acts as a selective barrier to substances entering and leaving the nucleus.<br>• Nuclear pores allow communication between the ER (see below) and the nucleus.<br>• Defines the boundary of genetic material such as DNA. |
| Nucleus | • Controls cellular activities.<br>• Contains chromosomes and thus genetic information.<br>• Site of transcription of mRNA from DNA.<br>• Ultimately responsible for protein production in the ribosomes.<br>• Nuclear division precedes cell division. |
| Chromosome | • Carries theoretical units of inheritance called genes.<br>• Contains DNA that is responsible for controlling the protein production.<br>• Capable of replication prior to cell division. |
| Endoplasmic reticulum (ER) | • Forms an internal cellular transport system.<br>• Enables communication between the cell membrane, the nucleus and the environment.<br>• Carries ribosomes that are responsible for the production of proteins (rough ER).<br>• Synthesises lipids from fatty acids and glycerol and transports these to the Golgi body (smooth ER). |
| Ribosomes | • Bind to rough ER.<br>• Bind to mRNA.<br>• Enable translation of mRNA to produce proteins. |
| Golgi body | • Receives proteins from the ribosomes via the ER and chemically modifies them for export (particularly in secreting cells).<br>• Produces vesicles to transport the modified proteins to the cell membrane for release.<br>• Receives and modifies lipids from the smooth ER for transport to the cell membrane.<br>• Produces lysosomes containing digestive enzymes. |
| Mitochondria | • Complete the oxidation of glucose (initially this begins in the cytoplasm) to release energy.<br>• Trap the energy released to form ATP, which is used to power the metabolic functions of the cells. |
| Cilia | • Transport mucus and other materials that may be stuck in them to the exterior by continuous rhythmic beating. |

## Assessment activity 13.1

Imagine that you have to teach a class about the microstructure of a typical animal cell and the functions of the main cell components. Produce a large diagram of a cell (similar to the one for Book 1, Unit 5) to show the detailed structures of the organelles and use annotations to describe the structure and functions of the main cell components. Your annotations should answer the questions:

1 What do the cell organelles look like?

2 And what do they do?

### Grading tip

**P1** The diagram could be drawn by you or compiled from a range of downloaded images. However, it must be a display of your own work and not simply a downloaded cell and description from the Internet. If you want to show transcription and translation, for example, you could add extra strips of paper that unfold to display the activities.

### PLTS

**Self-manager:** You can show your self-management ability by working towards goals (showing initiative, commitment and perseverance when preparing annotated diagrams of cell microstructure); dealing with competing pressures when completing annotated cell diagrams; and organising your time and resources to produce annotated diagrams.

# 2 Know the movement of materials into and out of cells

You are already aware that cells are separated from the tissue fluid that bathes them by the cell membrane and that most of the cell organelles have membrane boundaries. Cells are continuously needing to take in materials from their surroundings and, conversely, exporting or eliminating materials to their surroundings. This section will examine the methods by which materials are moved in this two-way process.

## 2.1 States of matter

Matter is material that has substance and occupies space. There are three states of matter that must be distinguished:

- solids
- liquids
- gases.

All these types of matter are made of atoms and molecules. Atoms are the smallest 'bits' of matter that can take part in chemical reactions, whereas molecules are composed of one or more atoms and are the smallest amount of a substance that can exist independently and keep its characteristic features. Even an atom is composed of smaller particles, known as protons and neutrons in a positively charged nucleus, and has negatively charged electrons present in a shell that orbits the nucleus. All atoms exhibit random motion and this is important in the state of matter.

## Solid matter

Bone, cartilage and skin are materials that you might think are solids because they are firm to the touch or because you know that they are not liquids or gases.

These responses are acceptable, but did you know that they are solids because the atoms/molecules are packed so tightly together that the motion is reduced to a very tiny vibration, so tiny that you cannot perceive it? These features define a solid – they cannot flow!

## Activity 5: Body fluids

Liquids form important parts of the body, as they enable materials to be transported. In pairs, answer the following questions:

1   Name three liquids found in the human body.

2   How do you know that these are liquids?

3   Discuss one characteristic function of a liquid you have named and say how its function relates to being a liquid.

## PLTS

**Independent enquirer:** Analysing and evaluating information on liquids will enable you to demonstrate your independent enquiry skills.

## Liquid matter

You probably chose blood, tissue fluid, lymph or urine and said that they were liquids because they could flow. The atoms/molecules are further apart than in a solid and so the atoms have more movement, resulting in flowing. Liquids take up the shape of their 'container', whether this is a vessel (as in blood and lymph), tiny spaces between cells or a hollow organ, like the bladder.

## Gases

Gases also occur in the human body – oxygen, carbon dioxide and nitrogen are common constituents of the air that we breathe in. The atoms/molecules of gases are much further apart from each other and are able to move about quite freely. Gases also flow. Most gases in the body are in a dissolved state.

## 2.2 Materials

In this section, you will learn about different types of material that you will meet in the body.

## Particulate material

Particles (e.g. dust from coal, asbestos, silica, and so on, and carbon particles in polluted air) can reach even the tiniest air passages, causing scarring and

disease. Such particles are very fine (as small as 0.005 mm in diameter). Particulate material can enter any open wound and rest in deeper tissues, where the macrophages will attempt to engulf and digest the particles. Invading bacteria digested by lysosomes will leave some debris behind, such as particulate matter. Images of the lungs of smokers or workers in 'dust' occupations show blackened tissues resulting from particulate matter.

## Ionic material

This is material containing atoms that may have a positive or negative charge as a result of gaining or losing electrons. Such atoms or groups of atoms are called ions or electrolytes. Ionic material is designated by the relevant charge shown against the atom – thus $Na^+$, $K^+$, $H^+$, $Cl^-$, $NH2^+$, $COOH^-$, etc.

In order, the above examples are positively charged sodium and potassium ions, hydrogen ion, chloride ion negatively charged, amine group positive and carboxyl group negatively charged.

Ions like these are continuously moving into and out of the cell, as they are often required or eliminated products from the thousands of chemical reactions occurring in cells.

## In solution

Substances that are capable of dissolving in a liquid are called solutes – the liquid is the solvent and the solute dissolved in the solvent is a solution. Water

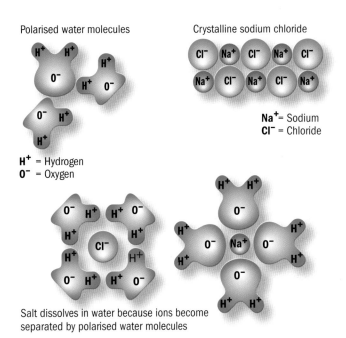

Polarised water molecules

Crystalline sodium chloride

$Na^+$ = Sodium
$Cl^-$ = Chloride

$H^+$ = Hydrogen
$O^-$ = Oxygen

Salt dissolves in water because ions become separated by polarised water molecules

**Fig 13.9:** Salt dissolving in water

is the most common molecule in the human body (9 out of every 10 molecules are water). Water is the most important solvent in the human body and most chemical reactions involve molecules dissolved in water.

Water is composed of two hydrogen atoms linked by chemical bonds to one oxygen atom. The hydrogen atoms have slight positive charges and the oxygen a slight negative charge, so water exists as a polar molecule. When a substance like salt (sodium chloride) is introduced into water, the water molecules are attracted to the positively charged sodium ions and negatively charged chloride ions and these become surrounded by water molecules. Sodium and chloride ions separate from the crystalline salt and thus are said to be dissolved.

Molecules having enough polar bonds or ionised groups will dissolve in water and are therefore hydrophilic. Molecules with electrically neutral groups do not dissolve in water and are hydrophobic. Such molecules will dissolve in non-polar solvents such as carbon tetrachloride (which is used as a dry-cleaning solvent for grease stains on clothes).

## Relevant colloidal forms

A colloid consists of larger particles (though they are too small to be seen with a light microscope), which are dispersed or scattered throughout a medium (gas, liquid or solid).

### Reflect

Uncooked egg white (a clear, sticky material) can flow but more slowly than liquid – this is called a colloid. Can you suggest the nature of the particles in egg white?

### Protein sols

Cytoplasm is an example of a colloid caused by the protein molecules that are not readily dissolved in water, so it is a protein sol. Blood plasma is another protein sol because of its plasma protein content. Polysaccharide molecules can also produce colloids when mixed with water. They are not readily soluble, as the molecules (like proteins) can be too large to simply dissolve.

### Emulsions

An emulsion occurs when one liquid is dispersed in droplets in another, such as fat in milk. Emulsifying agents cause one liquid to form very small droplets, which increases the surface area. This is what happens when bile salts are added to fats in chyme in the small intestine – the fats break up into thousands of tiny globules, producing a milky appearance. This provides an enormous surface area, which the pancreatic enzymes – dissolved in the water of the chyme – can act upon, causing fat digestion to break down to fatty acids and glycerol (see Book 1, Unit 5).

# 2.3 Movement of materials

You have learned about states of matter and materials and now you will learn about the ways in which materials are moved into and out of cells.

## Diffusion

You know that molecules, atoms and ions are in constant random motion and that this is most marked in gases and liquids because they are further apart. When there is a large number of molecules of a substance and a small number in another area, with no effective barrier between them, this random motion will cause the numbers to even up. This is known as **diffusion**.

Diffusion is the movement of molecules from a region of high concentration to a region of low concentration. Note the emphasis on concentration – the concentration of each region must be different and this is known as a **concentration gradient**. The greater the concentration gradient, the faster will be the rate of diffusion. Clearly, this will not happen instantly and so time is also important.

As the numbers of molecules become more evenly distributed, the *net* movement of molecules will slow down and eventually stop. This is said to be a state of **equilibrium**. However, it is important to understand that random motion is still occurring – it is just that as many move in one direction as in the other (in other words there is no net movement in one direction).

In the body, diffusion often takes place through cell membranes, but these are freely passable to the diffusing molecules provided that the barrier is thin. Note that in the lungs there are only two simple squamous epithelial cells separating the dissolved gases in the alveoli from the blood in the pulmonary capillaries. There is no source of energy required for diffusion of molecules.

# Facilitated diffusion

Some materials diffuse through the cell membrane by a related process known as **facilitated diffusion**. To facilitate something means to make it easier and the protein channels in the cell membrane assist in transporting molecules such as glucose and urea into and out of cells. Clearly, not only is the concentration gradient important here but also the number of channel proteins capable of allowing the materials through. The channel proteins have a shape containing a special receptor site for the molecule to be transported and then change shape to prevent further molecules binding until it is released on the opposite side of the membrane. One of the most vital systems depending on facilitated diffusion is the transport of glucose across cell membranes into the cell. Without the existence of the carrier proteins, the cell is virtually impermeable to glucose. When the glucose is released into the cytoplasm, it is almost immediately metabolised, thus maintaining the concentration gradient.

## Reflect

In the absence of insulin, a hormone produced by the pancreas, target cells are impermeable to glucose penetration.

Is it likely that insulin binds to the carrier proteins to cause them to open on the tissue fluid side and let glucose in?

## Osmosis

**Osmosis** is a special type of diffusion of water molecules. It is the movement of water molecules from a region of high concentration (of water molecules) to a region of low concentration (of water molecules) through a **selectively permeable membrane**.

Once again there is a concentration gradient *but* it is only concerned with numbers of water molecules. In addition, there is a selectively (sometimes also called partially) permeable membrane. You can think of permeable as meaning 'leaky'; a freely permeable membrane will allow most small molecules to pass through. A selectively permeable membrane allows some molecules through but not others. The molecules are usually too large.

Imagine a U-shaped tube in which there is a barrier of selectively permeable membrane in the centre. One limb of the tube contains water and the other a solution containing large molecules – say, a protein solution in equal volumes. The presence of the protein molecules takes up a lot of space – consequently there are fewer water molecules in that limb. There is a high concentration of water molecules on one side and a low concentration on the other. Water molecules will move through the selectively permeable membrane towards the low concentration on the 'protein' side, resulting in unequal volumes. This will continue until equilibrium has been reached.

Theoretically, pressure could be supplied to the top of the protein solution to prevent water molecules passing through the selectively permeable membrane from the water limb. This is known as the **osmotic pressure** of the protein solution.

Cell membranes can act as selectively permeable membranes to some substances. Osmosis occurs in the distal convoluted tubules of the kidney nephrons as they pass through a region of high sodium concentration in order to concentrate urine (see page 179).

## Key terms

**Diffusion** – The movement of molecules from a region of high concentration to a region of low concentration.

**Concentration gradient** – The difference between opposing concentrations.

**Equilibrium** – The state of having no net movement of molecules because the concentrations have evened up.

**Facilitated diffusion** – Diffusion down a concentration gradient that is dependent on energy-using carrier molecules or channel membranes.

**Osmosis** – The movement of water molecules from a region of high concentration to a region of low concentration (of water molecules) through a selectively permeable membrane.

**Selectively permeable membrane** – A membrane such as the phospholipid bilayer, which allows some molecules to pass through by osmosis but not others.

**Osmotic pressure** – The pressure exerted by large molecules to draw water to them. Plasma proteins in blood plasma have an osmotic pressure needed to return tissue fluid.

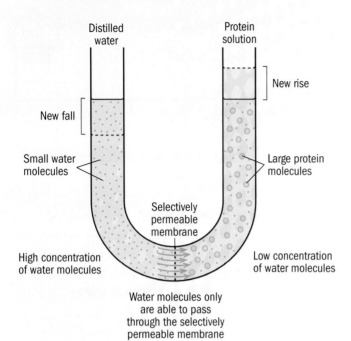

**Fig 13.10:** Osmosis

## Active transport

There are many examples of materials passing through living cells against a concentration gradient and neither diffusion nor osmosis can account for this type of movement. This is **active transport**; the word 'active' is used because this is an energy-using process powered by the release of energy from ATP in the cell (from the mitochondria). Carbohydrate digestion in the small intestine produces glucose and this may require active transport across cells of villi against a concentration gradient.

## Endocytosis

This is the process of taking materials that are outside the cell *into* the cell by **phagocytosis** or **pinocytosis**.

Phagocytosis literally means 'cell eating' and pinocytosis means 'cell drinking'. The process demonstrates the fluid nature of the cell membrane rather well. Areas of the cell membrane fold into the cell or invaginate, forming a pouch. The neck of the pouch gets narrower and eventually pinches off so that the material and a small volume of tissue fluid are enclosed within the cell in a membrane-bound pocket or vesicle. Larger particles such as bacteria and cell debris (from damaged cells) are taken in this

way; as the endocytic vesicle moves through the cell, it will merge with lysosomes and the material will be digested and broken down into basic raw materials.

**Endocytosis** can also be used to transport proteins and other chemicals across a cell to be released on the other side. Pinocytosis encloses only tissue fluid, or tissue fluid plus some specific molecules the cell requires. The specific molecules bind to carrier proteins in the membrane.

Pinocytosis occurs in all cells but phagocytosis occurs only in special cells such as macrophages and granulocytes (white blood cells, also called phagocytes). Endocytosis and **exocytosis** require energy from ATP to accomplish the tasks.

## Exocytosis

As you will anticipate from the name, exocytosis means the process of releasing materials from inside the cell out into the tissue fluid. Membrane-bound vesicles move through the cell to the cell membrane and fuse with it, releasing the contents as they do so. It is a way of introducing secretory molecules into body systems and also a method of replacing the cell membrane used up in endocytosis. This method is used for molecules that cannot pass through the cell membrane by diffusion or osmosis.

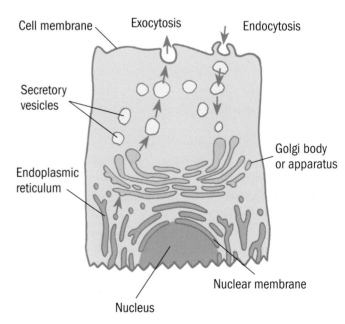

**Fig 13.11:** Endocytosis and exocytosis

## Key terms

**Active transport** – The movement of materials against a concentration gradient, using energy from ATP.

**Phagocytosis** – The engulfing and destruction of cell debris and foreign bodies by mobile cells which produce arm-like extensions to surround the material.

**Pinocytosis** – A process similar to phagocytosis but involving pinching off a vesicle filled with tiissue fluid to take into the cell.

**Endocytosis** – Transport of materials from outside a cell to the inside of the cell.

**Exocytosis** – The reverse of endocytosis, i.e. transporting materials from inside the cell to the outside.

## Factors affecting movement

The influences on movement will be considered in the next section. However, the availability of energy from ATP, and the fluidity of the cell membrane, are clearly important for all processes except diffusion and osmosis. The surface area and thickness of any intervening selectively permeable or freely permeable membranes will affect the rates of diffusion and osmosis. There are also complex cellular stimuli, which cause endocytosis and exocytosis to occur, that are beyond the scope of this unit.

# 2.4 Influences on movement of materials

There many known influences on why materials move in cells, into cells and out of cells and possibly many other influences that are not yet known. Here, you will learn about some of the known influences.

## Size

You have already learned that molecular size is important in osmosis; that a larger molecule cannot move through a selectively permeable membrane such as a protein like albumin, one of the plasma proteins. You have also learned that protein molecules cannot pass simply by diffusion and osmosis and are often transported across a cell by endocytosis.

The size of any surface for transport is vital, as it must be large enough to allow sufficient molecules or ions to be transported to accommodate the metabolic processes in a cell. For this reason, the surface area-to-

## Activity 6: Surface area/ volume relationships

Work in pairs and use a jelly cube (or a cube made of modelling clay or other soft material). Measure the length, width and depth of its sides and calculate the surface area and volume. Cut the cube into four even quarters and repeat the calculations.

1   Calculate the surface area/volume relationship of the original cube.

2   Calculate the surface area/volume relationship of the quarter cube.

3   Comment on the results.

4   Explain what this means for cell metabolism.

5   When the optimum size of a cell has been reached, what will happen next?

## Functional skills

**Mathematics:** This activity requires you to identify the problem and the method needed to tackle it. You can show your mathematical skills by finding solutions to the questions, drawing conclusions and providing mathematical justifications.

volume ratio for any cell is critical. Surface area is the area of cell membrane that must support the internal cytoplasmic and nuclear activities. Cells cannot just keep on growing larger, as the area of cell membrane will not be big enough for the exchange of materials for the volume of the cytoplasm.

Size is also important in terms of the width and length of a surface carrying out transport of materials. Here are a few examples:

* The surface area of single-celled alveoli in a person's lungs, if spread out flat on a surface, would total the area of a football pitch.

* The surface area of the villi in the ileum of the small intestine would be similar.

* There are over a million nephrons in a small organ like a kidney.

All these examples demonstrate the need for an enormous surface area for transport. This huge surface must be folded and folded again, to make organs that are compact enough to fit into the human body.

## Distance

As with size, so it is with distance. Any disease that affects the distance to be travelled reduces the efficiency of the transport process. For example, dissolved gases such as oxygen and carbon dioxide pass across the alveolar/capillary interface with ease in a healthy person. However, a patient with pneumonia has extra fluid and mucus in the alveoli and may suffer considerably from the lack of oxygen. Such a condition, often known as **cyanosis**, results in a bluish-purple tinge to blood vessels visible in the nail beds, ear lobes, cheeks and lips.

**Pneumoconiosis**, the dust disease of the lungs, produces fibrosis and scarring. Again, this results in cyanosis and of course respiratory difficulties.

Diffusion can distribute molecules quickly over a short distance but is very slow over more than a few centimetres. Vander, Sherman and Luciano (2003) state:

'It takes glucose 3.5s to reach 90 per cent equilibrium at 10 μm (10 thousandths of a millimetre) away from a source of glucose, such as the blood, but it would take over 11 years to reach the same concentration at a point 10 cm away.'

## Temperature

Increasing the temperature also increases **kinetic energy** (the energy of motion) and so molecules will move faster in diffusion and osmosis. The average speed of molecules depends on temperature and the mass of the molecule.

Vander *et al* (2003) report on diffusion thus:

'At body temperature, an average molecule of water moves at about 2500 km/h whereas a molecule of glucose, which is ten times heavier, moves at about 850 km/h. In solutions, such rapidly moving molecules cannot travel very far before colliding with other molecules. They bounce off each other like rubber balls, undergoing millions of collisions every second. Each collision alters the direction of the molecule's movement, so that the path of any one molecule becomes unpredictable.'

Source: Vander, A.J. (2003) *Human Physiology: The Mechanisms of Body Function* London: McGraw Hill.

Conversely, cooling temperatures mean that less kinetic energy is available, resulting in the slowing down of molecular movement.

Active transport, endocytosis and exocytosis systems will increase too, up to a point. However, as they depend on energy systems, carriers and the nature of the fluid cell membrane, a continually increasing temperature will begin to change the shape of protein molecules, rendering them inactive.

## Concentration gradient

This has been referred to in the section on diffusion (see pages 158–159).

## Osmotic potential

This is the power of a solution to gain or lose water molecules through a membrane. Weaker or more dilute solutions have higher osmotic potentials than concentrated solutions; it follows therefore that pure water has the highest **osmotic potential**. When tissue fluid returns to the blood, it does so by osmosis because the plasma proteins in blood plasma have a lower osmotic potential than the aqueous tissue fluid – the single-celled capillary wall acts as the selectively permeable membrane.

Under normal circumstances, some protein molecules inevitably escape from capillaries into interstitial spaces (spaces between cells filled with tissue fluid). In other circumstances associated with diseases of the renal system, excess protein can accumulate in the interstitial spaces.

Cells are capable of accumulating materials in low concentration from their surroundings and also capable of eliminating water found in high concentration outside the cell. In this way, osmotic potential energy is transformed from chemical energy.

# Activity 7: Practical work on movement into and out of cells

In this activity you will simulate osmosis across a cell membrane using a special material called Visking tubing, which is partially permeable. Visking tubing was originally made to separate materials within kidney machines.

Experiment 1:

1 Form a bag from Visking tubing by making a knot at one end.

2 Fill the bag with starch solution and wash and dry the outside.

3 Place the bag in a container of water, and add a few $cm^3$ of iodine solution to the water. (The test for starch is the formation of a blue-black colour when iodine is added.)

4 Observe what happens.

Soon the contents of the bag will begin to turn black, but the liquid outside the bag remains the same colour. What is moving across the Visking tubing membrane to cause this colour change?

The iodine solution outside the bag is passing through the membrane into the starch solution, turning it blue-black. Starch molecules are too large to pass through the membrane in the other direction and this mimics the cell membrane.

To advance the experiment, you could vary the strength of the starch solution you use or the temperature of the water and investigate the effects.

Experiment 2:

1 Make bags of Visking tubing, and fill them with different strengths of glucose solution. Mark the bags so you know which strength solution is in each one.

2 Weigh each bag and record the weights. Then immerse each bag in a container of water and leave them for a fixed length of time.

3 When the time is up, remove the bags, dry the outsides and weigh each one again.

Have the bags changed in weight? Can you explain what has moved across the membrane?

You could carry out a similar experiment but instead of varying the concentration of glucose, you could vary the temperature of the water.

You could also use dried weighed identical slices of potatoes immersed in different strengths of glucose solution (and water) to demonstrate the movement of water molecules by osmosis. Weigh the potato slices before and after they are immersed in different solutions and record the changes. Try varying the temperature of the water and different thicknesses of potato slices.

# Activity 8: Tissue fluid and the importance of protein

In pairs, answer the following questions:

1 In certain diseases protein builds up in the interstitial spaces between cells. Suggest why this can happen.

2 What effect will this excess protein have on the osmotic potential of tissue fluid?

3 How would this affect the circulatory system?

4 What sign would doctors notice?

5 Can you find out how doctors test for this in a patient examination?

6 Can you give this a clinical name?

## PLTS

**Independent enquirer:** Analysing and evaluating information on proteins, osmotic potential and tissue fluid formation will show your independent enquiry skills.

## Key terms

**Cyanosis** – Bluish colour of the skin and mucous membranes, indicating poor oxygenation of blood.

**Pneumoconiosis** – Industrial disease caused by inhaling dust particles over a period of time.

**Kinetic energy** – The energy of motion.

**Osmotic potential** – The power of a solution to gain or lose water molecules through a membrane.

## Electrochemical gradient

Cells have a difference in electrical charge across the cell membrane, the exterior of the cell membrane carrying positive charges and the interior negative charges. This is often referred to as a **membrane potential** and it will affect the diffusion of ions across the membrane. The result of this is that positively charged ions (like sodium and potassium) will be attracted into the cell and negatively charged ions (such as chloride ions) will be repelled. This force operates even when there is no concentration gradient. This is often referred to as the electrochemical gradient.

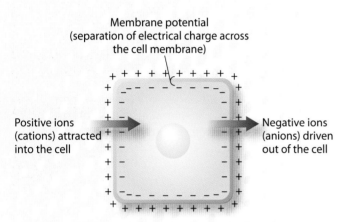

Membrane potential
(separation of electrical charge across the cell membrane)

Positive ions (cations) attracted into the cell

Negative ions (anions) driven out of the cell

Concentration difference and the membrane potential = electrochemical gradient across the cell membrane

**Fig 13.12:** The electrochemical gradient operating across a cell membrane

## Permeability of cell membrane

Most charged or polar molecules and ions diffuse across the phospholipid bilayer very slowly or even not at all, whereas non-polar molecules (those not carrying electrical charges) diffuse quite rapidly. This is possible because they dissolve in the fatty acid chains or the lipid layer of the cell membrane. Materials such as dissolved oxygen, carbon dioxide, fatty acids and steroid molecules diffuse in this way quite easily and rapidly. It appears then that the lipid part of the membrane acts as a selective barrier. Polar ion movement is dealt with in the next section.

## Channel proteins

The rates of entry of non-polar molecules through the cell membranes are very similar in different cells. This is not so for polar ions and molecules; different cells 'import' these at different rates and overall they are much faster than one would expect, given their relative insolubility in the lipid bilayer.

Experiments have shown that an artificial bilayer membrane containing no protein results in virtual impermeability to ions such as sodium, potassium, chloride and calcium. However, real cell membranes are permeable to these ions. This suggests that the protein channels are responsible for the permeability of the cell membrane to polar ions and molecules. Shapes of membrane protein channels are varied and related to the ions they allow through. The channels are extremely small so preventing other molecules from passing. The channels are selective as gate-keepers, and permeability to particular ions depends on the number and variety of protein channels in the cell membrane of particular cells.

## Carrier molecules

You have already learned about **carrier molecules** in the section on facilitated diffusion (see page 159). There are many types of carrier molecules in membranes, each specific to a particular substance or group of substances by way of its characteristic binding site. For example, amino acids and sugars have different binding sites and carrier proteins. Once again, the rate of movement will be influenced by the number of carrier proteins in cell membranes and by the number of binding sites occupied with transporting molecules at any one time.

### Key terms

**Membrane potential** – The potential difference across a cell membrane caused by different ions.

**Carrier molecules** – Molecules that bind to others, facilitating their transport.

## Assessment activity 13.2

P2 M1 D1 · BTEC

Write a report on the processes that enable materials to enter and leave cells. Your report should be arranged in the following three parts:

1 Describe the ways in which materials move in and out of cells.

2 Explain the factors that influence the movement of materials into and out of cells.

3 Analyse the role of the phospholipid bilayer in terms of the movement of materials into and out of cells.

### Grading tips

P2 For the first part, you need to explain the processes of diffusion, facilitated diffusion, osmosis, active transport, endocytosis and exocytosis, illustrating your answer where this helps understanding.

M1 For the second part, explain the relevant factors influencing the movement of materials. For example, size, distance, temperature and concentration gradient are all relevant to diffusion. This will give your writing structure and coherence.

D1 How is the phospholipid bilayer involved in the passage of materials to and from the cells? You need to read through the whole of this section on movement of materials and attempt some Internet research of your own as well. There is plenty of scope in the text to discuss the movement of polar and non-polar molecules/ions through the bilayer, illustrating your writing with examples and bringing in channel proteins and carrier molecules as well.

## PLTS

**Self-manager:** You can show your self-management skills by working towards goals showing initiative, commitment and perseverance when preparing a report on movement of materials in and out of cells. Dealing with competing pressures and organising your time and resources to produce the report will also demonstrate your self-management abilities.

# 3 Know the distribution and constituents of fluids in the body

In this section, you will learn about the importance of water, its role in the body and its unique properties. The distribution of water into body compartments and the types of material found in water are also included. The section will examine the role of electrolytes and the maintenance of pH in the body.

## 3.1 Constituents of body fluids

### Water

Water is the main component of all body fluids, comprising at least 90 per cent of blood plasma, lymph, urine, saliva, digestive juices, bile, cerebrospinal fluid and tissue fluid. Without water, the fluids could not flow, and flowing is essential. Stagnant fluid (i.e. fluid that does not flow because it has no outlet)

### Did you know?

Water is a polar molecule; the two hydrogen atoms are slightly positive and the oxygen negative. You can illustrate this by bringing a charged rod close to a thin stream of water from a running tap and actually seeing the water stream bend towards the rod. Rubbing a glass rod vigorously with a piece of silk converts it into a charged rod. This demonstrates the attraction of unlike charges.

is always a focus for infection, which can become potentially life-threatening. Water is essential to life because it provides the medium for all metabolic reactions and the transport of essential substances around the body.

## Case study: Becky

Becky is in the last stage of pregnancy and has complained of a burning feeling on passing urine. Her doctor explains that she has cystitis or inflammation of the bladder and that it is quite common in late pregnancy. He prescribes some tablets for Becky to take and the symptoms disappear in a few days.

1 Why are some cases of cystitis linked to late pregnancy?
2 Explain why the infection has occurred.
3 Can you think when a similar situation might arise in some men as clearly pregnancy would not be the cause?

Water molecules are constantly being moved between fluid compartments of the body. You will learn later that although some water is made as a by-product of metabolism, this is not sufficient to maintain life, so water is an essential part of our diet.

## Solutes

There are many solutes dissolved in water in body fluids, and you will explore the major solutes.

### Glucose

Glucose belongs to the class of organic molecules known as carbohydrates, which have the general formula of $Cn (H_2O)n$, where $n$ represents any whole number. As you see, there is a link between the name of the group and its chemical construction because each carbon atom has the elements of water or hydrate attached to it. In glucose, the $n$ is 6 so the accepted formula for glucose is $C_6H_{12}O_6$. A better representation can be seen in Figure 13.13, as this shows the two-dimensional shape of glucose (it is

actually three-dimensional but this cannot be shown on paper). Five carbon atoms and an oxygen atom form a ring, with hydroxyl and hydrogen groups attached to each carbon atom.

Glucose is a monosaccharide (this means single sugar ring). Disaccharides contain two such rings linked together and polysaccharides many rings. Glucose tastes sweet and is the most common carbohydrate in blood.

### Reflect

Other types of sugar are fructose (found in most fruits), sucrose (the type of sugar used to sweeten tea and coffee) and lactose (less sweet, found in milk).

Starch and glycogen (so-called animal starch) are polysaccharides that are less sweet.

Where is glycogen found in large amounts in the human body? What is the role of glycogen in these sites?

The normal range of blood glucose is 4.5–5.6 mmol per litre or 70–110 mg per 100 ml.

### Urea

Urea is a metabolic waste product of surplus amino acids.

Dietary proteins are digested to amino acids and absorbed into the blood. Both proteins and amino acids contain nitrogen atoms in their amino group ($-NH_2$) and excess amino acids cannot be stored because of the nitrogen component.

The nitrogen-containing amino group is converted into ammonia ($NH_3$) inside cells and then is easily transported through the cell membranes into tissue fluid and ultimately blood, from where it is transported to the liver. In the liver, ammonia combines with carbon dioxide to form urea. It is important to realise

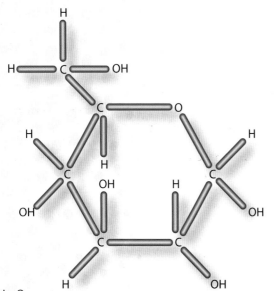

$C_6 H_{12} O_6$
Note the position of the single oxygen atom and the 'extra' C atom added on

**Fig 13.13:** The structure of glucose

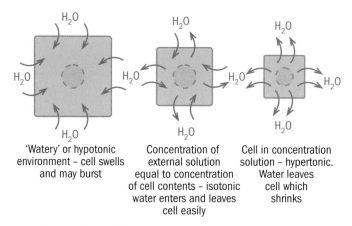

'Watery' or hypotonic environment – cell swells and may burst

Concentration of external solution equal to concentration of cell contents – isotonic water enters and leaves cell easily

Cell in concentration solution – hypertonic. Water leaves cell which shrinks

**Fig 13.15:** Cells in different osmotic environments

are rapidly returned. These salts assist in controlling osmosis through the cell membrane. When the osmotic pressure outside the cell is equal to that inside the cell, they are said to be isotonic to each other. As much water moves into the cell as moves out.

However, if cells are in more dilute solutions, the osmotic pressure is higher and water molecules will pass, by osmosis, from outside to inside, causing the cell to swell and possibly rupture. A swollen or damaged cell cannot function efficiently. Conversely, if cells exist in a more concentrated solution with a lower osmotic pressure than the cell contents, water molecules will leave the cell, resulting in dehydration and shrinkage. Once again, the cell cannot function effectively and may die. Sodium and potassium salts play a major role in controlling osmosis and osmotic pressure. The brain and the kidneys regulate the quantities of sodium and potassium salts in body fluids.

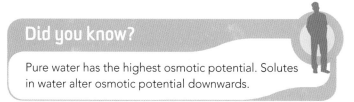

### Did you know?

Pure water has the highest osmotic potential. Solutes in water alter osmotic potential downwards.

## Maintenance of acid-base balance

This will be considered in detail in the next section. However, electrolytes have important roles in the maintenance of the balance between acids and bases in the body. This is accomplished by buffers in body fluids. A buffer is a chemical system that acts to prevent change in the concentration of another chemical substance.

Buffer systems consist of a weak acid and their soluble salt. You will recall that weak acids mainly remain as molecules and only a few dissociate. The salt, however, readily dissociates, producing large numbers of negatively charged ions. These ions readily accept hydrogen ions if more are produced as a result of metabolism, thus removing them from solution and keeping the pH more or less constant. Hydrogen carbonate and hydrogen phosphate are particularly important.

# 3.3 Acid-base balance

In this section, you will learn about the pH scale and buffer systems in more detail, and why it is so important to keep acidity and alkalinity within a narrow range of variables.

## pH

This is a measure of the quantity of hydrogen ions in a solution. It is an artificial logarithmic scale based around the ionisation of water. When water dissociates it produces equal numbers of $H^+$ and $OH^-$ ions and each has been determined as $1 \times 10^{-7}$ mol dm$^{-3}$. (Note that dm$^{-3}$ = 1 litre.)

This is such a small number that the pH scale was derived. It is based around the pH of water at 7, which is neither acidic nor basic. By making the scale logarithmic (denoted by the p) and reciprocal 1/X, the scale became easier to understand.

$$pH = -\log[H^+] \text{ or } 1 \div \log[H^+]$$

The greater the quantity of hydrogen ions, the greater the acidity and the lower will be the pH.

The pH scale begins at 1 and ends at 14, with 7 being the neutral point. Any substance between 1 and 7 is acidic in nature; and from 7 to 14 a substance is a base.

Strong acids have a pH near the bottom of the scale (such as 1–3) and strong bases have pH values that are nearer to 14.

## The importance of maintaining hydrogen ion concentration in body fluids

The importance of buffer systems in maintaining and stabilising the pH of cellular and body fluids cannot be over-emphasised. You have learned that metabolic activities are controlled by thousands of cellular and digestive enzymes and that enzymes only work efficiently within a narrow range of pH. Enzymes alter the rate of chemical reactions; in the human body, most enzymes speed up the rate of reactions many times. For example, carbon dioxide is carried in blood plasma mainly as the hydrogen carbonate and, without the presence of the enzyme carbonic anhydrase to improve the rate of formation of hydrogen carbonate, the elimination of carbon dioxide would be too slow to support life. Failure to keep blood pH between 7 and 8 usually results in death.

## Buffer systems

Blood and tissue fluid are buffered at around pH 7.2–7.4 by the system incorporating carbonic acid and sodium hydrogen carbonate as the weak acid and sodium salt as the weak acid.

$$H_2CO_3 \Leftrightarrow H^+ + HCO_3^{3-} \text{ (small dissociation)}$$

$$NaHCO_3 \Leftrightarrow Na^+ + HCO_3^{3-} \text{ (large dissociation)}$$

Extra hydrogen ions caused by metabolic reactions, such as vigorous exercise or diet, are accepted by the large numbers of hydrogen carbonate ions to form $H_2CO_3$, which exists mainly as molecules. In due course this will further push the reaction to the left and $CO_2$ and $H_2O$ will be formed. The $CO_2$ will be removed through increased ventilation and the water through sweating or urination.

Conversely, if the hydrogen ion concentration becomes too low, the buffer releases hydrogen ions into solution to keep the pH constant.

The main buffer that prevents large fluctuations in cells is the dihydrogen phosphate and monohydrogen phosphate buffer system. (Note that di- means two and mono- means one.) This system operates at around pH 7.2.

> ### Reflect
> The pH of blood is normally kept within the range 7.2–7.4. Does this mean that blood is slightly acid or slightly alkaline?

The phosphate buffer system operates mainly through kidney function. Tubular cells of the renal nephrons are stimulated to produce ammonia when the blood is becoming too acid. The ammonia replaces the sodium in the dihydrogen phosphate, causing increased acid secretion in urine. The pH of urine can vary from 4.0 to 8.0.

Finally, an important buffer operating in cells and plasma is that utilising proteins. At one end of a

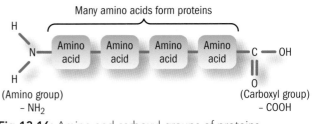

**Fig 13.16:** Amino and carboxyl groups of proteins

protein chain there is an amino group and at the other end there is a carboxyl group.

When there is a fall in pH, and therefore a corresponding rise in hydrogen ion concentration, the amino groups will accept the extra hydrogen ions. Conversely, where there is a rise in pH, the carboxyl groups will dissociate to release hydrogen ions to restore pH.

# 3.4 The role of water

You have learned that water is the main constituent of body fluids (see pages 165–166) and this section will examine the important properties of water in relation to this role.

## In relation to properties

### Specific heat capacity

Specific heat capacity is the amount of energy required to raise 1 kg of a substance by 1°K. The Kelvin scale is the SI temperature scale. You do not need to worry about the Kelvin scale if it is new to you. Water has a high specific heat capacity, which means that it takes a lot of energy to raise 1 kg of water by 1 degree of temperature.

This means that even in hot climates warm-blooded animals like humans will not have a massive rise in temperature – nor will they cool down too quickly. Water also has a high heat of vaporisation, meaning that it takes a lot of energy to convert liquid water into water vapour. This property is useful as it means that, when sweat is evaporated from the skin surface, a lot of heat energy from the skin surface is used up, thereby cooling the skin.

> ### Reflect
> On a hot summer day at the beach, you might feel the sand under your feet is so hot that you have to have your sandals on. However, when you go into the sea it is surprisingly cold. Think about this with reference to specific heat of water.

## Solvent

Water is an excellent solvent for many important substances in the body and you learned how this happens earlier (see page 166).

## Surface tension

Water also has a high surface tension, meaning that the quantity of water in contact with air or other material tends to have the smallest possible area. A fine watery film between the two pleural surfaces (one covering the lung and one lining the inside chest wall) creates a tension that literally pulls the lung surface along when the ribs move upwards and outwards during inspiration.

# 3.5 Distribution of water

In physiology, the weight of an average person is calculated at 70 kg, and about 60 per cent of this body weight would be water. This produces a figure of about 42 litres of total body water.

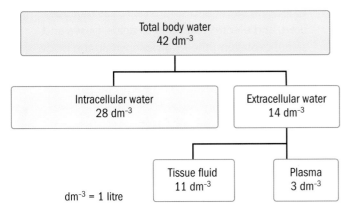

dm$^{-3}$ = 1 litre

**Fig 13.17:** The distribution of body water

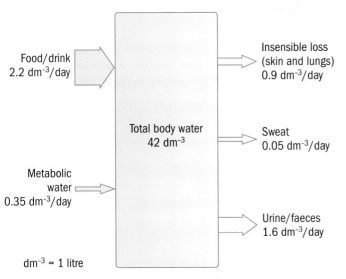

dm$^{-3}$ = 1 litre

**Fig 13.18:** Average daily water gain and loss

Total body water comprises the water inside cells, known as intracellular water (28 litres), and that which lies outside cells – called extracellular water (14 litres).

These two figures probably surprised you, as we tend to think of body water as blood, lymph, tissue fluid and urine and not as water inside cells. In fact only one-third of water is in plasma and tissue fluid. Tissue fluid, also known as intercellular and interstitial fluid, is actually the majority component of extracellular fluid, being 11 litres compared to 3 litres of plasma. Tissue fluid is of course derived from plasma and has the same constituents, apart from plasma proteins. Tissue fluid is a protein-free plasma filtrate. Lymph comprises about 10 per cent of the tissue fluid from which it forms, the remainder returning to plasma. Tissue fluid is not called lymph until it enters the branching network of the lymphatic vessels.

# Role of intercellular fluid in homeostasis

Intercellular or tissue fluid plays an integral part in **homeostasis**, maintaining the constancy of the **internal environment**.

Tissue fluid is driven out of the arterial end of a capillary by the remaining blood pressure after the blood has been driven through the medium of muscular arteries and arterioles. At this stage it has a high dissolved oxygen concentration and low carbon dioxide. It is also loaded with nutrients such as glucose, amino acids and salts. Tissue fluid circulates around and between cells (hence the name intercellular fluid) distributing raw materials by

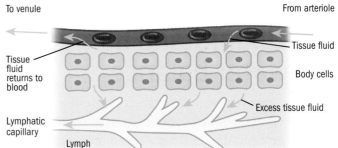

**Fig 13.19:** The formation and removal of tissue fluid

## Key terms

**Homeostasis** – Maintaining a constant internal environment around cells.

**Internal environment** – This is the physical and chemical composition of blood and tissue fluid that surrounds body cells.

diffusion, osmosis, facilitated diffusion, etc. Waste metabolic materials pass in the opposite direction from cells into tissue fluid and, if allowed to accumulate, would cause serious disruption and eventually cell and body death.

However, having collected the metabolic waste, most tissue fluid re-enters the venous end of the capillaries because the plasma proteins (still inside the capillaries) exert an osmotic pressure, drawing the fluid back into the capillary. This is assisted by the low blood pressure

at the venous end because of the volume of fluid forced out at the arterial end. The waste materials are carried away, to be excreted via the lungs or the liver and kidneys. Some proteins do escape the capillary (about 2 per cent) and, as they cannot either be allowed to accumulate or re-enter the capillary, they are removed, together with any surplus tissue fluid and waste products via the lymphatic system. In this way, the tissue fluid has a role in maintaining the stability or constancy of the internal environment.

## Assessment activity 13.3

**P3  M2**   BTEC

Design a poster showing an annotated diagram of a container with the various 'water' compartments of total body water, to answer the question:

How is water spread throughout the body and which solutes are present? You should include a description of the distribution and constituents of the body fluids. For M2, an explanation of the functions of the constituents of body fluids should also be included.

### Grading tips

**P3** Add annotations to your diagram, providing a short description and a list of the solutes found in each compartment.

**M2** Add to the annotations you have done for P3, as they are a logical progression. You will need to include water and solutes (such as glucose, urea, and electrolytes such as acids, bases and salts), explaining their purpose within the body. Try to think of more than one.

### PLTS

**Self-manager:** When carrying out this assignment, you can demonstrate your self-management ability by showing perseverance and commitment, being able to organise your time and being able to prioritise in order to produce written work while dealing with other pressures.

# 4  Understand homeostatic processes in relation to water balance

You have learned about the many features of water and solutes and you will now place this in context with reference to the renal system and how water is regulated to maintain homeostasis.

## 4.1 Water intake

Water is obtained from three sources for the body:

- fluids that are drunk
- water present in food
- water produced as a by-product of metabolism.

It will obviously vary from day to day but, generally speaking, an individual takes in approximately 1.2

litres in fluid such as water, soft drinks, beverages and alcoholic drinks like wine and beer. Surprisingly, as much as 1 litre is taken in as food; even the driest cracker has water in it, and vegetables and meat have a high proportion of water.

Only about one-third of a litre is produced from chemical reactions such as the oxidation of glucose and lipids. The total intake per day is around 2.5 litres.

In the previous section on the control of osmosis/osmotic pressure (see page 159) you learned about the effect of water gain on cells.

# 4.2 Water output/loss

Water is lost from the body in four ways:

- Through the skin – there is a constant loss from the skin that we are not conscious of. This is caused by evaporation and is known as insensible water loss – it can add up to 0.5 litre* to our total water loss. In addition, a variable amount can be lost through sweating to cool the skin. Clearly this depends on the climate and the season and ranges from about 50 ml to 2 litres.

- From the lungs – air breathed out is saturated with water vapour and this can range from 0.3 to 0.5 litre*.

- From faeces leaving the gastro-intestinal tract – water loss averages about 0.1 litre*.

- Through urine – in a temperate climate such as the UK this totals about 1.5 litres*.

- These figures take no account of loss by unusual circumstances, such as vomiting and diarrhoea, when water loss can be considerable and lead to dehydration and life-threatening situations (particularly in babies and older people who have less efficient water-regulating systems). It is also worth noting that the volume of urine generally declines in hot weather, as extra water is lost as sweat. Menstrual loss in women varies from one individual to another, with the average loss being 60 ml.

In the previous section on the control of osmosis/ osmotic pressure (see page 159) you learned about the effect of water loss on cells.

# 4.3 Renal system

## Gross anatomy

The renal system comprises two kidneys, their tubes (known as ureters), the bladder and the urethra.

The kidneys lie on the posterior or back wall of the abdomen, above the waist and partly protected by the lowest ribs. There is one kidney on each side of the vertebral column.

The bladder is a central pelvic organ connected to the kidneys by two ureters 20–30 cm in length. Both bladder and ureters have a lining of epithelium, surrounded by muscle and fibrous tissue.

## Activity 10: Where are the kidneys?

Most people believe that their kidneys are much lower down than they actually are. Try asking five people to point to their kidneys and liver. Then show them the correct positions. If you are unsure, check the positions out on an anatomical model or in Book 1, Unit 5.

1 What proportion of your small survey got the position of the kidneys wrong?

2 How many people got both positions wrong?

3 What proportion got the liver correct and the kidneys wrong?

## Activity 9: Fluid in your body

Keep your own or a friend's fluid balance sheet for 24 hours. A Saturday or Sunday is probably best and a day when you are not undertaking vigorous exercise.

You can research the volumes of water in the food you consume by consulting a nutrition manual and you will need two labelled plastic measuring jugs to measure the volumes of fluid and urine (keep them separate). Take the standards for faeces (0.1 litre*) and breath (0.4 litre) and the insensible perspiration as 0.4 litre*. Assume that metabolic water intake is 0.35 litre.

Design a fluid balance chart with three columns – input, output and comments.

- When the time is finished, add up the total water intake and total water output columns.

- Ignoring any difference under 50 ml, say whether you (or your friend) are in fluid balance. Do any of the comments listed make any difference? Estimate the difference and adjust the chart. For example, you may have spilled some fluid, not quite finished a drink, etc.

- If you are not in fluid balance, explain what would happen if the same imbalance was repeated daily for a week.

How much did environmental temperature influence your findings?

*Please note that the scientifically correct unit of measurement here is dm³ (Cubic Decimetres). 1 dm³ = 1 litre.

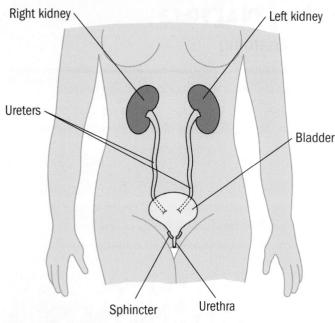

Right kidney
Left kidney
Ureters
Bladder
Sphincter
Urethra

**Fig 13.20:** The gross anatomy of the renal system

The bladder is connected to the exterior by the urethra, which is much longer in males than females. In males, the urethra just below the bladder is completely surrounded by the prostate gland. The urethra in males forms part of the penis.

## Associated blood supply

Two short renal arteries enter each kidney directly from the aorta and similarly two short renal veins come from each kidney to join the inferior vena cava. Each renal artery enters the kidney at the indented surface facing the aorta. This is known as the hilum of the kidney and it quickly breaks up into numerous smaller branches, which give off tributaries at right angles to supply each nephron with an afferent arteriole. Nephrons are the basic functional units of the kidney.

## Key terms

**Afferent arteriole** – The arteriole preceding the glomerulus.

**Bowman's capsule** – The cup-shaped beginning of a nephron.

**Glomerulus** – The tuft of capillaries located within the Bowman's capsule.

**Efferent arteriole** – The arteriole leaving the glomerulus.

The **afferent arteriole** breaks up into a tuft or knot of capillaries, closely pushed into the first cup-shaped beginning of each nephron, termed the **Bowman's capsule**. The knot of capillaries is called the **glomerulus**.

Emerging from the glomerulus is an **efferent arteriole**, which is narrower than the afferent arteriole. The efferent arteriole runs close to the tubules of the nephrons, breaking up into a separate network of capillaries around the tubules before re-uniting to form branches of the renal vein. As you will learn, this blood supply is of vital importance to kidney function.

## Physiological overview

The kidneys process blood by removing water, urea and excess mineral salts to provide a balance to enable the body to function efficiently.

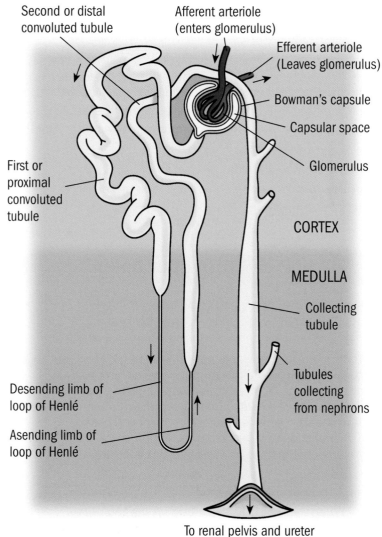

Second or distal convoluted tubule

Afferent arteriole (enters glomerulus)

Efferent arteriole (Leaves glomerulus)

Bowman's capsule

Capsular space

Glomerulus

First or proximal convoluted tubule

CORTEX

MEDULLA

Collecting tubule

Desending limb of loop of Henlé

Asending limb of loop of Henlé

Tubules collecting from nephrons

To renal pelvis and ureter

**Fig 13.21:** A nephron

The first part of each tubule is responsible for total re-absorption of glucose and amino acids and also for seven-eighths of the sodium and chloride reabsorption.

In performing these tasks, the kidneys regulate water, electrolytes and acid-base balance and eliminate the waste products of metabolism, such as:

- urea from surplus amino acids
- creatinine from creatine in muscle (this acts rather like ATP)
- uric acid from nucleic acids (all plant and animal cells comprising food have nuclei)
- the end products from the breakdown of haemoglobin (from old red blood cells).

Kidneys also remove unwanted chemicals from the blood – such as drugs, pesticides, food additives and toxins – and secrete hormones such as **erythropoietin**, which controls the production of red blood cells, and **renin**, which influences blood pressure.

### Urine production

The renal fluid undergoing modification as it passes along the nephrons' tubules is not called urine until the final changes are made in the last part of the tubule (see the next section). The filtrate enters the Bowman's capsule at a rate of 120 ml/min$^{-1}$* (ml per minute), but urine production averages only 1 ml/min$^{-1}$*, dripping into the pelvis (bowl) of the ureters, demonstrating the enormous changes that have happened in the tubules. Urine then moves down the ureters, partly by gravity and partly by peristalsis, to collect in the bladder.

### Composition of urine

The composition of a person's urine will vary, depending on their diet, intake of fluids, surrounding climate and degree of activity.

## Activity 12: Exercise and urine composition

Sweat produced during vigorous activity is a dilute salt solution. Explain how completing a 10 km run on a sunny day might change the composition of an athlete's urine for several hours afterwards.

You may find it useful to compare the average composition of urine and plasma in percentages. You can see these in the table below.

Table 13.3: Some principal components of plasma and urine

| Chemical | Plasma % | Urine % |
|----------|----------|---------|
| Water | 90–93 | 95 |
| Urea | 0.02 | 2 |
| Uric acid | 0.003 | 0.05 |
| Sodium | 0.3 | 0.6 |
| Chloride | 0.35 | 0.6 |
| Potassium | 0.02 | 0.15 |
| Phosphate | 0.003 | 0.15 |
| Ammonia | 0.0001 | 0.05 |

## Key terms

**Erythropoietin** – A hormone produced by the kidneys, which stimulates the production of red blood cells.

**Renin** – An enzyme released from the kidneys when blood pressure is low. It causes blood pressure to rise.

## Activity 11: Can you answer these?

Examine Table 13.3 (above), which shows the average percentage composition of plasma and urine. In pairs, answer the following questions:

1   Explain why there are no blood cells or plasma proteins listed in the table.
2   Explain why glucose and amino acids are not listed in the table.
3   Which substances are nitrogen-containing materials excreted from the body?
4   Calculate the concentrations of the following substances in urine:
- urea
- sodium.

*Please note that the scientifically correct unit of measurement here is dm$^3$ (Cubic Decimetres). 1 dm$^3$ = 1 litre.

### Storage of urine and micturition

Ureters enter a balloon-shaped muscular organ in the front of the pelvis called the bladder. The lower neck is guarded by a ring of muscle, which acts as a sphincter, relaxing to permit urine to be released when the bladder walls are stimulated by the pressure of a volume of urine. Urine is stored in the bladder for a period of time until the volume and pressure stimulate parasympathetic nervous impulses, causing the bladder muscle to contract and urine to be released. The technical term for the release of urine is micturition, although the word urination is commonly used.

# 4.4 Kidneys

Each kidney is bean-shaped and dark red in colour. The indented area faces the mid-line of the body and is known as the hilum. The ureter and renal vein emerge from the kidney, and the renal artery enters the kidney at the hilum. There is a capsule of membrane surrounding the kidney and each is topped by the conical adrenal gland. The kidneys and adrenal glands are surrounded by adipose tissue.

## Gross anatomy

When sectioned lengthways or longitudinally, the kidney shows an outer darker cortex and an inner paler medulla. The medulla is composed of a number of cone-shaped pyramids, with the tip of the cone projecting into the area where the ureter joins the kidney. This area is known as the pelvis of the kidney (pelvis means a bowl). Urine drips from the medullary pyramids into the pelvis.

The arterioles emerging from the branches of the renal artery tend to follow the border between the cortex and medulla, giving off smaller branches at right angles into the cortex to supply the million or so nephrons found in the kidney.

## Structure and functions of nephrons/kidney tubules

The nephron (see Figure 13.21) consists of a cup-shaped Bowman's capsule linked to a coiled tubule, which then runs into a hairpin-shaped section called the loop of Henlé, a second coiled tubule and then a straight collecting duct that empties at the conical tip of the pyramid. The coiled tubules and Bowman's capsule are located in the cortex but the loop of Henlé and collecting duct are chiefly located in the medulla. The blood vessels associated with the nephrons give the cortex its dark red colour.

The Bowman's capsule is made of two layers of simple squamous epithelium, with a small fluid-filled gap between them. The glomerulus is closely associated with the inner layer of the cup.

In fact, the inner layer of epithelial cells have been specially modified and have 'legs' with spaces in between for fluid to escape

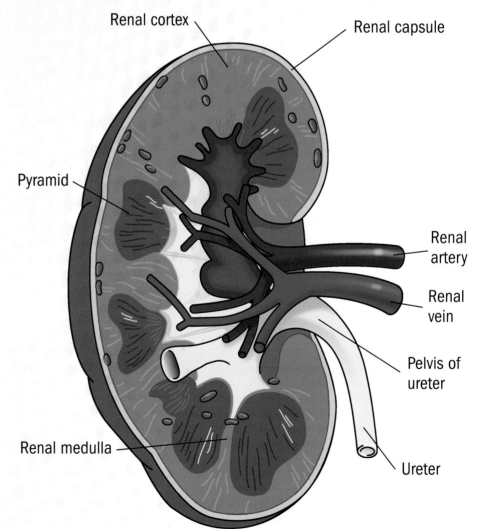

**Fig 13.22:** A longitudinal section through a kidney

## Did you know?

The glomerulus is a tuft or knot of capillaries. Capillaries have walls made of simple squamous epithelium. There are therefore only two flattened layers of cells separating the blood in the capillaries from the space in the Bowman's capsule. This is similar to the 'barrier' between dissolved gases in the alveoli of the lungs and the pulmonary capillaries. Clearly, when materials need to be transported, minimising thickness is vital.

through. The only barrier to the fluid is the basement membrane of the Bowman's capsule and the capillary wall, which you have learned is selectively permeable. These specially adapted cells are called podocytes and are visible with an electron microscope.

## Ultrafiltration

The afferent arteriole (see *Associated blood supply* on page 174) has a larger diameter than the efferent arteriole leaving the glomerulus. This contributes to high pressure in the glomerulus, as there is a 'traffic jam' of blood. Due to the shortness of the renal artery coming straight from the aorta, and this 'traffic jam', the blood in the glomerulus has a high pressure, which forces out fluid from the plasma. The fluid is a protein-free plasma filtrate – it contains no blood cells and no plasma proteins because they are too large to pass through the capillary/epithelial (podocyte) barrier.

## Did you know?

When glomeruli are damaged by very high blood pressure or an inflammatory disease process, the cells leak (plasma) protein, which passes into the filtrate and then into the urine. This is called proteinuria. Testing urine for protein is important, as it signals that glomerular damage has occurred. Protein in urine causes it to froth when passed (just as milk does when it is agitated). An experienced carer can tell that there is protein in urine because of the froth. Examining the appearance of urine is as important as using chemicals for testing.

## Selective reabsorption

You have learned that, on average, glomerular filtration rate (GFR) is 120 ml/min$^{-1}$* and urine formation is 1 ml/min$^{-1}$, so it is fairly clear that 119 ml/min$^{-1}$ must be reabsorbed along the renal tubule.

*Please note that the scientifically correct unit of measurement here is dm$^3$ (Cubic Decimetres). 1 dm$^3$ = 1 litre.

## Activity 13: Renal calculations

Cardiac output averages 5 litres or dm$^{-3}$* every minute and of this about 3 litres is plasma. Around 20 per cent of plasma in the capillaries is filtered as it passes once through the kidneys.

- Urine production averages 1 ml/min$^{-1}$. Calculate the volume passed in 24 hours and compare this with the average volume passed in water output (see page 171, fig 13.18).
- Calculate to the nearest whole number how many times the whole of the plasma is filtered every day.
- Explain how the figure obtained in question 1 is relevant to homeostasis of water.

The fluid is now known as glomerular filtrate or renal fluid. The average rate of glomerular filtration (GFR) is 120 ml/min$^{-1}$. The process is known as **ultrafiltration** because it takes place under high pressure. The pressure in the glomerular capillaries is 55 mmHg and this has to overcome:

- the filtrate pressure pushing outwards in the Bowman's capsule (15 mmHg)
- the osmotic pressure of the plasma proteins in the capillaries trying to draw fluid back into the bloodstream (30 mmHg)

so the net filtration pressure is 15 mmHg.

However, reabsorption is different for different substances, so it is called **selective reabsorption**. The first coiled part of the tubule (often referred to as the proximal convoluted tubule or PCT) is where the majority of reabsorption takes place into the capillary network surrounding the tubule. Here, seven-eighths of the water and sodium ions are reabsorbed. You will also recall that chloride ions tend to follow sodium so that returns as well. In addition, all the filtered glucose and amino acids are reabsorbed, so that there should be none of these molecules leaving in urine. It would be rather pointless to ingest food, and digest and absorb the

## Key terms

**Ultrafiltration** – The process driving a protein-free filtrate from plasma from the glomerulus.

**Selective reabsorption** – The process whereby some materials are reabsorbed back into the capillary network around the tubules but not others.

end products, only to have them leave in urine.

The glomerular filtrate is then significantly reduced by the time it reaches the entrance to the loop of Henlé.

### Activity 14: Just checking renal calculations

Some substances are reabsorbed in the proximal convoluted tubule (PCT). In pairs, answer the following questions:

1 Assuming that the dissolved products in glomerular filtrate have negligible volume, calculate the new volume of fluid entering the loop of Henlé.

2 Which nitrogen-containing compounds remain in the fluid after passing through the PCT?

3 Make a list of other substances remaining in the fluid.

4 What will happen to the concentration of substances not reabsorbed?

5 Why do the concentrations change?

You should also be aware that tubular cells can secrete certain substances from the plasma in the capillary network surrounding the tubule into the lumen of the tubule, the mechanism nearly always being by active

transport. This second process of materials entering the tubule (the first being glomerular filtration) is very useful in maintaining homeostasis. Common ions secreted are hydrogen and potassium ions, as well as creatinine. Many drugs are excreted in this way, such as penicillin. This process is called tubular secretion.

Under what circumstances might tubular secretion of hydrogen ions take place?

## Loop of Henlé and the counter-current mechanism

The two limbs of the hairpin-shaped loop of Henlé lie very close together in the medulla. The function of the loop was unknown for many years, although animals living in desert regions were known to possess very long loops and aquatic animals very short loops. It was concluded that the loop was concerned with water conservation. Later, it was discovered that the tissue fluid surrounding the loop was hyperosmotic (above normal osmolarity) and this was due to sodium ions. The mechanism works as follows:

- The tube is full of filtrate at normal osmolarity, say, arbitrarily 300.

- As this fluid rounds the bend of the loop and starts to climb up, sodium ions are passed from the ascending limb into the descending limb by active transport.

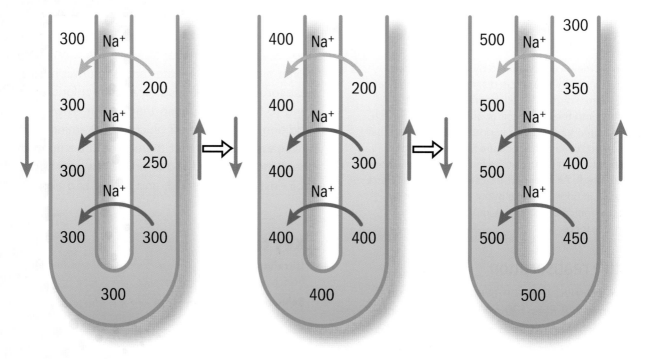

**Fig 13.23:** The counter-current mechanism

- The descending limb fluid now becomes 400 and the fluid leaving the loop becomes 200.
- As this fluid at 400 rounds the bend, more sodium ions are actively pumped across, making the descending limb now 500 and the ascending limb 300 and getting less as the end of the hairpin is achieved.
- The hyperosmotic fluid slowly diffuses into the tissue fluid surrounding the hairpin, but more sodium is actively pumped across to maintain the increased osmolarity.
- Eventually, the sodium ions will find their way back into the blood but the sodium ions keep on coming to maintain the high osmolarity.

This is known as the **counter-current mechanism**.

## Did you know?

The limbs of the loop of Henlé are not the only structures in the medulla – the last part of the tubules known as the collecting ducts are tightly packed in the medulla as well.

The purpose of this hyperosmotic region is to attract water molecules from the filtrate in the collecting ducts, but this only happens under the influence of a hormone. When water molecules are drawn across by osmosis into the tissue fluid and finally the blood, the urine will be more concentrated.

# Principles of osmoregulation, the role of the hypothalamus and anti-diuretic hormone

Osmoregulation is one process involved in homeostasis and it means 'controlling the osmotic potential of the blood'. In simple terms, osmoregulation ensures that the blood is at the right concentration. When blood becomes too concentrated, water is conserved until the correct concentration is restored. Less water is passed in urine, so it becomes more concentrated. When blood is too dilute, more water is passed in urine until the blood concentration is restored. This causes more dilute urine to be passed. A hormone is responsible for this phenomenon.

The hypothalamus in the brain lies just above the pituitary gland and contains modified neurones called **osmoreceptors**, which monitor the concentration of the adjacent blood. When blood is too concentrated, the osmoreceptors stimulate the posterior part of the pituitary gland to secrete a hormone called **antidiuretic hormone (ADH)**. ADH causes the cells of the distal convoluted tubule (DCT) and collecting tubules to become more permeable to water. As the collecting tubule passes through the hyperosmotic area in the medulla, water passes out by osmosis into the tissue fluid and the blood. When the osmoreceptors are not stimulated because blood is too dilute, little ADH is secreted and the tubules behave as if they are waterproofed and water passes onwards into the urine.

ADH secretion will be high in a hot climate where water is being lost as sweat to cool the skin. ADH will be low when an individual has been drinking a lot of fluid and not sweating.

Overall, volumes of urine are lower in the summer months than in the winter months.

## Activity 15: Diuretics

Some prescribed drugs can cause more urine to be produced. Patients often call these 'water' tablets. An increased flow of urine is known as diuresis. Water tablets are called diuretics.

Carry out a thought shower with your peers and consider which conditions may require a patient to need water removing from the bloodstream via urine.

## Key terms

**Counter-current mechanism** – A process involving active transport of sodium ions from the descending limb of the loop of Henlé to the ascending limb.

**Osmoreceptors** – Modified neurones sensitive to the osmotic pressure of blood.

**Antidiuretic hormone (ADH)** – A pituitary hormone causing tubular cells to become more permeable to water.

# 4.5 Dysfunctions in relation to water balance

Physiological problems arise when the balance between water intake and water output is disturbed and some of these are discussed below.

## Oedema

This is when too much fluid accumulates in the body tissues. It may be visible or not. Doctors will look for **oedema** either in the ankles, if a patient can walk about, or at the base of the spine if the patient is in bed. Until there is about 15 per cent extra fluid, the only sign would be an increase in weight. After that, when a doctor presses their thumb into the swollen tissues, an indentation appears, which takes some time to disappear. This is known as pitting oedema.

Heart failure can cause oedema because the heart is unable to drive blood onwards effectively and the pressure builds up in the congested veins. This results in a higher capillary pressure, which becomes greater than the osmotic pressure of the plasma proteins trying to return tissue fluid to the blood. Consequently, there is an accumulation of tissue fluid.

In renal failure, the kidneys cannot excrete enough sodium chloride from the body and it accumulates in tissue fluids. Sodium chloride attracts water to it and so there is a build-up in tissue fluid and oedema. In kidney disease, where there is damage to glomerular capillaries, protein is lost in the urine. This means that the plasma protein content of blood is lower than normal, so the osmotic pressure attracting fluid back to the bloodstream is low and oedema results. Any condition lowering the osmotic pressure of the plasma proteins in the blood can lead to oedema – for example, malnutrition, alcoholism or cirrhosis of the liver. Similarly, any condition involving salt retention in the tissues will also result in water accumulation (e.g. cirrhosis of the liver).

## Kidney failure

The kidneys have a reduced ability to excrete water, salts, urea, creatinine and uric acid from the blood in the condition generally known as kidney failure or chronic renal failure. This can lead to a multiplicity of problems such as disturbed water and acid-base balances, urea accumulation (uraemia), proteinuria, hypertension, anaemia, oedema and chemical disturbances in the blood.

Acute kidney failure can arise as a consequence of physiological shock such as severe injuries, haemorrhage or burns and even a heart attack. Chronic renal failure develops more slowly, arising from long-standing hypertension, diabetes, kidney defects, kidney stones and any condition that obstructs the flow of urine for a long time, such as prostatic enlargement. The number of nephrons also decreases with age. For example, at the age of 20 there are about 700,000 nephrons functioning but by 60 years of age the figure has dropped to around 250,000 in each kidney. At birth, there are a million nephrons in each kidney.

Chronic renal failure is a life-threatening disease and without treatment, coma and death will follow.

## Case study: Dai

Dai had a severe heart attack, which was thought to be the result of smoking and stress in his job as a professional football coach. He has had a bypass operation, to replace part of his right coronary artery, to open it up so more blood can flow through it. However, the cardiac muscle is permanently damaged and he has developed right-sided heart failure. Dai's legs and feet are very swollen and he has trouble breathing. He is being treated with drugs to strengthen and regulate his heartbeat and diuretics, which increase the output of urine from his kidneys.

1 What you think is meant by right-sided heart failure?

2 Can you explain the relationship between heart failure and swollen legs and feet?

3 From your knowledge of osmoregulation, suggest how and why diuretics might make Dai more comfortable.

No two kidney patients are on exactly the same medication regime, although there will be many similarities. Most will be on diuretics and antihypertensive drugs to increase urinary output and reduce blood pressure. Drugs to correct blood chemistry will depend on the specific disturbance and most will be on a particular diet regime. This will have common features such as:

- high carbohydrate for energy
- low protein to reduce the workload of the kidneys in excreting urea
- no added salt and special cooking methods to remove excess potassium
- limited fluid input to achieve a balance with output.

Inevitably, there is progress towards what is called 'end-stage renal failure' when dialysis or a kidney transplant becomes necessary.

Signs and symptoms might include:

- decreased urine production
- fatigue
- anaemia
- weakness and loss of weight
- nausea, vomiting and loss of appetite.

## Renal dialysis

There are two main types of dialysis – **haemodialysis** and **continuous ambulatory peritoneal dialysis (CAPD)**. Haemodialysis involves attaching a person to a kidney machine for at least four hours a day, three or four times a week. The person requires a **fistula** operation several months beforehand – usually in the arm. A fistula is an artificial connection between an artery and a vein, into which the needle attachment to the kidney machine is made. Multiple layers of special membrane material separate the person's blood from dialysing fluid in the kidney machine.

Any substance (waste products, toxic materials and excess water) needing to be removed from the blood is in low or zero concentration in dialysate so the substance passes across by diffusion and osmosis. Any substance not requiring elimination can be kept at a high concentration in the dialysate. The dialysate runs to waste and the 'cleaned' blood is returned to the person.

CAPD uses the inner lining or peritoneum of the abdomen as the dialysing membrane and the dialysate is introduced through a special tap and catheter. The process takes about one hour to complete (twice a day), i.e. to empty the old dialysate and introduce the fresh. The person may walk about with the dialysate inside (hence the use of the word 'ambulatory') and carry on with work. Although peritoneal dialysis can take place in hospital, most patients carry out CAPD at home and work.

### Reflect

Many hundreds of people are waiting for organ transplants to relieve their medical conditions. Many will die before they receive the vital organ. Research the British organ donation system and consider whether you will carry a donor card in future (many individuals do not).

Conversely a few clients have home kidney machines but most haemodialyse in hospital. Smaller portable dialysis kits have been invented but, as yet, these are not widely available and are costly.

Patients can be dialysing successfully for many years. However, the procedure is very expensive and kidney machines are in short supply. The semi-permanent answer is transplantation. Although the surgery and after-care are expensive, this is nowhere near the cost of many years of dialysis. Unfortunately there is also a problem with kidney donations, as these are in short supply.

### Key terms

**Oedema** – The accumulation of tissue fluid around the body cells.

**Haemodialysis** – The removal of metabolic waste products from the blood via a kidney machine because the kidneys are seriously damaged.

**Continuous ambulatory peritoneal dialysis (CAPD)** – A different form of dialysis carried out by running dialysing fluid into the peritoneal cavity of the abdomen for several hours and then running the fluid to waste and replacing with 'clean' dialysate.

**Fistula** – An artificial connection made between an artery and a vein for attachment to a kidney machine.

# Sarah McGough
**A dialysis nurse**

Sarah works on the haemodialysis unit of a large teaching hospital. Patients are mainly out-patients who have been allocated certain time slots on specific days of the week. The only day that the unit is not open is Sunday.

There is also an emergency dialysis ward in the hospital, which is open every day, 24 hours a day. As dialysis patients have many other problems, they often have to be in-patients and Sarah will see her patients off the wards as well.

After greeting the patient, Sarah will make the connection between the fistula and the kidney machine. This can be quite difficult, as the patient has so many needles that the veins will scar. During dialysis, the patient can have something to eat and drink – usually a sandwich and a cup of tea. Any problems can be sorted out and frequently Sarah will need to find a doctor – probably to change medication or admit the patient if they are poorly.

Sarah has to chart many figures shown by the machine and keep careful records. After dialysis is finished, the machine and bed must be cleaned and the small wound in the fistula is dressed. The next patient is usually waiting and the process begins again.

## Think about it!

1 Explain what is meant by a fistula.
2 Name two other problems common in renal patients.
3 Explain why Sarah often has to deal with emotional problems as well as renal problems.
4 Why is it important to keep careful records and charts in this unit?
5 Why is it important to clean kidney machines and bedding each time?

## Transplantation

In the UK, most transplant organs are only available from recently deceased people or close relatives.

The composition of the recipient individual's antigenic make-up is determined by means of blood tests and matched to a donor's make-up so that they are as closely matched as possible. This process is called **tissue-typing**.

Failing kidneys are usually left in place and the new kidney placed in the pelvis (groin area) and connected to the bladder by the donor's ureter. The donor blood vessels are connected to branches of the lower aorta and vena cava.

The client begins **immuno-suppressant** medication to prevent rejection and monitoring is carried out by urinalysis, blood tests and ultrasound scanning. The chief danger of rejection is in the first few months after the transplant.

More than 80 per cent of transplants are successful, enabling the client to live a normal life for many years while continuing on immuno-suppression.

Transplant organs age faster than normal body organs and, while some transplants may last for over 30 years, many also fail within the recipient's lifetime. This means that the individual would have to return to dialysis and the long wait for a repeat transplant. Individuals are tissue-typed and placed on a transplant waiting list. The potential recipient must be in reasonably good health to withstand surgery and not have any other untreatable life-threatening conditions.

Frequently, two kidneys become available for donations and this benefits two people, as only one kidney is transplanted at a time in an individual.

### Key terms

**Tissue-typing** – Identifying the protein markers on cell membranes to determine compatibility for transplantation.

**Immuno-suppressant** – Specific types of medication to suppress or reduce the immune response. Given to prevent rejection.

## Case study: Michael

Michael had moderately high blood pressure for years until it suddenly went dangerously high. He had been in the Far East while serving in the army and contracted malaria and other tropical diseases during his tour of duty. His GP referred him to a renal team at a teaching hospital.

Six months later, Michael had an operation to make a fistula in his arm, ready for haemodialysis when the team decided this was necessary. Meanwhile, Michael had medication to reduce his blood pressure but the damage to his kidneys was not reversible, due to long-term hypertension and the tropical infections.

About a year later, dialysis began for four hours, three times each week. Michael had to give up work, as he was often feeling weak after the treatment. Four years later he received a successful transplant and his health slowly improved. The transplanted kidney lasted 11 years and then slowly the old problems returned, meaning Michael had to return to dialysis.

The emotional effects of this were intense, as Michael knew his health had deteriorated again and he was unlikely to get another transplant, as he was now over 70 years old.

1 Why is a fistula operation necessary?

2 Explain how haemodialysis works.

3 Suggest why Michael's transplant failed after 11 years.

4 Why is Michael depressed about returning to haemodialysis?

## Assessment activity 13.4

P4 P5 M3 D2 · BTEC

Write a report on homeostasis and the renal system, in which you:

1  Explain the role of the kidney in the homeostatic control of water balance.

2  Briefly outline the main signs and symptoms of two or three medical problems concerned with water balance. Use three examples to explain each problem, or dysfunction, in relation to water balance and the possible treatments for each. Use physiological terminology in your explanation. Dysfunction means systems that are not doing their normal job, so renal dysfunction means when kidneys are behaving abnormally.

3  Discuss dysfunction by considering possible problems that may arise and how these might be overcome. You should consider possible ways in which water balance may be affected and the difficulties that may be associated with possible treatments.

4  Analyse the impact on the human body of dysfunctions in relation to water balance. What problems do people have when they cannot regulate their water input and output? How will you interpret the impact of an imbalance of water on the human body?

### Grading tips

P4  For this criterion, you need to give an explanation relating just to the kidney. This means that you are stating simply what happens in detail, referring to the whole organ and its control of water.

P5  For the second part of your report, you might choose as your examples food poisoning or viral diarrhoea in wards or nursing homes catering for babies and elderly people, as

these groups can become very seriously ill. Alternatively, you could research the effect of drought/starvation on people in Africa, looking at dehydration or kidney failure and the possible treatments.

M3  For an analysis, you will need to consider a range of different ways in which dysfunction can affect individuals, for example oedema and kidney failure or the alternatives mentioned above, and explain why water balance is disturbed and the possibility of short- or long-term disturbance. You must remember that a short-term dysfunction in vulnerable clients can still be life-threatening without treatment. Possible treatments will include rehydration methods, maintenance medication or different forms of dialysis and transplantation. If you are able to use short case studies to illustrate your work, that will be impressive. Try to visit a dialysis unit or ask a renal dialysis nurse to visit your class as a speaker.

D2  For the fourth part of your report, case studies will really help you, or you could invite a speaker who has renal problems or experience on a renal unit. You could discuss the implications of dietary restrictions including fluids, the social and emotional problems arising from dialysing, anaemia in kidney disease, the effects of being immuno-suppressed, the problems with iron build-up from treatment to combat anaemia, etc. Analysing these problems will mean providing reasons why these problems arise. Websites will also provide information on kidney diseases.

### PLTS

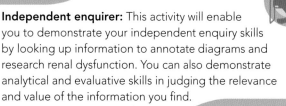

**Independent enquirer:** This activity will enable you to demonstrate your independent enquiry skills by looking up information to annotate diagrams and research renal dysfunction. You can also demonstrate analytical and evaluative skills in judging the relevance and value of the information you find.

### Functional skills

**English:** You can show your English skills by producing annotated diagrams and bringing together and organising images and text, producing written work that has been proof-read, and communicating ideas in a concise, clear and logical manner.

# Resources and further reading

Adds, J. *et al* (2003) *Molecules and Cells* Cheltenham: Nelson Thornes

Ashurst, S. *et al* (1995) *HAL Physiology* Churchill Livingstone

Baker, M. *et al* (2001) *Further Studies in Human Biology* (AQA) London: Hodder Murray

Boyle, M. *et al* (2002) *Human Biology* London: Collins Educational

Clancy, J. & McVicar, A. (2002) *Physiology and Anatomy* Hodder Arnold

Givens, P. & Reiss, M. (2002) *Human Biology and Health Studies* Cheltenham: Nelson Thornes

Indge, B. *et al* (2000) *A New Introduction to Human Biology* (AQA) London: Hodder Murray

Jones, M. & Jones, G. (2004) *Human Biology for AS Level* Cambridge: Cambridge University Press

Moonie, N. *et al* (2000) *Advanced Health and Social Care* Oxford: Heinemann

Myers, B. (2004) *The Natural Sciences* Cheltenham: Nelson Thornes

Pickering, W.R. (2001) *Advanced Human Biology through Diagrams* Oxford: Oxford University Press

Saffrey, J. *et al* (1972) *Maintaining the Whole* Milton Keynes: Open University

Stretch, B. & Whitehouse, M. (2010) *BTEC National Health and Social Care Book 1* Harlow: Pearson Education Ltd

Vander, A.J. *et al* (2003) *Human Physiology: The Mechanisms of Body Function* London: McGraw Hill

Ward, J. *et al* (2005) *Physiology at a Glance* Oxford: Blackwell

Wright, D. (2000) *Human Physiology and Health for GCSE* Oxford: Heinemann

## Journals

*Nursing Times* (and similar for case studies)

*New Scientist*

*Biological Scientist*

## Useful websites

BBC www.bbc.co.uk/science/humanbody

British Heart Foundation www.bhf.org.uk

NetDoctor www.netdoctor.co.uk

NHS Direct www.nhsdirect.nhs.uk

Surgery Door www.surgerydoor.co.uk

# Just checking

1 Explain the structural and functional differences between rough and smooth endoplasmic reticula.
2 What is meant by the term transcription?
3 How does transcription differ from translation?
4 Explain the terms active transport and facilitated diffusion.
5 Distinguish between intracellular fluid and intercellular fluid.
6 What are the components of a buffer system? Give one example of a buffer system.
7 Explain the pH scale.
8 What is a polar molecule and how is this relevant to the phospholipid bilayer?
9 Explain how anti-diuretic hormone may be important in an endurance race such as a marathon.
10 Explain why fluid and dietary restrictions are important in a patient undergoing dialysis.

edexcel :::

# Assignment tips

1 The unit will be internally assessed by your tutor and you can use illustrations carefully labelled and/or annotated where this will make the information clear and precise for your readers.

2 Any downloaded illustrations must be modified or adapted by you to become your unique work.

3 Where you have carried out primary research by interviewing individuals, remember to ensure confidentiality by changing names of individuals and establishments and obtain their permission beforehand.

4 Primary research is an important way of gathering information, particularly for P5, M3 and D2. You should consider how you will gather your information by careful planning before you visit an individual or establishment.

5 A questionnaire might be a useful tool for you but remember if the interview takes place during working hours with an appropriate health professional, they will not have the time to complete a lengthy questionnaire and verbal questions may be more appropriate.

6 If several students visit in a group, then plan together what you need to find out and share the questions. Select someone as a scribe to note the responses. You should acknowledge any research information that you obtain.

# 14 Physiological disorders

this unit, you will be able to apply your understanding of physiology to the
perience of individuals affected by physiological disorders. You will look at
w diseases are caused, diagnosed and treated. Understanding how individuals
ected by your chosen disorders are cared for by professionals, friends and family
undamental to the caring process.

will need to choose two physiological disorders and produce two leaflets to support the families
carers of individuals with the chosen disorders. You will research and explain their physiology
the processes involved in reaching a diagnosis. You will also investigate the roles of professional
support personnel and of informal carers involved in all aspects of the diagnosis, treatment and
of the individuals. Finally, you will conduct some secondary research to explore the possible
re progression of each disease.

unit will be valuable for anyone aiming to progress to professional training in the health and
ial care professions and those allied to health professions. Needs-based care planning and
port will form important parts of the unit investigations. There are strong links with several other
ts in the programme, including Unit 5 (Fundamentals of anatomy and physiology) and Unit 13
siology of fluid balance).

## Learning outcomes

After completing this unit you should:

1 understand the nature of physiological disorders
2 know the processes involved in the diagnosis of physiological disorders
3 be able to produce a care pathway for physiological disorders
4 understand the strategies used to support individuals with physiological disorders.

# Assessment and grading criteria

This table shows you what you must do in order to achieve a **pass**, **merit** or **distinction** grade, a where you can find activities in this book to help you.

| To achieve a pass grade, the evidence must show that you are able to: | To achieve a merit grade, the evidence must show that, in addition to the pass criteria, you are able to: | To achieve a distinction grade, the evidence must show that, in addition to the pass and merit criteria, you are able to: |
|---|---|---|
| **P1** Explain the nature of two named physiological disorders. **See Assessment activity 14.1, page 198** | **M1** Assess possible difficulties involved in the diagnosis of the disorders from their signs and symptoms. **See Assessment activity 14.2, page 204** | |
| **P2** Explain the signs and symptoms related to two named physiological disorders. **See Assessment activity 14.1, page 198** | | |
| **P3** Describe the investigations that are carried out to enable the diagnosis of these physiological disorders. **See Assessment activity 14.2, page 204** | | |
| **P4** Plan a care pathway for each physiological disorder including the roles of relevant practitioners. **See Assessment activity 14.3, page 216** | **M2** Discuss how the practitioners and agencies involved in the care pathways work together to provide the care needed for both physiological disorders. **See Assessment activity 14.3, page 216** | **D1** Evaluate the effectiveness of health and social care practitioners and agencies working together to deliver the care pathway for one of the chosen physiological disorders **See Assessment activity 14.3, page 216** |
| **P5** Explain the care strategies that can be used to support individuals with each of the physiological disorders. **See Assessment activity 14.3, page 216** | **M3** Discuss the care strategies that can be used to support individuals with each of the physiological disorders. **See Assessment activity 14.3, page 216** | **D2** Evaluate the care strategies that can be used to support an individual with one of the chosen physiological disorders. **See Assessment activity 14.3, page 216** |

# How you will be assessed

This unit will be internally assessed by your tutors and will probably consist of two assignments, which might be in the form of leaflets on dissimilar physiological disorders. The reports should be quite separate.

You need to demonstrate that you meet all the learning outcomes for the unit. The criteria for a pass grade set the level of achievement to pass the unit. To achieve a merit, you must also meet the merit learning outcomes and, to achieve a distinction, every pass, merit and distinction learning outcome must be demonstrated in your unit evidence.

## Trish, 17 years old

I panicked a bit when we researched the disorders that were appropriate. How on earth was I going to make the right choices and where would I be able to get all the information I needed? I was talking about it to my Mum and she reminded me that my Nan had Alzheimer's disease and I could ask her if she minded me writing about her. Nan is in a nursing home, as she can't look after herself any more. I felt a bit guilty because I knew after I had asked her, she wouldn't remember it again; Mum said that as long as I changed all the names so that no one could recognise her or the setting it would be all right. That was one sorted out! My father goes for regular blood sugar tests. He isn't diabetic but the GP says he is 'borderline' so I thought that would be good to do, as I will know more about it.

I decided to use Nan as the main disorder because I need to try and get a distinction. The hardest part was the evaluations because if you are not there all the time, it is difficult to know the strengths and weaknesses and because of my Nan's disorder she couldn't tell me anything useful. In the end, I used my eyes and ears and interviewed other clients and some of the staff. Diabetes was tricky and had to be done by research mostly although we had a diabetic nurse who came and talked to us in class. I was pleased with my assignment when it was finished – the difficult part turned out be getting two disorders done on time.

### Over to you!

1  What do you need to consider when making your final choices of physiological disorders?

2  How will you present your work – as a leaflet or report? The quantity of information may be a factor.

3  Will you work on both disorders at the same time or complete the first one before starting the second? Good record-keeping will be essential for the first option.

# 1    Understand the nature of physiological disorders

### Planning your first case study

Which disorder will you choose for your first case study? You will need to think about both the type of disorder and the individual. If you choose a disorder that a friend or family member has, and you aim to use primary research to help you, then you might need to spend significant time with your individual. Get together in small groups and bounce ideas around. How will you manage to get your information? Can you ask a care professional to visit your class?

You will need to consider confidentiality at all times, so never include photographs, copies of clinical reports and images such as x-ray films and scans.

How will you show sensitivity to the feelings of people living with the disorder? Bear in mind that the disorder won't go away once you have finished your case study.

## 1.1 Physiological disorders, as appropriate

You can study disorders other than those in the following list but you must check your choice with your tutor:

- diabetes (type 1 insulin dependent or type 2 non-insulin dependent)
- coronary heart disease
- stroke (cerebral haemorrhage, cerebral thrombosis or cerebral infarction)
- hypertension
- Parkinson's disease
- Alzheimer's disease
- motor neurone disease
- multiple sclerosis (MS)
- rheumatoid arthritis
- osteoporosis
- Crohn's disease
- inflammatory bowel syndrome (IBS)
- cancer – lung, bowel, skin, breast, prostate gland, liver
- leukaemia
- deficiency diseases.

## Activity 1: Where do we begin?

In groups of three or four, choose two disorders each and using primary (if possible) and secondary research prepare a short presentation lasting about ten minutes. You can include statistical information to enhance the presentation.

Give your presentation either to your own group or to a whole class.

When you have heard the presentations, decide which two you will investigate for your assignment. Can you obtain information from an individual as a primary source? This should inform your decision.

Discuss your decisions, with reasons, with your tutor.

### Functional skills

**ICT:** This activity requires you to select, interact with and use ICT systems independently for a complex task to meet a variety of needs by accessing appropriate websites for research on physiological disorders.

### PLTS

**Independent enquirer:** You can show your independent enquiry skills by planning which disorders to investigate, and carrying out research.

# 1.2 Nature of the disorder

## Causes of the disorder

The causes can be varied and may not be clearly defined, as in Alzheimer's disease or multiple sclerosis. The disorders may be genetically inherited from either a dominant **allele** or two recessive alleles, in which case there may be a clear family history. Other diseases may not be a clear case of inheriting faulty alleles but the condition may 'run in the family', indicating that there is a susceptibility to the condition which – under certain circumstances – may result in the development of the disease, such as breast cancer or diabetes.

Lifestyle may be an important cause of the disease, although it is often linked to other factors as well – coronary heart disease, stroke, melanoma, liver and lung cancer fit into this type. Some disorders fall into a category known as **auto-immune disorders**, where the individual's body is believed to produce antibodies that attack particular tissues in their bodies because they are not recognising them as 'self' and treating them as foreign cells that need to be destroyed. Rheumatoid arthritis and multiple sclerosis are believed to be auto-immune disorders. Diabetes mellitus type 1 is also considered to be an auto-immune disorder, which may have been triggered by a specific viral infection to which the individual has an inherited vulnerability. Type 2 is often related to being overweight and having a resistance to insulin.

Leukaemia and other cancers arise from abnormal cells that multiply rapidly and destroy normal cells. Inflammatory bowel disease is thought to be an undue sensitivity of the bowel muscles to food, anxiety, stress, etc. The causes of disorders then are often multiple, varied and not transparent.

## Changes to the relevant physiology of the body systems as a result of the disorder

You will need to write about the body systems affected by the disorder. There may be more than one – in fact there may be several systems involved with a complex disorder. However, you will only be required to identify and explain the major systems affected.

In diabetes, for example, this would include the endocrine and digestive systems (the role of pancreas, liver and carbohydrate digestion). At some stage, you might have to discuss how diabetes affects the cardiovascular and nervous systems but you would only need to describe the organs and tissues that are involved.

Table 14.1 on page 192 summarises the major systems involved in all the physiological disorders listed in the specification and reproduced on page 190.

As you progress with the requirements of this unit, you will follow a case study of Joe, who has Parkinson's disease. This should help you determine how to set out and research your own chosen disorders and prepare your leaflets.

## Key terms

**Allele** – Unit of inheritance derived from one or two parents; an allele can be thought of as half a gene.

**Auto-immune disorder** – A disorder in which an individual produces antibodies that attack specific tissues in the body.

## Activity 2: Primary research

You need to be aware of ethical issues and respect the confidentiality of all information supplied to you for the purpose of writing your two reports.

Compile a short leaflet demonstrating how you will manage ethical issues and confidentiality. Discuss the leaflet with any individual you might use in your primary research and note any concerns they may have. Even when an individual expresses a lack of concern about confidentiality, remember you still have an ethical duty to preserve it.

**Table 14.1:** Disorders and the major body systems involved

| Disorder | Major body systems involved |
| --- | --- |
| Diabetes | Endocrine and digestive systems |
| Coronary heart disease | Cardiovascular and respiratory systems |
| Stroke | Cardiovascular and nervous systems |
| Hypertension | Cardiovascular and renal systems |
| Parkinson's disease | Nervous and musculo-skeletal systems |
| Alzheimer's disease | Nervous system |
| Motor neurone disease | Nervous and musculo-skeletal systems |
| Multiple sclerosis (MS) | Nervous and musculo-skeletal systems |
| Rheumatoid arthritis | Musculo-skeletal system |
| Osteoporosis | Musculo-skeletal system |
| Crohn's disease | Digestive system |
| Deficiency diseases | Digestive system, cardiovascular system |
| Inflammatory bowel disease (IBS) | Digestive system |
| Cancer | Cardiovascular – leukaemia<br>Respiratory system – lung<br>Digestive system – bowel<br>Skin<br>Reproductive system – breast<br>Reproductive system – prostate |

## Case study: Joe

Joe suffers from Parkinson's disease. The major body system involved is the nervous system, although other systems (such as the musculo-skeletal system) become involved.

1  Describe the body system involved in Parkinson's disease.

2  Using secondary research, investigate the physiological changes caused by Parkinson's disease.

3  Research probable causes of Parkinson's disease.

You will find it helpful to revise the appropriate body system by returning to Book 1, Unit 5.

## Functional skills

**ICT:** Access, search for, select and use ICT-based information and evaluate its fitness for purpose when accessing different websites for information on Parkinson's disease.

## Did you know?

Road traffic accidents used to be a major cause of death in Parkinson's disease (due to skeletal rigidity, shuffling gait and head fixed downwards) before new medication reduced these symptoms.

# Changes to overall body functions

After investigating how the physiology of the body system has changed as a result of the disorder, you will have to engage in a discussion of how body systems have changed overall. For example, individuals with diabetes often get tired very easily and are prone to repeated infections. Their eyesight may deteriorate, particularly in type 2, with vascular changes in the retina or the beginnings of cataract formation. Individuals with MS find that stress, heat and tiredness worsen their symptoms and they have a tendency to forget things and find it difficult to focus on a task for a long time. You will discover these extra changes from your primary and secondary research.

For example, if you are investigating breast cancer, you will need to identify and explain how the macroscopic structure of the breast might change. The breast might be enlarged, swollen or distorted. The skin overlying the breast might appear dimpled (this is called peau d'orange because it resembles the skin of an orange). The nipple might become inverted (sunken) or there could be a bloody discharge from the nipple ducts. You would then go on to explain the microscopic changes usually revealed as a result of a needle biopsy or lumpectomy. The pathologist looks for evidence of abnormal cells.

Another example, motor neurone disease, might show **muscle wasting** macroscopically and degeneration of nerve fibres and muscle fibres microscopically.

As well as structural changes, there are also likely to be physiological changes resulting from the disorder. For example, in motor neurone disease, there is muscle weakness, commonly beginning in the hands or the legs. Other physiological disturbances are cramps, unusual stiffness or irregular, spontaneous contractions of areas of muscle. In a stroke, caused by an interrupted flow of blood to part of the brain or bleeding in the brain, there can be weakness or paralysis of one side of the body, slurred speech, visual disturbance, difficulty in swallowing, confusion and headaches. With a stroke, the effects depend on which particular part of the brain is affected.

## Case study: Joe

Joe had suffered from mild depression for many years and his doctor had prescribed medication from time to time to lift his mood. Several weeks ago he saw his doctor on a routine visit and his GP noticed that Joe's hand was trembling when he was just resting. This is known as a tremor. The GP also felt that Joe had slowed down considerably in his movements and speech. Joe was referred to a specialist in nervous disorders (a neurologist). Among other tests, Joe had a CT scan of his brain to examine its condition and check that there were no other causes of the tremor. The CT scan showed nothing of significance.

1 Explain the purpose of tests such as a CT scan or MRI (magnetic resonance imaging) using secondary research.

2 Find three other disorders where these tests are useful.

3 Assess the value of CT scans and MRIs.

4 Research the physiological changes in Parkinson's disease.

## PLTS

**Creative thinker:** You can demonstrate your creative thinking abilities by asking questions about Parkinson's disease and connecting other ideas and experiences.

## Functional skills

**ICT:** You can show your ICT skills by following and understanding the need for safety and security practices when accessing appropriate websites.

## Key term

**Muscle wasting** – Observable diminishing muscle mass.

# Physiological changes due to treatments for the disorder

Treatment can cause both structural and physiological changes too. Nearly all invasive procedures will inevitably cause some structural damage. Invasive procedures involve cutting or piercing the skin or inserting instruments or material into the body. **Needle biopsies**, injections and blood transfusions are examples of invasive techniques. Physiotherapy after injuries such as fractures, or in conditions like arthritis or the early stages of motor neurone disease, can reduce joint stiffness, retrain muscles after a stroke, reduce muscle spasms and minimise pain and inflammation. Clinical drugs can restore blood chemistry, as insulin does in diabetes, hormones do in endocrine disorders and iron supplements in anaemia.

The range of treatment for disorders is vast and you will need to explain how the treatment and the disorder affect the physiology of the body for your chosen disorders.

Parkinson's disease involves a reduction in muscle control due to a lowered level of a chemical known as a neurotransmitter, which enables nervous impulses to pass across junctions between nerve endings and muscle. This chemical transmitter is called dopamine and it is reduced in Parkinson's disease. One possible form of medical treatment is to prescribe drugs that increase the level of dopamine. This affects physiology by restoring the balance of neurotransmitters. Unfortunately, using one drug has a limited effect time-wise but other drugs can then be substituted. It is important to note that only limited information is given here so that any learner choosing Parkinson's disease will still need to carry out more extensive research.

Many of the disorders you will study are long-term, non-communicable (not infectious) disorders with limited treatment and management. Some might be curable in the accepted sense, such as breast cancer or coronary heart disease, but many will get progressively worse, such as Alzheimer's and Parkinson's diseases.

Disorders like these can have psychological effects as well as physiological effects and most of these will be negative effects such as bouts of **depression** and anxiety. Individuals who have these disorders will naturally be concerned for themselves but also for their family and especially their dependants. Physiological changes resulting from treatment of side effects may also be considered.

Pain is often associated with worry, depression and fear of the unknown. When a diagnosis has been made, the perception of pain and its effects is often less, especially if the sufferer can be reassured. Individuals have very different **pain thresholds**, especially if they have been incapacitated or ill for a long time and are 'used' to the pain experience.

In a few disorders, such as multiple sclerosis, the individual may have periods of intense or exaggerated well-being (for no apparent reason) interspersed with periods of depression. This state of exaggerated well-being is known as **euphoria**.

## Did you know?

It is common to feel tiredness and weakness – for example, after influenza or food poisoning. Glandular fever and chronic fatigue syndrome (which used to be called ME) are examples of conditions where tiredness and fatigue are often excessive.

## Activity 3: Depression

Research the effects of depression and compare them with how you felt after your last illness. Depression has more signs and symptoms than a temporary feeling of unhappiness.

## Key terms

**Needle biopsy** – This is when a fine needle is inserted into a lump or organ to remove material for microscopic examination. Needles may have cutting tips to remove small sections of tissue or have a hollow stem for removing fluid (containing cells). The material is prepared for microscopic examination. The search is for abnormal cells that might be enlarged, peculiarly shaped or have actively dividing nuclei.

**Depression** – Extreme sadness or melancholy. Reactive depression occurs as a result of illness. Some types of depression have no known cause.

**Pain threshold** – The level at which the agony becomes unbearable. Individuals have different pain thresholds and the levels can be affected by past experiences of pain.

**Euphoria** – An inflated sense of well-being when circumstances do not warrant it.

# Influences on the development of the disorder

After a disorder has been diagnosed, the cause may or may not be apparent. In most cases of the types of disorders you may be studying, the causes will not be transparent but there may be underlying factors or influences that have played some part.

Some of these factors are discussed below.

## Inherited traits

As knowledge and understanding of inheritance grows, we become aware that many disorders such as cystic fibrosis, phenylketonuria (PKU) and Down's syndrome are inherited from one or both parents or that a mutation of a gene or chromosome has occurred at or before conception. Other medical conditions are not openly inherited in this way but research has shown that they tend to run in families and there is said to be an inherited trait that predisposes family members to certain conditions.

Breast cancer is a well-known disorder that runs in some families and it is not uncommon nowadays for female family members to have breast removals or mastectomies as a preventative strategy.

Multiple sclerosis also runs in families. Research has shown that relatives of individuals with multiple sclerosis are eight times more likely to develop the condition than those without an affected family member. There are also inherited traits in osteoporosis, and relatives are advised to take preventative measures by leading a healthy lifestyle including no smoking and moderate alcohol intake, a calcium-rich diet and significant exercise. Post-menopausal women may be prescribed hormone replacement therapy, as the female hormone oestrogen is important in maintaining bone density.

## Lifestyle choices

You learned above that lifestyle choices are important in preventing osteoporosis in vulnerable individuals and you will be well aware of the role smoking plays in the possibility of developing lung cancer. Excessive exposure to ultraviolet light is a major factor in the development of skin cancer, yet a summer tan is still seen as evidence of 'health' and looking well. Only very slowly are we becoming used to the idea of using a high-factor sunscreen and covering up exposed skin, especially around noon, in the summer months. It is taking a long time to change the summertime culture among young adults in the UK.

People with sedentary lifestyles and jobs, who do not regularly take exercise, are prone to coronary heart disease, diabetes and strokes.

Diets rich in saturated fats and refined sugars influence the development of non-insulin-dependent diabetes (type 2), coronary heart disease and stroke. Diets rich in meat and fat and low in fibre are thought to be significant in the development of bowel cancer. Emphysema is regularly associated with chronic bronchitis, as a result of smoking.

You are almost certainly going to find that some lifestyle choices influence at least one of the physiological disorders you will choose.

## Employment

The work of an individual can exert an influence on the development of the disorder. We are now very familiar with the effects of exposure to asbestos. In the past, many environments contained asbestos, as it was commonly used to reduce the risk of fire. Catering establishments, schools, many manufacturing plants and even homes were built using asbestos. An aggressive form of cancer called mesothelioma became linked to asbestos exposure and this caused cancer of the pleura lining the lungs.

## Case study: Joe

Joe had spent his early adult life as an officer in the army, where he excelled in boxing with an army team. Since leaving the army, Joe has had a career in engineering sales, driving long distances, but he continued to box as an amateur until he was in his late thirties. Discuss the effects of lifestyle factors on Joe's health and well-being.

1 Explain how Joe's employment may have had an effect on his health.

2 Evaluate the possible influences on Joe's physiological disorder.

### Diet

You have learned about the influences of some dietary choices on the development of diabetes, coronary heart disease and strokes in the previous section on lifestyle choices. People who do not eat healthy, balanced diets are prone to obesity, bowel disorders and bowel cancer. Fibre is thought to be particularly important in preventing gastro-intestinal disorders and the Change 4 Life and '5 a day' health promotion campaigns, which encourage people to eat more fruit and vegetables, are attempting to introduce more fibre into the diets of people in the UK (as well as preventing obesity).

Convenience foods have come under attack in recent years due to their high saturated fat and sugar content. So-called healthy meals, advertised as being low in fat, are often high in refined sugar and can result in dental disease and diabetes.

Alcohol, as well as being a major cause of road accidents and a significant factor in unwanted pregnancies and criminal activities, may lead to cirrhosis of the liver, a serious life-threatening disorder. Alcohol is contraindicated (should not be mixed) with many types of medication.

### Environmental influences

Under this heading, you might consider the quality of air and water, noise and light pollution, housing, crime levels, climate, altitude, natural and man-induced radioactivity levels, etc.

Fortunately in the UK, most environmental influences are strictly regulated and their influence on disease is minimised. However, poor-quality housing, particularly rented accommodation, still exists in many large inner cities and can lead to the spread of tuberculosis, respiratory illnesses and infestations. Air pollution, including fumes from traffic, while not believed to cause asthma, certainly makes attacks more frequent and severe.

Research has shown that more cases of cancer occur in inhabited areas close to some nuclear plants. Mobile phone masts and wind farms have been coming under increasing scrutiny because of concern that they may affect the health of nearby inhabitants, particularly children, in various ways but as yet no definitive proof has been found.

The environment can potentially have a huge effect on the development of some disorders so you will need to investigate this carefully for your chosen disorders.

Have you read media reports on possible health risks posed by mobile phone masts/ wind farms? What were the main concerns?

# 1.3 Signs and symptoms of both disorders

A **diagnosis** is usually made by a doctor. When it is based on the **signs** and **symptoms**, it is sometimes called a **clinical diagnosis** and, if these might fit more than one disorder, a **differential diagnosis** is made. A family doctor might need another health care professional's opinion and make a **referral** to the appropriate professional or professional service.

Physiological disorders will be characterised by the signs and symptoms experienced by the individuals suffering from the disorders.

# Case study: Joe

Joe had no symptoms of a disorder and thought the trembling in his hand was just a feature of getting older. The GP noticed that his tremor was worse at rest and that he was generally slower – these are signs. Joe sometimes felt unwell but could not describe why, except to say that he always felt tired. He had started to take hot drinks in a mug that he could hold with two hands and never filled it completely (he had previously caused minor scalds with a cup and saucer). This is known as compensation.

1  Many people complain of 'just not feeling right'. Find out the correct medical term to describe this.

2  Can you think of other methods of compensation Joe might have developed?

3  Chronic diseases often start slowly and develop over several months so they can be difficult to diagnose early. Why is an early diagnosis preferable for patients?

It is not possible to explain every sign and symptom for all the disorders you might investigate but some common manifestations could include those shown in Table 14.2.

**Table 14.2:** Common signs and symptoms

| Common signs | Common symptoms |
| --- | --- |
| Pallor/red flush/jaundice | Pain/discomfort/general malaise |
| Sweating/dehydration | |
| Trembling/tremors | Thirst |
| Smell (breath, body) | Palpitations |
| Changes in appearance of urine/faeces | 'Pins and needles' |
| | Paralysis |
| Changes in heart rate | Headache |
| Changes in breathing rate/wheezing | Visual disturbances |
| Rash/spots | Unsteadiness/muscle weakness |
| Changed blood pressure | |
| Changes in sensation | Changes in urination |
| Loss/gain in weight | Changes in bowel habit |
| Changes in consciousness | Loss/gain in weight |
| Changes in mobility | Cough |
| Changes in skin/mucous membranes (e.g. colour, texture, etc) | Seizure |
| | Presence of lump/blood |
| | Nausea/vomiting |
| Changes in temperature | |

In each case study of a physiological disorder, from your primary and secondary research you will describe and explain the signs and symptoms that are characteristic of the illness.

## Key terms

**Diagnosis** – The process by which the nature of the disease or disorder is determined or made known.

**Sign** – An objective indication of a disorder noticed by a doctor (or nurse).

**Symptom** – A feature complained of by the individual or patient.

**Clinical diagnosis** – A diagnosis made on the basis of signs and symptoms.

**Differential diagnosis** – The recognition of one disease from among a number presenting similar signs and symptoms.

**Referral** – Handing over to another professional (usually a specialist) or type of service such as physiotherapy.

## Assessment activity 14.1

P1 P2 · BTEC

You work on behalf of agencies that support the families and carers of individuals with particular physiological disorders and have been asked to produce an information leaflet for two different disorders.

You can either produce a detailed leaflet or a written report or (with the agreement of your tutor) you can make an oral presentation but this must be supported by your notes and a detailed witness statement.

1 Explain the nature of of two named physiological disorders.

2 Explain the signs and symptoms related to two named physiological disorders.

### Grading tips

P1 Do you feel that you have an understanding of each disorder? Try to collect the information together in order, under the following headings:

- the cause/s of the disorder
- physiological changes as a result of the disorder
- overall changes
- physiological changes as a result of treatment
- the factors influencing the development of the disorder.

P2 What is likely to make the person go to their GP in the first place? Did the GP notice signs that the patient had not noticed? What signs and symptoms develop later?

Remember to complete a leaflet/report/make a presentation for **two** different disorders.

### PLTS

**Independent enquirer:** Planning which disorders to investigate, planning and carrying out research will allow you to demonstrate your independent enquiry skills.

### Functional skills

**ICT:** You can show your ICT skills by finding and presenting information to suit your leaflet's meaning and purpose, designing your leaflet, presenting a leaflet or written report and by using images that are scanned for a leaflet.

# 2  Know the processes involved in diagnosis of physiological disorders

There can be several stages between the first time an individual visits their GP with a complaint and the diagnosis being reached.

## 2.1 Referral

This can be self-referral, professional referral or third party referral.

### Self-referral

This is when the patient refers themself to a health professional, usually their GP. Self-referral to a specialist is unusual and occurs only if the patient is known to the specialist from a previous consultation and has been told to return if symptoms recur. People may refer themselves to private health professionals outside the NHS such as a remedial physiotherapist.

### Professional referral

Occasionally a doctor will examine a patient and be extremely anxious about the diagnosis, and telephone or provide a letter for immediate attention by a hospital doctor, usually a consultant.

When the patient has private health insurance or is financially well off, he or she can be seen within a day or two at a private health hospital.

More usually, however, the family doctor will see the patient a few times before deciding on referral to a consultant or specialist in that field of medicine or continuing to treat the patient at the surgery. There may be several weeks before the patient can actually be seen by a specialist consultant or his team. In either case, the family doctor may also arrange for the patient to have x-rays, blood tests, physiotherapy or other services. A GP will refer a patient whose diagnosis is in doubt, needs specialist treatment, or whose condition is urgent and/or likely to be serious.

### Third party referral

This can happen when a relative or friend decides that an individual should be seen by a health professional such as a GP because they are unable to do this for themselves. It may also occur when a member of an ancillary profession notices something that should be investigated. Ophthalmic opticians may write to a GP, for example, if their examination suggests an underlying disease such as diabetes.

## 2.2 Investigations that may be undertaken

A simple investigation based on signs and symptoms is the taking of your own temperature when you don't feel well. When a patient complains of a burning sensation on passing urine; cloudy, smelly urine or blood in urine; or needing to pass urine more often than usual, then the GP will ask for a specimen of urine so that any abnormal constituents can be investigated.

A patient complaining of dizzy feelings and getting breathless on climbing stairs will have a blood investigation; and an individual complaining of a phlegm-producing cough will be asked to produce a specimen for examination. Investigations are not always laboratory tests, however, and in the next section you will learn how a physical examination (also based on the signs and symptoms) is carried out.

Men are advised to carry out regular testicular examination to check for swellings or lumps and women are similarly encouraged to examine their breasts regularly by inspection and touch. Current practice allows and encourages individuals to have regular checks on their blood pressure and blood glucose. Cheap and easy-to-use equipment is available for such tests and many high street pharmacists now offer these services. An individual who is not feeling well might take their own temperature over several hours and this is also a simple investigation.

## 2.3 Investigations for each individual

Any investigations carried out will be specific to each disorder but will always include a medical history and standard blood tests, such as a blood count and haemoglobin level (see Blood tests, page 200).

### Medical history

To take a medical history, the doctor listens to what the patient has to say and asks appropriate questions about the patient's symptoms and any previous disorders that might have had an influence on the development of the current disorder.

The patient's account can be vital in providing clues to the nature of the illness and, in an ideal world, it should not be rushed. The doctor is searching for significant clues that will form a pattern to establish the exact nature of the complaint or diagnosis. In many instances, the doctor can elicit information that will point to two or more conditions and they will then try to establish which one is the most likely (this is known as a differential diagnosis). The GP is likely to enquire into the family history in some disorders, as this might be useful in indicating family traits (characteristics that run in the family).

It is important to establish the likelihood of the illness. If the patient is in pain or distress some form of treatment may be necessary. The treatment itself might then mask the original symptoms and make the diagnosis more difficult.

After recording the medical history, the doctor will carry out a physical examination. This may be short or extended, depending on the nature of the disorder. For example, the doctor is extremely unlikely to examine anything other than the chest area if a patient is complaining of difficulty in breathing. A patient who has symptoms related to the digestive tract will have the abdominal area examined. During a physical examination, the doctor is likely to listen to the patient's heart and lungs and measure blood pressure, especially if the patient has not been seen before or for a long time.

## Palpation

This is a technique for feeling organ shapes, sizes and surfaces with the hands. It is particularly useful on the abdomen because doctors are taught to examine for larger than normal organs such as the liver, spleen, bladder, etc. Areas of unusual tenderness or rigidity are noted, together with any abnormal masses or lumps.

## Blood tests

Samples of blood can be obtained in two ways, by venepuncture (inserting a syringe needle into a vein) or by a finger-prick, using a small, sterile lancet. Venepuncture is used when several millilitres of blood are required for clinical analysis.

An examination of blood provides a good indication of the health and well-being of a patient. Many

substances normally present in blood can be reported on, including:

- haemoglobin level (for anaemia)
- levels of blood salts, technically known as electrolytes (for renal disorders, diabetes, metabolic bone disorders)
- hormone levels (for pregnancy, endocrine disorders)
- blood gases, such as oxygen and carbon dioxide (for respiratory disease)
- specific enzyme tests (for heart attacks)
- plasma proteins (for bleeding disorders)
- pH (for renal disorders, diabetes – see page 180).

A special test known as a blood cell count will reveal whether the different types of blood cells are present in normal quantities and appearance.

The finger-prick test is used when only small quantities of blood are required to measure the presence of a particular substance. For example, diabetics use small quantities like this, soaked into paper, in a special device for monitoring their blood glucose. Health visitors will use a heel-prick on newborn babies to collect tiny amounts of blood to test for phenylketonuria (PKU test).

There are also other special blood tests for various purposes – for example, blood culture to determine whether septicaemia or blood poisoning is present.

## Urine tests

The physical characteristics (such as colour, smell, clarity, pH, concentration) and chemical composition of urine – glucose, **urea** (which results from the liver breaking down excess **amino acids**), protein, drugs, hormones, blood, etc. – can reveal underlying conditions such as kidney diseases, pregnancy and

### Key terms

**Urea** – A nitrogenous substance resulting from the liver breaking down excess amino acids from the digestion of proteins. Nitrogenous material not required for metabolism cannot be stored in the body. If allowed to accumulate, urea is toxic to body tissues and can result in death.

**Amino acids** – The nitrogenous end products of protein digestion normally used to build up new structural and physiological body proteins such as enzymes and hormones. However, many Western diets contain too much dietary protein, and after digestion the unwanted amino acids will be broken down by the liver and eliminated by the kidneys.

diabetes. More specific tests can estimate kidney function and inherited metabolic disorders. Urine, like blood, can be cultured to detect microbial infections.

## Radiological investigations

You will most likely have seen plain black and white x-rays, which are ideal for viewing the skeleton in a non-invasive way. Modern equipment produces high-quality images without exposure to too much radiation.

Despite this, all radiation is harmful and every effort is made to minimise exposure. Radio-opaque materials can be used to fill hollow organs, such as the alimentary canal, and if the part is viewed from more than one angle, filling defects (black areas not filled by the radio-opaque material) caused by tumours and polyps, or bumps caused by ulcers or erosion, will be displayed. The most common radio-opaque material is a barium compound and a patient will drink this (a barium meal) or have it poured into the rectum as an enema (barium enema), depending on whether the upper or lower part of the alimentary canal needs to be examined.

Different radio-opaque substances can be introduced into the cardiovascular system to display particular blood vessels – this is known as angiography. Radio-opaque iodine compounds are used to display the urinary tract, as these compounds can be excreted by the kidneys and show the pelvis of the ureters (where the ureter enters the kidney), the ureters, bladder and urethra. This is useful to determine whether there is anything blocking the passage of urine.

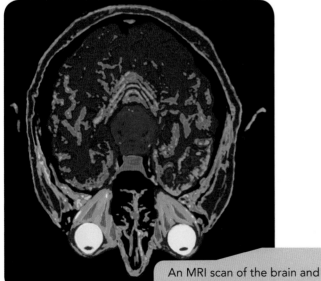

An MRI scan of the brain and skull taken at the level of the eyes

## Scans

The most common form of scan is an ultrasound scan and the technology is now so advanced that it is used for many things. Most people associate ultrasound scans with pregnancy monitoring, but they are also used for visualising the liver, gall bladder, pancreas, breast and kidneys. Ultrasound works by bouncing high-frequency sound waves off internal organs but has difficulty where there is a lot of gas, such as in the lungs, or a casing of bone like the adult brain (new-born babies' brains can be scanned through the so-called 'soft spot'). It is used to detect tumours, foreign bodies, cysts and abnormalities of structure. Ultrasound scanning is considered very safe.

MRI (magnetic resonance imaging) scans are also safe because they do not use radiation either. Powerful magnetic fields and radio waves are used to provide high-quality three-dimensional images of organs and structures within the body. MRI equipment is still not available everywhere, as it is very expensive.

CT or CAT (computerised (axial) tomography) scans use x-rays passed at different angles through the body, transformed using a computer to produce cross-sectional images ('slices'). This is particularly useful in producing 'serial slices of brain tissue' but is also used for other organs.

## Function tests

These are tests that have been specially designed to determine the degree of function of particular parts of the body, to assist with diagnosis and assess the value of treatment. Examples of these would be glucose tolerance tests for diabetes and liver function tests. Function tests for an organ may include imaging techniques as well (see Radiological investigations, above).

Liver function tests are commonly ordered by GPs and specialists to assess liver function in people who are suspected of having liver damage, liver disease or a partial loss of function. These tests look for chemical compounds that the liver manufactures or breaks down, and are helpful in distinguishing between a disease of the liver and a blockage of the bile duct. Bilirubin is made by the liver from the breakdown of old, unwanted red blood cells and passed into bile. When bile flow is blocked, bilirubin levels will be higher than normal. Albumin is a plasma protein made by the liver and passed into blood. When liver cells are damaged or diseased, albumin levels will be lower than normal.

Kidney function tests will include an examination of the urine (see Urine tests, pages 200–201). More precise results can be obtained from clearance tests (see below).

Urea and creatinine are two substances excreted into urine by healthy kidneys. In a clearance test, the person collects all urine over a 24-hour period in a plastic container and the amount of creatinine excreted can be compared with the blood levels, to determine how well the kidneys are removing creatinine (or urea).

Brain function tests assess mental state and abilities, sensation and **reflexes**. Electrical activity can be measured using an **electroencephalogram (EEG)**, and movement and muscle tone can be estimated.

Pancreatic function tests can include enzyme measurements in blood or the duodenum.

Reproductive and endocrine function tests can measure hormone levels in the blood.

# 2.4 Measurements

Certain measurements are taken routinely, such as pulse rate, breathing rate, blood pressure, body temperature, and body weight and height (which

enable the body mass index (BMI) to be calculated). BMI is calculated by dividing a person's weight in kilograms by their height in metres squared (this means multiplied by itself). (See also Book 1, Unit 5.)

More caution has been seen in interpreting BMIs in recent years and it is now recognised that body fat may be overestimated in athletes, sportspeople, and body builders who have a muscular build.

## Key terms

**Reflexes** – These are automatic responses to stimuli. The patellar or knee-jerk reflex is a common reflex that doctors use as a test. It enables doctors to determine whether there is damage to the nervous pathway and also whether the speed of nervous impulses has been increased or decreased.

**Electroencephalogram (EEG)** – This is a tracing of the electrical activity of the brain. An abnormal rhythm may be found in epilepsy, dementia (Parkinson's disease) and brain tumours.

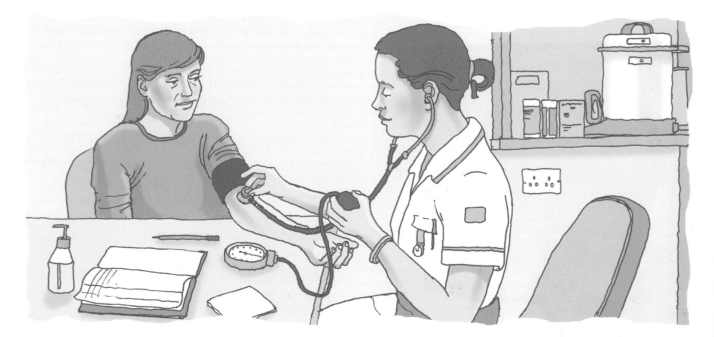

**Fig 14.1:** Taking blood pressure using a sphygmomanometer

## Did you know?

Systolic blood pressure (BP) corresponds to the pressure of the blood when the ventricles are contracting. Diastolic BP represents blood pressure when the ventricles are relaxed and filling. BP is usually written as systolic/diastolic (e.g. 120/80) and the units are mmHg or millimetres of mercury. Few establishments have converted to SI units or kilopascals (kPa).

120/80 mmHg is taken as standard young healthy adult BP and in kPa this is 15.79/10.53.

The force blood exerts on the walls of the blood vessels it is passing through is known as the blood pressure. It can be measured using a special piece of equipment called a sphygmomanometer, often abbreviated to 'sphygmo' (pronounced sfigmo). Blood pressure should only be measured by a competent operator.

Other measurements are taken that are specific to particular disorders. For example, people with asthma are encouraged to monitor their own disorder using peak flow measurements.

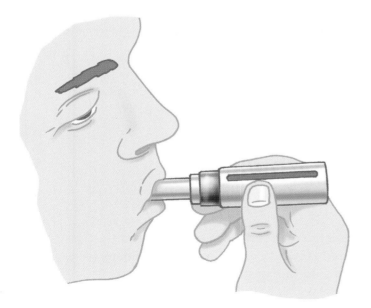

**Fig 14.2:** Measuring peak flow

Peak flow measurement is now important in lung function testing and is quite easy to do. It measures the maximum speed of expiration and is associated with the calibre of the subject's main airways. A baseline is often obtained using a medical spirometer with a skilled operator and then a simple peak flow meter is used, particularly in domestic settings, for monitoring. Special sizes are available for children. Electronic peak flow meters are available but expensive. Many children and adults with asthma use peak flow meters twice daily to monitor their condition and modify their therapy. They are asked to record the readings and take the records with them when they visit clinics or hospitals. Patients with chronic bronchitis and emphysema will be asked to monitor their lung function in the same way. Athletes in training and patients requiring physiotherapy of the chest may also find peak flow readings useful.

## Activity 4: Designing a storyboard

Sarah had just had her third child and her recovery seemed to be taking a long time. Her GP visited her regularly and could find nothing wrong on examination. Sarah continued to feel weak and her mood was low. Post-natal depression was considered but this didn't account for the weakness. Blood tests and counts were carried out and when Sarah was found to be very slightly anaemic this was treated.

Sarah continued to feel weak and complained of her limbs feeling heavier than normal. Her parents came to stay, to help her care for the baby and other children, as she could not do this on her own.

She also complained of dizziness at times and that colours were blurred. An ophthalmologist examined her vision and could not detect any abnormalities. The GP arranged for a lumbar puncture and also referred Sarah to a specialist for nervous diseases. The lumbar puncture showed slight abnormalities.

Six months later, Sarah was diagnosed with MS and treatment commenced.

1   In groups of three or four, design a storyboard to illustrate how Sarah's diagnosis was made.

2   Show how it was differentiated from other possible causes.

## Assessment activity 14.2

For each of your chosen disorders, carry out the following tasks:

1 Describe the investigations that are carried out to enable the diagnosis of physiological disorders. What measurements and investigations are appropriate to your chosen disorder?

2 Assess possible difficulties in the diagnosis of the disorders from their signs and symptoms for both physiological disorders. What problems arose in making a final diagnosis from the presentation of the signs and symptoms?

### Grading tips

**P3** You will need to research how each investigation was carried out to enable a diagnosis. It would be useful to identify the potential of modern methods of diagnosis, such as CT and MRI scans, even though the equipment was not available or called upon in your primary research. If you wish, you can add the information derived from the tests and measurements to your leaflet or report from

Assignment 14.1. However, if you prefer to do this separately, you can chart the tests and measurements carried out and state how the results will lead to a diagnosis of the disorder.

**M1** Some disorders (such as MS and Alzheimer's disease) are notoriously difficult to diagnose, especially in the early stages. Initially, diagnosis may be made by eliminating other disorders with similar signs and symptoms. On the other hand, coronary heart disease and diabetes can be diagnosed more easily, although there are always some patients who are difficult to diagnose. If you have chosen coronary heart disease for your investigative study, you will learn that some patients in later adulthood do not display the characteristic signs of a heart attack. Small strokes can have confusing effects and in elderly people can prove challenging to diagnose. Likewise, people with MS may display symptoms for only a short while and then have a remission lasting for many years, or never have another occurrence.

### PLTS

**Creative thinker:** You can show your creative thinking skills by asking questions about the nature of the disorders, and connecting other people's ideas and experiences.

### Functional skills

**ICT:** You can use your ICT skills to communicate and exchange information safely, responsibly and effectively, including storing messages and contact lists and researching and presenting relevant information for the assignment work.

# 3 Be able to produce a care pathway for physiological disorders

## 3.1 Care pathways

What is a **care pathway**? It is a description of the way in which services are brought together to meet an individual's needs over a period of time.

A definition used by care workers and using specialist vocabulary might be:

'Integrated care pathways are structured multi-disciplinary care plans which detail essential steps in the care of patients with a specific clinical problem and describe the expected progress of the patient' Campbell et al, 1998.

Other terms used for care pathways are integrated care pathways or ICPs, **multi-disciplinary** pathways of care and care protocols.

### Key terms

**Care pathway** – A coming together of services to meet an individual's needs.

**Multi-disciplinary** – Describes teams, care plans, etc; indicates that different care professionals from different fields are working together.

## Purpose of care pathways?

Care pathways offer many benefits. For example, using a care pathway:

- ensures a consistent standard of care in the same department
- empowers patients and staff
- reduces duplication (doubling up)
- identifies costs and resources
- ensures that everyone involved, including the patient, knows what care will be received
- eliminates unnecessary or repetitive documentation.

An individual's basic needs are the most important requirements to achieve a state of health and well-being. Maslow is best known for his hierarchy of needs theory and you will be familiar with this from Book 1 Unit 8 and Book 2 Units 10 and 29.

### Activity 5: Sarah's needs

Sarah has been diagnosed with MS and has three children including a six-month old baby. She lives in a warm, well-furnished house with a good income but her husband works as a captain on oil tankers and is away for several months at a time. Her elderly parents live 8 km (5 miles) away and, although supportive, cannot stay at Sarah's home indefinitely.

Working alone or in small groups, produce a pattern diagram of Sarah's needs.

### Functional skills

**English:** You can demonstrate your speaking and listening skills by contributing and making effective presentations in a wide range of contexts through discussion of Sarah's needs.

## Assessment of needs

An initial assessment of need is required to agree a starting point or level, which can then be used to determine improvement and justification for the care pathway. It is carried out by a professional who is trained in assessment and is often the first contact for the individual. Assessment should involve the individual and their carers and also involve the outcomes they wish to achieve and the methods

they wish to use to get there. For adults, there is a single assessment process (SAP) but for children and young people it is through a Common Assessment Framework (CAF). Assessment is shared by all professionals and is coordinated with all agencies likely to be involved with the individual, including voluntary and informal carers.

In Sarah's case (see Activity 5), her parents may agree to help with daily living activities for the family after school and at weekends.

The care pathway will indicate other agencies involved during the week and provide a timescale for a review of care needs as Sarah improves with medication.

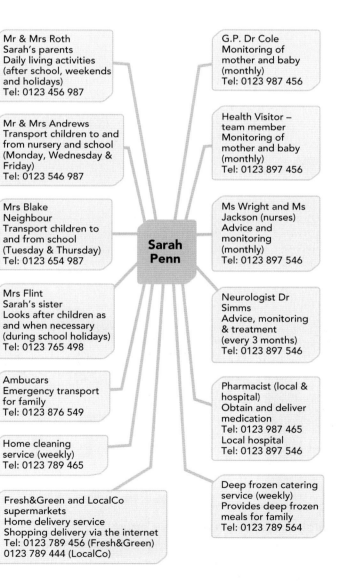

**Fig 14.3:** A simplified part of Sarah's care pathway, one year after diagnosis

A **care plan** is drawn up to detail who is going to do what and when, together with the details of all agencies involved, such as telephone numbers. The individual is central to the care planning process.

## Primary care

This is the type of care that occurs in the community, outside hospitals. It usually involves the GP and other staff connected to the practice. Dentists, opticians and pharmacists also carry out primary care in the community, although they are not attached to a health practice. Services like these, provided in the community, are called primary care services. **Health centres** are now offering many more services than doctors' surgeries used to, thus relieving some of the pressure on hospitals.

### Activity 6: Primary care services

In a small group, create a pattern diagram on a flip sheet to demonstrate the type of services carried out in modern health centres. Display your work in the classroom to stimulate ideas for use in care pathways. To extend this work, indicate whether the clinic is likely to be run by a specialist nurse attached to the health centre or a doctor.

### Key terms

**Care plan** – The term used to outline and record the care, therapy and/or treatment for an individual carried out by the multi-disciplinary team.

**Health centre** – A multi-agency community-based facility where teams of health professionals work together. They are often purpose-built. Teams consist of GPs, nurses, midwives, counsellors, community nurses, speech and occupational therapists and sometimes dentists.

How do modern health centres compare with old-style doctors' surgeries? What extra services do they offer?

## Secondary care

This is the care carried out in a general hospital, usually after referral by the GP, a primary carer. General hospitals provide emergency services, medical and surgical beds, laboratory testing, scans, gynaecological and obstetric services, physiotherapy, occupational therapy and radiology services, to name only a few examples. Out-patient and in-patient care is also provided by hospitals.

## Tertiary care

These are specialist care establishments such as stroke rehabilitation clinics, spinal injury units and cancer care (oncology) units.

## 3.2 Practitioners involved in the delivery of the care pathway

Formal and informal carers can be included in care pathway delivery. Formal carers are professional carers, either employed by the individual (fairly unusual) or by an organisation. They should be trained and qualified in their roles and follow professional codes of conduct. Informal carers (also known as family carers and caregivers) are a very large group of people who support individuals both physically and emotionally. It has been estimated that there are over 6 million informal carers, some of whom are children, in the UK. Many work exceedingly long hours for no money and save the government billions of pounds.

### Involvement of other agencies

Many local authorities now contract out services to other agencies rather than supplying the services directly. For example, cars are provided to take children in need to school and other people to hospital appointments such as outpatient and dialysis units. The drivers use and pay for their own vehicles but are usually paid by the mile. They belong to a not-for-profit organisation. The same applies to services to supply meals to individuals who cannot manage their own daily living activities such as shopping and cooking. Charities serving older people, such as Age UK, may offer daycare centres, where meals, activities and companionship are provided. Some may carry out laundry, bathing and barbering services for individuals without family to help.

### Reflect

Sarah's parents lived at her home for three months after her baby was born and before she was diagnosed with MS. With three children, including a young baby, and a sick mother to care for, just imagine how many thousands of pounds they saved the health authority and social services!

## 3.3 Care strategies

Care strategies need to be reviewed at regular intervals to ensure that they are still in the best interests of the individual's health. Medication has to be reviewed, as it may have reached a specified time limit, as in the case of some antibiotics. Checks also need to be carried out to make sure that the medication is still effective and that side effects have not become unduly troublesome. New or alternative medication may suit the individual better.

Patients may be required to attend special clinics until treatment is considered to be optimum. Individuals with cardiac problems may be prescribed Warfarin which reduces the risk of blood clotting and often requires constant monitoring before final effective doses are reached. Likewise, diabetic patients may need 'trial and error' dosages until insulin injections are at the right level. Progressive deteriorating conditions may require different medication at different stages of the disease.

Scans and x-rays may need to be repeated to check on the progress, or lack of progress, being made by the care strategy in place.

Therapies may no longer be required, such as occupational therapy, and others may not be effective, such as radiotherapy, or conversely need to be added to the strategy. Patients can be referred back to the GP for monitoring, knowing that any change requiring specialist input will once again be referred.

Care strategies need to be reviewed to effect these types of changes to improve the patient's health, avoid duplication and waste of resources and ensure that the NHS is delivering the most cost-effective care to all patients.

# 4 Understand the strategies used to support individuals with physiological disorders

In this section, you will learn about:

- the different care settings that the individual will experience
- the people responsible for providing the care
- the type of care that will be given.

The information here can only be generic, as there are many types of physiological disorder that you may be investigating. You can use this information as a 'pick and mix' selection to apply to your case studies.

## 4.1 Care provision

### Statutory

This type of care provision is required by law and is governed by legislation. Local and health authorities, primary care trusts and hospitals are all subject to the laws of the land in delivering services and meeting set targets.

### Non-statutory

This type of care is composed of the private and voluntary sectors. Health and social care services are often delivered by companies in the business of care, who are aiming to make a profit. Local authorities frequently contract out services to other organisations. In this way people may be cared for in their own homes (domiciliary care) or in residential homes in a process sometimes called 'buying in'.

Many organisations purchase catering from another organisation. Such an arrangement still needs careful planning, monitoring and reviewing.

Voluntary organisations deliver services on a not-for-profit basis and many are registered as charities. There are usually some paid workers and also people who help without being paid.

## 4.2 Care settings where support can occur

A care setting is the name given to any location where care is dispensed. Care settings will change, as an individual with a disorder is diagnosed, treated and care-managed.

### GP's surgery

This is likely to be the first (or primary) setting in which the patient seeks help for symptoms they are experiencing. There might already be a long-term relationship between the patient and the doctor, which will be advantageous to both. A medical history will be taken, if it is not already known, and the doctor will ask relevant questions about the new symptoms.

As a result of their questioning, the doctor will soon have in mind a possible list of disorders from which the patient may be suffering, and will then carry out a physical examination to support or narrow their differential diagnosis. The physical examination will be enhanced by taking routine measurements such as blood pressure, body temperature, pulse and breathing rates.

The doctor may quickly decide that the patient needs to be referred to a hospital specialist, write a letter explaining the findings at the initial consultation and make an out-patient's appointment with an appropriate specialist or consultant at the earliest opportunity. More usually, however, the doctor will arrange to use services allied to the hospital for x-rays, blood tests or other early investigations and request that the patient returns at a date when these results are likely to be available.

After further consultations, the doctor might still refer the patient to hospital or treat the condition for a time.

### Health centre

More and more GPs are grouping together in purpose-built health centres where extra services and facilities can be offered. Such facilities might include maternity services, counselling, alternative therapy sessions, various specialised clinics, phlebotomists, mobility aid specialists, family planning, health promotion, etc. Such services relieve the pressure on hospitals, serve the local community well and may save patients having to travel long distances to hospitals. They are often located close to pharmacies so that medication can be more easily obtained.

### Hospital care

Individuals may access hospital care as out-patients or in-patients.

People with serious disorders such as cancer will be admitted as soon as possible for investigations and treatment. When the condition is less acute, they may make out-patient visits for a long time – for example, in cases of Parkinson's disease or Alzheimer's disease. Diabetic patients may be admitted for a short period to stabilise their condition with appropriate medication, followed by annual checks.

Hospitals have varied facilities and a person may need to be taken from one hospital to another for specialist facilities such as scans. This is usually for a short period only. Smaller hospitals have limited facilities and specialist consultants may visit, for example, for one day every month.

People are likely to be admitted as in-patients for any surgery, except for minor complaints.

## Home

Most people who are ill would prefer to stay in their own homes while being cared for, especially if they have a loving family around. Older people often have a particular fear of hospitals or going into residential care and would prefer to stay at home, with familiar things around them. They often feel that if they leave home, they will not return.

Many of the disorders listed on page 190 will allow people to be cared for at home until the later stages of the illness. Where special aids are required, such as stair lifts, bath hoists and disabled access, these can be provided after a professional assessment. It is also more cost-effective for the NHS for people to continue living independently for as long as possible. Services such as home carers, Meals on Wheels and chiropody can be arranged to support people in their own homes as part of a care package of assistance.

## Social care settings

People in the late stages of disorders such as Parkinson's and Alzheimer's disease, rheumatoid arthritis, stroke and coronary heart disease may have to be cared for in a social care setting such as a residential care home because of their increasing disability and the need to keep them safe. Other people may be able to stay at home and go to a daycare setting several times a week for specific care, company and relaxation. This can be particularly important if the family is working during the day or the individual lives alone.

## Educational settings

Children with special educational needs have a right to access education at a local school and a school is obliged to be accessible to all children. This means that a school has to supply additional provision. There is a coordinator within each school who is specially trained to take responsibility for all special needs provision. This teacher is known as the Special Education Needs Coordinator (SENCO) and there may be other specially trained teachers in the team, depending on the size of the school and needs of the area. Special schools are centres providing an educational setting, where children with major needs who are not able to benefit from attending local schools may be cared for in a learning environment.

## 4.3 Formal carers

We have looked at a general range of care settings above but it is mainly the people who work in these settings who are fundamental to the caring process. They include the following professionals and care workers.

Care strategies may include social care settings. What are the advantages of these settings for the patients?

## General practitioners

You have already learned about the role of the GP in the GP's surgery section (see page 208).

## Clinical specialists

Clinical specialists have taken further qualifications in their particular field of medicine or surgery and become 'experts'; you may be more familiar with the term consultant.

They are often called by their specialist field with '-ist' on the end, so, for example, a cardiologist specialises in heart disorders, a nephrologist in kidney disorders and a rheumatologist in bone diseases. These types of clinical specialists are usually physicians – people who practise medicine as opposed to surgery.

A doctor who has specialised in heart surgery will be a cardiac surgeon, a kidney surgeon is a renal surgeon and a bone surgeon is an orthopaedic surgeon.

There are also specialists for some particular life stages; a paediatrician is an expert in diseases found in children and a geriatrician is concerned with diseases of older patients.

An oncologist is a specialist in tumours and a radiologist studies both the diagnosis and treatment of disease using radiological techniques.

There are clinical specialists in biochemistry, haematology, pathology and cytology, who patients rarely see but who work behind the scenes in departments that assist other clinical specialists.

The list of clinical specialists is very long and, if you come across an '-ist' name you do not recognise, you can either ask a professional or consult a dictionary.

Clinical specialists cannot see every individual and they usually head a team of people consisting of registrars, senior house officers and house officers (in descending order of rank). The specialist will often see the person on a first visit to make a diagnosis and order investigations.

## Nurses

Many years ago, nurses used to be seen as the 'handmaidens' (servants) to doctors. Now they are rightly recognised as expert professionals in individualised client/patient care, emanating from sound research and knowledge-based practice.

Like doctors, there are several tiers of nurses, all working to a value-based system. The system of nurse education underwent significant reforms several years ago and is now a recognised degree programme. Nurses also specialise in different areas, such as mental health, children, health visiting and midwifery, to mention only the major branches.

Nurses are taking on more and more of the traditional roles of doctors, such as prescribing medicines. Nearly every individual receiving care will have contact with nurses at most levels. Patients rely on nurses to meet their everyday caring needs, as they tend to see doctors infrequently.

## Professions allied to medicine

These include:

- occupational therapists
- physiotherapists
- radiographers
- radiotherapists
- chiropodists.

These professionals can all undertake specialist degrees in their fields.

Occupational therapists are rehabilitation experts and, although this may involve rehabilitation looking towards employment or getting back to work, their work is also vital to ensure that people have the abilities and competencies to manage at home. For example, an occupational therapist will be involved in the care of any individual who has musculo-skeletal problems before they can transfer from hospital to home. They will assess the person and, if necessary, visit the home to see which mobility aids will assist them in everyday living.

Physiotherapists are concerned with the treatment and rehabilitation of movement, mainly muscles, by the use of heat, light, electricity, massage, remedial exercises and manipulation.

Radiographers, who should not be confused with radiologists (see Clinical specialists, left), are professional health care workers in either a diagnostic x-ray department or a radiotherapy department. They position the individual for the correct angle of the radiation and manage the process of radiography or radiotherapy. Radiotherapists will be important to cancer patients, in particular.

Chiropodists, also sometimes known as podiatrists, care for the feet and treat diseases of the feet. The care of feet is particularly important for older diabetic people, as they are prone to gangrene from open cuts (inflicted by scissors when cutting toenails).

## Care managers

This is a professional carer who carries out an initial assessment of care needs and then commissions a 'package' of care to meet those needs. Person-centred planning is now widely used; this is where the individual is the centre of the plan and the focus is always positive. The plan is to look at what the individual is able to do for themselves and to provide extra support where it is needed.

## Social workers

These are qualified, registered professionals who provide social work services to statutory, independent or voluntary organisations. Social work helps people to overcome barriers and become full citizens with equal rights.

## Pharmacists

Pharmacists work in hospital settings, dispensing medication for in-patients and some out-patients, and also in pharmacies or chemist shops serving communities. Pharmacists are allowed to give advice and some forms of treatment to the community. Many offer extra services such as blood pressure or blood glucose monitoring.

People use pharmacists for more or less instant advice because it is less frightening and more informal than going to the surgery. It's also more convenient to pop in while shopping and people 'don't like to bother the doctor with unimportant things'! Hospital pharmacists will advise hospital doctors on inappropriate combinations of drugs and side-effects and often confer with others at a 'case conference', where multi-disciplinary health professionals discuss the best form of care for a particular individual.

## Phlebotomists

A phlebotomist is a person skilled in taking one or more blood samples by puncturing a vein, usually close to the inner side of the elbow, and withdrawing blood through a syringe. Many blood samples have to be placed in special bottles for specific tests, and taking blood from some individuals is notoriously difficult! Most phlebotomists work in hospital settings. Although nurses are also competent at taking blood samples, the sheer volume of blood that needs to be taken from all the patients would occupy the time of many nurses so specialist care workers are employed.

## Laboratory workers

Blood samples, urine samples, stool samples and biopsies all have to be analysed and hospital laboratories employ many people. Patients rarely see laboratory personnel but the work they do is essential.

## Care assistants

Care assistants undertake most of the care associated with daily living and will, in a hospital setting, be the carers most involved in meeting the needs of patients. They undertake more practical National Vocational Qualifications. Many progress after achieving these qualifications to degree programmes in nursing. Care assistants are also employed to carry out similar tasks in social care and domestic settings.

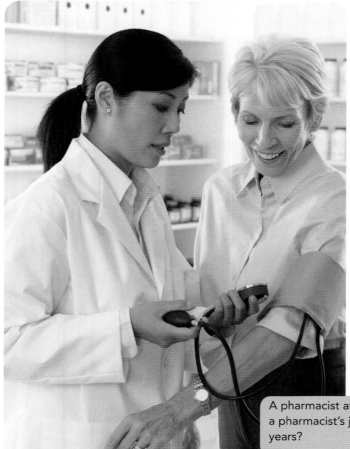

A pharmacist at work – how do you think a pharmacist's job has changed in recent years?

## Counsellors

Counsellors provide guidance and psychological support, usually for a specific problem, but also where feelings and attitudes are important. Counsellors work in cancer care, abortion and HIV support as well as many other areas. Such areas might include mental health, family therapy, marriage guidance, sexual difficulties, substance abuse, terminal illness, disability and bereavement.

Although sessions are usually with one individual, there can also be group therapy sessions.

Counselling can be of great benefit for people with MS, motor neurone disease, cancer and stroke conditions. It helps people to take a realistic view and to remain positive in difficult circumstances.

## 4.4 Informal carers

So far in this section we have looked at formal carers, i.e. those individuals who work in the health and social care field as professionals. Informal carers are individuals who have not taken any care qualifications but nevertheless carry the main burden of looking after a family member, relative or friend who is not fully independent. Informal carers are family members (sometimes children), friends, neighbours, faith-based organisation members, etc. There are massive numbers of informal carers doing a fantastic job, often 24 hours a day, seven days a week, with very little support either

financial or practical. Many informal carers are tied, unable to work or enjoy free time but continue to provide care quite selflessly.

When an individual is almost or permanently house-bound, having contact with the activities in the outside world helps to prevent an inward-looking mentality. Family and friends will offer practical support, as well as emotional and social support, by doing household chores and shopping.

Clearly, this is a very important source of care for individuals with physiological disorders.

### Reflect

Have you ever thought about the feelings of individuals who cannot carry out daily tasks for themselves? Write down positive and negative feelings associated with being immobile or housebound. Discuss them with your peers.

## Lay carers

Lay carers are individuals who are outside the health professions and not necessarily known to the patient. They include informal carers and voluntary workers from organisations that may be faith-based, such as the St Vincent de Paul Society (SVP), or those specialising in particular disorders, such as Mencap for learning disabilities. They are not paid for attending to an individual with a disorder but may be part of a care plan.

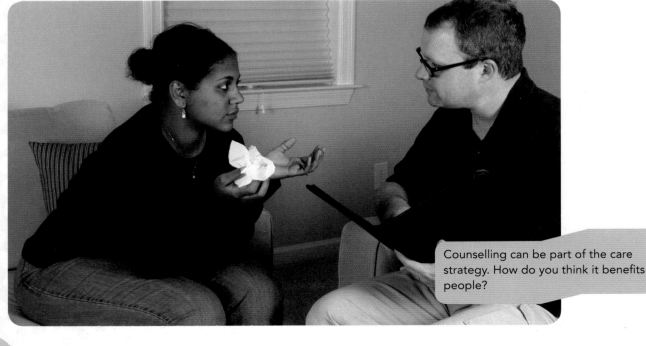

Counselling can be part of the care strategy. How do you think it benefits people?

# Ken Lowe
## Meals delivery driver

Ken is a driver for a catering organisation. This part of the firm is non-profit-making and they supply deep-frozen meals to people with disabilities and sick people who are unable to leave their homes easily to shop or who cannot manage to cook meals for themselves.

The service isn't free but it isn't expensive either. The local authority provides the contracts for selected individuals and Ken delivers the meals to their doors. He works weekdays only, usually starting the deliveries around 10 a.m. after the refrigerated van is loaded and he finishes at 4 p.m. if he's lucky. Apart from holidays and sick leave, he tries to see the same clients every week, although there are one or two part-time relief drivers.

He delivers regularly to Joe who has Parkinson's disease. Joe lives alone and can't do much cooking. His hands shake a lot and his muscles are very stiff. They always have a little chat about the weather and Joe's football team. He also delivered to Sarah and her children for about six months. Sarah has MS and her husband is a captain on oil tankers and he is away for half of every year. When he finished this time, Sarah had improved a lot so, between them, they were then able to manage.

All his clients have the firm's number and Ken's mobile so they can let him know if they have appointments and are going to be out. It is a problem if they forget, as he has to contact friends or relatives. He loves his job and feels that he is doing something worthwhile.

## Think about it!

1  Hot meals used to be provided by the WRVS every day, but most authorities are now contracting-out for frozen meals. Why do you think this change has occurred?

2  Explain why drivers like Ken see the same clients whenever possible.

3  How do you think clients are selected for this service by the local authority?

4  Why has Ken got to contact friends or family if no one answers the door when he makes a delivery?

# 4.5 Care

There are many different care strategies for physiological disorders and the strategies studied in detail will depend on the particular disorders you choose. However, certain strategies are useful in many disorders. We will look at some below.

## Medication

There are many types of medication – too many to include all of them – but some include:

- analgesics (painkillers)
- antibiotics (to combat infection)
- anti-inflammatory drugs
- antihypertensives (to lower blood pressure)
- metabolic dysfunction drugs (to correct or limit impaired chemical functions)
- immunosuppressive drugs (to suppress the immune response)
- carcino-chemotherapeutic drugs (to combat cancer; may be used in conjunction with radiation therapy)
- anti-allergic drugs (to suppress symptoms of allergic reactions)
- diuretics (to increase urine flow, thus removing surplus fluid from the body)
- bronchospasm relaxants (asthma and emphysema)
- hormone replacements
- muscle relaxants (stroke, MS)
- anti-depressants
- drugs for cardiac failure, angina, arrhythmias (changes in the heart's rhythm).

You will need to explore the types of medication used in your chosen disorders.

## Aids for living

Mobility aids may be required by people with arthritis, stroke, motor neurone disease, MS and in other conditions when the individual with the disorder is becoming frail and requires support. Such aids may include walking sticks, Zimmer frames or wheelchairs. People may need a variety of other aids such as stair lifts, bath hoists, support splints (to support weak muscles), special chairs, special cutlery and untippable dishes. Aids should be supplied to enable people to manage their daily living activities for as long as possible to retain their independence, self-respect and dignity.

Some people, especially those with lung cancer, bronchitis and emphysema and coronary heart disease, may require oxygen cylinders at home to ease breathing difficulties.

## Surgery

Surgical operations may play a significant part in the progress of some disorders. For example, a person may have a heart bypass operation (see Figure 14.4 on page 215) if they have coronary heart disease. This is where a short length of leg vein or artificial tubing is joined to a section of healthy coronary artery to avoid a blockage and rejoined beyond the obstruction, so forming a bypass. This may be done two or three times if the coronary arteries are seriously diseased – in so-called double or triple bypass operations.

Tumours will often be removed, especially in the early stages of cancer. Removing a lump from the breast (a **lumpectomy**) or removing the whole breast (mastectomy) may be necessary to try to halt the spread of the disease. Likewise, removal of the prostate gland in males (prostatectomy) may be required in some cases of prostate cancer.

Skin cancers are usually surgically removed and parts of the lung in the early stages of cancer only.

Surgery may play a part in the management of bowel cancer, Crohn's disease, ulcerative colitis and inflammatory bowel disease if symptoms are severe and not responding to other treatment. When parts of the bowel are removed, the person may be left with a temporary or permanent **ileostomy** or **colostomy**, after which faeces are passed into a bag attached to the abdominal wall and removed periodically.

## Blood transfusion

Anaemia can be a feature of several physiological disorders, such as MS, ulcerative colitis and also if surgery has been used to treat the main disorder.

### Key terms

**Lumpectomy** – An operation to remove a suspect lump, which is then sent for microscopic examination.

**Ileostomy** – An artificial opening from the ileum to the abdominal wall to evacuate faeces and bypass the large intestine.

**Colostomy** – This is the same as an ileostomy except that the artificial opening is from the colon. The artificial opening is known as a stoma, and faeces are evacuated into a bag attached to a belt or by adhesive.

Whole blood transfusions may be necessary to correct the impaired oxygen carriage and give a better quality of life. Saline (physiological salt solution) transfusions may be given to carry some forms of medication, correct dehydration (which can occur in diabetes) or reduce shock after surgery.

## Transplant

This is the surgical transfer of an organ or part of an organ from one individual (known as the donor) to another (the recipient). Donors are usually recently deceased or a very close relative. Individuals are tissue-typed to minimise problems of rejection and usually need to take immunosuppressant drugs for the remainder of their lives. Kidneys, corneas, hearts and lungs are commonly transplanted and other organs are being tried out.

## Advice on lifestyle changes

You will understand that this can be extremely varied and may extend from reviewing lifestyle factors (such as smoking in respiratory and cardiovascular disease) to dietary advice (such as a recommendation to increase or lower the amount of fibre in the diet). Advice may be given on the degree of activity to be undertaken and the correct use of aids. Advice will be given by doctors, nurses, people in professions allied to medicine, pharmacists and dieticians, to name but a few.

Advice may be verbal (given at consultations) or written in the form of instruction leaflets, information leaflets or simply how to take medication correctly, such as before food, after food and the dosage.

Information leaflets are easily available in supermarkets, health centres, out-patient departments, dental surgeries, pharmacies and health promotion units.

## Support for managing the disorder

You have already learned about professional advice and aids but support may come in the form of visits to or from specialist organisations, or volunteers concerned with the disorder itself, such as the Alzheimer's Society, Age UK, Mencap, Multiple Sclerosis Society, British Diabetic Association, British Colostomy Association and Arthritis Care. All these voluntary organisations have websites where information can be obtained to support individuals and their families.

There are also specialist nurses who are designated to help people in their own homes, health visitors, stoma nurses (dealing with the management of ileostomies and colostomies), diabetic nurses and, of course, school nurses who help a lot of children with asthma. Macmillan nurses help cancer patients (especially in the later stages) and you will learn about other types of support in the sections below.

## Rehabilitation programmes

These programmes are particularly important after a heart attack or coronary thrombosis and stroke and aim to return the person to living as independently as possible. Rehabilitation may include professional advice on maintaining a healthy lifestyle, counselling, relaxation techniques, physiotherapy, occupational therapy and psychotherapy as necessary. Complementary therapies may prove useful in improving health and well-being in people with cancer. It is clearly wise to attempt to re-educate or improve someone's quality of life to prevent further incidents of ill-health where this is possible. For example, another heart attack might be prevented by dietary changes and an exercise regime.

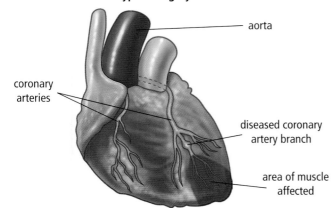

**Before bypass surgery**

aorta

coronary arteries

diseased coronary artery branch

area of muscle affected

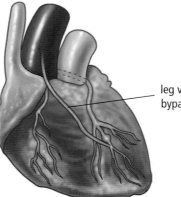

**After bypass surgery**

leg vein bypass

**Fig 14.4:** Heart bypass surgery

## Complementary therapies

Complementary therapies include practices such as aromatherapy, reflexology and naturotherapy. You will be able to find more details of these on the Internet. A brief outline will be given here.

Aromatherapists choose special oils impregnated with plant extracts for external massage. The practice is used particularly for psychosomatic and stress-related disorders.

Reflexologists massage the feet in the belief that parts of the body are reflected on the soles. Many will use herb-impregnated oils as they work.

Naturopaths believe that symptoms are related to the body attempting to eliminate the build-up of waste toxins in the body. Consequently, to be healthy, they say you must only consume natural foods and avoid environmental pollutants.

Acupuncture is a form of Chinese medicine where needles are inserted into the skin to treat disorders. Some conventional doctors suspect that the needles act as a counter-irritant (in the same way as heat pads and pain-relieving creams), causing temporary relief by distraction.

Many people suffering from chronic disorders may wish to use complementary therapies to relieve their symptoms, even if the relief is only temporary.

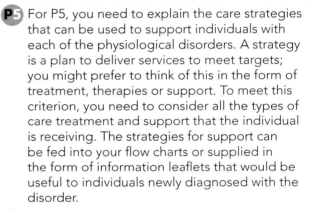

## Assessment activity 14.3    P4 P5 M2 M3 D1 D2   BTEC

As part of your work, you have been asked to conduct primary research into the care pathways and strategies available for individuals diagnosed with physiological disorders and write a report based on your research. You may wish to present your work in the form of detailed flow charts that also show the roles of relevant practitioners.

1. Plan a care pathway for each physiological disorder including the roles of relevant practitioners. If you are not conducting primary research by interviewing individuals with your chosen disorders, you will have to obtain information from an appropriate care practitioner who has experience of such pathways.

2. Discuss how practitioners and agencies involved in the care pathways work together to provide the care needed for both physiological disorders. For M3, you have to discuss the care strategies that can be used to support individuals with each of the physiological disorders.

3. Evaluate the effectiveness of health and social care practitioners and agencies working together to deliver the care pathway for one of the chosen disorders. For D2, you need to evaluate the care strategies that can be used to support an individual with one of the chosen physiological disorders.

### Grading tips

**P4** There is also information available on the Internet. A simple example of part of a care pathway is provided in this unit (see page 205).

**P5** For P5, you need to explain the care strategies that can be used to support individuals with each of the physiological disorders. A strategy is a plan to deliver services to meet targets; you might prefer to think of this in the form of treatment, therapies or support. To meet this criterion, you need to consider all the types of care treatment and support that the individual is receiving. The strategies for support can be fed into your flow charts or supplied in the form of information leaflets that would be useful to individuals newly diagnosed with the disorder.

**M2** You will need to examine the links between practitioners, from the first referral for initial assessment when care practitioners consult with the individual and the lead professional about their input into the care pathway, right through to the monitoring and review stages. Think about questions to ask your primary research sources, e.g. how do practitioners communicate with one another? What role does the lead person take with reference to other practitioners? How is everybody's commitment maintained? How is feedback of results carried out? How is ongoing improvement of the pathway effected?

**M3** You will need to provide details of the strategies and discuss the circumstances in which they might be used or contra-indicated. This might involve being used in the short or long term or for a period until a target is met.

**Assessment activity 14.3** *continued*

**D1** To achieve distinction, you will need to tease out the strengths and weaknesses of this combination of people working together to achieve the best possible care for the individual. This will be easier if you have interviewed an individual with the disorder because you can ask them how well it all works. Try to balance this information with a practitioner source as well, as individuals with disorders may well have a 'wish list' that is not practical in terms of time, resources (both human and equipment) and costs. When you have determined the strengths and weaknesses, try to reach a sensible conclusion as to how effectively the care pathway is working. Provide reasons for your conclusion, remembering the practical considerations already referred to.

**D2** This is similar to D1 but with relevance to care strategies. Strengths, weaknesses and conclusions justified by reasoning will need to be demonstrated to show your higher skills. You will find this easier if you have some primary sources of information.

## PLTS

**Reflective learner:** You can demonstrate this skill when setting goals for completing a care pathway plan.

## Functional skills

**English:** This assignment will enable you to demonstrate your reading and writing skills.

# Resources and further reading

Baker, M. *et al* (2001) *Further Studies in Human Biology* (AQA) London: Hodder Murray

Boyle, M. *et al* (2002) *Human Biology* London: Collins Educational

Campbell *et al* (1998) 'Integrated care pathways' *BMJ* (316:133–137)

Givens, P. & Reiss, M. (2002) *Human Biology and Health Studies* Cheltenham: Nelson Thornes

Indge, B. *et al* (2000) *A New Introduction to Human Biology* (AQA) London: Hodder Murray

Jones, M. & Jones, G. (2004) *Human Biology for AS Level* Cambridge: Cambridge University Press

Moonie, N. *et al* (2000) *Advanced Health and Social Care* Oxford: Heinemann

Myers, B. (2004) *The Natural Sciences* Cheltenham: Nelson Thornes

Pickering, W.R. (2001) *Advanced Human Biology through Diagrams* Oxford: Oxford University Press

Saffrey, J. *et al* (1972) *Maintaining the Whole* Milton Keynes: The Open University

Stretch, B. & Whitehouse, M. (2007) *BTEC National Health and Social Care Book 1* Oxford: Heinemann

Vander, A.J. (2003) *Human Physiology: The Mechanisms of Body Function* London: McGraw Hill

Ward, J. *et al* (2005) *Physiology at a Glance* Oxford: Blackwell

Wright, D. (2000) *Human Physiology and Health for GCSE*, Oxford: Heinemann

## Journals

*Nursing Times* and similar for case studies

# Useful websites

BBC www.bbc.co.uk/science/humanbody

British Heart Foundation www.bhf.org.uk

British Lung Foundation www.lunguk.org

NetDoctor www.netdoctor.co.uk

NHS Direct www.nhsdirect

Surgery Door www.surgerydoor.co.uk

Voluntary organisations exist for almost all the diseases on the list for this unit. You can find the addresses and websites in a library or by surfing the Internet. There is also a Voluntary Agencies Directory 2009 published by the National Council for Voluntary Organisations.They provide helpful information and recommend literature as part of their services. For example:

British Heart Foundation

British Lung Foundation

Motor Neurone Disease Assocation

The Alzheimer's Society

Parkinson's Disease Society of the UK

# Just checking

1 Name the main body systems affected by the following disorders:
  - MS
  - Alzheimer's disease
  - Coronary heart disease.
2 Explain the term palpation.
3 Name two factors that may influence the development of a disorder.
4 Which types of scans do not expose the individual to radiation?
5 Explain the role of a phlebotomist.
6 Name three purposes of a blood test.
7 Describe one form of complementary therapy.
8 Explain the purpose of two physiological measurements.

edexcel

# Assignment tips

1 Try to find two dissimilar disorders to investigate. You must maintain strict confidentiality throughout. You might need access to individuals and health care professionals, so friends, neighbours or relatives you know well will be easier to access than people in care settings. You must get their permission and use sensitivity at all times.

2 If you are seeking to obtain primary information from a patient or care worker, draft a consent form to be signed by the chosen individual and an eyewitness. Check it with your tutor and save and print out two copies. If you are going to involve a care setting, you still need to prepare a form for consent.

3 Although a case study is not the same as a research proposal, it has many related issues, such as deciding what methods to use to collect information and data. Ethical issues are just as central and so is the importance of respecting the confidentiality of the data obtained.

4 It is also your duty in health and social care to respect confidentiality, and you could give reassurance by saying that you have to plan your report confidentially as part of your task. This of course means not using their names, addresses, true ages or any details that might be used to identify the individuals.

# 19 Applied sociological perspectives for health and social care

Despite the United Kingdom being one of the wealthiest countries in the world, the gap between rich and poor is growing. Life expectancy is higher for the rich than for the poor. The average wage for women is lower than the average wage for men. Unit 19 covers issues such as these, which are of central concern to health and social care professionals. You will also be introduced to terms used to describe and analyse social inequalities. The unit then discusses recent changes in the size and make-up of the population and the impact of these changes on health and care provision. Finally, it describes the links between social inequalities and health and well-being.

This unit extends knowledge and understanding of the topics introduced in Book 1 – in Unit 2 Equality, diversity and rights in health and social care and Unit 7 Sociological perspectives in health and social care. In particular, it explores the impact of poverty and other social inequalities on the health and well-being of people in modern Britain. Those of you who have completed Unit 7 will be familiar with this approach to analysing the health of the nation. Here you will have the opportunity to apply this and additional knowledge to a wider range of social groups. This will include examining the evidence for the higher incidence of truancy, teenage pregnancy, mental illness and suicide, among the disadvantaged in our society.

## Learning outcomes

After completing this unit you should:

1 understand the concept of an unequal society
2 know social inequalities in society
3 understand the nature of demographic change within an unequal society
4 understand potential links between social inequalities and the health and well-being of the population.

# Assessment and grading criteria

This table shows you what you must do in order to achieve a **pass**, **merit** or **distinction** grade, and where you can find activities in this book to help you.

| To achieve a **pass** grade, the evidence must show that you are able to: | To achieve a **merit** grade, the evidence must show that, in addition to the pass criteria, you are able to: | To achieve a **distinction** grade, the evidence must show that, in addition to the pass and merit criteria, you are able to: |
|---|---|---|
| **P1** Explain the concept of an unequal society. **See Assessment activity 19.1, page 226** | **M1** Discuss the impact of social inequalities on groups in society. **See Assessment activity 19.1, page 226** | **D1** Evaluate the impact of social inequalities in society. **See Assessment activity 19.1, page 226** |
| **P2** Describe social inequalities that exist in society. **See Assessment activity 19.1, page 226** | | |
| **P3** Explain recent demographic change within their home country. **See Assessment activity 19.2, page 234** | **M2** Assess the impact of demographic changes within their home country. **See Assessment activity 19.2, page 234** | |
| **P4** Explain how demographic data is used in health and social care service provision. **See Assessment activity 19.2, page 234** | | |
| **P5** Explain potential links between social inequalities and the health of the population. **See Assessment activity 19.3, page 246** | **M3** Assess the impact of social inequalities on the health of one group in society. **See Assessment activity 19.3, page 246** | **D2** Evaluate the potential links between social inequalities and the health and well-being of one group in society. **See Assessment activity 19.3, page 246** |

# How you will be assessed

This unit will be assessed by internal assignments that will be marked and assessed by the staff at your centre. It may be subject to sampling by your centre's External Verifier as part of Edexcel's ongoing quality assurance procedures. Various exercises and activities are included here to help you prepare for the assessment activities. There will be opportunities to apply your sociological knowledge, and especially your knowledge of the effects of inequality and disadvantage, on social groups that are supported by the health and care services in your home country. This will include older people, members of ethnic minority groups, people with disabilities and learning difficulties and people with mental health problems.

Your assignments could be in the form of:

- presentations
- written assignments
- case studies
- reports
- essays.

Guidance is included throughout this unit to help you prepare and present your work.

## Jo, 18 years old

I have been on work experience, as part of my BTEC course, at a centre for girls of school age who have had babies. The girls have lessons while I help look after their children. Some are working for their GCSEs.

Two of the girls are from the local grammar school and they stand out as different but the others are really girls who rejected school. They don't seem to have any friends or family who have been to college. Most of their friends are young mums who have only ever had unskilled jobs. All the girls are struggling for money and their families are not able to help them in this way. Some of the girls, I know, have been in care. When I talk to them, they say they love their babies but most say they wish it had never happened. Another curious thing is that many of their own mums had babies when they were teenagers too.

From this unit I discovered that all this is not uncommon. Teenage pregnancies are highest in areas of poverty. Most schoolgirl mothers are girls who did not fit into school, who did not plan to go on to college or have a career. But neither did most of them plan to have their babies.

I begin my nurse training in September and I want to specialise in health education with young people. I'd like to be a school nurse. This unit has really opened my eyes. The high teenage pregnancy rate seems to be linked with poverty and a poor education. That has really started me thinking about how we could start to tackle the problem.

### Over to you!

1 Why do you think that teenage pregnancy rates are highest in areas of poverty?

2 Why do you think that teenage pregnancy rates are higher among girls who have not achieved at school?

3 What do you think could be done to address the high teenage pregnancy rate in the UK?

# 1 Understand the concept of an unequal society

**Get started**

### Youth unemployment

Get into small groups and discuss the following questions:

1 What factors might lead to young people being unemployed?
2 How might unemployment affect their physical, intellectual, social and emotional well-being?
3 How might social attitudes towards the unemployed affect their health and well-being?
4 Are there any support services in your school or college to help students who may be vulnerable to unemployment when they leave?

Social inequalities are a characteristic of almost all known societies and of many social groups. This is because some people or groups of people are seen as having a higher social status or more prestige and importance than others. Disadvantaged groups in society often become the subject of **prejudice**.

Prejudice is a term that is not easy to define but it refers to a set of rather fixed attitudes or beliefs about particular social or ethnic groups. People are normally unwilling, unable and often uninterested in changing these attitudes. For example, an example of a prejudiced view would be that people of working age who are on benefits are lazy; they do not want to work and, if they did, they would find a job because there are plenty advertised. If people were really prejudiced, they would not easily change their minds about this, even if you presented clear examples of unemployed people who had applied unsuccessfully for many jobs.

Normally, prejudicial attitudes are negative and based on oversimplified views of a social group. It is a concept closely linked to the term **stereotyping**, which defines a group (in this case the unemployed, or job seekers) as if they all share the same characteristics and ignores their individual differences. When a stereotype is widely held, it is sometimes said that the group is the subject of **labelling**. This means that the stereotypical qualities and characteristics are applied to them, their individual differences are ignored and they are treated accordingly.

## Activity 1: Prejudice and stereotyping

In small groups identify two different groups in your home country who suffer from:

- prejudice
- stereotyping and/or
- labelling.

1 Identify the characteristics that are often linked with those groups.
2 Are they positive characteristics or negative?
3 What do you think is the impact of stereotyping on these groups of people?

Be prepared to share your ideas with the rest of your class.

## PLTS

**Creative thinker:** This activity will require you to use creative thinking to question your own and other people's assumptions about other groups in our society, particularly the disadvantaged and marginalised groups.

Prejudicial attitudes, which in themselves are a state of mind, can easily lead to **discrimination**. This means treating a person differently (usually less favourably) because of particular personal characteristics such as their age, race, colour or gender. Groups who are discriminated against can quickly feel **marginalised** by the general society or more dominant group. They feel 'out on the edge' and excluded from the life and status enjoyed by the rest of the group or society.

Why do you think groups who are discriminated against can often feel marginalised?

## Case study: Employment of men in the early years sector

Pete has a level 3 child care qualification. He has decided to become a childminder. He has approval from the local authority. He has been working in the early years sector for over ten years and he has very good references from all previous employers. Although there is a shortage of childminders in the area he has had very few enquiries.

1  Could the concepts introduced in this chapter (e.g. prejudice, stereotyping and labelling) help explain why Pete has had few enquiries?

2  Do you think he has evidence to suggest he is being discriminated against because he is a man working in a field with an almost exclusively female workforce?

3  What do you think could be done to remedy the situation?

## Activity 2: How does it feel?

1  Can you think of an occasion or a time when you felt:
   - stereotyped
   - labelled and/or
   - discriminated against?

2  What did this feel like?

3  What did you do?

4  How do you think you should have reacted?

If you feel able, discuss these points in your group.

## Key terms

**Prejudice** – A fixed set of attitudes or beliefs about particular groups in society that people are normally unwilling, unable and often uninterested in changing.

**Stereotyping** – Defining a group of people (e.g. women) as if they all share the same characteristics and ignoring their individual differences.

**Labelling** – A term closely linked with stereotyping, where the stereotypical characteristics are applied to a person and their individuality is ignored.

**Discrimination** – Treating a person differently (usually less favourably) because of particular personal characteristics, such as their age, race, colour or gender.

**Marginalise** – Make individuals or groups of people feel 'out on the edge' of a society and excluded from the way of life and the status enjoyed by others.

**Social exclusion** – The situation for people who suffer from a combination of linked problems such as unemployment, poor housing, high crime rates and poor health.

**Social exclusion** is a term closely linked with issues of inequality, discrimination, stereotyping and marginalisation. However, it also refers to wider issues of participation in society. The Social Exclusion Unit (set up by the Labour government in 1997) defined exclusion as follows:

> Social exclusion is a shorthand term for what can happen when people or areas suffer from a combination of linked problems such as unemployment, poor housing, high unemployment, poor skills, low incomes, poor housing, high crime environments, bad health, poverty and family break down.

The Social Exclusion Unit was set up to address the problems that arose from inequality and its consequences for individuals and groups in society. The problems were seen as having interlinked causes and the Social Exclusion Unit was seen as a way of addressing them. When launching the unit, Tony Blair said that social exclusion wasn't only due to financial deprivation. He also blamed problems involving housing, health, education, transport and, most of all, unemployment.

In September 2004 the government published a further report, 'A New Direction for the Social Exclusion Unit 2004–2005'. Responding to new research, the Prime Minister and Deputy Prime Minister set a new direction for the work of the Social Exclusion Unit, which was given the task of improving the life chances of the most vulnerable groups in society.

---

### Activity 3: Social exclusion

In small groups identify four groups of people who you think might feel socially excluded.

1 Discuss your reasons for identifying these particular groups.
2 What do you think will be the impact of social exclusion on their opportunities in society?

Present and be prepared to discuss your views with the rest of your class.

---

### PLTS

**Creative thinker:** This activity will require you to think creatively in order to ask questions and challenge each others' views and perhaps stereotypes of different groups in our society.

---

# 2   Know social inequalities in society

**Social class** is a term that is difficult to define but is used to describe social hierarchies in most modern industrialised societies. It is largely based on economic factors linked with income, the ownership of property and other forms of wealth. Sociologists have been particularly interested in the links between our social class position and other aspects of our lives. In this unit we will consider the links between social class and the incidence of abuse or substance abuse, crime, mental illness, teenage pregnancies, bullying and eating disorders.

British governments first started to use an official social class classification system to measure and analyse changes in the population in 1851. In 1921 the Registrar General identified five social classes, based largely on perceived occupational skill, and these categories remained in place until 2001. Until very recently, this system was used by government

statisticians and others to analyse population trends and to compare levels of health and ill health, life expectancy, lifestyle choices and life events by social status or class. The five social classes are shown in the following table.

**Table 19.1:** The Registrar General's scale of social class, 1921–2001

| Class | Description |
|-------|-------------|
| Class 1 | Professional class |
| Class 2 | Managerial and technical occupations |
| Class 3 | Skilled occupations<br>Non-manual (3N)<br>Manual (3M) |
| Class 4 | Semi-skilled occupations |
| Class 5 | Unskilled occupations |

Since 2001, the National Statistics Socio-Economic Classification (NS-SEC) has been used for government official statistics and surveys. It is still based on occupation but has been altered in line with employment changes and has categories to include the vast majority of the adult population, as shown in Table 19.2 on page 225.

---

### Key term

**Social class** – Social hierarchies in most modern industrialised societies, largely based on economic factors linked with income, the ownership of property and other forms of wealth.

**Table 19.2:** National Statistics Socio-economic Classification (NS-SEC), 2001 to present day

| Class | Description |
|-------|-------------|
| Class 1 | Higher managerial and professional occupations |
| Class 2 | Lower managerial and professional occupations |
| Class 3 | Intermediate occupations |
| Class 4 | Small employers and own account workers (mainly the self-employed) |
| Class 5 | Lower supervisory and technical occupations |
| Class 6 | Semi-routine occupations |
| Class 7 | Routine occupations |
| Class 8 | Never worked and long-term unemployed |

## Activity 4: Social class

1   In groups, identify the likely differences in the lifestyles of
   • young people
   • retired people
   • people with disabilities
   in the highest social classes, compared to those in the lowest two groups.
2   Consider the reasons for these differences.

Different sociologists define the term 'social class' in slightly different ways, but despite these difficulties of definition and different views on the continuing importance of class in our society, there is overwhelming evidence that

• standards of health
• the incidence of ill health or morbidity
• and life expectancy

vary by social group and especially by social class. Members of the higher social classes live longer and enjoy better health than members of the lower social groups. The most influential modern studies that consider the reasons for these differences are the 1980 *Black Report* and the 1998 *Acheson Report*. Both reports provide detailed and comprehensive explanations of the relationships between social and

environmental factors and health, illness and life expectancy. There is also evidence that patterns of health and illness vary with:

• gender
• age
• culture and ethnicity
• disability
• sexuality.

Evidence also shows that:

• men have a shorter life expectancy than women, although women have longer periods of ill health
• people from most minority ethnic groups in the UK have greater periods of illness and shorter life expectancy than the host population
• one in six people in the UK (10.3 million) living in a private household have an illness or condition that limits their daily activities – a limiting long-term illness (Census of the population 2001)
• gay men and lesbians reported more psychological distress than heterosexual people (Mind 2003).

However, if people from any of these groups are also poor, the differences are even greater.

## Activity 5: The impact of the environment on health and well-being

In groups draw spidergrams or mind maps identifying the possible range of social and environmental factors that might lead to:

• higher levels of ill health among the poor compared to the rich
• higher levels of mental illness in women than men
• longer life expectancy for women than men.

Be prepared to share and discuss your views with the rest of your class.

## PLTS

**Creative thinker:** This activity allows you to demonstrate your creative thinking skills by asking questions and discussing the reasons for differences in the health and well-being between social groups.

## Case study: Two different families

Lisa is a lone parent. She has two children: Tom who is three years old and Sam who is 18 months. Her husband has recently left her and she doesn't know where he is living. She has no other family support and her only income is state benefits. Lisa and her children live in a two-bedroom flat on the second floor of an old Victorian house. The flat is damp. She is frightened of using too much heating in case she cannot afford the electricity bills.

Felicity and Paul are in a very happy long-term relationship. They have two children: Adam who is three years old and Lucy who is two. Paul is an accountant. They are financially secure and enjoy a high standard of living. They have a four-bedroom house with a large garden, they enjoy regular holidays and have a varied and stimulating social life.

1 Compare the socio-economic circumstances of the two families.

2 Discuss the possible impact of the differences on the physical, social, emotional and intellectual development of the children in the two families.

## Assessment activity 19.1

 **P1 P2 M1 D1** **:BTEC**

Write a report that will:

1 explain the concept of an unequal society
2 describe social inequalities that exist in society
3 discuss the impact of social inequalities on groups in society
4 evaluate the impact of social inequalities in society.

### Grading tips

It could be useful to review your learning from Unit 7 Sociological perspectives in Health and Social Care before starting this unit.

 To achieve P1, you will need to explain what is meant by the term 'unequal society' using the sociological terms and concepts introduced at the beginning of this unit (e.g. prejudice, stereotyping, marginalisation and exclusion). You will need to ensure that you give clear definitions of these inter-related terms and provide appropriate examples to illustrate their meaning.

 For P2, you should briefly describe the social inequalities for people in different social groups. You should describe differences in opportunities, quality of life and/or levels of health and well-being for people of different:

- social classes
- ages – children or older people
- gender
- ethnicity
- disability and/or
- sexuality.

**M1** To achieve M1, you should develop the material introduced in your answer to P2. Use the sociological terms and concepts introduced at the beginning of this chapter (e.g. prejudice, stereotyping, marginalisation and exclusion) when discussing how social inequalities can affect the health and well-being of different social groups

**D1** For D1, you will need to consider the overall effect and impact of social inequalities (in terms of the poorer quality of life, including levels of health and well-being) on society. You should also think about questions such as: is there sufficient reliable evidence to suggest that the shorter life expectancy and higher levels of reported illness are significant? You need to weigh up the evidence and come to your own conclusion. You will not have all the evidence needed to reach a firm definitive conclusion. The research continues. You have to make a judgement and come to a conclusion based on the evidence you have found.

### PLTS

**Self-manager:** To complete this assignment, you will need to use your self-management skills to organise your time and resources, prioritise your activities and meet the assessment deadlines.

# 3   Understand the nature of demographic change within an unequal society

## 3.1 Demographic change

Demography is the technical term used to describe the study of changes in the size and structure of the population. Social scientists, commercial institutions, governments and other policy makers all study changes in the size and make-up of the population. At first governments were concerned with measuring:

- natural changes in the population – changes in the birth rates and death rates
- changes in migration (emigration and immigration).

Now demographers examine wider changes in the population, such as changes in educational achievements, employment, spending patterns and the use of leisure time.

### Birth rates and death rates

Natural changes in the population include changes in the **birth rates** and **death rates**. The birth rate, measured as a proportion of live births per thousand of the population, fell during the twentieth century from an average of some six children per family in 1870 to 1.7 children in 2007. The 2001 census (for more information on the census, see page 233) showed for the first time that there were fewer children under the age of 16 than people over the age of 65. If this trend continued, by 2033, 23 per cent of the population would be aged 65 and over, compared to 18 per cent

aged 16 or younger. (Source: National Statistics Online 27.8.09)

It is not possible to explain this trend with full certainty but it is reasonable to account for it by considering the changing social circumstances of the twentieth century:

- reliable contraception became available to women from the late 1960s
- women began to pursue their own careers and chose not to have large families
- people chose to have smaller families to sustain a higher standard of living
- the development of the welfare state meant that large families were not necessary to care for parents in their old age.

The **infant mortality rate** is defined as the number of deaths of babies under the age of one year, per thousand live births over a given period, normally a year. The **perinatal mortality rate** refers to babies who die during the first week of life. The number of babies who die in infancy has declined in the UK during the twentieth century but the numbers are still higher than those of other developed countries. A high infant mortality rate will often point to inadequacies in a range of social and economic services and to high levels of poverty and economic hardship.

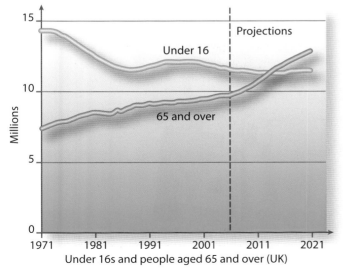

**Fig 19.1:** Ageing (source: National Statistics Online 27.8.09)

## Key terms

**Birth rate** – The number of live births per thousand of the population over a given period, normally a year.

**Death rate** – The number of deaths per thousand of the population over a given period, normally a year.

**Infant mortality rate** – The number of deaths of babies under the age of one year, per thousand live births over a given period, normally a year.

**Perinatal mortality rate** – The number of deaths of babies who die during their first week of life per thousand live births over a given period, normally a year.

## Activity 6: Changes in mortality rates

Divide into three groups and use flip chart paper to create spidergrams that identify the likely reasons for the:

- fall in the infant mortality rate in the past 100 years
- the higher infant mortality rates in social classes 7 and 8, compared to social classes 1 and 2
- the increase in life expectancy over the past 100 years.

Be prepared to defend and discuss your findings with the rest of your class.

## PLTS

**Independent enquirer:** Through this activity you can demonstrate your independent enquiry skills by investigating the reasons for these demographic changes in your home country.

## Migration: immigration and emigration

Britain has, for many years, been a country of many races. Very often **immigration** occurred because people were escaping religious or political persecution. For example, in the seventeenth century, French Huguenot Protestants came to Britain to escape religious persecution, and Jewish people sought refuge in Britain at the time of the Second World War. During the same conflict, men and women from Commonwealth countries (notably India, Pakistan and the Caribbean) and from Eastern Europe, particularly Poland and Czechoslovakia, served in the British armed forces. In the mid-twentieth century, people from former Commonwealth nations were offered inducements to emigrate to the UK to help solve labour shortages in:

- the health services
- textile industries
- public transport.

Since the expansion of the European Union in 2004, to include the Czech Republic, Cyprus, Latvia, Lithuania, Malta, Estonia, Hungary, Poland, Slovakia and

Which groups of people came to the UK in the mid-twentieth century?

Slovenia, there has been increasing migration from Eastern Europe. In 2008, an estimated 163,000 more people entered than left the UK. Source: Office of National Statistics Online, 26.11.2009

In the late nineteenth century, and until the 1930s, **emigration** was more common than immigration. There were more emigrants from the UK starting new lives in other countries than immigrants making new homes in Britain. However, in most years since the early 1930s, the reverse has been the case. There have been more people entering the country than leaving. **Net migration** refers to the difference between the number of immigrants and the number of emigrants over a given period.

## Multiculturalism

For many years, Britain has been a diverse society made up of people from many nations and many different ethnic groups. **Multiculturalism** promotes the view that people from all ethnic and cultural groups should feel free to celebrate their varied beliefs, customs and traditions. Furthermore, there should be an atmosphere of interest and tolerance, and people should learn about each other's cultures with respect and understanding.

## Changes in life expectancy

Since the mid-nineteenth century, there has been a steady fall in the death rate or, to look at it another way, an increase in **life expectancy**.

The fall in the death rate in the mid-nineteenth century was certainly linked to the public health measures of the time, including improved sanitation and cleaner water (in place from the 1840s onwards). In the twentieth century, further public health measures included:

- improved housing
- child immunisation programmes
- improved diets
- the introduction of the NHS and other welfare services
- a general increase in the standard of living.

### Key terms

**Immigration** – The arrival in a country of people who have left their home country and who wish to make the new country their permanent place of residence.

**Emigration** – The movement of people from their home country to make a permanent residence in a different country.

**Net migration** – The difference between the number of immigrants and the number of emigrants in a country over a given period, normally a year.

**Multiculturalism** – The celebration of the culture of all people living in the home country.

**Life expectancy** – A statistical calculation that predicts the average number of years a person is likely to live. This is usually based on the year of birth but can be calculated from any age.

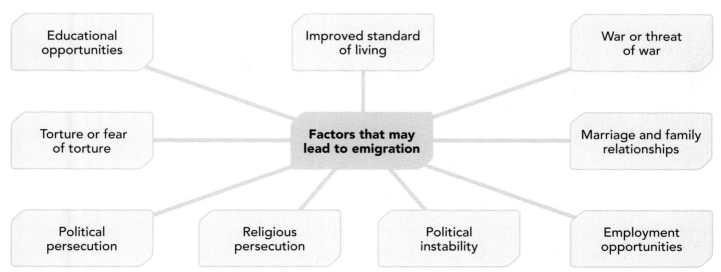

**Fig 19.2:** Factors that may lead to emigration

# Aleksy Janic
## Care assistant

Aleksy is a care assistant who works at The Maples, a day centre for people with disabilities. The centre is based in an ethnically mixed community on the eastern edge of a large industrial city, where there is considerable racial tension. There have been many instances of racially motivated violence and, most recently, race riots.

The centre was opened just four months ago. So far, there are 15 people who regularly attend the centre who are gradually getting to know each other. They represent five main religious groups, including Muslims, Hindus, Jews, Sikhs and Christians. There are others who do not have any clear religious affiliation.

The staff are committed to ensuring that people who use the centre and other visitors should feel welcome. The centre is decorated with pictures and images representing many different countries and cultures. The staff prepare a diverse range of food and have asked the people who come to the sessions for their preferences and ideas. They are hoping to recruit staff and volunteers from diverse backgrounds to work at the centre.

The Maples has an equality and diversity policy, which is understood by the staff and shared with the attendees and their carers. However, there are difficulties in communication. Some of the attendees have a very limited vocabulary and some have difficulties in speaking at all. Furthermore, over ten different languages are used by the families and carers of those who attend the centre.

The equality and diversity policy states that The Maples:

1  supports the celebration of diversity

2  is committed to providing an environment that ensures that everybody is made welcome, everybody is treated fairly and the views and beliefs of others are fully respected

3  is committed to eliminating discrimination against all users of the centre, particularly on the grounds of:

- age
- disability
- ethnic origin
- gender
- religion or belief
- sexual orientation
- socio-economic group.

## Think about it!

1  Why it is important that the equal opportunities policy is understood by all users of the centre?

2  What are the particular challenges of ensuring that they all understand the policy at The Maples?

3  What are the measures that should be in place to ensure that everyone who comes to the centre feels welcome?

4  What is meant by 'celebrating diversity'?

5  How can staff and other users of the centre ensure that diversity is celebrated at The Maples?

Many people over retirement age lead busy and active lives. Many remain in paid employment and contribute to a wide range of voluntary and community activities. Lots of retired people give very practical support to their children and grandchildren and often say that they don't know how they found the time to work!

Growing older is a natural process and, while it may lead to slower reactions, poorer eyesight, loss of hearing and restricted mobility, this need not itself be an issue or a problem. However, it does become a problem if there is insufficient support and if day-to-day activities become too big a challenge. The fall in the death rate, or the fact that people are living longer, presents new and pressing issues for health and care workers.

more likely to be provided by adult daughters than by adult sons.

Changes in family networks, however, mean that families can find it increasingly difficult to provide this kind of support. Adult children may not necessarily live near their ageing parents – they might have moved for reasons of employment, education, or in search of suitable and affordable housing. To compound this, modern houses are often too small to accommodate three generations. In addition, increasing numbers of women are in paid work and unable to provide daily care for older parents. The increase in divorce, and the high proportion of one-parent families, place further financial and emotional pressures on adult children, and the fall in family size often means that the support needs of ageing parents cannot easily be shared.

## Activity 7: Never had it so good?

As a homework task:

- search through newspapers, magazines, websites and any other aspects of the mass media for positive images of older people
- in the first 20 minutes of your next lesson, create a poster display using the images or articles you have collected
- write a 100-word newspaper article that celebrates the life of older people in the community and compare your article with others in your group. Have you identified similar issues and activities to celebrate?

## Activity 8: Services for older people

In groups:

1 Identify the services you think governments should provide for frail older people in our society. Present your main points to the rest of the group.

2 Using the Internet, the library and experience from work placements, write a short report identifying the range of services actually provided for frail older people in your local area.

## PLTS

**Self-manager:** For this activity you will need to organise your time and resources, prioritise activities and keep to the timetable agreed.

## Functional skills

**ICT:** Select and use a variety of sources of information independently for a complex task.

## The implications of an ageing population

For those people over retirement age who do need practical care and support, it is very likely to come from family, friends or neighbours. The 2001 census showed a big increase in the number of people over the age of 85, to over 1.1 million (or 1.9 per cent of the population), and it is this age group who typically need more intensive support in order to live independently. When this support comes from the family, despite changes in attitudes and equality legislation, it is still

Services for older people are of course costly and the increasing numbers bring significant financial responsibilities for the working population. Retirement pensions and the costs of providing appropriate care services have to be met at least partly from the taxes of those in work. This is currently impacting on government policy. High taxes are unpopular but government-funded care has to be paid for.

Throughout much of the twentieth century, older people who needed more support, in addition to that provided by family and friends, were cared for in large institutions and often in the geriatric wards of hospitals. Many of the hospitals carried the stigma and shame of the workhouse. However, the NHS and Community Care Act (1990) provided the legislative framework and financial support required for planned care in the community. This led to the closure of many large institutions and to the provision of care in people's homes or in smaller establishments more closely linked with their community. The community care services include:

- adaptations to homes
- regular home care services
- meals on wheels
- attendance at day centres or lunch clubs
- full-time care in a residential home (long-term care in large institutions rarely happens now).

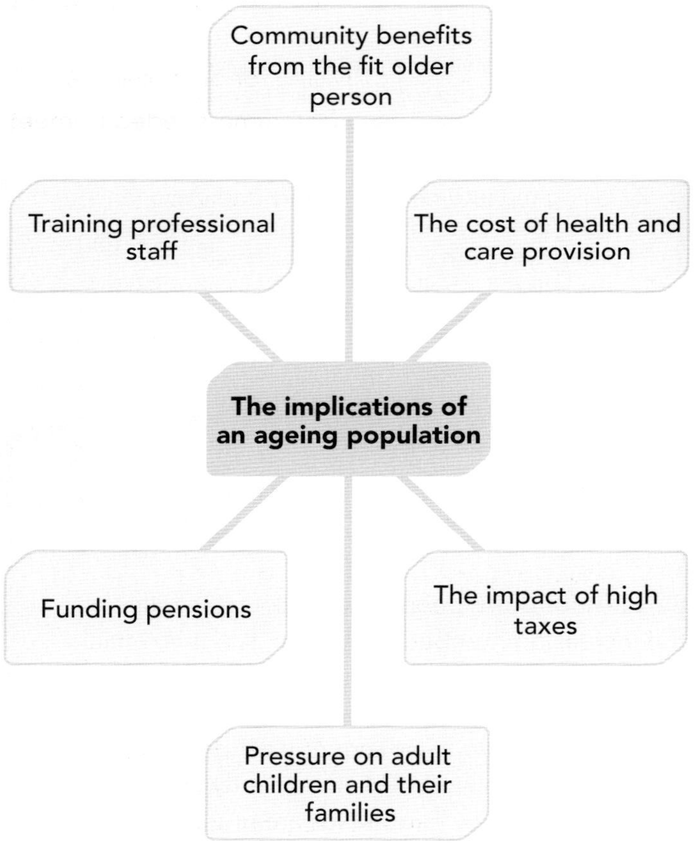

Fig 19.3: The implications of an ageing population

## Activity 9: Long-term care for frail older people

The sociologist Peter Townsend, in his classic study 'The Last Refuge' (1962), carried out a survey of older people living in large institutions. He found that people suffered from:

- isolation
- lack of choice in day-to-day activities
- lack of control over their lives.

Drawing on work placement experience in care settings for older people, identify how the setting aims to overcome the negative factors identified by Peter Townsend.

## PLTS

**Independent enquirer:** Through this activity you will draw on experience and your independent enquiry skills to investigate the links between inequalities, the quality of care provision and the health and well-being of clients.

## Activity 10: The implications of demographic change

In groups:

- Identify reasons why governments will need to study changes in the size and structure of the population.
- Draw a spidergram to summarise the key points that you make.
- Present your reasons to the group.

Make sure that you have individual notes on all the key reasons presented during the full class feedback.

## PLTS

**Independent enquirer:** In this activity you will use your independent enquiry skills to analyse and report on the importance of collecting demographic data for governments, and the health and social care sector in particular.

# 3.2 Demographic data

## Birth and death rates

The impact of birth and death rates on the planning and provision of health and care services was discussed earlier in the unit (see page 227).

## The census

Every ten years, since 1801 (apart from 1941), the government has carried out a **census** of the population; this is an attempt to count the total number of people living in the UK. The most recent census took place on Sunday, 29 April 2001. The census is managed by:

- the Office for National Statistics – England
- the General Register Office – Scotland
- the Northern Ireland Statistics and Research Agency – Northern Ireland.

On the night of the census every household is required, by law, to provide information about the people staying in their house. Those people living in institutions (e.g. prisons, hospitals boarding schools or convents) are recorded by the head of the institution and every effort is made to record the number of people who are homeless.

In its earliest forms, the census provided a simple record of the size of the population, the age structure, sex and marital status and the levels of employment. In more recent times, questions have been asked about levels of education, types of housing and housing conditions, car ownership and religion. A record of the size and structure of the population at the time of the last census can be found on the government website: www.statistics.gov.uk/census2001.

The next census of the population is due in 2011. The Office for National Statistics is working with local authorities and communities to ensure that the count of the population is as accurate as possible. Special attention is being paid to collecting accurate data from groups where the response has been historically low. This includes people with disabilities, older people, ethnic minority groups, faith communities, migrants, non-English-speaking people, unemployed people, people on low incomes, students and other young adults, gypsy, traveller and other groups.

## Electoral registers

Electoral registers, which are compiled by the local council, list the name and address of everyone who is eligible to vote in national and local government elections. People are only eligible to vote if their name appears on the register.

## Using demographic data

Governments need to measure and monitor changes in the size and structure of the population in order to plan provision and anticipate changes in social need. For example:

- an increase in car ownership has implications for transport policies
- an increase in life expectancy has implications for care provision for older people
- a fall in the birth rate has implications for child care provision.

Demographic information of this type will be used to set specific targets for planners, for example:

- the number of child care places needed in nurseries and schools over the next decade
- the range and size of provision for older people
- the size of the building programme needed to meet these demands
- the training needed to support the plans.

## Key term

**Census** – A compulsory and detailed count of the population in the UK held every 10 years.

## Activity 11: Why have a census of the population?

In pairs identify three implications for the government of each the following trends that have been identified in recent censuses of the population:

- a rise in life expectancy
- an increase in the number of immigrants for whom English is not their first language
- an increase in teenage pregnancies
- an increase in the number of one-parent households
- a fall in the number of children under 16.

Be prepared to share your ideas with the class.

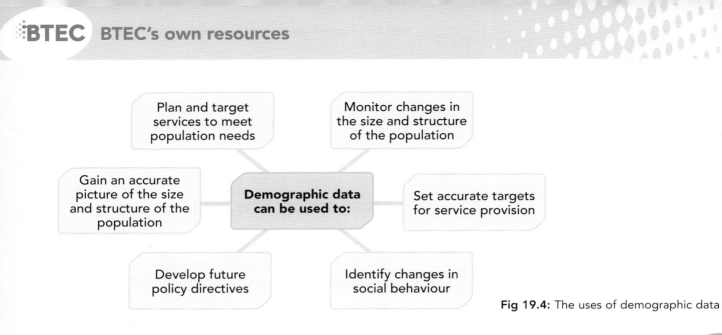

**Fig 19.4:** The uses of demographic data

## Assessment activity 19.2

**P3** **P4** **M2** BTEC

Ruth works for a large social care provider and has been asked by her employer to investigate which social groups are most in need of care services. In order to do this, she will need to examine the size and structure of the population and how this is changing. This information will be used to inform the planning of health and care services.

Write a report that will assist Ruth in her investigation of health and social care provision, in which you:

1 explain recent demographic changes in your home country

2 assess the impact of demographic changes within your home country

3 explain how demographic data is used in health and social care service provision.

### Grading tips

**P3** When explaining recent demographic change you must refer to natural changes in the population (changes in birth rates and death rates) and changes in patterns of immigration and emigration.

You will need to refer to the number and in some cases the proportion of people of different social groupings in the population of your home country. For example, the number and/or proportion of:

• older people

• babies and young people of school age

• immigrants and emigrants

• people wit h disabilities.

You will need to give clear reasons for the changes identified. For example, provide explanations or reasons for the fall in the birth rate, increase in life expectancy and increased migration from Eastern Europe.

**M2** For the pass grade, you are required to explain the recent demographic changes in the population of your home country. To achieve M2, you need to assess the impact or consequences of these changes.

Refer to your data (e.g. the fall in the birth and death rates or changing patterns of migration) and show how the changes will affect the level of need and the type of care provision required.

**P4** In the concluding section of your report, explain how this statistical information is used in the planning and provision of health and care services.

Provide specific examples to show how information about the population changes can and will be used to inform planning and type of provision.

Remember that the benefits of using accurate and up-to-date demographic data will be felt by the planners, the care providers (both paid and unpaid) and also by the individuals using health and care services.

# 4 Understand potential links between social inequalities and the health and well-being of the population

## 4.1 Social inequalities

Poverty is difficult to define. What might seem like poverty to one person could be regarded as great riches by another. In our society, if someone cannot afford electrical goods for their home and can never afford a holiday or the occasional meal out in a café or restaurant, this would be seen by many as significant deprivation, if not actual poverty. However, most people living in Africa would not regard it as a sign of either.

### Activity 12: What do we mean by poverty?

1  Write a list of ten items that you regard as necessary (i.e. if someone did not have them you would regard them as being in poverty).

2  Compare your list with the person sitting next to you.

3  Can you come to an agreement?

### PLTS

**Creative thinker:** When completing this activity you will use your creative thinking skills to question your own and others' assumptions as to the nature of poverty and deprivation.

The earliest large-scale studies of poverty were conducted at the turn of the nineteenth century. Seebohm Rowntree (1871–1954), a Quaker and more famously a chocolate manufacturer, studied poverty in his home city of York; and Charles Booth (1840–1916) conducted a similar study of poverty in London. Booth and Rowntree were probably the first researchers to make clear the links between low wages, unemployment, disability, poor housing, family poverty and levels of health and illness.

People with an income below the level seen as necessary to support 'physical efficiency' were considered by Rowntree to be in **absolute poverty**. This level of income was very low – there was no possibility of buying newspapers, presents or even sending letters to family members and certainly no allowance for sweets, toys, alcohol or tobacco.

**Secondary poverty** was defined by Rowntree as a situation where people had an income above that allowed for absolute poverty but chose to spend their money on other 'unallowable' (non-essential) items.

This approach to defining poverty introduced the concept of the **poverty line** – a level of income below which people were regarded as being in poverty. The idea of the poverty line is still used to inform the benefit system in modern Britain. The level of income support is calculated and set at a level that should allow claimants to sustain good health – a poverty line.

### Reflect

Which groups of people in our society do you think are most likely to be in poverty?

### Key terms

**Absolute poverty** – A term introduced by Seebohm Rowntree, referring to people on a level of income below that which will maintain 'physical efficiency'.

**Secondary poverty** – A term also used by Seebohm Rowntree, referring to a situation where people had sufficient money but were in poverty because they spent it on non-essential items.

**Poverty line** – A term introduced by Seebohm Rowntree and still used by policy makers to refer to the level of income necessary to keep people out of poverty.

Studies of poverty in the second half of the twentieth century approached the issues slightly differently, introducing the concept of **relative poverty**. This defined poverty as a level of income that prevents people participating in the life of the society in which they live. Peter Townsend was key in the development and use of relative poverty in studies of inequality and deprivation. In 1979, Townsend's view was that:

'Individuals, families and groups in the population can be said to be in poverty when they lack the resources to obtain the type of diet, participate in the activities and have the living conditions and amenities that are customary or at least widely encouraged or approved, in the societies to which they belong. Their resources are so seriously below those commanded by the average individual or family that they are, in effect, excluded from the ordinary living patterns, customs and activities.'

In 1983, London Weekend Television supported a study of poverty known as 'Breadline Britain'. It used the concept of relative poverty, or relative deprivation, developed by Peter Townsend; it was conducted by Joanna Mack and Stewart Lansley. This was updated in 1990 and again in 1999. These large-scale studies attempted to identify both the extent of poverty and those groups most vulnerable to poverty in our society.

The numbers of people in poverty were found to be:

- 7.5 million people (approximately 14 per cent of the population) in 1983
- 11 million people (approximately 20 per cent of the population – two-thirds of whom relied on state benefits for their main source of income) in 1990.

The 1999 study (Gordon *et al* 2000) found that poverty had increased again. The 1999 researchers found that the proportion in poverty had risen from the 1983 level of 14 per cent to 24 per cent in 1999.

The most commonly used measure of poverty, and the one normally used by government agencies, is that if a household income is 60 per cent below the average household income for that year (after this has been adjusted to account for the size of household) the household is regarded as being in poverty – another reference to a poverty line. In 2006/7, 13.5 million people in Great Britain were living in households below this 'income threshold'.

### Key term

**Relative poverty** – A level of income that deprives a person of the standard of living or way of life considered normal in a particular society.

Fig 19.5: Groups who are vulnerable to poverty

# Income and wealth distribution

Inequalities in society can be measured by comparing differences in the levels of income and wealth by different social groups. Income is a term used to describe the regular flow of money earned from work or income from pensions, benefits or savings, and wealth normally refers to property, shares or other personal possessions that could be sold to generate an income. These terms are difficult to define and also difficult to measure accurately. Reliable data on levels of income and wealth is not easily available. However, data from government sources consistently show that wealth and income are not evenly distributed through the population. A large-scale report commissioned by the Labour government announced in January 2010 that the richest 10 per cent of the population are now 100 per cent better off than the poorest and that Britain had become more unequal over the 30 years since 1980 (*Guardian*, 27.1.2010, quoting from 'An Anatomy of Economic Inequality in the UK').

# Unemployment

Closely linked with issues of poverty are the specific issues of unemployment, especially long-term

## Activity 13: The impact of unemployment

In pairs, using government statistics, identify the areas in your home country that have the highest unemployment.
1  Identify and discuss the likely impact of long-term unemployment on families and communities.
2  Be prepared to share your findings with the rest of the class.

## PLTS

**Independent enquirer:** This activity will enable you to demonstrate your ability to carry out independent research, analyse data and discuss the potential links between unemployment and health and well-being.

## Functional skills

**English:** Making a range of contributions to discussion and giving effective presentations will allow you to demonstrate your speaking and listening skills.

unemployment. State benefits are set at levels linked with Rowntree's concept of the poverty line and kept at very low levels (arguably for political reasons). High taxes are unpopular and state benefits are a direct cost to the taxpayer. There is also an ongoing concern that people should not be able to receive more money in benefits than they could earn from paid employment. In addition, the long-term unemployed potentially suffer the personal consequences of prejudice and discrimination, marginalisation and social exclusion, as well as the continuing impact of poverty.

# The ageing society

In many societies, social status increases with age. Older people, or elders, have a high status and an important role in the family and wider community. In China and many parts of Africa, and on the Indian subcontinent, older people are treated with great respect. In modern Britain, however, older people have a less clear position in society. They may feel they have less of a stake in society, or that, as they are not at work, they are less important. They may very well be unclear as to what their new role should be.

There is widespread evidence that older people are the subject of discrimination. In 2006, the Age Discrimination Act was passed – a response to the extent of discrimination against older people.

There have also been a number of studies pointing to the higher incidence of poverty among older people, compared to the population as a whole. However, recent research supported by the Joseph Rowntree Foundation confirmed that poverty was not evenly spread across the older people in our society. Studies found that the risks of having a low income after the age of 60 were strongly related to:

*   occupational group
*   continuity of employment.

People who had worked continuously in professional and managerial jobs were far less likely to face a poor retirement than people who had worked in manual or unskilled occupations. The manual workers will typically have earned lower wages, enjoyed less secure employment and will be less likely to have a private pension.

Males in professional classes have a life expectancy at birth of 80 years, compared to 78.1 years in the manual unskilled classes. Females in the professional classes have a life expectancy of 85.1 years, compared to 78.1

years for the unskilled classes. (Source: The Office of National Statistics, October 2007).The causes of death also vary by social class. The incidence of lung cancer, respiratory diseases, coronary heart diseases and strokes are lowest in the higher social classes. The incidence of these causes of death increases with social disadvantage.

## Activity 14: Respecting our elders

In groups, discuss the following questions:

1 Why do you think that older people in our society may not feel that they are respected in the way that elders are revered in many developing nations?

2 How may this affect their health and well-being?

### PLTS

**Creative thinker:** Through discussion, this activity will enable you to use your creative thinking skills to explore the impact of values and attitudes on the health and well-being of older people.

## Gender and health

Probably the most noted social change since the Second World War has been the changing role of women in wider society. In society, and in the more private sphere of the family, there have been moves towards equality. For example, more women continue in full-time employment after marriage and after the birth of their children, and women are taking a more significant role in public life and within the community. However, despite these changes, there is considerable evidence that inequalities between men and women still exist. Women's hourly rate of pay, despite equality legislation, stubbornly remains lower than men's.

### Did you know?

The average (median) weekly earning for full-time employees in 2008 was £412 for women (an increase of 4.4 per cent over 2007), compared to £521 for men (an increase of 4.6 per cent over 2007). The gap had increased.

Source: Office for National Statistics, 14.11.08

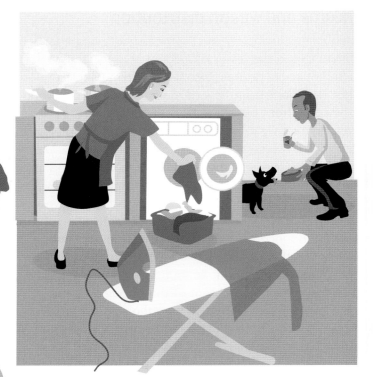

Fig 19.6: Women are still seen as having the principal responsibility for the home!

Despite changes in attitudes, and significant evidence that men take a fuller part in childcare and housework than in the past, women are still seen as having the main responsibility for the home and family.

## Activity 15: Gender and the division of labour at home

Think about a family (either your own or another you know well) that is headed by a man and a woman who are both in full-time paid employment. Identify who normally takes responsibility for the following domestic tasks:

- making evening meals
- cooking
- washing and ironing
- small repairs around the house
- household cleaning
- household shopping
- looking after sick members of the family.

Collate the information gathered by each member of your class and present it as a bar chart.

Do the results confirm or disprove the view that women take a larger responsibility than men for household tasks?

There are differences between the sexes in life expectancy and health in older age. Life expectancy for babies born between 2006 and 2008 was 77.4 years for males and 81.6 for females.

Source: National Statistics Online, 21.10.09

Women can expect to live longer than men but they are likely to spend more years in poor health or with a disability. Women are more likely to suffer from arthritis and rheumatism than men. In 2006 the rate of these conditions for people between the ages of 65 and 74 was 144 per 1,000 men in the UK, but for women was much higher at 229 per 1,000 women. Although the death rate for circulatory diseases (including heart disease and strokes) has declined, overall it is still considerably higher for men than women. In 2006 2,462 per million men and 1,559 per million women died from circulatory disease.

Source: National Statistics Online, 26.9.08

## Mental illness and suicide

Mental illness is another term that is difficult to define and therefore difficult to monitor. What is regarded as normal and acceptable behaviour varies from one society to another and at different times in history. In addition, the evidence available is derived largely from medical statistics, recording the number of people who present themselves for treatment. However, there may be many reasons why people with mental health problems do not seek professional help. They may not regard themselves as mentally ill, perhaps just thinking that they are 'having a hard time at the moment – you can't expect to be happy all the time'. They might not want to admit that they have a mental health problem – some people feel that there is a particular stigma linked to mental illness that they do not associate with physical illness. They may be frightened to

seek medical help, worried that being diagnosed as depressed or phobic would affect their employment prospects. There is some basis for this concern as people with mental health problems have the highest rate of unemployment among people with disabilities.

The most common types of mental illness include:

- depression
- anxiety
- panic attacks
- phobias
- obsessive-compulsive disorders
- schizophrenia.

Difficulties in defining and diagnosing particular mental illnesses can lead to problems in measuring and monitoring levels of mental ill health. However, there is evidence that the poorest and most deprived people in the community have the highest incidence of mental illness. A statement from Mind claims:

*These groups are not only more likely to experience higher infant mortality rates and lower life expectancy but also a higher lifetime prevalence of major mental health problems and relatively poor access to mental health care.*

Furthermore, the Social Exclusion Unit report 'Rough Sleeping' (1998) estimated that up to half the people who sleep rough each night have mental health needs but less than half of them are getting treatment. It was estimated that one in two had a serious alcohol problem and one in five misused drugs.

Rates of mental illness and distress also vary between men and women.

- The National Institute for Health and Clinical Excellence (NICE) reports that the incidence of anorexia nervosa is around 19 per 100,000 of the population per year for women and 2 per 100,000 per year for men.

- The recorded rate of anxiety and depression is 11.2 per cent in women, compared to 7.2 per cent in men.

- Lone mothers have particularly high rates of recorded mental illness.

Source: Mind Fact Sheet, March 2008

### Did you know?

Depression is the most common mental health problem in later life. Research suggests that only about 15 per cent of all older people with clinical depression receive treatment.
Source: www.ageconcern.org.uk 15.2.2010

## Disability and dysfunction

Until recently, many people with disabilities were cared for in large institutions or hospitals and were almost invisible to much of society. In recent years, however, there have been significant changes. The Community Care Act (1990) increased the number of people with disabilities being cared for and supported in the community rather than in large institutions. Very importantly, the Disability Discrimination Act (1995) provided legal protection from discrimination in employment, access to public buildings and in the renting of accommodation. However, despite recent progress, disabled people are more likely to:

- be on low incomes
- be without paid employment
- have difficulty in accessing public transport and public buildings
- be without the necessary social support to live full lives.

The poverty rate for adults with disabilities is twice that for adults without a disability. The main reason for this, despite the Disability Discrimination Act, is the high rate of unemployment among people with disabilities. Approximately one in five adults with a disability who wants to work is unable to find employment. This compares with one in 15 for those without a disability. Furthermore, people with disabilities face extra costs related to managing their impairment, such as the extra expense of paying for adaptations to their homes, social care support and the cost of other mobility and communication aids.

In 2009 the Disability Alliance launched a manifesto of recommendations for routes out of poverty, with the aim of eliminating disability poverty by 2025.

Source: Leonard Cheshire Disability (17.1.08) *Disability Poverty in the UK*

### PLTS

**Independent enquirer:** This activity requires you to use your independent enquiry skills to investigate and discuss links between poverty and health and well-being.

### Did you know?

Around a third of all adults with disabilities aged 25 to retirement are living in low-income households.

Source: Joseph Rowntree Foundation, The Poverty Site (www.poverty.org.uk), 15.2.2010

## 4.2 Factors affecting life chances

The concept of **life chances** was first introduced by Max Weber, a nineteenth-century sociologist. He described and discussed the privileged position of the rich and powerful in society and how that privilege provided the opportunity to purchase and enjoy those things regarded as desirable and highly valued. In our society, these 'desirable and highly valued' things include:

- good housing
- a good education
- holidays
- satisfying work
- job security
- good health.

## Case study: Disability and relative poverty

Guy is 35 years old. He has multiple sclerosis and is now unable to work. Guy lives with his partner, Rob, who has an unskilled job and is quite often unemployed, as he needs to be available to care for Guy. They live in a one-bedroom flat, which is expensive to heat. They do not have a car. Guy and Rob have not been on holiday for five years. Their social life is limited to a Friday evening visit to the pub. They never eat out and they normally buy all their clothes from charity shops.

1 Define the term 'relative poverty'.
2 Would you say that Guy and Rob were in absolute or relative poverty?
3 Identify the factors that are linked with their difficult financial circumstances.
4 Discuss the likely impact of their circumstances on their health and well-being.

# Regional patterns in health and illness

There are regional variations in patterns of health and illness. Mortality and morbidity rates vary in different parts of the country and also within towns and cities within the UK. It should come as no surprise that the poorer regions and the poorer parts of cities have higher recorded levels of illness.

For example, research has shown that there are regional trends in the incidence of lung cancer across the UK. Rates for lung cancer are highest in Scotland, and higher in the north than the more affluent south of England.

Source: http//info.cancerresearch.uk.org.

# Social class and family background

The social class system allows for social mobility and may generally be regarded as a **meritocracy**, i.e. people achieve their social position largely on merit. The view is that there is **equality of opportunity** for all and, if people work hard, and achieve good qualifications, opportunities will open up for them. They will be able to improve their position in society.

However, as we have seen, the social class that a child is born into can have an important impact on their life chances. Where many factors linked with poverty and deprivation come together (long-term unemployment, poor housing, pollution, low income and poor health), this often leads to a sense of social exclusion – a situation referred to as **multiple deprivation**. This can have serious implications for people's life chances.

# Culture and ethnicity

In the UK the majority population is white English. At the time of the 2001 census, the minority ethnic population was 4.6 million or 7.9 per cent of the population. Just over 5 per cent of the population identified themselves as non-white.

Minority ethnic groups are groups within the population who share a particular and distinctive way of life, which is seen as different from the majority population. Often this may be linked with nationality or religion. Many ethnic groups have identifiable and different dress codes, diets and music; they may share a different language and celebrate different festivals from the host population.

Evidence from a wide range of sources shows that ethnic minority groups suffer significant economic hardship. Compared to the white majority ethnic group, there is evidence of:

- a higher incidence of unemployment
- a higher proportion of people in low-paid work

## Case study: Equal opportunities

Laura is 18 years of age and taking her A levels. Her father is a university professor. He is, as you might expect, very supportive and involved in her education. Laura attends a very successful fee-paying school and it is expected that she, along with several of her friends, will go to Oxford University when they leave. She loves school, has worked hard and hopes to study medicine at university.

Aisha is also 18. She has never known her father, and her mother has only ever had part-time unskilled work. Nobody in Aisha's family has ever been to college or university. Aisha formally left school when she was 16, but actually had hardly attended since year 9.

1  Define and explain the terms:
   - equal opportunities and
   - life chances.
2  Compare the life chances of Laura and Aisha.
3  Would you say that Laura and Aisha have equal opportunities to secure a successful career?

## PLTS

**Independent enquirer:** This activity requires you to use your independent enquiry skills to consider and discuss the link between inequality and opportunities for educational success and wider intellectual development.

## Key terms

**Life chance** – The opportunity to achieve and acquire the way of life and the possessions that are highly valued in a society.

**Meritocracy** – A society where social position is achieved by ability, skill and effort rather than ascribed at birth. High achievements are open to all.

**Equality of opportunity** – A situation where everybody has the same chance of achieving and acquiring the way of life valued in a society.

**Multiple deprivation** – A situation where many factors linked with poverty and deprivation come together (e.g. long-term unemployment, poor housing, pollution, low income and poor health).

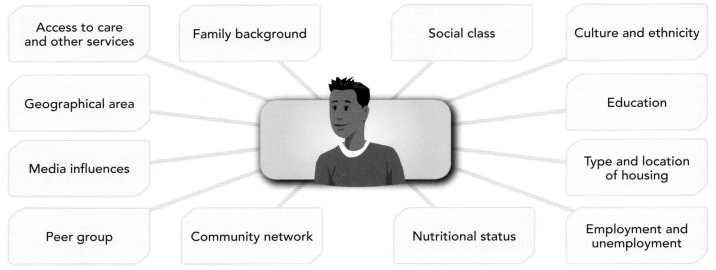

Access to care and other services

Family background

Social class

Culture and ethnicity

Geographical area

Education

Media influences

Type and location of housing

Peer group

Community network

Nutritional status

Employment and unemployment

**Fig 19.7:** Social and environmental factors that affect life chances

- a higher incidence of rickets in children from the Asian subcontinent
- shorter life expectancy
- and higher infant mortality rates

among members of minority ethnic groups.

In addition to the health implications of higher levels of poverty, there are issues of access to health services. Full use of services may be limited by language and other cultural barriers. Asian women are often reluctant to see a male doctor. There may be language barriers and, despite improvements, translators are in short supply and much important information is not translated into minority languages. In addition, racism (or the fear of racism) is stressful.

Unless health and care workers understand the religious and cultural beliefs and practices of minority ethnic groups, their care needs are unlikely to be fully met, leaving them vulnerable to higher levels of ill health.

## Activity 16: Cultural diversity

In four groups briefly describe the key
- religious practices
- dietary needs
- marriage patterns
- cultural festivals

of one of the following religious groups:
- Muslims
- Jews
- Sikhs
- Hindus

Present your information as an A4 handout and distribute it to all members of your class.

## Functional skills

**English:** You can use your reading skills to access textbooks and the Internet to gather information and your writing skills to produce a report summarising the key points.

## Case study

Mr Abdul speaks very little English. He has lived in Pakistan all his life and has come to this country to live with his son Mohamed and his family. To his surprise, Mohamed and his wife Tamsila both work full time. Tamsila is a childcare worker and Mohamed is a teacher. They live in a quiet village. They are the only Asian family for miles. The Abduls are a Muslim family. There is no mosque nearby and no other Muslim families in the area. Mohamed has arranged for his father to attend a day centre with a lunch club in the village hall, but Mr Abdul is reluctant to go. He's been told he would find a warm welcome.

1 Describe the reasons why Mr Abdul may feel isolated in this community.

2 Explain why Mr Abdul might be reluctant to try the day centre.

3 Discuss what could be done to help Mr Abdul become part of the community and to access the day centre and other care services more easily.

## Nutritional status

A balanced diet, appropriate to the individual's age, is central to health and well-being. You might think that what we eat is a matter of personal choice and the power to eat a healthy diet is in our own hands. However, factors that affect our decisions include the cost and convenience of different foods, cultural habits, and the preferences and choices made within the family. Research has indicated that people in the poorer social economic groups tend to eat less fruit and vegetables and a lower proportion of high-fibre foods than people in the higher social groups. The Low Income Diet and Nutrition Survey (2007) carried out for the Food Standards Agency also found that the poor diets of the low-income population were accompanied by higher levels of smoking, higher alcohol intake and lower levels of physical activity, compared with the general population.

## Media and peer group influences

Life chances can be affected by the influence of the media, TV, newspapers and magazines – through advertising and by reinforcing stereotypical images of particular social groups. For example, women are too frequently portrayed as being solely concerned with fashion, beauty, childrearing and housework. This is likely to influence young girls' aspirations and ambitions. Young people are often presented as a 'problem' group, involved in anti-social behaviour, often in groups or gangs, negatively influenced by their peers.

## Access to services

Despite equality legislation, there is considerable evidence that members of disadvantaged groups derive less benefit from local amenities and services than people from more advantaged groups. Access to many schools and colleges, shops, restaurants and other public buildings, and to many people's homes, is still limited for people with disabilities. Claiming health and social care services and welfare benefits can also be very confusing. Many people, including those with literacy problems, or for whom English is not a first language,

do not claim the benefits to which they are entitled. On their Poverty Site (www.poverty.org.uk), the Joseph Rowntree Trust reported that in June 2009 around one-third of pensioners entitled to Pension Credits (approximately 1.4 million households) and almost half who were entitled to Council Tax Benefit (approximately 2 million households) were not claiming it.

## The family and social support networks

The values, culture and economic circumstances of the family and neighbourhood affect individual attitudes and aspirations. They will also affect life chances. For example, in a family and neighbourhood where education is valued, children are more likely to value achievement at school highly too. Their family and friends are more likely to support a serious attitude to work and hence the possibilities of achievement increase.

# 4.3 Potential effects of social inequalities

## Teenage pregnancies

The UK has the highest teenage birth rates in western Europe. One in every ten babies born in the UK is to a teenager. In addition, the infant mortality rate for babies born to teenage mothers is approximately 60 per cent higher than the average according to the government report 'Teenage Pregnancy: Accelerating the strategy to 2010' (2006). There is also a higher risk of maternal mortality for young women under the age of 18. The UK government target is that by 2010 the births of babies to young women under the age of 18 should be reduced by 50 per cent compared to the figure in 1998. However, the incidence of teenage pregnancy varies by social group. Young women from homes with low incomes are four times more likely to become pregnant than those from materially more advantaged homes.

## Activity 18: Teenage pregnancy and infant mortality

Why do you think there is a higher infant mortality rate for babies born to teenage parents?

What measures should be taken to address this problem?

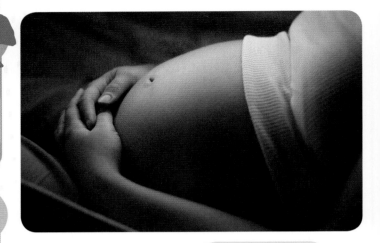

The UK has the highest teenage birth rate in western Europe. Can you think of any reasons for this?

### Did you know?

Teenage motherhood is eight times as common among those from manual social backgrounds as for those from professional backgrounds.

Source: Joseph Rowntree Foundation, The Poverty Site (www.poverty.org.uk), 15.2.2010

### Case study: Teenage pregnancies

Ryan has just discovered that his 17-year-old girlfriend Mandy is pregnant. They are both at college in the first year of a business studies course. They have decided to keep their baby. He is very anxious, but committed to supporting her.

Compile a booklet for teenage fathers explaining:

1 some of the risks of teenage pregnancies
2 how Ryan can best support Mandy during the pregnancy
3 their options for the immediate future.

### PLTS

**Independent enquirer:** This activity will require you to use your independent enquiry skills to investigate the potential link between a social inequality and health and well-being.

## Truancy

A study carried out by Ming Zhang (published in *Community Care*, Issue 1554, 2004) found that children who come from families with low levels of income are more likely to truant. They found the social and emotional problems that arose from poverty were very closely linked with the non-attendance of primary schoolchildren. Parents who were questioned said

they 'sometimes forgot about their younger children's schooling when they hit money troubles'. For secondary school children, especially among low-achieving pupils, truancy was more linked to peer pressure:

Ming Zhang found that threatening parents with prison sentences had no long-term impact on improving attendance rates. Despite government strategies to reduce truancy, there has been very little improvement in truancy rates since the 1920s.

### Reflect

Think about people you know who have truanted from school. What personal and social factors do you think are linked with truancy?

## Crime

Official statistics have consistently pointed to the link between social class, deprivation and offending. The 'Home Office Youth Lifestyles Survey 1998/1999' reported that 41 per cent of prisoners were from social classes IV and V, which are represented by only 19 per cent of the population as a whole, and 18 per cent from the higher social classes 1, 2 and 3, which make up 45 per cent of the population. Offenders from the higher social classes are less likely to be involved in violent crime and more likely to commit fraud and theft from employers (which is more difficult to detect). Persistent offending is closely linked with social deprivation and is likely to cause continuing financial difficulties, as employment prospects are measurably poorer for offenders.

However, simply because more members of the working class are convicted of crimes than members of other social classes doesn't mean that we can automatically assume that the working classes are somehow 'more criminal' than the middle or upper classes. Working-class criminals tend to be involved in crimes that are highly visible, such as crimes of violence, in situations where detection, arrest and conviction rates are likely to be higher. Meanwhile, crimes such as fraud and insider dealing tend to be much less visible to the police and general public. Since the police do not routinely involve themselves in companies, offices and so forth, it is possible that more of these 'white collar' criminals go undetected.

## Mental health issues

Earlier in the unit we discussed issues of mental health, the difficulties of definition and of knowing the true levels of mental illness in our society. The Joseph Rowntree Foundation reported in 2009 that, although the risk of mental illness is the same across all regions of England, adults on low incomes were much more likely to be at risk of developing a mental illness than those on higher incomes. Furthermore, people employed in manual occupations were more at risk than people from non-manual backgrounds. Persistent mental distress is also linked with higher levels of unemployment. In 2006, the Disability Rights Commission reported that only 20 per cent of people with mental health problems are in employment and with that follow the issues of poverty.

## Eating disorders

Beat Eating Disorders (BEAT), formerly known as the Eating Disorders Association, has estimated that 1.6 million people in the UK are affected by an eating disorder. Anyone, regardless of age, sex or ethnicity can develop an eating disorder, but the most likely group to develop this problem are young women between the ages of 12 and 24. (Source: BEAT, www.b-eat.co.uk, 9.4.2010). Eating disorders, particularly anorexia and bulimia, are normally regarded as mental health conditions and are certainly closely associated with persistent mental health problems. The physical and emotional consequences of anorexia or bulimia impact negatively on educational achievements

and employment prospects. There is no evidence, though, to suggest a link between eating disorders and deprivation. On the contrary, although eating disorders may affect people of all classes there is some evidence to suggest that anorexia, in particular, is more prevalent in the higher social classes of industrialised countries, where being slim is highly valued.

## Substance abuse

Substance abuse and dependence can arise from the excessive use of a range of drugs or toxins, including alcohol, prescribed drugs, illegal drugs and solvents. The term 'substance abuse' is usually used when it leads to personal and social difficulties (e.g. failure to meet school, work or family obligations, poor timekeeping, oversleeping, and theft to finance the habit). Substance abuse is found in all population groups and across all social classes, though its consequences are often more serious for the poor. They do not have the financial resources to fund their habit, or savings to fall back on when their addiction leads to ill health, unemployment and debts. Poverty may be a result of substance abuse, drug or alcohol addiction or other factors leading to social exclusion, including mental health problems.

## Bullying

Similarly, the impact of persistent bullying is not confined to particular social groups but the consequences can impact very negatively on social, emotional, physical and intellectual development. The discriminatory behaviour directed at marginalised groups (e.g. the poor, members of minority groups and the mentally ill) may lead to a higher incidence of bullying of disadvantaged people. According to a Northern Ireland study, 'School Bullying in Northern Ireland – It hasn't gone away you know' by Stephanie Burns (2006), young people from 'not well off families' reported higher levels of bullying than young people from more affluent families.

## Physical health

We have already discussed the links between poor diet, poverty and disadvantage. The challenge of leading a healthy lifestyle, eating well, taking sufficient exercise, and keeping safe and warm, when living on a low income in an area of deprivation, is considerable, and this may help to explain why there are higher levels of ill health among the poor.

## Abuse

Abuse can take many forms – physical, emotional, sexual and neglect abuse. Bullying and domestic violence are also forms of abuse. All of these can cause distress to the victim and their family and friends. Although people of all social groups may be victims of abuse, help and support may be accessed less often by people from disadvantaged groups, including people from ethnic minorities, with learning difficulties or other literacy problems and with disabilities. All these individuals may have more difficulty locating and accessing support services, e.g. the NSPCC, Rape Crisis or the National Domestic Violence Helpline.

## Increased motivation and developing skills and abilities

If people do not live in poverty, and if they have the chance to get appropriate employment and are paid a just and fair wage, with the opportunity to enjoy the financial rewards of their work, then the issues of poor physical and mental health, crime and social exclusion may well be reduced. People are likely to feel more optimistic about the future and be motivated to develop the skills and abilities that support a healthy lifestyle.

## Assessment activity 19.3

**P5** **M3** **D2**   BTEC

Prepare a presentation for your class that addresses the impact of social inequalities on the health of the population. You are required to:

1 explain potential links between social inequalities and the health of the population

2 assess the impact of social inequalities on the health of one group in society

3 evaluate the potential links between social inequalities and the health of one group in society.

### Grading tips

**P5** You will need to access accurate and up-to-date statistical information to provide evidence for the links between social inequalities and the levels of health and ill health of the nation. Remember to accurately record the source of any statistics or other evidence that you use. This must include accurate references to websites as well as paper-based evidence. You might find the websites of charities and other voluntary organisations a helpful source of up-to-date evidence.

**M3** To achieve M3, you need to select and provide detailed information that relates to one chosen social group, e.g. older people, people with disabilities or with mental health problems.

- You will need to draw on a wide range of current evidence
- When considering the health of this group remember that health can include physical, social, emotional and intellectual health.

**D2** To achieve D2, you will need to develop further your work for M3 by weighing up the strengths and weaknesses of your evidence. You will need to consider the difficulties of defining the terms that are used in this section, e.g. the difficulties in agreeing a definition of:

- social class
- poverty
- health and ill health
- disability.

If it is difficult to define a term, it is difficult to accurately measure the potential links and their impact on health. You will need to discuss the reliability of data. For example:

- some may be published in a newspaper to satisfy the views and prejudices of their readers

- even official documents such as death certificates may not give a true picture of the range of causes of death in the population (sometimes a doctor may record a condition that is one of a number of contributory reasons, selecting one that will cause least distress to the deceased's relatives)

- some may be collected by particular groups or organisations in order to persuade and gather support

- medical records only record people who have presented themselves for treatment, and diagnosis may vary.

You will need to point to the fact that statistics must be used with great care.

**Assessment activity 19.3** *continued*

To achieve the distinction grade, you will need to discuss these issues and then weigh up the evidence. Is there sufficient evidence to argue that there are links between social inequalities and the health status of the social group you are considering?

## PLTS

**Self-manager:** In order to complete this assignment successfully you will need to use your self-management skills to organise your time and resources, prioritise your activities and meet the assessment deadline.

# Resources and further reading

Acheson, D. (1998) *Independent Inquiry into Inequalities in Health* London: HMSO

Age UK (15.2.2010) www.ageuk.org.uk

Booth, C. (1889) *Life and Labour of the People of London*

Burns, Stephanie (2006) *School bullying in Northern Ireland* ARK, Northern Ireland Social and Political Archive

*Guardian* newspaper (4.7.2009) 'Caste divide is blighting Indian communities in the UK'

*Guardian* newspaper (27.1.2010) 'Unequal Britain'

Gordon, D. (2000) *Poverty and Social Exclusion in Britain* York: Joseph Rowntree Foundation

HM Government (1998) *The Independent Inquiry into Inequalities in Health* London: HMSO

HM Government (1988) *Community Care: an Agenda for Action* London: HMSO

HM Government (1988) *Residential Care: a Positive Choice (The Wagner Report)* London: HMSO

HM Government (2004) *New Directions for the Social Exclusion Unit*

HM Government (2006) *Teenage Pregnancy: Accelerating the Strategy to 2010*

Joseph Rowntree Foundation (15.2.2010), The Poverty Site www.poverty.org.uk

Leonard Cheshire Disability (17.1.2008) *Disability Poverty in the UK*

Mack, J. & Lansley, S. (1985) *Poor Britain* London: Allen and Unwin

Mack, J. & Lansley, S. (1992) *Breadline Britain 1990s* London Weekend Television

National Centre for Social Research *British Social Attitudes Survey 2007*

New Policy Institute (2003) *Monitoring Poverty and Social Exclusion* Joseph Rowntree Trust

Office of National Statistics (1999) *Labour Force Survey*

Office for National Statistics (2006) *Social Trends 2006*

Office for National Statistics (2007) *Social Trends Volume 36*

Office for National Statistics *National Statistics Online 21.10.09*

Office for National Statistics *National Statistics Online 27.8.09*

Rowntree, S. (1901) *Poverty: A Study of Town Life* London: Macmillan

Tossell, D. & Webb, R. (2000) *Social Issues for Carers* London: Hodder & Stoughton

Townsend, P. (1962) *The Last Refuge* London: Routledge and Kegan Paul

Townsend, P. (1979) *Poverty in the United Kingdom* Harmondsworth: Penguin

Townsend, P., Davidson, N. & Whitehead, M. (eds) (1980) *Inequalities in Health: The Black Report* Harmondsworth: Penguin

United Nations World (2006) *Population Prospect Report 2005–2010*

Zhang, M. cited on news.bbc.co.uk/1/hi/education/2094292.stm

(1998) *Rough Sleeping* Cabinet Office Social Exclusion Unit

# Useful websites

Age UK www.ageuk.org.uk

Centre for Economic and Social Inclusion www.cesi.org.uk

Child Poverty Action Group www.cpag.org.uk

Equality and Human Rights Commission www.equalityhumanrights.com/

Beating Eating Disorders www.b-eat.co.uk

Mind www.mind.org.uk

National Statistics Online www.statistics.gov.uk

# Just checking

1   Define the terms: prejudice, discrimination, stereotyping, labelling, marginalisation.
2   Identify four groups who are often treated unequally in our society.
3   Define the following key terms used by demographers: birth rate, death rate, life expectancy, immigration, emigration, net migration.
4   Identify four reasons for the fall in the birth rate and four reasons for the fall in the death rate.
5   Explain why governments collect demographic data.
6   Define the concept of life chances.
7   Identify four factors that might improve a person's life chances.
8   Identify and briefly explain three types of inequality that might arise from: poverty, older age, disability, mental ill health and unemployment.

edexcel

# Assignment tips

1   To achieve the pass grades in this unit, you are required to *describe* or *explain* ideas and issues, such as inequalities that exist in our society and the impact of inequalities on health and well-being. Explanations and descriptions require more detail than a definition or identification of the issues. To achieve the pass grade, you will need to provide examples and often statistical data to support the claims you make.

2   To achieve the merit grade, in addition to meeting the pass criteria you are required to discuss or assess the impact of issues. Make sure you plan your work carefully, devoting one paragraph to each impact or consequence that you present.

3   To achieve the distinction grade for this unit, you are required, in addition to meeting all other grading criteria, to *evaluate* the consequences of inequalities. Draw on the evidence you presented earlier in your assignment and consider the strengths and weaknesses of the evidence you have presented. In the final paragraph, present your conclusion based on the information and evidence that you have considered.

4   In this unit you will refer to government and other statistics. Always make sure that your data is up to date and that you accurately quote the sources of your information.

# 20 Promoting health education

The government recognised in its white paper *Choosing Health: Making Healthy Choices Easier* (published by the Department of Health in 2004) that, while we now live longer, and the major causes of premature death of the last century are largely under control, the same cannot be said for today's main killers. In this unit we are going to explore how we tackle these modern-day diseases.

The aim of this unit is to explain the principles of health education, the approaches used and to introduce you to health education campaigns. Health education is a central component of health promotion, which in turn is a major component of public health. This unit therefore links with Unit 12 (public health) and aims to extend some of the concepts introduced there.

Health education could be described as any activity that promotes health-related learning and therefore brings about some relatively permanent change in the thinking or behaviour of individuals. You are going to consider a range of different approaches to health education, including the role of the mass media and social marketing. You will then examine different models of behaviour change, relating these to the social and economic context.

Finally, you will gain an understanding of health education campaigns by actively planning, designing, implementing and evaluating a small-scale campaign.

## Learning outcomes

After completing this unit you should:

1 understand different approaches to health education
2 understand models of behaviour change
3 understand how health education campaigns are implemented
4 be able to implement a health campaign.

# Assessment and grading criteria

This table shows you what you must do in order to achieve a **pass**, **merit** or **distinction** grade, ar where you can find activities in this book to help you.

| To achieve a **pass** grade, the evidence must show that you are able to: | To achieve a **merit** grade, the evidence must show that, in addition to the pass criteria, you are able to: | To achieve a **distinction** grade, the evidence must show that, in addition to the pass and merit criteria, you are able to: |
| --- | --- | --- |
| **P1** Explain three different approaches to health education. **See Assessment activity 20.1, page 269** | | **D1** Justify the proposed approaches and methods in their health education campaign, relating them to models of behaviour change. **See Assessment activity 20.2, page 278** |
| **P2** Explain two models of behaviour change that have been used in recent national health education campaigns. **See Assessment activity 20.1, page 269** | **M1** Assess how the social context may influence the ability of health education campaigns to change behaviour in relation to health. **See Assessment activity 20.1, page 269** | |
| **P3** Explain how to plan a small-scale health education campaign relevant to local or national health strategies. **See Assessment activity 20.2, page 278** | | |
| **P4** Carry out a health education campaign, relating it to models of behaviour change. **See Assessment activity 20.2, page 278** | **M2** Assess factors that influenced the effectiveness of their health education campaign. **See Assessment activity 20.2, page 278** | **D2** Make recommendations for improving their health education campaign. **See Assessment activity 20.2, page 278** |
| **P5** Explain ethical issues involved in the health education campaign. **See Assessment activity 20.2, page 278** | **M3** Discuss how ethical issues that arose were addressed. **See Assessment activity 20.2, page 278** | |

# How you will be assessed

Assessment of this unit is largely based on your success in planning, designing and implementing a small-scale health education campaign. This will be assessed by your tutor. You will need to demonstrate that you have considered recent or current health policy, have gathered the relevant information, set clear targets and have described clear aims and objectives for the campaign, outlining the target audience and the approach you have selected. Guidance about the grading for this exercise is included towards the end of this section.

## Nicky, 17 years old

This unit helped me to think through what a health education project might be, and how to plan and organise it.

I enjoyed looking at the different theories about what influences attitudes and behaviour change. I found myself becoming very aware of how these theories were operating in my day-to-day life as I watched 'peer pressure' and 'social learning theory' happen in real life. It really made me think about my own health attitudes and reconsider why I hold them.

There were lots of practical tasks and activities for this unit, which helped me think about how the theory works in practice. Some of them were about people who work in health education but many of them were asking me to think about my own life or the lives of my family and friends.

The most important part of the unit for me was the work on the health education project. This section helped me think through my topic choice, my approach and all the planning I needed to do.

### Over to you!

1    What areas of this unit might you find challenging?

2    Which section of the unit are you most looking forward to?

3    What topic might you want to consider for your own health education project?

# 1 Understand different approaches to health education

**Get started**

### Promoting health – where to start

A key component of this unit is the planning and delivery of a small-scale **health education** project. You need to prepare this piece of work right from the beginning so now is the time to start your planning by considering the following questions:

• What health education issues are of particular interest to you and why?

• Which groups might these issues be relevant for? (It is probably sensible to look for issues that are relevant to your peers, i.e. other students.)

• Is this a suitable subject for a health education project?

• What might your aim be for the project?

As the unit unfolds, you will learn more about the planning and delivery of a health education project.

Health education is usually defined as the process of giving information and advice and of facilitating the development of knowledge and skills in order to change behaviour that affects health. Health educators come from a wide range of professions including teachers, social workers, practice nurses, health visitors and leisure centre staff. In some cases, such as health visiting and practice nursing, health education is an acknowledged part of their role. However, in others, it might not be so easy to recognise the potential for a health education role. For example, a community police officer walking the local streets will frequently come across groups of young people who might be smoking and/or drunk – this clearly presents a health promotion opportunity that they may not appreciate or be trained to deal with effectively.

## 1.1 Historical perspective

Unit 12 provides more detail on the history of public health but the key health promotion landmarks are set out below.

**Key term**

**Health education** – An aspect of health promotion that largely relates to educating people about good health and how to develop and support it.

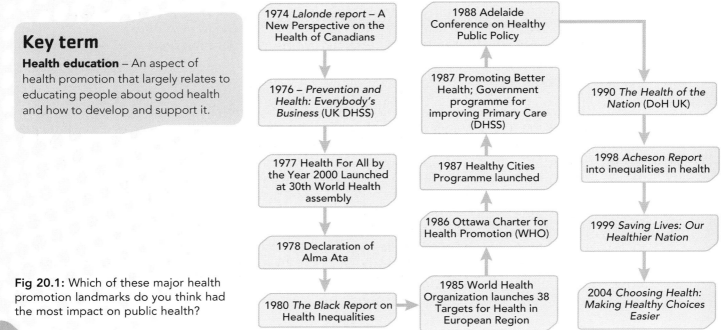

1974 *Lalonde report* – A New Perspective on the Health of Canadians

1976 – *Prevention and Health: Everybody's Business* (UK DHSS)

1977 Health For All by the Year 2000 Launched at 30th World Health assembly

1978 Declaration of Alma Ata

1980 *The Black Report* on Health Inequalities

1985 World Health Organization launches 38 Targets for Health in European Region

1986 Ottawa Charter for Health Promotion (WHO)

1987 Healthy Cities Programme launched

1987 Promoting Better Health; Government programme for improving Primary Care (DHSS)

1988 Adelaide Conference on Healthy Public Policy

1990 *The Health of the Nation* (DoH UK)

1998 *Acheson Report* into inequalities in health

1999 *Saving Lives: Our Healthier Nation*

2004 *Choosing Health: Making Healthy Choices Easier*

**Fig 20.1:** Which of these major health promotion landmarks do you think had the most impact on public health?

# 1.2 Health educators

Almost any agency can act as a potential health promoter. However, some (listed below) are acknowledged as leaders or key players in the field of health education.

## Key term

**Social marketing** – The systematic application of marketing techniques and concepts to achieve specific behavioural goals with the aim of improving health and reducing health inequalities.

# 1.3 The social marketing approach

In recent years there has been a recognition that health education needs to adopt more sophisticated marketing approaches – the kind that are used so successfully by commercial companies to advertise unhealthy products such as fast food, chocolate and alcohol. This type of marketing is called **social marketing**.

**Table 20.1:** Leading organisations in health education

| International organisations | |
| --- | --- |
| The World Health Organization (WHO) | The WHO has been instrumental in shaping and influencing health policy across many nations through its landmark *Health For All by the Year 2000* programme. This has been crucial in moving the health promotion agenda away from medically dominated models to a broader-based approach, which encompasses social and environmental influences. |
| **National organisations** | |
| Government | Government action to make improvements in health takes place across all departments, as was seen in the first health strategy, *The Health of the Nation* (1992). The Department of Health has the lead role for health, managing the delivery of health services through the National Health Service (NHS). |
| The Health Protection Agency (HPA) | The HPA (see also Unit 12) provides support and advice on preventing and reducing the impact of infectious diseases, chemical and radiation hazards, and major emergencies. This includes a health education role (e.g. informing people about the role of vaccination in reducing the spread of infectious diseases and providing information about other communicable diseases such as food poisoning and water-borne infections). |
| NHS Direct | NHS Direct is best known for its year-round, 24-hour telephone health line, run by a specially trained team, including nurses and dental nurses. The service helps to avoid unnecessary trips to the doctor, dentist and hospital accident and emergency department. Every caller is assessed to establish the severity of their symptoms, so as to re-route any urgent or life-threatening situations to the emergency services as quickly as possible, or to offer advice on the best course of action. It operates a website with an online symptom checker to give advice on cold or flu symptoms, contraceptive advice and sexual health issues. The website also offers a confidential web chat service for those needing advice about unprotected sex or emergency contraception. |
| **Local agencies** | |
| Primary Care Trust (PCT) | Putting national policy into practice at the local level requires a range of local agencies to work together effectively on health issues with a common purpose. A key local partner is the Primary Care Trust (PCT), which has the following responsibilities: <br>• to improve the health of the local population <br>• to develop local primary health care services <br>• to commission other local health services in line with local health needs. <br>The PCT has a key role in local health promotion programmes with several key staff groups, including health promotion staff, the public health team and community nurses such as health visitors and school nurses. |

**Table 20.2:** The main features of social marketing

| | |
|---|---|
| **The customer or consumer is placed at the centre** | Starts by trying to understand *where the person is at now*, rather than where someone might think they are or should be, i.e. it is needs-led. |
| **Clear behavioural goals** | Aims to achieve measurable impacts on what people *actually do* (not just on their knowledge, awareness or beliefs about an issue). Describes the aim of an intervention in terms of specific behaviours and manageable steps towards a main goal. |
| **Developing insight** | Driven by an understanding of why people behave as they do, particularly what people think, feel and believe about the subject. |
| **The exchange** | Puts a strong emphasis on understanding what is to be 'offered' (e.g. the advantages of being more active). Also requires an appreciation of the 'full cost' of accepting the offer, (e.g. having to be more active, having to invest money, time and effort and sacrifice other social activities, etc). Aims to maximise the potential 'offer' and its value to the audience, while minimising all the 'costs' of adopting, maintaining or changing a particular behaviour. |
| **The competition** | Examines all the factors that compete for people's attention and willingness to adopt a desired behaviour. Looks at both external factors (e.g. competitor advertising) and internal competition (e.g. habits, the desire to take risks, etc.). |
| **Segmentation (audience analysis)** | Considers alternative ways that people can be understood and profiled by looking at how different people respond to an issue and what moves and motivates them. |
| **'Intervention mix' and 'marketing mix'** | The range of options or approaches that could be used to achieve a particular goal. Single approaches are generally less effective than multi-layered approaches, so use a 'marketing mix' of different approaches, e.g. a campaign aimed at young people to promote safe sex might include:<br>• radio adverts<br>• promotional club events<br>• branded giveaways such as wrist bands, condom packs, etc. |

## Activity 1: Your local PCT

Use a search engine to find the website of your local PCT.

- What is its name? Does it use the title 'PCT' or has it been re-branded to NHS (followed by the name of your local district, e.g. Salford)?
- Why do you think the organisation might have changed its name in this way?
- What types of services does it provide within the local community?
- Can you find the organisation's strategic plan for the next five years? If so, what are the priorities it has set out in its plan?
- What does the plan suggest that the key health challenges are for your local area?

### PLTS

**Independent enquirer:** This activity will help you demonstrate your independent enquiry skills by doing the required research.

### Functional skills

**ICT:** ICT skills will be required to find and utilise information on the Internet.

Table 20.3: What the mass media can and can't achieve

| Mass media can: | Mass media cannot: |
| --- | --- |
| Raise awareness of health and health issues | Convey complex information, e.g. about transmission routes of HIV |
| Deliver a simple message, e.g. that there is a national advice line for young people wanting information about sexual health | Teach skills, e.g. how to deal assertively with pressure to have sex without a condom or to take drugs |
| Change simple one-off behaviours (e.g. get someone to phone for a leaflet) that people are already motivated to carry out | Change more complex behaviour, e.g. it is unlikely to persuade those who are not motivated to be active to take up walking |
| Reach large numbers of people | Shift people's attitudes or beliefs; if a message challenges a person's basic beliefs, they are more likely to dismiss the message than change their belief |
| | Provide two-way communication – mass media work is almost exclusively information giving, with little or no dialogue |

## 1.4 The role of the mass media

Many people view the use of the media (newspapers, magazines, billboards, leaflets, posters, radio and television) as the most effective means of putting health on the agenda for the majority of the population. People might assume that because the media reaches a large number of people, its effect will be correspondingly great. However, this is not necessarily the case.

The success of a health message conveyed by the mass media will depend upon the attitude and viewpoint of the individual who receives the message. Therefore it is not surprising to find that many research studies have shown that the direct persuasive power of the mass media is limited. So how much success can

realistically be expected when the mass media is used in health promotion work?

The use of mass media should be viewed as part of an overall strategy that includes face-to-face discussion, personal help, and attention to social and environmental factors that help or hinder change.

## Different forms of media

### Local media

While most people are familiar with national and regional media, i.e. the main national newspapers, local evening papers, national radio and television stations, it is far more likely that you will be dealing with local media. The local media can still be a very effective way of reaching people. For example, the local free newspaper will probably reach every house in your area, but how many people will actually read it? Providing a press release will enable you to give them the information you want them to put in the story, including:

- a title (if it's catchy they may use it directly)
- a brief summary of the main message you are trying to get across (usually three points at the most)
- what is happening, where and when
- the names of any important people who might be attending
- a photo, if possible (or they could send a photographer)
- a quote about the news item from someone the media might be interested in
- some background facts
- the name and details of the person to contact to follow up the press release.

If you write a good press release the paper may use it more or less verbatim (word for word), or the radio station may read it directly. If they like your story they might want to interview you. If that happens, make sure you ask to see their questions beforehand. Tell them this will help you prepare the necessary background information and improve the quality of your answers and therefore of the interview.

**Fig 20.2:** How would you prepare for an interview?

## Leaflets

Leaflets are the backbone of health education activity. They can serve a wide variety of purposes such as:

- informing people about local services
- providing information about specific health conditions
- giving advice about specific health promotion issues
- engaging people in thought about broader health considerations.

## Activity 3: Adult literacy and leaflet design

When we use print materials it's easy to forget that many adults struggle with both numeracy and literacy. Find out:

- what proportion and/or number of adults in England could be described as lacking basic literacy (i.e. have not reached the standards of reading and writing currently expected for children aged 11)?
- what proportion of leaflets are unreadable by this group of people, i.e. any evidence that shows what proportion of information leaflets is of too high a reading age for the target population?

The *Choosing Health* white paper refers to some of these points and can point you towards the surveys where this information can be found.

Find a couple of health education leaflets and evaluate their design, asking:

1 Who is this leaflet for?

2 Is the language level used appropriate for the target audience?

3 Will it connect specifically with the target audience?

4 When was the leaflet first produced and is the information still relevant or accurate?

5 Is it well designed, i.e. will it grab the reader's attention if it is displayed among other leaflets and posters?

6 Are the key messages clearly identified or are there too many other visual distractions?

7 Who produced the leaflet? Was it produced by an organisation with a vested interest in the issue?

**Fig. 20.3:** Look at these publicity materials from the '5 a day' campaign and consider how well they deliver their message to different groups in society

You can find examples of well-designed publicity materials for healthy eating campaigns on the Department of Health website under '5 a day'. These illustrate two particular points relating to good poster design:

1   the use of colour to make the material attractive and draw attention to it

2   the simplicity of the message.

### Key term

**Holistic health** – An all-encompassing view of health that includes, physical, mental, emotional, spiritual, social and environmental aspects of health.

### Posters

Posters provide an excellent tool for catching the attention of the target audience. A poster should support the key broad messages which you will then develop in more detail within a leaflet.

# 1.5 The community development approach
## The holistic concept

In order to understand how community development for health fits in with health education, you first need to understand what is meant by **holistic health**.

Using the holistic view of health community development, as defined by Ewles and Simnett (1992) in *Promoting Health: A Practical Guide*, can be seen as a health-promoting activity:

> 'A process by which a community identifies its needs or objectives, orders or ranks them, develops the confidence and will to work at these needs or objectives, takes action in respect of them, and in so doing develops co-operative and collaborative attitudes and practices in the community.'

**Community development** might include activities that directly influence health (e.g. a community food co-op) and other activities that address aspects of more holistic health (e.g. a community organisation formed to resist racism could be seen as promoting societal health). In this context, 'community' might be a network of people linked by:

- where they live (such as a housing estate, town, county, country)
- the work they do (such as the mining community)
- their ethnic background (such as the Muslim community)
- the way they live (such as 'New Age' travellers or homeless people)
- or other factors they have in common.

## Participation and development

A community development approach to health emphasises **empowerment** and **participation**. It involves working with groups of people to identify their own health concerns, and to take appropriate action. Examples of this type of work might include:

- supporting a group of people with learning difficulties and their carers to consider their sexuality and sexual health needs
- youth and community workers working with young people where they congregate on street corners or in parks to address their substance use issues.

### Key terms

**Community development** – Development that is based on a commitment to equality, an emphasis on participation and valuing the experiences and lay knowledge of communities. It also requires empowerment of the community and its individuals through training, skills development and joint action.

**Empowerment** – The process of transferring decision-making power from influential sectors to communities and individuals who have traditionally been excluded from it.

**Participation** – A process through which stakeholders influence and share control over development initiatives and the decisions and resources that affect them.

## Activity 4: Poster design

Good poster design has a number of key features or characteristics. See what you can find about the following aspects of poster design. Try to source two or more sample posters to illustrate the following points:

- size
- intensity and boldness of headings
- use of colour
- use of pictures
- novelty aspects
- items of interest for target audience
- entertainment or humour.

## PLTS

**Independent enquirer:** You can demonstrate your independent enquiry skills by carrying out additional research for this activity.

# Mathew Jessop
## Health improvement team member

Mathew works for a local PCT in their health improvement team, supporting people in the neighbourhood in addressing health issues that are relevant to them.

His work tends to fall into two broad areas: directed (where he tries to set the agenda); and non-directed (where he works with people on whatever they feel is important to them).

Examples of directed work include the community mentor scheme, which tries to recruit local people as volunteer supporters for people who are making lifestyle changes.

For example, a volunteer might go to the local leisure centre with people who are trying to lose weight or they might support people who are trying to give up smoking. The volunteer network may be available closer to the community and at times when the PCT services may not be.

Another scheme is time banking, where local people offer services to others in return for services they need themselves. For example, 'I will paint your front room, which will gain me X number of credits with the bank, which I can then use to get my garden cleared up.' Mathew has been encouraging the time bank to generate health-based offers such as supporting people to quit smoking and going walking with people who are trying to be active.

In his non-directed work Matthew supports groups of people with any issues they choose. Last year he helped a group of men reclaim some derelict land and turn it into a community garden. This benefited the community and also engaged a group of men who had become detached and isolated because they were all unemployed and suffered varying degrees of depression.

## Think about it!

1 What differences might you expect between non-directed and directed work for Matthew?

2 What challenges would Matthew have been likely to meet in trying to find and engage with a group of men like the ones in this case study?

3 What advantages can you see in using local people to support others with their lifestyle changes?

4 How could he evaluate the success of these activities to demonstrate the worth of this activity?

## Benefits and limitations of community development activity

**Table 20.4:** The benefits and limitations of community development

| Benefits | Limitations |
|---|---|
| Based on locally identified concerns so there is stronger support | Can take a long time to engage the community and address the underlying issues |
| Focuses on the root causes of ill health | Results are often not tangible or easily measured |
| Builds confidence in the local community | Difficult to evaluate |
| Develops skills in the community (many of which are transferable), e.g. lobbying, numeracy and literacy skills | Funding can be difficult to attract and sustain without clear evaluation |
| Extends democratic accountability (all participants have equal value) so employed workers do not have overall control | Health promoters can be in a difficult position if the needs of the community conflict with the position of their employer |
| | Direct work is often only carried out with a small number of people. |
| | Tends to draw attention towards small communities and away from larger structural issues |

# 1.6 Two-way communication

It is hard to quantify the extent to which individual face-to-face interaction can contribute to health campaigning. However, it is clear that the general public holds certain groups, such as doctors, nurses and teachers, in high regard and values the information provided by these professionals. This creates considerable potential for promoting key health messages simply through the day-to-day work routine. For example, a doctor could suggest to someone attending a health check that they consider giving up smoking, or a district nurse who is visiting an older individual at home could suggest that moderate activity is still possible and potentially beneficial.

It is quite normal for health campaigns to engage these health promoters when they are trying to communicate a key message. For example, on National No Smoking Day many health practitioners plan specific events to link with the national campaign and offer support to people wishing to give up smoking. Three examples of one-to-one activity are considered in more detail below:

1  Pre-conceptual health: For anyone thinking about becoming pregnant, especially for the first time, there may be opportunities for their GP, health visitor, midwife and practice nurse to discuss possible health education issues such as:

   - smoking (associated with low birth weight and prematurity or early delivery)
   - alcohol (consumption of alcohol in large amounts has been associated with abnormalities in newborn babies called foetal alcohol syndrome).

2  Promoting safe sex: The UK is currently facing a major sexual health challenge with rates of almost all sexually transmitted infections (STIs) rising. Alongside this, the UK has one of the highest rates of teenage pregnancy in Western Europe. Therefore it is important that safe sex messages (i.e. encouraging correct and consistent condom use) are promoted by all professionals who have the opportunity to do so. This might be a youth worker talking to a young person who they know is having sex with their partner or a GP talking to a woman who wants to start taking the pill.

3  Immunisation: Children are routinely immunised against diphtheria, typhoid, polio, measles, mumps, rubella, etc. However, recent inaccurate publicity about the MMR vaccine has undermined public confidence in it (see Unit 12, page 127). Therefore, health professionals who work with young families have an important role to play in promoting childhood immunisation. For example, midwives and health visitors can both explain the immunisation programme (i.e. what vaccination at what age) and can also discuss the parents' concerns about immunisation and provide factual information to re-boost public confidence.

## Theatre in Health Education (TIHE)

Theatre in health education (TIHE) was first developed as a tool for exploring issues relating to HIV and AIDS within schools in the 1980s. Consequently it has a particularly strong tradition of involvement with sex and relationship education (SRE). A number of activities belong under the umbrella term of TIHE but the key feature is that projects use participatory approaches. This means that performances are often accompanied by:

- preparatory work by actors or teachers
- workshops where issues raised in the performance can be explored
- follow-up activities led by teachers in the weeks after a TIHE event.

A key feature of theatre in health education is that the performances use participatory approaches.

## Peer-led approaches

Peer-led approaches aim to use the interactions between peers (usually young people but not in all cases) to promote health-related behaviours. Peer leaders are often seen by young people as having greater credibility than professionals (who are inevitably adults).

The main method is to use young people (not necessarily the same age as the target audience) who

are seen as credible by the audience, to provide all or some of the health education input. The decision as to who might be a credible peer leader must be based on the views of the target audience – this ensures that the peer leaders selected are appropriate and effective. Peer leaders need to be good communicators and unconventional (i.e. they don't try to conform with the people they are leading) but they also need to demonstrate responsible attitudes.

### Activity 5: A peer mentor scheme for local schools

Your college has offered to work with three local high schools to provide mentors for young people in years 10 and 11 who are at risk of under-achieving in their GCSEs. The college is asking you and a group of friends to each support a young person from one of the schools. You will need to coach them in their subject and help them with the issues that may be leading to them performing poorly at the moment, for example, managing stresses associated with study.

However, the scheme depends upon you providing answers to the following queries raised by staff and governors in the high schools:

1  What criteria would you use to identify suitable peer mentors?

2  How would you expect them to operate in their role with the young person?

3  Would you need a range of different mentors to suit different young people's needs?

4  What training or development might these people require to enable them to fulfil their role effectively?

5  How could the college evaluate the success of the project?

6  How could this be linked to work in the curriculum, particularly the *Personal, Social and Health Education and Citizenship* aspects of the curriculum?

### PLTS

**Creative thinker:** This activity will help you demonstrate your creative thinking skills as you consider the challenges of this work and find answers to the questions raised here.

## Interactive video and computer packages

In the past, health education frequently made use of videos, workbooks, worksheets and other paper-based media. However, with the widespread use of ICT in schools, there is now an emphasis on using interactive computer packages (either on disk or on websites). These media allow a discovery learning approach for young people, where health education can often be conveyed through a game format, a medium that young people are both familiar with and engaged by. A good example is the online alcohol game for primary age children at www.lookoutalcohol.co.uk, which was designed with the help of primary school children in Lancashire.

**Fig 20.4:** Lookout alcohol's online game. Why would this game appeal to young people?

# 1.7 Models (or approaches) used in health education

## Victim blaming

The concept of **victim blaming** is firmly rooted in the view that people have control and responsibility over their own lives and their health behaviours. In this model the decision to take up smoking is seen as a matter of personal choice, as is the decision to stop.

This is a relatively unsophisticated view and cannot explain, for example, the fact that smoking is not equally distributed within society, with those in lower socio-economic groups smoking more frequently. The *Choosing Health* white paper (2004) echoed this point:

'On paper, the answers can look deceptively simple – balance exercise and how much you eat, drink sensibly, practise safe sex, don't smoke. But knowing is not the same as doing. For individuals, motivation, opportunity and support all matter … Healthy choices are often difficult for anyone to make, but where people do not feel in control of their environment or their personal circumstances, the task can be more challenging. People who are disabled or suffer from mental ill health, stretched for money, out of work, poorly qualified, or who live in inadequate or temporary accommodation or in an area of high crime, are likely to experience less control over their lives than others.'

### Key term

**Victim blaming** – People frequently simplify health choices by blaming the person who chooses to adopt an unhealthy behaviour for making that choice. In reality things are rarely that simple. For example, people say lack of time, due to work pressures, is the major reason why they don't take enough exercise.

## Empowerment

This approach is based on enabling people to express their own concerns, and gain the necessary knowledge and skills to address those concerns. It tries to address the wider determinants that may be influencing poor health in a person or a community, instead of just focusing on specific medical health concerns. This might mean a community addressing issues such as local traffic, or street violence, or access to nutritious food.

### Reflect

Are you aware of any local issues where people have felt sufficiently strongly to want to do something about the situation? What was the issue and what action did they take to make things change? Was the action successful? If not can you find any reasons as to why not?

## Activity 6: A holistic view of the alcohol problem

Alcohol is one of the most challenging public health issues we currently face. Although consumption rates are stabilising they are doing so at an all-time high, with massive economic, health and social consequences. Television routinely covers this issue with programmes about teenage drunkenness that paint an unsympathetic picture of young people's drinking behaviour. There is little discussion of the wider context in which drinking happens but a heavy focus on the individual's drunken behaviour.

This is a classic example of victim blaming in action so let's look at the complex issues that may underpin alcohol consumption.

List as many factors as possible that contribute to young people drinking to excess and/or getting drunk. Now try and group them into those issues that are about:

- their individual responsibility
- the influences within the local community
- the national agenda, e.g. legislation.

How did the balance appear between the individual and the wider local and national issues?

Now try to suggest changes that could be made to reduce teenage alcohol consumption at each of the levels identified.

**PLTS**

**Creative thinker:** This activity will help you demonstrate your creative thinking skills as you consider the broader contextual issues that influence alcohol consumption and find solutions to the questions raised here.

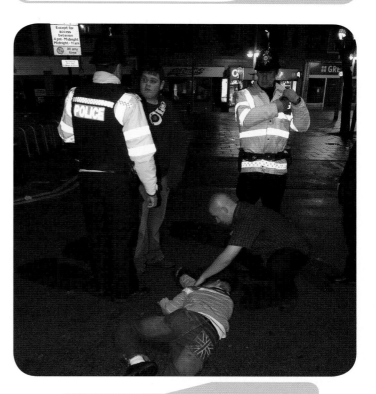

What impression does the photograph give about young people and alcohol?

# 1.8 National campaigns

Mass media campaigns can be an easy response to many health problems. Sometimes they can be driven by a need to be seen to be doing something, even though there is little evidence that a media campaign on the issue is likely to make much difference. National campaigns tend to be used primarily to raise an issue with the public, and to encourage people to reflect on their behaviour. At best, they can direct people to services where the necessary support may be available.

## Physical activity and diet

Obesity is a global problem. According to recent reports, over 30 per cent of children in England are currently overweight or obese. It is a complex issue and, as yet, no country has found a way to stop the rise in obesity. The UK Department of Health developed the Change4Life programme, which highlights the links between poor diet, sedentary (inactive) lifestyles and preventable illnesses, and emphasises parents' responsibility to ensure that their children eat better and take regular exercise. It offered accessible, friendly and encouraging support to implement changes, and highlighted the links between poor diet, sedentary lifestyles and preventable illnesses such as diabetes, heart disease and cancer. It also emphasised the importance of ensuring that children eat better and take regular exercise in order to avoid these conditions in later life.

## Smoking

The UK government ran a new anti-smoking campaign in 2009 that aimed to show parents how much their teenage children worry about their future health because of their tobacco habit. The 'Worried' campaign adverts were supported by a new survey commissioned by NHS Stop Smoking Services, which questioned 400 youngsters between the ages of 11 and 15 whose parents were smokers. Researchers found that 46 per cent of teenagers were more worried by their parents' smoking than by money, bullying or the prospect of divorce.

## Heart disease

The British Heart Foundation (BHF) campaigns specifically on the issue of heart disease, and is a member of the national coalition of voluntary organisations with an interest in promoting and protecting cardio and vascular health in England. The BHF runs many smaller campaigns under this one umbrella issue, working to prevent heart disease through campaigns such as:

- *Food Labelling* – calling on all supermarkets to embrace the traffic light food labelling model.

- *Cigarette machine ban* – calling for a ban on sales of cigarettes through vending machines to reduce their availability to children.

The BHF also works to enable people to survive a heart attack and live better after it through campaigns such as:

- *Cardiac Rehab* – campaigning to increase access to cardiac rehabilitation (60 per cent of heart patients who needed cardiac rehabilitation didn't have access to it in 2009).

- *Heart attack* – raising awareness among the general public of the symptoms of a heart attack so that they can recognise when a person is experiencing a heart attack and deal with it quickly and effectively, which could save the person's life.

## Reducing teenage pregnancy and improving sexual health

Condom Essential Wear is a campaign that focuses on ensuring that young adults have enough information to make informed choices about safer sex and know how to improve their sexual health. It also raises awareness of the prevalence and invisibility of sexually transmitted Infections. It was devised to make condom use appear more normal and to address the barriers that prevent people carrying and using condoms as a part of an active sex life. It primarily targeted those whose behaviour can be considered 'sexually risky', e.g. 18–24-year-old adults, and men and women who have active sex lives with multiple or serial partners, plus sometimes having unprotected sex.

The first phase was a media-led campaign, including public relations, advertising (on TV, radio and in magazines) and digital media, delivering a 'call to action' across the 'sexually risky' primary audience, encouraging them to carry and use condoms. The campaign also brought together a variety of partners, such as fashion retailers, universities and nightclubs, in order to promote condoms as an essential everyday item. For example, the haircare brand Fudge ran a competition that offered consumers the chance to win a year's supply of Fudge styling products and Mates condoms, while Yellow Hammers Bars allowed people to queue-jump at its nightclubs upon presentation of a condom.

## Mental health

Mental illness is often referred to as the silent epidemic, with large numbers of people affected by conditions such as depression and anxiety but little national-level campaigning to address the issues. Instead, it is largely left to voluntary sector organisations like the Mental Health Foundation to run campaigns on this issue. For example, in 2009 it launched a national campaign to raise awareness about the impact that fear and anxiety can have on our lives.

# 2 Understand models of behaviour change

## 2.1 Models

For a health educator to be effective in their role, they must understand the complex processes that might influence a person to change their behaviour. There are several different models of behaviour change.

## The health belief model

This was originally developed as a way to explain and predict preventive health behaviour. The model suggests that an individual is most likely to undertake the recommended preventive health action if they believe:

- a threat to their health is real and serious
- that the benefits of taking the suggested action outweigh the barriers.

In many cases they might also need to be cued to take action.

Key concepts in the model are:

- perceived susceptibility – a person's perception of how likely it is that they will get a particular condition that would adversely affect their health

- perceived seriousness – a person's beliefs about how a disease or condition would affect them (e.g. the difficulties that a disease would create, including pain and discomfort, loss of work time, financial impact, difficulties with family)

- perceived benefits of taking action – once they have accepted their susceptibility to a disease and recognised it is serious, someone may then feel motivated to act and attempt to prevent the disease (but this will also require them to feel there are real benefits from taking action)

- barriers to taking action – action may not take place, even though a person believes in the benefits of taking action. This is because of perceived barriers relating to the nature of the treatment or preventive measures (which may be inconvenient, expensive, unpleasant, painful or upsetting)

- cues to action – a person may also require a 'cue to action' for the desired behaviour (e.g. a call to participate in a screening programme).

## The theory of reasoned action

This theory provides a framework to study the attitudes that underpin behaviours, suggesting that the most important determinant of a person's behaviour is **behaviour intent**. This is the individual's intention to perform a behaviour, which is formed from a combination of their attitude toward performing the behaviour and the **subjective norm**.

If a person believes that the result of adopting a behaviour will be positive, they will have a positive attitude towards that behaviour.

*If other people* important to that person also view this action in a positive way, then a *positive subjective norm* is created. Taken together, these two influences would strongly suggest that the person would follow the health advice.

For example, if a person thinks that it is important to lose weight and believes that this will make them healthier and happier, and their family and friends support this view, then it is more likely that they will adopt the necessary lifestyle changes to reduce their body weight.

However, if someone is considering quitting smoking, but they are concerned about the impact on their social life because all their friends smoke and these friends are not actively supportive, then it is less likely that this person will choose to quit.

### Key terms

**Behaviour intent** – The individual's intention to perform a behaviour. This is a combination of their attitude towards performing the behaviour and the subjective norm.

**Subjective norms** – The influence of people in someone's social environment on his/her intention to carry out a particular behaviour.

## The theory of planned behaviour

This is actually a development of the theory of reasoned action, based on recognition that behaviour is not 100 per cent under an individual's control. This led to the addition of a third influence, *perceived behavioural control*, which is defined as our perception of the difficulty of performing a behaviour.

The theory suggests that people view the control they have over their behaviour on a continuum, which ranges from behaviours that are easily performed to those requiring considerable effort, resources, etc. The difficulties that might influence the perception of control could include:

- the time needed to do something (e.g. to prepare fresh food as opposed to using ready meals)

- the financial cost (e.g. to go swimming regularly)

- the difficulty (e.g. the skills needed to negotiate condom use, etc).

However, if the person has a positive behaviour intent and a strong positive subjective norm towards a behaviour, then it is also highly likely that they will view the perceived control favourably. Thus, they will feel they have few barriers to deal with and a high degree of control over the behaviour change.

## The theory of social learning

Social learning theory (SLT) is a category of learning theories grounded in the belief that human behaviour is determined by interaction between three sets of factors:

- cognitive (knowledge and attitudes)

- behavioural (e.g. personal skills)

- environmental (services in the community, attitudes of peers).

This three-way relationship can be seen in the diagram below.

There are three main aspects to social learning theory:

1 the likelihood that a person will perform a particular behaviour again in a given situation is strongly influenced by their perception of the likely consequences (e.g. the previous rewards or punishments which they experienced when performing the behaviour)

2 people can learn by observing others (this is called vicarious learning), in addition to learning by participating in an act personally

3 individuals are most likely to adopt behaviour observed in others they identify with (this has obvious links to peer education approaches).

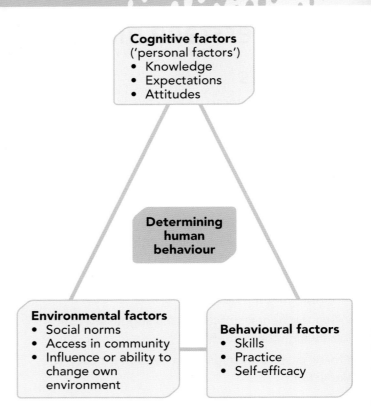

**Fig 20.5:** What does this diagram tell you about the relationship between cognitive, environmental and behavioural factors?

If social learning theory is applied to condom use among young men, the cognitive factors might include:

- the understanding of the risks associated with unprotected sex

- attitudes to teen parenthood

- their expectations of sex.

The environmental factors might include:

- their peer group's views about condom use

- their ability to access condoms from local services

- their ability to change their own views on the subject (perhaps after a class discussion at college).

The skills might include:

- how to put a condom on correctly

- how to negotiate its use with their partner.

## Activity 7: Behaviour intent and young people's access to services

Now consider the 'Be Smart' substance use service for under-25s.

1 Suggest some relevant cognitive factors for people considering accessing the service.

2 What environmental factors might influence the likelihood of people making use of the service?

3 What skills might someone need in order to access this service?

## The stages of change model

This model is now widely accepted and routinely used in substance use services, for smoking, alcohol and many illegal substances. It suggests the process of behaviour change can be broken down into five stages:

1 *pre-contemplation* – there is no intention to change behaviour in the foreseeable future (many individuals in this stage are unaware or under-aware of their problems)

2 *contemplation* – people are aware that a problem exists and are seriously thinking about overcoming it but have not yet made a commitment to take action

3 *preparation* – individuals in this stage are intending to take action in the next month and have unsuccessfully taken action in the past year

4 *action* – individuals modify their behaviour, experiences or environment in order to overcome their problems; this requires considerable commitment of time and energy

5 *maintenance* – people work to prevent relapse and consolidate the gains made during action.

The model is frequently illustrated as a wheel, and many people may have to repeat the process several times to successfully leave the cycle and achieve a stable changed behaviour. For example, think about the people you know who may have tried to quit smoking on several occasions – each of these attempts is part of the learning process that builds their chances of achieving the desired long-term behaviour change. For this reason, the process is often portrayed as a spiral, with the person gradually moving up the spiral to the desired change.

## Reflect

Is there anything you have considered changing in order to improve your health? Do you smoke? Are you less active than you could be? Do you drink more than the recommended guidelines? Think about any aspect of your health where you know your behaviour doesn't conform to recommended advice.

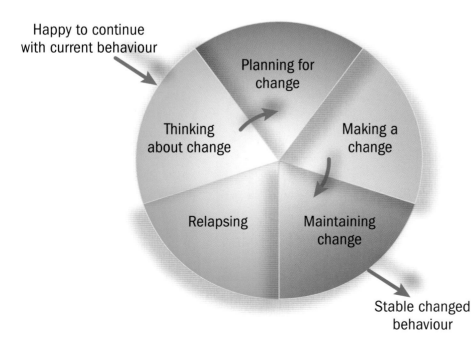

Happy to continue with current behaviour

Planning for change

Thinking about change

Making a change

Relapsing

Maintaining change

Stable changed behaviour

**Fig 20.6:** The stages of change model – how well does it reflect your experience of the process of changing behaviour?

# 2.2 Social and economic context

It is important to remember that not everyone has the same ability to bring about change in their health behaviours (as discussed in the section on victim blaming, page 262). If you think back to Unit 12 (Public health), you were introduced to the impact of social factors that influence health status and the importance of income in particular. Therefore, while we can consider the theoretical approaches to behaviour change, we also have to take into account people's social and economic circumstances and the way these circumstances can affect their success in making a change for the better.

## Financial

In Unit 12 we saw how income was closely related to health. The fact that income is the strongest predictor of health inequalities is best illustrated by the life expectancy gap between richer districts, like Kensington and Chelsea in London, and poorer districts like parts of Manchester.

## Social class

In Unit 12 we also saw how social class was closely related to health. For example, children in the lowest social class are five times more likely to die from an accident than those in the top social class.

## Peer pressure

Peer pressure may happen in the workplace, at school or within the general community. It can affect people of all ages and backgrounds. Peer pressure occurs when we are influenced to do something we usually would not do, or are stopped from doing something we would like to do, because we want to be accepted by our peers. A peer can be anyone we look up to, or someone we think of as an equal in age or ability. A peer could be a friend, someone in the community or even someone on TV. We may experience peer pressure as we live up to either the individual's or group's expectations or follow a particular fashion or trend. Peer pressure may be a positive influence and help to challenge or motivate us to do our best, but it can also result in someone doing something that may not fit their sense of what is right and wrong. It can influence us in a number of ways, including:

- fashion choice
- alcohol and other drugs use
- the decision to have a boyfriend or girlfriend
- our choice of friends
- academic performance.

> ### Reflect
>
> Over the course of the next week, observe the behaviour of the students in your college. Can you see peer pressure in action? How did the people you observed respond to it? Were there some people who handled this pressure better than others? How did they do that?

Peer pressure can be:

- *direct* – for example, someone telling you what you should be doing
- *indirect* – a group of friends may have particular habits or activities that they do together (e.g. a person may only smoke when they are with certain friends)
- *individual* – sometimes the pressure comes from within; sometimes we choose to do things to make sure we feel like the rest of the group.

**Fig 20.7:** Smoking when you don't really want to is often a result of peer pressure. Have you been affected by this yourself?

## Assessment activity 20.1

**P1** **P2** **M1**

**BTEC**

The assessment for this unit will be based on the design, delivery and evaluation of a small-scale health education campaign. Throughout the activities, you will be guided through the assessment criteria for your own project and given an opportunity to think about what these mean. Here we use a worked example about young people's substance use services.

This activity breaks down into three parts:

1   identify the education approaches you intend to adopt (from the text) to promote the substance misuse service

2   describe in practical terms what your role as the health educator would be in order to promote a local substance use service, using each approach as the basis

3   explain how this approach might encourage students to utilise the service.

To achieve P2, you must describe the key parts of two models of behaviour change and then show how some of these features are evidenced in national health campaigns. You can draw on more than one campaign to illustrate all the features of the models.

For MI you need to consider the impact of social context on health education approaches and assess how this will limit the abilities of a project to deliver behaviour change. For this activity you can consider an apparently simple act like condom use:

- What socioeconomic factors might affect the choice to use a condom or not?

- How will these factors impact on campaigns which promote condom use?

### Grading tips

**P1** The first part of the project brief is to describe the need for the service.

You will find detailed information on the Home Office website, where annual trends in use are published.

- Check back in Unit 12 (pages 128–129) and summarise the current trends in substance use by young people. Young people's substance misuse services offer support regarding alcohol and tobacco use as well as illicit drugs.

- Find out what local substance use services exist for you and your peers.

- What type of premises do they operate from?

- What type of support do they offer?

This might mean searching for local service information on your PCT or Drug Action Team (DAT) website. You could even contact the service and interview someone to get a better understanding of how the service works.

**P2** Identify up to three recent national health education campaigns, which have aspects of two of the following applied within them:

- the theory of reasoned action

- the social learning theory

- the stages of change model.

For each model, summarise the key features and then show how they have been applied in one or more of the campaigns.

**M1** You will need to start by considering what might happen at the point when someone needs to use a condom, i.e. just before they have sex. Consider all the different factors that might influence their decision to use or not to use. This might include quite a wide range of issues, e.g. communication skills the person might need, financial cost, availability, acceptability, etc.

Look at how each of these factors might influence the person's decision. What would need to be done to address each of these issues in turn? To what extent can these be dealt with through a campaign approach?

Finish by drawing some conclusions about the challenges within what appears to be a simple act (promoting condom use) and what the limitations might be of a high-level national campaign like those you have read about.

When you are considering your own project you will also need to consider the social or economic factors that might affect the behaviour you are trying to change, as well as considering how two models of behaviour change could be applied to your project design.

# 3 Understand how health education campaigns are implemented

Clearly, there are several different influences that can shape a health promotion campaign and these subtly interlink to define the way in which the campaign is delivered on the ground. The starting point for any project should be needs assessment, i.e. understanding of local or national patterns of ill health. This assessment will determine what conditions need to be addressed to bring the greatest health gains, and which people suffer those conditions most. This information frames the type of activity and the target audience.

Take smoking, for example. In 1997, new statistics suggested that smoking rates among young adults (16–24-year-olds) were on the increase – against an overall reduction in smoking across the whole population. As a result, the target audience for mass media campaigns, which had previously been smokers aged between 25 and 40, was changed to a lower 16–24 age range, leading to the *Testimonials* campaign, with a target audience of C2DE (lower socio-economic groups, reflecting the higher smoking rates in those groups).

This media campaign works alongside the development of local initiatives such as the development of stop smoking services. Here, allocations from the Department of Health are targeted at the areas with the highest indictors for deprivation, i.e. the poorest areas of the country, again recognising that this is where the levels of smoking will be highest.

## 3.1 Health strategies

### National health campaigns

We looked at the key government health strategies of recent years in Unit 12. *Choosing Health: Making Healthy Choices Easier*, *Saving Lives: Our Healthier Nation*, the Acheson Report and other key policy documents are considered in detail in that unit.

### Every Child Matters

In 2003 the government published a Green Paper called *Every Child Matters: Change for Children*. This was published alongside the formal response to the report into the death of Victoria Climbié, the young girl who was abused and eventually killed by her great-aunt and the man with whom they lived.

The Green Paper built on existing plans to strengthen preventative services by focusing on four key themes:

1  increasing the focus on supporting families and carers

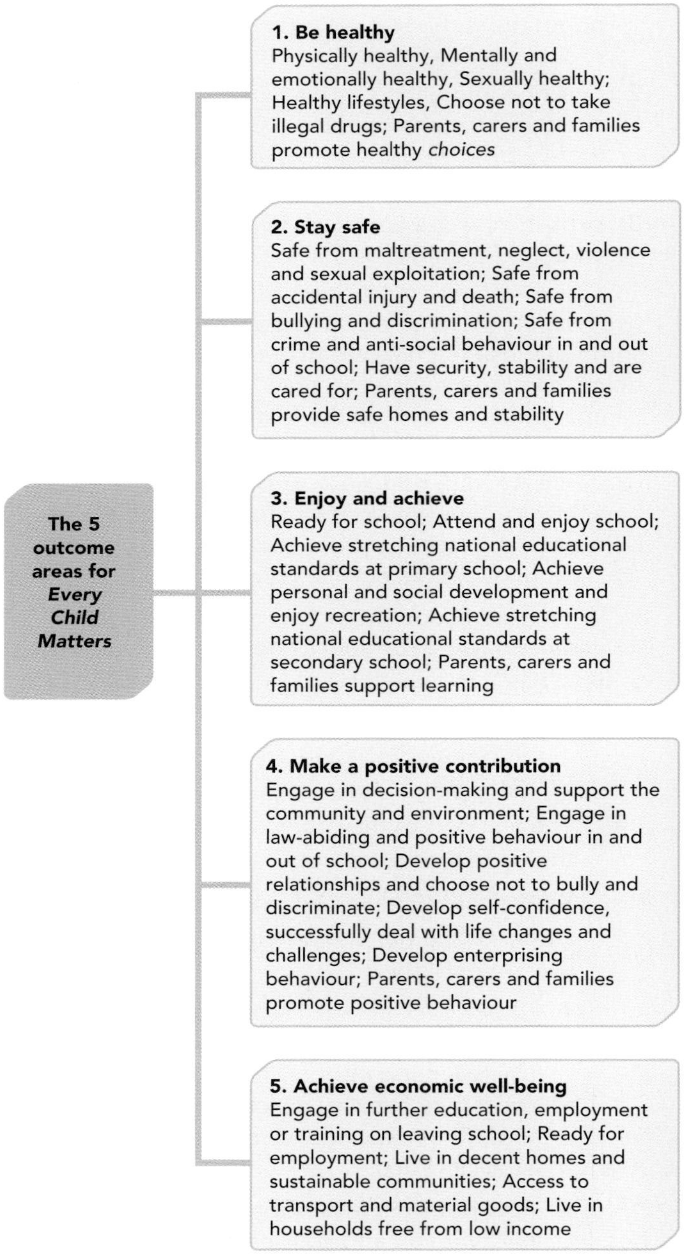

**The 5 outcome areas for *Every Child Matters***

**1. Be healthy**
Physically healthy, Mentally and emotionally healthy, Sexually healthy; Healthy lifestyles, Choose not to take illegal drugs; Parents, carers and families promote healthy *choices*

**2. Stay safe**
Safe from maltreatment, neglect, violence and sexual exploitation; Safe from accidental injury and death; Safe from bullying and discrimination; Safe from crime and anti-social behaviour in and out of school; Have security, stability and are cared for; Parents, carers and families provide safe homes and stability

**3. Enjoy and achieve**
Ready for school; Attend and enjoy school; Achieve stretching national educational standards at primary school; Achieve personal and social development and enjoy recreation; Achieve stretching national educational standards at secondary school; Parents, carers and families support learning

**4. Make a positive contribution**
Engage in decision-making and support the community and environment; Engage in law-abiding and positive behaviour in and out of school; Develop positive relationships and choose not to bully and discriminate; Develop self-confidence, successfully deal with life changes and challenges; Develop enterprising behaviour; Parents, carers and families promote positive behaviour

**5. Achieve economic well-being**
Engage in further education, employment or training on leaving school; Ready for employment; Live in decent homes and sustainable communities; Access to transport and material goods; Live in households free from low income

**Fig 20.8:** Five key areas of *Every Child Matters*

**2** ensuring that services intervene early before children reach crisis point

**3** addressing the underlying problems identified in the report, i.e. weak accountability and poor integration of services

**4** ensuring that the people working with children are valued, rewarded and trained.

The Green Paper prompted an unprecedented debate about services for children, young people and families. There was a wide consultation with people working in children's services, and with parents, children and young people. Following the consultation, the government published *Every Child Matters: The Next Steps*, and passed the Children Act 2004, providing the legislative basis to develop more effective and accessible services focused around the needs of children, young people and families. In its outcome framework, *Every Child Matters* describes five key areas of entitlement for all children and young people.

## Legislation

Other examples of health-promoting legislation, relevant to all aspects of health, include:

- the Factory Acts of the nineteenth century, which limited the hours that children, women and men could work

- the Public Health legislation in 1848 that required towns to take steps to improve sanitary conditions

- the Clean Air Acts of the 1950s, which significantly reduced city 'smogs' (pollution-laden fogs)

- the Water (Fluoridation) Act of 1985, which enabled health authorities to ask water companies to add fluoride to drinking water to reduce dental decay.

# 3.2 Design principles for health education activities

## Importance of national health policy and planning

There are certain accepted principles that guide effective planning for health education activities. The starting point for any project should be an identified need. This could be due to a national priority or target. For example, a current priority is to reduce the waiting time for access to GUM (genito-urinary medicine) services (i.e. sexual health clinics which deal with the treatment of sexually transmitted infections). To support this aim, a major national TV campaign was launched to promote the adoption of safe sexual practices (using a condom) and therefore reduce the demand on GUM services, an equally effective means of achieving the national target.

In order to plan effectively, you need a clear understanding of what you are trying to achieve. Planning should provide you with the answers to three questions:

**1** What am I trying to achieve?

**2** What am I going to do?

**3** How will I know whether I have succeeded?

## Identifying your target audience and need

As a health promoter, your first action should be to identify the source of the need you are considering. This will identify who you are targeting. Identifying your target audience for a campaign starts with the question: 'What is the health need that I should be addressing?' The need for a campaign will usually come from one of four sources:

**1** *Normative need* – defined by an expert or professional according to their own standards. For example, a person with a body mass index above 30 is classed as obese.

**2** *Felt need* – the needs that people feel, i.e. the things we want. For example, people might want their food to be free of genetically modified (GM) products.

**3** *Expressed need* – a felt need that is voiced. For example, the felt need to have GM-free food may become a public debate, with pressure groups focusing on the issue.

**4** *Comparative need* – this arises from comparisons between similar groups of people, where one group has access to a health promotion activity and the other does not. For example, one college might employ a student counsellor where another might not.

## Information gathering/statistics

The evidence of need for your own project can be established from national, regional and/or local health information. There are many sources for this type of information, including:

- your local Primary Care Trust (the health promotion unit or public health department in particular)
- the local authority
- key websites where you can access data, in some cases for areas as small as individual electoral wards. These include the Public Health Observatories, the Office for National Statistics, the Department of Health and, in the case of drug and alcohol use, the Home Office.

## Activity 8: Identifying local needs

If you were to carry out a health promotion activity locally, how would you start to identify local needs? What felt or expressed needs are you aware of, within the student body of your college?

List possible sources of useful information for the needs you may be aware of. How can you add substance to the expressed need with some normative information? How would you decide whether this information is a reliable basis for your decision-making?

## Target setting

As a health promoter, you need to set targets, which means defining clear aims and objectives before you do anything else. An *aim* is a broad overall goal for the whole project. It is often a very broad statement of the underlying intention and will be hard to use to assess the success of a project. An *objective* is a specific goal to be achieved as part of delivering the aim.

## SMART objectives

Your objectives need to be SMART, which means they must be Specific, Measurable, Achievable, Relevant and Timely (i.e. possible to achieve by a certain time). For more on this, see Book 1, Unit 6 Personal and professional development, page 269. In addition, for health education to succeed, the objective has to acknowledge the starting point of the audience. In other words, it should be based on an understanding of *where the person is at now*, rather than *where someone might think the person should be*.

## Choice of approach

Is this a media-driven campaign, or one that would work best through a one-to-one approach (for

example, using peer educators), or a community development project? Whichever approach you adopt, you will need to be able to explain it and justify why it has been selected.

## Clear and accurate information communicated appropriately

The information you are using must be accurate and up to date, and this can be particularly problematic for printed materials. Information can become outdated but it is still available because people don't regularly check the content and remove leaflets and posters from circulation.

Having ensured that your information is clearly worded and accurate, you need to choose which media to use (e.g. newspapers, radio or TV) and this decision could be crucial. For example, radio stations tend to have very specific target audience age ranges so selecting the wrong radio station for your campaign could mean that a campaign about drug use is targeted at the over-60s!

## Misinformation and prejudice challenged and corrected

In the section on immunisation on page 127 you saw that one person's views can distort the perception of a large part of the population. This illustrates the responsibility of health educators to make sure the information they are giving out is both accurate and free from prejudice.

## Consultation with other agencies

The causes of ill health are so broad that it requires a wide range of agencies to work together to have a positive influence on health. When you are working with other agencies, it is important to know who you need to work with and at what stages.

## Obtaining feedback from participants

A key aspect of any health promotion activity is to ensure that the people who have participated are given an opportunity to evaluate the activity. The feedback gained from previous participants, e.g. through questionnaires or satisfaction surveys about the activity, given to participants after the event, should also be a key part of the information you build into the planning process. The refining that takes place through incorporation of participant feedback ensures that the activity improves with each repetition.

## 3.3 Resources

As communication methods become increasingly diverse and complex, the range of resources available to the health promoter grows. In many cases, paper-based materials are less effective than, for instance, podcasts, online quizzes, moving images, games, three-dimensional models and drama performances. Increasingly, new media are favoured by younger audiences, as in the following examples:

- Chlamydia screening services can use SMS texting to deliver results.
- Campaigns can use Bluetooth technology to send messages direct to people's mobile phones.
- Internet sites can be used to provide comprehensive campaign packages built into games and activities to engage the audience.
- Younger children may prefer models or toys; teenagers might prefer podcast, Internet or SMS communication.

## 3.4 Local and national targets

Activities that are likely to gain the most support are those that are linked in some way to national and/or local health targets. Targets are defined for issues that are identified as being important. Therefore they will be recognised and supported either financially or in kind with people and materials. In Unit 12 you saw how national health strategy is driven by a range of targets such as those within *Our Healthier Nation*. These targets are frequently used as the basis for developing health education activities.

# 4 Be able to implement a health campaign

## 4.1 Aims and objectives

### Improving the health of individuals and society

While we might be trying to improve the health of individuals and society as a whole, this is at best an overall aim and not easily measurable or attributable to specific health education projects. Therefore, when you are trying to define objectives for your project, you might think about objectives like the ones in the table below.

**Table 20.5:** Different types of objectives

| Objective type | A possible example |
| --- | --- |
| Health-related learning | To improve the knowledge of parents who are attending a workshop to learn how to discuss drug use with their children |
| Exploring values and attitudes | To provide an opportunity for a group of local community members to explore attitudes to racism in their locality |
| Promoting self-esteem and self-empowerment | To increase self-awareness and self-belief in a group of people from a local community in order to encourage them to be active in decision-making |
| Providing knowledge and skills for change | To develop the knowledge and skills of a group of people to enable them to stop smoking for a period of at least four weeks |
| Changing beliefs | To reduce the proportion of parents holding negative views about the MMR vaccine through a health visitor-led awareness event at a local surgery |
| Changing attitudes | To increase the numbers of people who are thinking about stopping smoking after an awareness-raising session in a local workplace |
| Changing behaviours | To increase the numbers of young people who are using a condom when having sex |
| Changing lifestyle | To increase the numbers of people who report they are using active forms of transport to get to and from work on a local industrial estate |

Table 20.6: Different target audiences

| Group | Issues to consider | Planning considerations |
|---|---|---|
| **Children** | • Young children largely have their choices made for them by their parents.<br>• However, young children can influence parental behaviour, e.g. young people can persuade parents to quit smoking or to change the family diet (this is sometimes referred to as 'pester power'). | • Campaigns usually have to influence the behaviour of parents as well as children. |
| **Older people** | • May hold fatalistic views (e.g. *'It hasn't done me any harm so far so why change now? I'm not going to be around long enough to feel the benefits'* or *'I've done well to get this far – I can't really expect my health to be great now'*).<br>• People are generally living longer, but not necessarily extending their *healthy life expectancy* (i.e. people live longer but may be sick and disabled for many of their extra years). | • Key to success will be a focus on how quickly they are likely to feel the benefits of any health behaviour change and how much it will improve the *quality* of life, not just quantity. |
| **Pregnant mothers** | • If a midwife avoids a direct message by saying that 'continuing to smoke *might* harm your unborn child', the mother may interpret this as saying that it equally *might not*.<br>• Take care not to give conflicting messages, e.g. *'If you smoke, your baby may be small'* could be seen as beneficial because this may make for an easier birth. | • Using a clear, direct message is key to influencing behaviour.<br>• Must not suggest the mother is a bad person or this could jeopardise working relationship.<br>• Ensure that risks of having a small baby (e.g. being premature and slow in development) are clear to mother. |
| **Young people** | • Young people rarely consider long-term issues (e.g. the impact of a particular behaviour on their health in ten or twenty years' time) so any health campaign needs to deal with a very short-term effect.<br>• They can be encouraged to react against the exploitative action of big business (e.g. tobacco or alcohol trades), which seek to recruit young people as lifetime consumers. | • Ensure messages are relevant to the target audience and deal with what they value (e.g. for young women it will be things like their appearance and the attitudes of celebrities they aspire to be like).<br>• Emphasise immediate positive impact (e.g. saving money).<br>• Focus on more immediate harms (e.g. liver damage from alcohol abuse may take tens of years to develop but they are more likely to be hit by a car while drunk or be beaten up or have unprotected sex).<br>• Focus on exploitation by commercial companies. |

# 4.2 Target audience

The target audience for any health education initiative is a key concern. It is important to consider the attitudes and values of the audience you are addressing in order to get the message, and the vehicle for its delivery, right.

# 4.3 Context

What type of intervention are you planning?

Is it for a group of people? If so, you will need to consider a range of things such as:

- What is the nature of the group activity? This is usually educational so you will need to define some clear learning objectives (e.g. 'by the end of the session participants will be able to…').
- Room size – how many people are you expecting to attend?
- Materials – will you be using audio-visual equipment (e.g. TV, DVD or PowerPoint)?
- Type of delivery – are you planning it to be a presentation or are you planning smaller group-based activities with more participant involvement?
- Managing the task – if you are using small groups, how will you manage the task you set for the group?

However, if you are planning a one-to-one interaction the considerations are usually different, and this is likely to require more of a counselling approach. For example, if you are likely to be discussing someone's health, which is a sensitive and highly personal issue, you will need to consider:

- Setting – where are you planning to discuss the issue with the person? A quiet room, with comfortable furniture laid out to enable conversation, would be ideal.
- Confidentiality – the person is likely to want to know how you will treat any information they divulge.
- Your own skills – have you had any experience of carrying out this type of discussion before?

# 4.4 Ethical issues

To act ethically is to act in a principled way. Health promotion is founded on a set of principles that define an ethical approach. These principles include:

- a respect for autonomy, i.e. the right of others to make their own choices and determine their own life
- not doing harm
- doing good
- a commitment to justice, i.e. being fair and equitable.

Health education can present serious challenges to the educator. For example, if a health promoter works with a person, gradually exploring their health needs and supporting them towards making an informed choice, the individual might still decide not to follow the health promoter's advice and still choose to adopt a health-damaging behaviour. The educator has respected the individual's right to autonomy but should they accept and respect that decision and not try to persuade the person to adopt a different choice because of their concerns about the impact on their health?

Unit 12 (The *Choosing Health* white paper) introduced a variation on this principle, i.e. informed choice but with two important qualifications:

- you should protect children
- you shouldn't allow one person's choice to adversely affect another (e.g. passive smoking).

In other words, one person's choice should not compromise the rights of another.

The danger with health education activity is that health promoters become fixated on the goal of improved medical or physical health, to the detriment of other aspects of holistic health. It is all too easy for professionals to adopt a victim blaming approach, deciding what is best for the individual to the exclusion of that person's right to self-autonomy. However, it is important to remember that empowering people is an integral part of effective and ethical health promotion work.

Although discussing a patient's health behaviour may seem relatively safe, and in some cases it may be discussed quite openly in public (e.g. someone's desire to be more active would easily be seen as public information), as with any other health intervention, the health educator must maintain client confidentiality. There may be aspects of the discussion that are more personal, or the nature of the discussion itself (e.g. about a person's sexual health risk-taking) may demand that the information is managed in the same way as any other health information.

# 4.5 Evaluation

**Evaluation** is something we actively engage in on a daily basis, when we ask ourselves questions such as:

*'Do I enjoy my job or should I apply for another one? Will I go to that club again?'*

Or, on a professional footing:

*'How did that session go? Did I achieve what I set out to do? Did that person really understand what I was explaining to her or was she just being polite when she said she did?'*

In other words, evaluation is about assessing the value or worth of something, and it necessarily includes an element of subjectivity (i.e. our own appreciation of it).

## Key term

**Evaluation** – A judgement of the worth of something.

When evaluating health promotion activity, it is usually necessary to take a fairly formal approach to evaluation. This type of evaluation may be more public or open to scrutiny by outsiders, and it has two key aspects:

1 defining what we hope to achieve, i.e. aims and objectives

2 gathering information to assess whether we have met these aims and objectives.

## Evaluation – measures, strengths, weaknesses and targets

In your assessment of your own project, you will need to reflect upon its strengths, weaknesses and areas where it could have been improved upon. This is part of an outcome evaluation, which tries to establish the worth of work when it is finished. Evaluation that involves feedback during the course of a project, when things are still taking shape, is termed formative evaluation, or an *evaluation of process*.

An outcome measure is the end point of the piece of work a health promoter undertakes. This can be a target as challenging as those seen in *Saving Lives* (which refers to reductions in disease, see Unit 12, page 119) or something quite small-scale, such as improving the knowledge and skills of people from a specific geographical community about healthy cooking. There will be considerable overlap between

**Table 20.7:** Sample evaluation of a theatre in health education project

| Objective | Use a TIHE approach to engage young people in an accessible, fun but rigorous discussion about the legal, health, personal and social consequences of decisions made in relation to drugs, sex and crime. Plan and deliver this activity within the next school term. |
| --- | --- |
| Key tasks/ activities | Briefly describe what service or activity you will provide and evaluate to achieve this objective. |
| Results | What do you hope will change as a result of this activity? |
| Measures | How will you measure the described change? |
| Standards | What will be the best you could hope for? What will you be happy with? What will you be unhappy with? |

outcome measures and objectives here but it is important not to confuse the two.

So for your assessment activity you need to ask yourself, 'How will I know that this has been a worthwhile activity?' You will need to identify the information that enables you to state categorically that your aim has been achieved. You might want to scale down some of your objectives and outcomes when you begin to do this, as you might realise how ambitious you have been!

Good evaluation starts with clearly defined objectives and clear measures for the level of performance, i.e. how well the activity has performed. This is illustrated using a theatre in health education example below:

To evaluate the work, you need to have both an outcome and a quality measure (i.e. the standard for the activity). For example, in this case you might find that the activity raised the awareness of both pupils and staff but that they thought the story wasn't very realistic and wouldn't recommend it to other schools. In other words, you achieved the outcome you hoped for but the performance wasn't the right quality to enthuse people and ensure that it could be repeated for other issues. This is where you begin to assess what worked well (the strengths) and the areas for improvement (weaknesses). In this case the medium is the strength (i.e. you would use TIHE again) but the storyline is the weakness (i.e. the script needs to be rewritten with the help of feedback from some of the target audience).

## Case study: Anne

Anne is a health visitor who works in a challenging neighbourhood where income levels are in the bottom 20 per cent for the country. She has worked here for the last nine years. She has been working with Kylie, a 22-year-old woman who has two children, aged five and two. Anne is worried that both Kylie's children are overweight at an early age. Using the growth chart, she can see that Sean, Kylie's youngest, is already in the top 10 per cent weight range for his age and her daughter Katie has a high BMI.

Anne has tried to discuss her children's diet with Kylie but she says that her mum fed her similar food at that age and it doesn't appear to have done her any harm. Anne can see that Kylie is likely to be overweight or obese but she hasn't been weighed recently so she doesn't know for certain. She is increasingly concerned that both the children are at risk of obesity-related conditions and may suffer bullying at school as a result of being overweight, a common situation for children locally.

1 Should Anne be telling Kylie more forcefully to change their diet?

2 What would the appropriate messages be for her to convey to Kylie?

3 Is she failing in her role as a health visitor if she accepts Kylie's wish to continue feeding them the food she chooses?

4 In this situation, who is better placed to judge what is right for Kylie and her family? And how do you justify that opinion?

5 If Anne was very directive, how might this affect her relationship with Kylie? And what might be the implications of any change in the relationship?

6 Should health behaviour be a matter of personal choice, or is it too important to leave to the individual?

**Fig 20.9:** Why is it so important for health professionals to consider ethical issues when discussing health-damaging behaviours such as smoking?

## Assessment activity 20.2

P3 P4 P5 M2 M3 D1 D2 **BTEC**

All the evidence for this final assessment activity will be generated through planning and implementing a small-scale health education campaign that you will carry out yourself. The campaign must be relevant to local or national health strategies and your own contribution could be part of a bigger campaign that you plan cooperatively with others in your class group. However, for assessment, you will produce a resource for the campaign and an individual report of the campaign, focusing particularly on your own contribution to it.

For P3 you should explain how you have planned your campaign (this could be the **Methodology** section of the report). You should explain how you took account of the design principles that underpin the campaign. These will include:

- how you developed an overall plan for the campaign
- how you developed an individual action plan of what you (individually) would be contributing to the campaign
- how you decided which methods would be used for the campaign – how the campaign fits with local and national strategies and targets
- how its aims and objectives, in relation to local and/or national strategies and targets, were developed, particularly in relation to the model of behaviour change to be targeted
- the audience for the campaign
- which resource, e.g. written literature, film, drama, 3D model, ICT you will develop for the campaign and what planning will be necessary to develop this
- the consultation with others that might be necessary, e.g. with your peers in the class group, staff at your school/college, external agencies
- how you will check the accuracy and appropriateness of the information used in the campaign
- how you will obtain feedback about the outcomes from the campaign (i.e. how well/accurately have the audience received the health education message?).

You should identify the key tasks or actions that will be necessary to implement the campaign and should produce an action plan.

For D1 you will need to justify the approaches and methods and relate them to models of behaviour change. You should ensure that your explanation includes reasons for the decisions you made, as well as the reasons why you rejected other alternatives, particularly in relation to the models of behaviour change selected. This could be a section of the report titled **Rationale for selected approach**.

For the P4 criterion you will need to produce evidence to show what you actually did in the planning and implementing stage of the campaign, rather than whether it worked. Evidence could be presented as the **Implementation** section of the report. You should consider how the actual (as compared to the planned) implementation of the campaign relates to models of behaviour change.

For P5, your report must explain ethical issues associated with the campaign, relating to the planning and/or implementation phases of the campaign. For M3 you will also need to discuss how the ethical issues that arose were addressed, again considering different possibilities. This section of the report could be called **Ethical Issues**.

Evidence for M2 could be presented in a section of the report called **Impact of the Campaign**. You should assess how effective your own campaign was in relation to achieving its aims and objectives, as intended in the campaign planning. You should consider the factors that contributed to its success and those that limited its effectiveness. You might also consider any unexpected outcomes from the campaign as part of your assessment.

For D2 you should add a **Recommendations** section to the report that makes suggestions for improving your health education campaign for a future occasion.

### Grading tips

**P3 Aims and Objectives**

- be clear about the aims and objectives of the campaign
- relate the aims and objectives to specific local and/or national targets
- apply SMART principles to develop an action plan
- prioritise the actions in the action plan by using different deadlines

**Assessment activity 20.2** *continued*

- if you are working in a group, be clear about who is responsible for each action.

**P4** You should be explicit in reporting on the contribution to the overall campaign made by the individual resource that you develop. Evidence you submit with your assignment could include:

- a log documenting what actions you took (and on what dates) relating to the development of your resource, and how your own actions contributed to the class effort in planning and implementing the overall campaign

- an action plan – annotated and updated – to show you have monitored your progress against your plan

- a witness testimony from your teacher to confirm your participation in the campaign. Your teacher could also sign and date your action plan on each occasion that you monitor your progress

- a photograph or copy of your resource

- if the resource was developed as a group, e.g. a video, a description of what your individual contribution was.

**D1** This requires you to demonstrate how you use theory to influence practice. For example, show how your knowledge of social learning theory has been used in the design of your project and why you selected this approach over the other models of behaviour change as the foundation of your work. In this context the word 'justify' means that you should assess the different approaches and explain why you have chosen those models.

**P5** **Ethical issues**

Ethical issues that might arise could relate to the type of literature you use in your campaign, relative to the target audience and obtaining appropriate consent to carry out the campaign.

Go back to the section on ethical practice in health education on page 275; now think about the ethical issues this project might raise for you. For example, if your project is about substance use, some of your friends may be putting themselves at risk by using illegal substances and/or alcohol and tobacco.

Imagine that your work is about substance use and as the work progressed, you uncovered three pieces of information that you hadn't anticipated:

- one student contacted you and divulged that someone was dealing drugs on the college premises

- another person admitted they thought that they may have been date-raped while under the influence of a mixture of drink and drugs

- a member of your project team said they were in a difficult position because their father worked in the drugs unit of the police and they now know about the allegations of dealing on the premises.

In other words it requires you to have reflected upon what ethical issues might be raised by a group of students designing a campaign for their peers particularly if you choose to focus on sensitive subjects such as sex and drugs? Being under the influence can have serious risks attached, including rape, drink/drugged-driving or violence. Have any of your friends been in a situation where these might have occurred? Is it possible this work might uncover these types of issues?

For each situation, identify what the ethical issues might be for this scenario and explain clearly how you would deal with it and why you would adopt that approach.

**M3** The activity above will give you a worked example of possible ethical issues which a campaign focusing on substance misuse might raise. To achieve this grade it is the final part of that activity that you will need to focus on, i.e. what ethical issues might be raised by your own work and how did you plan to deal with them?

**M2** Refer back to the points given in the task guidance in P3 and P4 to help you assess the factors that affect the effectiveness of your campaign. You could also use the key tasks in

**Assessment activity 20.2** *continued*

your action plan to help organise your thinking for the assessment of the health education campaign. Consider identifying success criteria against which you can judge how effective the campaign was in meeting its aims and objectives. Any feedback you have obtained from participants amongst the target audience could be helpful here.

Remember to include explicit comments about the effectiveness of the resource you developed within your assessment.

One important consideration is whether there were factors that influenced the outcome which could have been foreseen and therefore could have been planned for, or if they were unknowns that couldn't be.

You could frame your assessment around three aspects of the project:

Its delivery: i.e. how well the plan was delivered, which things went well and on time and which didn't and why

The reach: i.e. did you contact the numbers of people you expected and how many of them engaged with the issues you were raising

The impact: what happened as a result of the contact you had with those people, did

anything change, how do you know it changed? Is the change sustainable?

**D2** Finally, you need to make recommendations for improvements to your own health education campaign. This requires you to:

- identify the problems that led to poor or less good performance in some areas of the project
- be able to identify a range of measures that could be taken in future to prevent that happening again.

For each of the areas that went less well in your project, it is crucial that you identify at least one and up to three actions that would prevent a repetition.

The recommendations usually form the final section of any project report. Their purpose is to inform future planning and repetition of the activity and ensure that learning points are built into the redesign process. Your recommendations will work best if they follow this format:

*'I found that…*

*Therefore in any future repetition of this work I would recommend that…'*

# Resources and further reading

Benzeval, M., Judge, K. & Whitehead, M. (1995) *Tackling Inequalities in Health: an Agenda for Action* London: Kings Fund Publishing

Downie, R.S., Tannahill, C. & Tannahill, A. (1996) *Health Promotion Models and Values* Oxford: Oxford University Press

Draper, P. (ed) (1991) *Health Through Public Policy: Greening of Public Health* Green Print

Ewles, L. & Simnett, I. (1992) *Promoting Health: A Practical Guide* London: Scutari Press

HM Government (2004) *At Least Five a Week: Evidence on the Impact of Physical Activity and its Relationship to Health* London: HMSO

HM Government (2004) *Choosing Health: Making Healthy Choices Easier* London: HMSO

HM Government (1992) *The Health of the Nation* London: HMSO

HM Government (1998) *Independent Inquiry into Inequalities in Health* London: HMSO

HM Government (2006) *It's our health! Realising the potential of effective social marketing* London: HMSO

HM Government (2001) *National Strategy for HIV and Sexual Health* London: HMSO

HM Government (1997) *The New NHS: Modern, Dependable* London: HMSO

HM Government (1997) *Saving Lives: Our Healthier Nation* London: HMSO

Jones, L., & Sidell, M. (1997) *The Challenge of Promoting Health: Exploration and Action* Milton Keynes: Open University

Katz, J. & Peberdy, A. (1997) *Promoting Health: Knowledge and Practice* Buckingham: Macmillan/OU Press

Moonie, N. (2000) *Advanced Health and Social Care* Oxford: Heinemann

Naidoo, J. & Wills, J. (1996) *Health Promotion: Foundations for Practice* London: Baillière Tindall

Townsend, P., Whitehead, M., Davidson, N. & Davidsen, N. (1987) *Inequalities in Health: The Black Report and the Health Divide* Harmondsworth: Penguin Books

# Useful websites

British Heart Foundation www.bhf.org.uk

Calculate your Body Mass Index www.nhlbisupport.com/bmi/bmicalc.htm

Department of Health www.doh.gov.uk

Food in Schools www.foodinschools.org

NHS Stop Smoking www.givingupsmoking.co.uk

Healthy School Lunches www.healthyschoollunches.org

National Drugs Strategy www.homeoffice.gov.uk/drugs/index.html

National Institute for Health and Clinical Excellence (NICE) www.nice.org.uk/

National Social Marketing Centre www.nsms.org.uk

NHS in England www.nhs.uk/nhsengland/Pages/NHSEngland.aspx

NHS immunisation information www.immunisation.nhs.uk/Vaccines/MMR

School Food Trust www.schoolfoodtrust.org.uk

World Health Organization www.who.int/en/

# Just checking

1 Why might a 'victim blaming' approach to health education be described as being over-simplistic?
2 List two advantages and two disadvantages of a community development approach to health education.
3 What are the seven main features of a social marketing approach?
4 When designing a leaflet, what are the key questions you would need to consider?
5 What are the stages described in the stages of change model? Why is it sometimes represented as a spiral rather than a circle?
6 What were the underpinning principles for the *Choosing Health* white paper?
7 If you were to undertake a health promotion project to reduce the unsafe level of alcohol consumption in a particular estate in your locality, you would first need to identify the need for this project. Describe examples of: a normative need; a comparative need; a felt need; and an expressed need.
8 What does SMART stand for when defining objectives?
9 What is the difference between an outcome evaluation measure and a formative evaluation measure?
10 A friend of yours has had unprotected sex on several occasions, usually while under the influence of alcohol. You are worried that they are regularly putting themselves at risk of catching a sexually transmitted infection and also that they are making themselves vulnerable when they are intoxicated. What are the ethical considerations you need to think about if you wish to discuss this with them?

edexcel

# Assignment tips

1 This unit has clear links to Unit 12 so you can expect to find lots of overlaps (e.g. key policy drivers). Unit 12 is primarily about policy and programmes (i.e. collections of projects), whereas this unit is more focused on the individual, e.g. on the theories of behaviour change that apply to individual people.

2 You can practise some of the key skills you learned in Unit 12 here, e.g. the assessment of need to define your project at the outset.

3 What is different in this unit is the focus on your own project. It's important to focus on all aspects of your project from the beginning. For example, a common mistake is for people to leave evaluation until the latter stages of the project, assuming that they won't need to evaluate until the end. However, evaluation often requires the collection of information at the beginning to provide a baseline, to enable you to demonstrate the change you have delivered when you re-measure at the end. You should therefore make sure you have read through all the guidance on planning and delivering your project before you begin.

4 A critical aspect of this process is the definition of clear objectives for the project – what is it that you are trying to achieve? It's important to think about this carefully and describe an objective that meets the criteria set out in the text.

5 This emphasis on time spent planning might seem frustrating but the old adage holds true: 'Fail to plan – Plan to fail'.

# 29 Applied psychological perspectives for health and social care

ychological perspectives are ideas and theories about what makes people
have in a particular way. Since behaviour, feelings and thoughts have a big
fluence on health, it is important to have a working knowledge of psychology
d how it impacts upon people in health and social care. For example, why
e some of us optimistic and others pessimistic? What causes prejudice and
crimination? Psychology can shed light on these issues by giving insight into
man development and behaviour. Different life stages and events also affect
haviour quite dramatically so that some people become disempowered and
ybe even depressed when they enter residential care and lose their role.

e nature–nurture debate is of major significance in understanding development and behaviour,
h some theorists focusing on one aspect more than the other. You will learn how to recognise
ure accounts of development and differentiate them from nurture accounts, as well as knowing
en to seek to understand behaviour by looking at the interaction between the two. You will
 study the mind–body connection by learning how our perceptions, and experience, of stress
uence the functioning of our immune system. Some of the perspectives and theories covered
 be familiar from Unit 8, but there is considerably more focus in this chapter on developmental
chology, including the theories of Piaget, Vygotsky and Bowlby, which will enable you to deepen
r understanding of human behaviour.

## Learning outcomes

After completing this unit you should:

1   understand the contribution of psychological perspectives to the understanding of
the development of individuals

2   understand the contribution of psychological perspectives to the understanding of
specific behaviours

3   understand the contribution of psychological perspectives to the management and
treatment of specific behaviours

4   understand the contribution of psychological perspectives to residential care
provision.

# Assessment and grading criteria

This table shows you what you must do in order to achieve a **pass**, **merit** or **distinction** grade, a
where you can find activities in this book to help you.

| To achieve a **pass** grade, the evidence must show that you are able to: | To achieve a **merit** grade, the evidence must show that, in addition to the pass criteria, you are able to: | To achieve a **distinction** grade, the evidence must show that, in addition to the pass and merit criteria, you are able to |
|---|---|---|
| **P1** Explain the principal psychological perspectives applied to the understanding of the development of individuals. **See Assessment activity 29.1, page 308** | **M1** Discuss the principal psychological perspectives applied to the understanding of the development of individuals. **See Assessment activity 29.1, page 308** | **D1** Evaluate the principal psychological perspectives applied to the understanding of the development of individuals. **See Assessment activity 29.1, page 308** |
| **P2** Explain the contribution of complementary psychological theories to the understanding of two specific behaviours. **See Assessment activity 29.2, page 312** | **M2** Assess the contribution of complementary and contrasting psychological theories to the understanding of the two specific behaviours. **See Assessment activity 29.2, page 312** | |
| **P3** Explain the contribution of contrasting psychological theories to the understanding of two specific behaviours. **See Assessment activity 29.2, page 312** | | |
| **P4** Explain the contribution of psychological perspectives to the management and treatment of two specific behaviours. **See Assessment activity 29.3, page 323** | | |
| **P5** Explain the contribution of psychological perspectives to the promotion of good practice in residential care services. **See Assessment activity 29.4, page 328** | **M3** Discuss the contribution of two psychological perspectives to the promotion of good practice in residential care services. **See Assessment activity 29.4 page 328** | **D2** Evaluate the contribution of two psychological perspectives to the promotion of good practice in residential care services. **See Assessment activity 29.4, page 328** |

# How you will be assessed

You will be assessed by means of two written assignments and a presentation with accompanying materials. The first assignment takes the form of an information leaflet, in which you will explain how principal psychological perspectives are applied to the development of individuals. For the second assignment, you will need to produce two case studies, which will enable you to show your understanding of how psychological perspectives can be used in the management and treatment of specific behaviours. For your third assignment, you will prepare a presentation, with accompanying relevant materials, explaining how psychological perspectives can be used to promote good practice in residential settings.

## Kwame, 17 years old

When I first looked at the chapter contents I felt overwhelmed. But I found a few strategies to use and I ended up really enjoying it all. To begin with, I knew far more than I realised. My tutor advised us to keep a notebook with the terminology for each perspective and this helped me when I was working on the assignments.

I had two weeks' work experience in a residential care setting for children and was able to compare their development with that outlined by Piaget. I found I disagreed with him on some aspects but it was really helpful to be able to put the theory into practice. I want to work as a play therapist in a hospital and found attachment theory particularly useful, as it explains children's behaviour so well when they are separated from parents. I also thought social learning theory could be used in my future career, as the children I work with would be able to learn by observing others.

## Over to you!

1   What do you think you will find most interesting about this unit?

2   Do you know about any psychological perspectives at present?

3   Why do you need an understanding of psychological perspectives in order to work in health and social care?

# 1 Understand the contribution of psychological perspectives to the understanding of the development of individuals

**Why do people behave the way they do?**

Do you ever wonder why people behave the way they do? Some are sunny and positive all the time, others pessimistic and moody. Some people seem to want to pick a fight, others to smooth things over. Where does intelligence come from? Why are some toddlers clingy and whiny, while others are adventurous and confident even when they first go to nursery or playgroup? Why are some people artistic, musical or sporty and others academic? How much of our behaviour are we born with? And how much is due to our upbringing? Psychology does not have definite answers but provides a framework to examine these questions and will help you to understand people's behaviour and development in much more depth.

Consider some of the behaviours mentioned above, or choose your own topic. How much of behaviour is due to nature and how much to nurture? Can behaviour be changed? We shall explore these questions in more depth in this unit but make a note of your ideas now because you probably know a lot more about psychology than you think you do!

## 1.1 Debates in developmental psychology
### Nature versus nurture

For more information on this debate, see Book 1, Unit 4.

The essence of this debate is whether our behaviour is determined by **nature** (what we are born with) or **nurture** (how we are brought up and socialised). Different psychological perspectives tend to have different (though sometimes complementary) views on the relative importance of nature and nurture. Behavioural psychologists take the view that we are born as 'blank slates' and our behaviour and personality develop as a result of interactions with our environment (nurture). Biological psychologists believe that many of the influences on our development come from our genes and the influence of biochemistry on our behaviour (nature). Others believe that there is an interaction between the two factors.

### Nature

A nature account of development, personality and behaviours focuses on what is innate (what we are born with) such as left-handedness, the genes we have inherited, etc. Issues such as temperament (are you shy and withdrawn or outgoing and confident?), intelligence and susceptibility to developing certain illnesses or diseases bring this debate into focus; there are arguments in favour of the nature perspective, stating that our inheritance has a very large influence on the type of people we become.

### Nurture

Nurture refers to all that happens within the environment (even in the womb) that influences the growing child. It involves the way someone is brought up (socialisation) and the way they are treated by important people in their lives such as parents, teachers and peers. All of this influences behaviour and development and goes towards building a personality.

One way of exploring the nature versus nurture debate is by looking at intelligence. If intelligence is an inborn quality that merely develops, then the environment should have no influence on it. This seems unlikely, though, since children who are exposed to enriching environments, where they get the opportunity to develop their talents to the full, seem to do better than those who have fewer educational opportunities.

## Continuity versus discontinuity

This debate is about whether development is a smooth process with no distinct changes taking place (**continuity**) or a discontinuous process where development takes place in stages (**discontinuity**).

### Continuity

A continuity account of development looks at quantitative rather than qualitative change. Change involves smooth growth – for example, the skull expands, the number of words in a child's vocabulary increases. The analogy of a sponge is sometimes used to explain this, where growth simply drips in, just as water soaks into a sponge (which gets heavier and more laden with water but does not change shape).

### Discontinuity

In this characterisation of development, the differences between stages are qualitative rather than quantitative. This can be likened to the development of a butterfly, which moves from the caterpillar stage to the chrysalis stage to the final emergence of a butterfly – all very distinct stages involving qualitative change. This can be seen in children in the development of walking rather than crawling and the emergence of social smiling. Stage theories in psychology, as suggested by Freud, Piaget and Erikson, are examples of discontinuity.

## Nomothetic versus idiographic

**Nomothetic**, as applied to psychology, is concerned with the study of features that are common to a group or class of individuals. The cognitive psychologists (for example, Piaget) researched into why all children made similar errors in logic, problem solving and reasoning at a certain age.

**Idiographic** refers to the study of an individual and those unique characteristics that distinguish them from others. Case studies in psychology take an idiographic approach, as they are concerned to find out why a particular individual developed in the way they did.

### Key terms

**Nature** – All aspects of a person that involves genetic inheritance.

**Nurture** – Aspects of a person that result from socialisation, parenting and other environmental factors.

**Continuity** – Development that takes place slowly, smoothly and continuously (for example, a growth in height).

**Discontinuity** – Development occurring in discontinuous stages. Each stage is qualitatively different from the preceding and following stage.

**Nomothetic** – An approach that seeks to find out what traits and behaviours a group of individuals share.

**Idiographic** – An approach that investigates the full richness of experience of just one individual.

# 1.2 Principal psychological perspectives

## The behaviourist perspective

This perspective is widely used to understand the development of human behaviour. The basic assumption is that all human behaviour can be understood as the result of learning. There are two types of learning: classical and operant conditioning.

### Classical conditioning

This refers to an association being made between two events. The first event is called a stimulus and the second is a response. Suppose, for example, a young child runs up to a large dog and puts out her hand to pat the dog. The dog barks loudly (the stimulus), causing the child to have an automatic physiological reaction of being startled and afraid (the response). The pairing of these two events creates an association, leading the child to fear dogs in the future.

For more detail on the process of classical conditioning, see Book 1, Unit 8.

## Operant conditioning

This theory says that behaviour is learned according to the **consequence** of that behaviour. If the consequence is positively **reinforcing** (i.e. it provides something the individual wants or values) it will be repeated. Over time the behaviour is strengthened and becomes a typical pattern of behaviour. If the consequence is unpleasant (**punishment**) there is a possibility that this unpleasant consequence will lead to a lessening of the behaviour. However, in operant conditioning it has been found that punishment is much less effective than reinforcement. Negative reinforcement occurs when the consequence of something we do removes an unpleasant stimulus or event. For example, if taking a painkiller stops a headache, we are negatively reinforced for this action. For more detail on operant conditioning see Unit 8 Psychological perspectives.

A very simple example would be a child having a tantrum in a supermarket. If this behaviour leads to the consequence of Dad buying her a bag of sweets to keep her quiet, she will learn to repeat the behaviour in order to receive this consequence. The bag of sweets (consequence) is experienced as **positive reinforcement**.

## Social learning theory

Social learning theory is sometimes called a theory of **observational learning**. It was developed by Albert Bandura (born 1925), who stated that behaviour can develop as a result of observing and imitating others. The person we imitate is known as a model. When we observe others behaving, dressing or speaking in a particular way, we notice what kind of response they get. If a schoolchild is disruptive in class, others are likely to observe whether or not this behaviour is reinforced, and this will influence their decision about whether or not to imitate this behaviour – if not now, then at a later stage. When behaviour is learned but not performed until later, this is called **latent learning**.

For performance of the learned behaviour to take place, we need to have the **motivation** to perform the behaviour. Motivation depends on a number of factors, including how attractive or prestigious the model is. We are more likely to imitate behaviour performed by someone we admire and want to be like than someone we dismiss as not being important. The consequences for the model also influence motivation. If the model gets punished, we are less likely to imitate behaviour.

However, if the model gets a reinforcing consequence, we are more likely to imitate behaviour.

## Key terms

**Consequence** – Something that happens as a direct result of what you do (your behaviour).

**Reinforcer** – Something that acts to reinforce (strengthen) behaviour. In the case of positive reinforcement this could be something tangible like payment or a sweet, or intangible such as a smile or praise.

**Punishment** – A response to behaviour that is experienced as unwanted and therefore reduces the likelihood that the behaviour will be performed again.

**Positive reinforcement** – A response to behaviour that is experienced as wanted (it may, for example, be desired or pleasurable). It increases the likelihood of the behaviour being performed again.

**Observational learning** – A type of learning where we do not experience a consequence directly, but learn from watching others perform a behaviour and noting the consequences they receive.

**Latent learning** – This refers to a situation where a new behaviour has been learned via observational learning but has not yet been (and may never be) performed.

**Motivation** – This is the key factor that determines whether someone will put what they have learned into practice. Motivation is strongly governed by the individual's own emotions, thoughts, wishes, beliefs, values, etc.

Fig 29.1: The characteristics of the model influence whether or not people will imitate them. If the individual being observed has characteristics we aspire to, we are more likely to imitate their behaviour

Sometimes there can be more than one consequence. In the example of the disruptive schoolchild, the teacher is likely to respond with a verbal punishment or some other sanction. However, if the rest of the class roars with laughter or encourages the child, the consequence that he or she pays attention to is likely to be this reinforcing response from classmates.

**For more information on social learning theory, see Book 1, Unit 8.**

### Case study: Learning to be the class clown

Joe is eleven years old and has recently started secondary school. He initially felt out of place as he was struggling with his schoolwork. However, he has discovered that he can make other children laugh by mimicking the teacher and has, on one occasion, caused his science teacher to cry. His best friend Jason always sits next to him in class.

1  Has Joe learned the behaviour of mimicking the teacher?

2  What motivational factors may be involved in Jason either imitating or not imitating this behaviour?

## Psychodynamic perspective

This perspective takes the stance that many of our motivations and behaviours come from unconscious drives, which means that we are often not aware of the meanings motivating our behaviour. The psychodynamic perspective is covered in more depth on pages 299–302.

## Humanistic perspective

This perspective understands human development according to how 'the self' develops. From a very early age, children develop a sense of self in terms of self-concept and self-esteem. Self-concept refers to how we see ourselves. It includes:

- physical and biological characteristics such as being female, tall, blue-eyed
- skills and competencies such as being good at sport or swimming, being a leader

- psychological aspects such as being kind, shy, outgoing, lively, thoughtful, carefree
- relational aspects such as being a daughter, sister, mother, uncle
- occupational aspects such as being a fire-fighter, a care-worker, a solicitor, a baker, etc.

Self-esteem refers to how much value we give to ourselves and how lovable and likeable we believe ourselves to be. It develops from the way we are loved, listened to, respected and valued by others. A child who is neglected, ridiculed, criticised, told they are unwanted or ignored will develop very low self-esteem. By contrast, being treated with respect, told one is loved and valued will lead to high self-esteem. There is a close link between self-esteem and self-concept.

## Cognitive psychology

*Cognosco* is the Latin for 'I know'. Cognitive comes from this verb and refers to all aspects of an individual's cognitive processes that are involved with learning, thinking, knowing about, reflecting on and understanding the world. Cognitive psychologists study the following human cognitive processes:

- thinking
- memory
- intelligence
- language development
- perception
- problem-solving
- reasoning

## Developmental psychology

Developmental psychology is a perspective that looks at development over the life course – from the foetus in the womb to old age and death. Subjects of interest to developmental psychologists include:

- the development of the physical self including the brain and the body
- social and emotional development
- sex differences and development of gender roles
- moral development
- development of language and communication skills
- the development of intelligence
- cognitive development (all aspects of thinking, learning, memory, attentional processes, visual perception and problem solving).

# 1.3 Application of psychological theories to the development of individuals

## Cognitive development

This refers to all aspects of cognition as outlined above. Although recent research shows that newborn babies have a number of abilities, they do not resemble the fully formed human being in terms of language, memory, the ability to reason, solve problems and so forth. These abilities develop over time and, although many theorists believe they cannot be separated out from other types of development (such as social and emotional), cognitive capacities can be investigated fairly clearly.

## The Piagetian approach

Jean Piaget (1896–1980) held the view that children develop intellectually as a result of informal experiences with the environment – instruction from others is relatively unimportant. Their interactions with the environment need to provide intellectual challenges for development to take place.

Piaget spent many years researching the way in which children seemed to move forward in stages in terms of their ability to use knowledge and to process and organise information. He was especially interested in the development of the ability to:

- think logically
- reason
- solve problems.

His was a nomothetic approach to the study of children. Rather than being concerned with what was unique about each child, he was interested in what was common to all children of a certain age. He thus developed a stage theory of cognitive development.

Piaget believed that children develop schemata for both physical and mental actions. A **schema** (plural: schemata or schemas) is an internal representation of an action. He sees the reflex responses of the newborn as innate (i.e. inborn) schemata – for example, a schema for sucking, grasping, etc.

As the child grows and develops cognitively, these schemata become more elaborate and they develop and change using the processes of **assimilation** and **accommodation**. Assimilation involves using an existing schema to make sense of a new object. Suppose, for example, a two-year-old boy has an existing schema of a bird – an object that flies through the sky. If the child sees a kite on a string flying through the sky, he may well say 'Look, daddy, a bird!' The child has 'assimilated' the kite into his schema for 'objects that fly through the sky'. When the child's father corrects him, and explains that kites are a different category from birds, the child can create a new schema for 'other objects that fly through the sky but are not birds': this is 'accommodation'. The original schema has thus been used to understand the object, but modified to allow for a clearer and more detailed understanding of the environment.

### The four developmental stages

Piaget's theory postulates four developmental stages. The child cannot move from one stage to the next until a biological **maturation** point has been reached. Although some children may move through the stages rather more quickly or slowly than others, this is due to maturational processes rather than stimulation in the environment.

## Key terms

**Schema** – A mental short cut used to understand physical and mental objects, thoughts, situations and events in the world. Each schema is built upon prior experience. For example, an interview schema contains information about how to behave at interview, and what to wear.

**Assimilation** – The process of adapting to new problems and situations using existing knowledge and schemata to make sense of incoming knowledge and events.

**Accommodation** – A process that works alongside assimilation and enables an individual to modify their understanding and internal representation of concepts in order to create new understanding.

**Maturation** – The biological changes that take place as the child develops. Intellectual growth and development cannot move forward until this maturational process reaches a point where the child is ready to move to the next stage.

**Table 29.1:** Piaget's four developmental stages

| Stage | Age | Key features |
|---|---|---|
| Sensorimotor stage | Birth to about 2 years | The child learns to understand the world through its senses and through physical (motor) activity. They lack memory, as we would understand it, and are incapable of **abstract thought**. |
| Pre-operational stage | 2–7 years | The child develops language and thought. She tends to see things from her own perspective (**egocentrism**) and is unable to 'de-centre' (see below). |
| Concrete operational stage | 7–11 years | The child now becomes capable of a level of abstract thinking that enables him or her to handle the concept of reversal. This means they can perform conservation tasks. They still need to use concrete objects to understand problems. If a child aged between seven and eleven years is asked to solve the problem: 'Joan is taller than Susan; Joan is smaller than Mary; who is the smallest?' they will not be able to solve it in their head (using abstract thought) but can do so if given three dolls to represent Joan, Susan and Mary. (Cited in Birch and Malim, 1988.) |
| Formal operational stage | About 11 years onwards | Abstract thought is now present and the child can reason and solve problems much like an adult. |

### Did you know?

Below the age of about two, if you cover up an object a child is playing with, the child acts as though it has disappeared! This is because the child lacks the concept of **object permanence**.

### Investigating egocentrism

Egocentrism is illustrated in Piaget's famous 'Three mountains experiment'. The child is asked to sit in a particular place in front of a model landscape of three mountains, all of different shapes and sizes. The child is then asked what another person seated in a different position (for example, at the back of the landscape) would see. The child at this stage, however, is only able to describe what they see themselves.

### Investigating centration and decentration

The term **centration** refers to a tendency to focus on only one property of a situation and ignore all others. (The opposite tendency is called **de-centration**.) Piaget tested centration by means of famous experiments called **conservation** tasks.

### Conservation of number

In this experiment, Piaget showed children two identically spaced lines of counters. Each child was asked, 'Are there the same number of counters in each row?' The children agreed they were the same.

### Key terms

**Abstract thought** – Representing a problem mentally and manipulating ideas in one's mind. For example, solving the problem '3 + 3' in one's head rather than using counters.

**Egocentrism** – An inability, both literally and metaphorically, to imagine that anyone has a viewpoint which is different from their own.

**Object permanence** – Awareness that an object continues to exist even if it can no longer be seen.

**Centration** – A tendency to focus only on certain key elements of an object, without seeing its other properties (e.g. using height to judge volume).

**De-centration** – The ability to move from one classification system to another. For example, an object is no longer judged by its external properties, such as height, but by its internal properties such as mass.

**Conservation** – The ability to recognise that objects do not change when their appearance changes and that nothing has been added or taken away.

In the second part of the experiment, the experimenter changed the arrangement of the counters (in full view of the child) and then asked the same question, 'Do the rows still contain the same number of counters?'

At this point, most children believe there are more counters in row A than in row B. Once again, the child is paying attention to one feature only and is unable to conserve or perform the operation of **reversibility** (i.e. imagine back to when the counters were first shown to him or her, before the experimenter moved them).

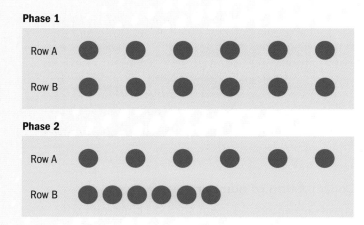

**Phase 1**

Row A

Row B

**Phase 2**

Row A

Row B

Fig 29.2: An experiment to examine conservation of number

## Key term

**Reversibility** – An ability to represent mentally something that has just happened and to perform logical processes on the action. For example, to know that if water is poured into a new beaker, it can also be poured back (reversed) and will stay the same, regardless of physical appearance.

## Summary

Piaget believed that cognitive development takes place in stages. Until the child has reached the right point of maturity, he or she cannot proceed to the next stage. Each stage involves qualitative differences in problem-solving, thinking and logic.

## Activity 1: Piaget's conservation experiments

Research the following experiments used by Piaget to test children's cognitive capacities:

- conservation of volume
- conservation of substance.

## PLTS

**Independent enquirer:** By carrying out this activity you may be able to demonstrate your skill in planning and carrying out research and appreciating the consequence of decisions.

## Critics of Piaget

Despite his influence on psychologists and educators working with children, Piaget is not without his critics.

### Margaret Donaldson (born 1926)

Margaret Donaldson suggested that children might understand more than Piaget thought, and that there was something about the 'decontextualised' nature of the task in his conservation experiment that made children appear less aware than they really were. The experimenter was quite a powerful person and the children may have been confused by the second question (asking whether there was the same number/amount) when the experimenter repeated the question. They may have thought that they had got it wrong and that the experimenter was hinting that they should change their mind!

James McGarrigle, a colleague of Donaldson's, set up an experiment to investigate children's ability to conserve number, this time using a toy ('naughty teddy') to make the transformation, instead of the experimenter. When the naughty teddy intentionally moved the counters for the second part of the experiment, 34 per cent of children got the correct answer (cited by M. Donaldson, 1978).

### Lev Vygotsky (1896–1934)

Vygotsky was a Russian psychologist whose study of psychology was strongly influenced by sociology. He suggested a more social model than Piaget, believing that we need social interaction with more mature, skilled people in order to develop our own skills. He believed that children need to acquire language in order to develop new concepts. Language is seen as a tool that allows the child to develop abstract thought. As we learn language, the structure of language becomes internalised.

Vygotsky further disagreed with Piaget on the need for social interaction. Whereas Piaget believed that the child was rather like a mini-scientist, working things out on his own by experimenting with objects and ideas in the environment, Vygotsky believed that social interaction and language drive cognitive development. For example, a child who breaks a crayon while drawing might be distressed that he can no longer complete the drawing. Upon being told by someone that 'you can use either piece of crayon to continue the drawing', the child learns that a crayon still performs the same functions, whether it is whole or broken into pieces. This cognitive development has been driven by language.

Although Piaget and Vygotsky agree that, at the age of about four, the child changes cognitively, the reasons for such cognitive changes are explained differently. Vygotsky refers to the 'zone of proximal development', by which he means that a child who is nearly ready to grasp something can be speeded up in this process by working with a slightly more advanced child.

According to Vygotsky, older children 'scaffold' (support) younger children's development. How does this photograph illustrate this process?

In summary, whereas Vygotsky saw language as driving cognitive development, Piaget believed that cognitive development leads to language acquisition.

### Jerome Bruner (born 1915)

Like Vygotsky, Bruner emphasised the role of language and interaction with others in enhancing cognitive development. He believed that teaching children to use symbols could speed up their cognitive development.

He agreed with Piaget on the following points:

- children are born with basic cognitive structures that mature over time, enabling more complex organisation of information
- children are intrinsically motivated to explore their environment and adapt by interacting with it.

However, rather than seeing development as a series of stages, he focused on underlying internal representations (ways of understanding the world) called modes.

*Enactive mode:* Here, thinking develops as a result of physical actions. When a baby plays with a toy, it develops an internal representation of that toy. This learning operates throughout life – for example, riding a bike, throwing a ball and swimming.

*Iconic mode:* In this mode, the child is able to form mental images in all senses – visual, tactile, olfactory and auditory. These help the child to build a 'picture' of the environment although he or she is as yet unable to represent this verbally. Various images are stored in the memory, which are not suited to enactive representation (for example, remembering someone's face).

*Symbolic mode:* Once the child develops language, he or she can use the symbolic mode and can develop systems for language, number, music, etc. The capacity for abstract, flexible thought is enhanced and the child can begin to manipulate and transform ideas.

### The information-processing approach

This approach is part of the cognitive perspective, which focuses on the way we take in and interpret information. An example of this is the use of schemas. These can be viewed as packets of information based on previous experience, which enable us to process information quickly. Schemata (plural of schema) are generally shared, as can be seen in the following activity.

## Activity 2: Testing schema theory

Form groups of five or six and describe in as much detail as possible a librarian. Include details such as gender, personality type, hobbies, preferred holiday type and destination, appearance and so on. When you have finished, join with the other groups and write down all the descriptions you have agreed upon. You will probably find that there is considerable similarity between the groups.

NOTE: Do not "censor" your ideas. This activity acknowledges that we share common schemas but in no way does it advocate that we should act on them!

### The views of Aaron Beck (born 1921)

Aaron Beck developed a widely used form of cognitive behavioural therapy (see pages 313–314) that can be used with all age groups, even children as young as eight. Beck views all emotional distress as originating from negative or irrational thoughts. Thoughts influence feelings, which in turn influence behaviour. So an individual who believes themselves to be unpopular may well feel unwanted and take steps to avoid social company. This in turn confirms the view of the self as being unwanted. Beck believes that by breaking this cycle, by changing thoughts, people can be helped to develop more positive views of themselves and raise their emotional spirits.

### The views of Albert Ellis (1913–2007)

Albert Ellis founded a form of cognitive therapy called Rational Emotive Behaviour Therapy. Rather like Beck, Ellis believes that if we can reach an understanding of how our thinking may be irrational or unhelpful, we can challenge these thoughts and replace them with thoughts that are more beneficial to our emotional well-being and personal growth. The underlying philosophy of this therapy can be summed up in the following extract from the 'Serenity Prayer', written by Karl Paul Reinhold Niebuhr (1892–1971) and used by Alcoholics Anonymous:

*'Grant me the courage to change the things I can change, the serenity to accept those that I cannot change and the wisdom to know the difference.'*

### Encoding

'Encoding' means the way in which we receive information from the outside world and 'represent' it in our minds. For example, if I see a beautiful sunset I will encode this as a visual image, which I can then re-create when I want to remember it. Some people have trouble encoding information securely, and may find it difficult to know which parts of incoming information to pay attention to and how to co-ordinate this activity with what is happening within their mind. This sheds some insight on what it is like to have attention deficit hyperactivity disorder (ADHD).

ADHD consists of three main symptom clusters:

- an inability to sustain attention
- hyperactive behaviour
- a tendency to be impulsive.

The symptoms of inattention (attention deficit) are detailed in the *Diagnostic and Statistical Manual of Mental Disorders* (latest version DSM-IV-TR), published by the American Psychiatric Association. They are reproduced below:

- often becoming easily distracted by irrelevant sights and sounds
- often failing to pay attention to details, and making careless mistakes
- rarely following instructions carefully, and completely losing or forgetting things like toys, or pencils, books and tools needed for a task
- often skipping from one uncompleted activity to another.

It should be remembered that children who just have an inability to sustain attention may not be hyperactive or impulsive. Hyperactive children are often fidgety, unable to sit still, constantly 'on the go' and have a tendency to move around and touch things or, when sitting, tap their feet or a pencil. In adolescence and adulthood this manifests itself as an internal restlessness. Impulsive children tend to say whatever is on their mind without considering the consequences. They act on the spur of the moment and are quite likely to hit another child if they get in the way or have something the impulsive child wants.

# Language development

Spoken language is learned easily and rapidly without explicit teaching. It is almost impossible to prevent children learning language and they acquire a large vocabulary with ease. By contrast, written language is quite slow and difficult to acquire – and requires explicit teaching. So how does language develop?

## Behaviourist perspective on the development of language: the views of Skinner (1904–1990)

As with his theory of other types of learning, B. F. Skinner proposed that children learn as a result of reinforcement. There are three key principles to this:

1 The child initially imitates a sound made by others (this is called an **echoic** response). Those hearing the sound then react with pleasure, which in turn increases the probability of the child repeating the word.

2 When the child produces a request word or gesture, called a **mand** (for example, 'banana', 'open'), people around respond by fulfilling the request (for example, bringing a banana, opening a box). This response reinforces the child in its use of requests.

3 When a child imitates a word in the presence of an object this is again met with approval (called a **tact response**). This increases the likelihood of the word being produced in the correct circumstances in future.

In this manner, through trial and error, reinforcement and imitation, the child develops a repertoire of language which matches that of an adult.

## Nativist perspective on the development of language: the views of Chomsky

A nativist perspective is one where humans are seen as biologically programmed with a particular skill or competence. Noam Chomsky (born 1928) disagreed with Skinner's explanation of language development, arguing that the structure of language is too complex to be learned through trial-and-error learning and simple reinforcement. Chomsky proposed that we are born with an innate structure that enables us to understand not just language but the rules of grammar, syntax, etc. He called this a **language acquisition device**.

As long as children are exposed to language, this innate device will be available to make sense of the language usage around them and to internalise new

rules of language. For example, children who are able to use the word feet as a plural for foot may begin by saying 'foots' instead of 'feet'. This suggests that they have understood that the rule to make a word plural is to add an s to the end (for example, sock becomes socks) and are over-applying this rule. They are definitely not imitating others, since adults do not say foots! This phenomenon certainly supports Chomsky and the nativist approach rather than Skinner.

## Prelinguistic language development

Up until the age of between 10 and 13 months, a child is said to be in the **prelinguistic** period. This means they cannot yet use meaningful words but they are still very responsive to language.

The prelinguistic child communicates using sounds. The first of these is a cry. Different types of cry signal different needs (e.g. hunger, pain, discomfort) and they vary from infant to infant. Crying thus reflects the infant's state both psychologically and physiologically.

This is followed by vocalisations such as chuckling, burbling, etc. When you watch a mother and baby together you will find that these sounds take on a language-type quality. The infant makes a vocalisation, which is then repeated by the mother, and thus the communication skills are developed. These vocalisations are probably not of an imitative nature because deaf children also make them.

## Key terms

**Echoic** – A sound uttered by the child in imitation of a sound that they have heard (a bit like an echo).

**Mand** – A verbal or non-verbal command that is regularly reinforced with a predictable consequence. For example, when a child gestures to a parent with their arms open, they are reinforced by the parent picking them up.

**Tact response** – Reinforcement of a child when they recognise that a word (the tact) is being used to name a given object.

**Language acquisition device (also called LAD)** – Chomsky believed this to be an innate system that prepares us to develop language. The device is thought to be located somewhere within the brain.

**Prelinguistic** – Meaning, literally, 'before language', this refers to all types of communication used before language takes over. It includes things like pointing and turn-taking.

### Phonological language development

Babbling eventually develops into **phonemes**. Phonemes are the basic units of sound, of which there are about 45 in English but no more than 60 in any language. Every language has a set of rules for combining phonemes. For example, we put together *st* for *street*, *start*, *station*, etc. but we do not use the combinations *sg* or *sb*. It seems we are born with an innate capacity to develop any language. For instance, in the English language we can hear the difference between *z* and *s*, but in some languages listeners cannot differentiate between *sip* and *zip*. It seems we 'tune in' to the language of our culture and, during the first year of life, 'tune out' phonemes and sounds we do not encounter.

### Syntax

Syntax refers to a system of grammar that governs how one sign is related to another. For example, in the statement 'John hit Richard' John is the agent who did the hitting, whereas Richard is the object who was hit. The meaning of the sentence would be completely altered if it were expressed as 'Richard hit John'. We all know these rules implicitly and can use them effortlessly but cannot explain them verbally, as we are unaware that we know them!

### Semantic language development

Semantic language development refers to understanding the expressed meaning of words and sentences. Using words to name objects is fairly easy – we associate the sound with the object. However, words such as *in*, *on* and *under* are more abstract.

## The development of the self

Hard as it may be to remember a time when we were not aware of ourselves, we are not born with a separate sense of self. A baby, for example, is just a bundle of sensations and cannot differentiate between themselves and their mother. The development of a sense of self and all that goes with it has long been of interest to both philosophers and psychologists.

Psychologists are primarily concerned with aspects of the self, such as the development of self-concept and self-esteem. The next two theorists we shall examine both operate from the humanistic perspective.

### Carl Rogers (1902–1987)

The starting point for Rogers' concept of self is that people are fundamentally whole, healthy and basically good. He takes an optimistic view of the development of the self, showing a belief in the ability of the self to develop throughout life and to give us the capacity to make choices that will help us in our lives.

Rogers believed strongly in the **actualising tendency**, which ultimately leads to **self-actualisation**. This refers to a desire to grow as people, to develop all our capabilities and creativity. He focused on the importance of the way people perceive the world, believing that this gave a far greater insight into the individual than an investigation of their real, external reality. This reflects his belief that we construct our own reality and, in doing so, we also construct our sense of self. This includes what is known as the **ideal self** – a view of ourselves 'as we should be', which we try to live up to. We may experience distress when our ideal self is unrealistic or too idealistic. We then judge ourselves as constantly failing.

### Key terms

**Phoneme** – A unit of sound used within a language.

**Actualising tendency** – An innate drive to become the very most and best that we can be: to use our skills, abilities and qualities, both physical and psychological, to the full.

**Self-actualisation** – The achievement of the actualising tendency. People who have achieved self-actualisation include Albert Einstein.

**Ideal self** – An internal view of ourselves as we would like ourselves to (and often believe we should) be. Our ideal self is a standard against which we judge ourselves.

### Abraham Maslow (1908–1970)

Maslow saw individuals as seeking self-actualisation. When self-actualisation is achieved, the individual is able to be warm and giving, autonomous, non-judgemental, realistic and accepting of both self and others. Maslow saw people as progressing towards self-actualisation through a series of stages, represented in Figure 29.3 on the next page.

For more information on self-actualisation and the views of Carl Rogers and Abraham Maslow, see Book 1, Unit 8.

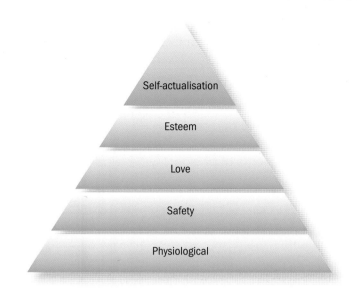

**Fig 29.3:** Maslow believed our needs at the bottom of the pyramid had to be satisfied before we could move up towards the top of the pyramid.

### The cognitive–developmental approach to the development of self

This combines features from the cognitive approach and more general social and emotional features of development. A key thinker is Robert Selman, who examined the developing ability of children to see things from the perspective of others. He suggested that this occurs as a result of role-taking and becomes

more sophisticated over time. Five stages have been identified, as shown in Table 29.2.

As their ability to understand perspective-taking becomes more sophisticated, children similarly develop a more complex view of friendship. They move from seeing friends as people who give them things, or do nice things for them, towards a recognition that friendship involves give and take and forgiveness of one another's mistakes. The ability to role-take is associated with sociability and popularity. Children who are able to infer the needs, feelings and emotions of others seem to be more socially skilled than their peers who lag behind in these areas.

### Environmental psychology

This type of psychology investigates the way the individual's environment affects behaviour. There is a particular focus on the roles that people take within different social settings. For example, the roles to be adopted in church or school are fixed and known by all and thus determine behaviour while in that setting. However, on a beach or in a party we have more freedom to express other aspects of ourselves. See Book 1, Unit 8 for more information.

### Learning theory

The views of Bandura (outlined on page 288), suggest that we develop a sense of self by observing and imitating others, as well as by direct reinforcement and

**Table 29.2:** A child's ability to take the perspective of others develops over approximately five stages

| Five stages of development | Main features of each stage |
| --- | --- |
| Egocentric or undifferentiated perspective (3–6 years) | Children are unable to imagine any perspective other than their own. |
| Social–informational role-taking (6–8 years) | Children know that other people have different perspectives but believe this is because others have been given different information. |
| Self-reflective role-taking (8–10 years) | Children recognise that other people can have the same information as they do and still take a different perspective. |
| Mutual role-taking (10–12 years) | By now a child is able to form their own views, and place themselves 'in the shoes' of another person. They are also aware that other people can do this too. |
| Social and conventional system role-taking (12–15 years+) | The adolescent is able to consider their own and others' perspectives, and also to compare them with the perspective an average person in his society would take. Perspective-taking is thus very complex. |

punishment. Our sense of self is largely influenced by the degree of **self-efficacy** we believe ourselves to have. Self-efficacy is built upon mastering experiences, and influences how motivated we will be to take on new challenges and how we feel about ourselves if we succeed or fail. Someone with a high sense of self-efficacy is likely to have a strong belief that if they try something they will probably succeed – if not at first, then eventually. Unfortunately, the reverse is the case for someone with a low sense of self-efficacy. You probably all knew someone at school who was convinced they would fail at whatever they did and was therefore reluctant to try anything new.

### Key term

**Self-efficacy** – A judgement we make on ourselves in terms of our ability to master events in the environment. It is based on past experience and can generalise to our expectations of success or failure in new situations. It can be positive or negative.

### Interpersonal theory

The views of two sociologists, Charles Cooley (1864–1929) and George Herbert Mead (1863–1931), have been very influential. A fundamental principle of their approach was that the self develops out of social interactions with others.

Cooley used the term 'the looking-glass self' to explain the development of the self. Other people's judgements of our behaviour, our appearance and other aspects of ourselves give us information about who we are, and what we should think about ourselves. However, we do not just receive one 'reflection', as everyone we encounter acts as a slightly different looking glass.

Mead has a different interpretation of the development of self. He sees the self as lying within the individual. We can communicate within ourselves as well as with others around us. We therefore have beliefs about ourselves to begin with. The influence of others is incorporated into this sense of self, largely through the taking on of roles. For example, a child playing the role of a teacher does more than just copy what a teacher does. They actually take on the role of a teacher and in their pretend play will develop aspects of themselves to do with authority, values, manners of speech and so forth. This constant taking on of roles

allows us to reflect upon who we are and thus develop a sense of a multi-faceted self.

## The acquisition of behaviour

This section investigates how we acquire behaviour. Some theorists see personality as no more than a set of fairly consistent behaviours, so there will be an overlap with other accounts of personality development.

### Activity 3: Reflect on your own behaviours

Ask a friend to describe you, using as many adjectives as possible (e.g. competitive, assertive, outgoing, shy, daring, nervous, kind, etc.).

1 Do you think you inherited these behavioural traits or did they develop as a result of upbringing?

2 Make notes on which aspects of your personality and behaviour you believe are innate, and why.

3 Note also those that you believe are a result of your upbringing, and why.

### The behaviourist account of the acquisition of behaviour

The American behaviourist John Watson (1878–1958) famously stated:

'Give me a dozen healthy infants, well formed, and my own specified world to bring them up in and I'll guarantee to take any one at random and train him to become any type of specialist I might select – doctor, lawyer, artist, merchant, chief, and yes, even beggar-man and thief, regardless of his talents, penchants, tendencies, abilities, vocations and race of his ancestors. There is no such thing as an inheritance of capacity, talent, temperament, mental constitution, and behavioural characteristics.' (Watson, 1925, cited in Shaffer, 1993, p. 44)

What Watson is referring to here is the importance of environmental experiences. For example, a child who grows up in a loving, caring environment may develop into an optimistic, confident individual. If the same child, however, were to grow up in an environment where they were neglected, they might become withdrawn and quiet.

## Classical conditioning

This theory explains behaviour as arising out of a series of learning experiences. It is concerned with reflex responses (involuntary responses such as the eye blink or the startle response). The founder of this theory of learning, Ivan Pavlov (1849–1936), investigated the basic principles when working with dogs. He discovered that a dog was salivating not just when it saw or smelled food (a natural reflex) but when it saw the white coat of the lab assistant or an empty food bowl.

He then conducted a series of experiments to investigate this type of learning. His aim was to see if he could train a dog to have a reflexive response to a stimulus (an object presented to create a response) that does not by itself cause a response.

Before conditioning – the stimulus is initially called an unconditioned stimulus or UCS. It is unconditioned because no learning has taken place and it automatically leads to an unconditioned response of salivation.

A bell is then rung (the conditioned stimulus) and this leads to no response.

During conditioning – every time food is presented a bell is rung. The combination of food + bell leads to an unconditioned (unlearned, reflex) response of salivation.

After conditioning – the dog has now learned to associate the bell with the response of salivation. When the bell is rung the dog will now salivate. Salivation has thus become a conditioned response.

Pavlov believed that a number of behaviours, especially anxiety and fear responses, could be learned in this way.

### Activity 4: Aversion therapy

Do some Internet research on the use of the principles of classical conditioning to treat addictions. This method is known as aversion therapy.

### PLTS

**Independent enquirer:** By carrying out this activity you can demonstrate your ability to plan and carry out research, appreciating the consequence of decisions.

## Operant conditioning

According to B. F. Skinner, behaviour is acquired as a result of a series of learning experiences in which the consequences of behaviour (reinforcement or punishment) provide the building blocks of the development of behaviour (and personality). So a child who is shy may have been punished for being noisy and boisterous ('Oh for goodness sake, Sally, nobody wants to listen to you singing now!') and reinforced for being quiet and retiring ('Well done, Sally, you were so good we hardly noticed you were there. Good girl').

## The social learning theory perspective

The social learning theory of personality development relies heavily on external, environmental factors. It is associated with two theorists: Albert Bandura and Walter Mischel. According to this approach, the learning experiences acquired as an individual grows up will determine personality. Behaviour that is reinforced will be produced more often; behaviour that is punished, less often. In this way a whole range of personality traits can develop over time. So if a child is consistently punished for behaving aggressively but, equally consistently, is positively reinforced for being polite and helpful, the aggressive behaviours will gradually drop away, while the behaviours associated with being polite and helpful will increase.

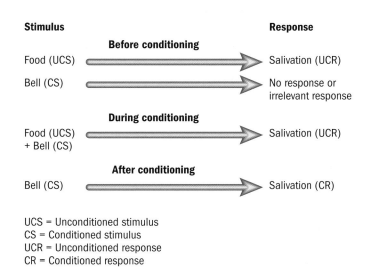

UCS = Unconditioned stimulus
CS = Conditioned stimulus
UCR = Unconditioned response
CR = Conditioned response

**Fig 29.4:** The process of classical conditioning

### The psychodynamic perspective – the development of personality

This perspective is associated with Sigmund Freud and Erik Erikson. Freud developed an internal model of personality in which unconscious structures influence development. Development is seen as a dynamic process that proceeds in stages.

It is a rather pessimistic account of personality, where there is perpetual conflict between the urges of the **id** and the ruthless civilising influences of the **ego** and **superego**. Personality is thought to be relatively fixed by the age of five.

### Sigmund Freud (1856–1939)

There are three strands to Freud's theory of the acquisition of behaviour and the development of personality. These are:

- forces within the psyche
- progression through psychosexual stages
- ego defences.

#### The psyche

The psyche is a hypothetical structure that is roughly equivalent to the mind. There are three parts to the psyche, which are continually in conflict. The id, which is present at birth, operates on the **pleasure principle**. This means that it is devoted entirely to satisfying instincts and needs. It is insatiable (meaning it can never be satisfied) and has no sense of reality – the focus of this part of the psyche is simply to get its own way when it wants something.

The second structure of the psyche, the ego, develops around the age of two. This operates on the **reality principle**: its purpose is to negotiate between the id and the superego and to find a rational course to follow.

The id is in conflict with the superego, the third structure of the psyche, which develops last. Roughly equivalent to a conscience, the superego contains all the moral values and the socialisation practices that have taught us right from wrong, all of which are internalised. The superego also contains our 'ideal self'. It develops around the age of five.

A healthy personality is characterised by a balance between the id and the superego. Too much id energy will create a personality that is reckless, selfish,

### Key terms

**Ego** – The part of the psyche that attempts to mediate between the id's demands for instant gratification and the superego's for restraint. The ego operates on the reality principle and tries to steer a course that will keep the person on an even keel.

**Id** – The part of the psyche that is determined to get its own way. It contains all the drives without knowing any bounds – aggression, sexuality, happiness.

**Superego** – The part of the psyche that develops last (at about three to five years of age). It is composed of all the morals and requirements of socialisation. Resembling a conscience, the superego is the part of the psyche that governs reason and restraint.

**Pleasure principle** – A drive towards self-gratification. It has to be kept in check by the ego and superego.

**Reality principle** – An awareness of what is socially acceptable and necessary for the individual to negotiate safely through life. This is the prime function of the ego.

unconcerned with others or aggressive. Too much superego energy will lead to a personality type that is shy, unassertive, guilty and maybe over-moralistic. If the ego can balance these energies then a personality will emerge that is able to be assertive rather than aggressive and able to enjoy themselves without going over the top or feeling guilty. A strong ego is needed to create this balanced personality.

If the id dominates, an erotic personality type will emerge. This person will be most concerned with sex, love and the pursuit of pleasure. A dominant ego with a weak superego results in a narcissistic personality, where the individual is only concerned with meeting their needs and indifferent to their effect on others. In extreme cases this may be connected with criminal behaviour. An individual with a very strong superego is likely to be guilty, with a tendency towards being obsessional.

#### The psychosexual stages

Progression through psychosexual stages involves libido (life force) centring upon a particular body part that is relevant to the individual's stage of physical development. If the stage is not worked through satisfactorily, the individual becomes 'fixated' and this affects later personality and behaviour.

Table 29.3: The features of Freud's psychosexual stages

| Stage and age | Key features | Behaviour |
|---|---|---|
| The oral stage (birth to about 2 years) | The libido is centred on the mouth, with the focus on feeding and exploring objects orally | If weaned too early, the person may be envious and greedy with a tendency to addiction. A child who is weaned very late may be optimistic, gullible and full of admiration for others around them. They are symbolically sucking for the rest of their lives. |
| The anal stage (2–3 years) | The libido is centred on the anus and the key focus is potty training | If the child defies parents and 'refuses to go' they may become **anally retentive** in later life, characterised by being obsessive and miserly. If there is too much pleasure in expulsion the individual may become **anally expulsive** – disorganised, defiant and reckless. |
| The phallic stage (3–5 years) | The libido is centred on the genitals and the superego develops | The desire for the opposite-sex parent is replaced by identification with same-sex parent. Fixation may lead to a very vain, proud individual. |
| The latency period (5–11 years) | The libido lies dormant | |
| The genital stage (puberty onwards) | The libido is again centred on the genitals | The individual is now able to form mature relationships with members of the opposite sex. |

## Key terms

**Anally retentive** – A child in the anal stage who feels pressured by their parents into being potty trained may rebel by 'refusing to go'. This is associated with later personality traits such as obstinacy and miserliness.

**Anally expulsive** – A personality type originating in the anal stage, when the infant rebelliously expels their faeces anywhere. Adults fixated at this stage tend to be messy and creative.

In the genital stage (from puberty onwards) the child's energy once again focuses on their genitals, and they become interested in heterosexual relationships.

### Ego defences

Finally, ego defences are strategies used by the mind when something happens which is so threatening and painful that it cannot be dealt with. It is pushed into unconsciousness so the individual isn't aware of it. Common ego defences are denial, when the individual refuses to recognise something painful (e.g. a diagnosis of a terminal illness), and repression, when the person buries painful memories so they do not have to be aware of them (e.g. after a traumatic event).

For further details of the psychodynamic approach, see Book 1, Unit 8 (pages 344–347).

### Erik Erikson (1902–1994)

Erikson's theory sees development occurring in a series of stages that continue throughout life. He called these the Eight Stages of Man.

*Stage 1: Trust versus basic mistrust (ages 0–1)* – at this stage the infant is totally helpless and relies entirely on others to meet their needs and provide good-quality emotional and physical care. If the main parenting figure is able to meet the infant's needs in a satisfactory, responsive and caring way, the infant learns a sense of *trust*. Self-confidence grows and the world is believed to be a dependable and predictable place. They learn that they have some influence over others and this will transfer to later stages.

If, by contrast, the carer is unresponsive, lacks warmth and affection and doesn't meet the infant's needs or is inconsistent the infant will develop a basic *mistrust* of others. They will feel a fundamental sense of not being able to influence others. In terms of later personality development, this child will be fearful and suspicious and possibly withdrawn or apathetic.

*Stage 2: Autonomy versus shame and doubt (ages 1–3)* – the child is now more mobile. They want to be independent and to do things for themselves. Toilet training is an important crisis to work through. If this is begun too early, or is very harsh, the child may feel a sense of shame at having a lack of control over their bowels.

**Autonomy** – the child is allowed to experience things without being controlled. They are supported, not criticised, through failure/accidents, etc. They feel competent and have a sense of self-belief.

**Shame and doubt** – the child is controlled and this induces doubt about their own abilities. The child fails frequently (perhaps they are being expected to do too much too soon) and/or criticised (which induces shame). The child feels powerless and may revert to thumb sucking and is likely to become attention seeking. The child rejects others and becomes closed off.

**Stage 3: Initiative versus guilt (ages 3–6)** – there is rapid social, emotional, physical and intellectual growth and development at this stage. The child is acquiring new skills through interaction with the world and others. If development is impeded, the child may lose their sense of initiative and become passive and unwilling to try new things.

**Initiative** can be fostered when the child's curiosity about life is welcomed and met with encouragement to explore new ideas and learn new skills. When play of all varieties is encouraged, this enhances the development of initiative, as does physical activity, which helps the child to develop skills. The negative potential outcome of the crisis at this stage is *guilt*. This may occur if parents dampen their child's curiosity about the world – perhaps by ignoring their questions or telling them not to be silly. Similarly if fantasy play is discouraged and physical activities are banned as 'too dangerous' the child's sense of growing competence and their ability to take initiative will dwindle. They will be left with a sense of guilt and a belief in their own lack of competence.

**Stage 4: Industry versus inferiority (ages 6–12)**

The child is concerned at this stage with understanding how things are made and how they work (including making things by themselves). Significant others now begin to include teachers and other adults as well as parents. The peer group begins to be important – children compare themselves in order to assess their own achievements. This is influential in the child's development of the self.

A sense of *industry* is developed when the individual is encouraged to take on realistic tasks where there is a

high degree of success and they are encouraged to try things out. This results in high self-esteem and a sense of competence. *Inferiority* results if the child is pushed to do things they are not ready for, without enough guidance, and then criticised for failure. If unfavourable comparisons are made with others (either by the child or by others), a sense of inferiority will develop, leading to a negative self-concept and low self-esteem.

**Stage 5: Identity versus role confusion (ages 12–18)**

Erikson saw adolescence as a time of *storm and stress* – a period of psychological turmoil that has a far-reaching effect on the self-concept. The self-concept is affected by the following factors:

- physical changes bring about an altered body image, which affects one's sense of self
- intellectual development allows the adolescent to become aware of what is potentially possible as well as what currently exists
- emotional development involves increasing emotional independence
- the individual is also involved in making decisions about careers, values and sexual behaviour.

The main goal of the individual at this stage is to achieve a lasting and secure sense of self, or *ego identity*. This has three parts – a sense of:

- consistency in the way one sees oneself
- continuity of the self over time
- mutuality (i.e. agreement between one's own perceptions of self and the perceptions of others).

The peer group is very important in this process and the developmental task of the adolescent is to establish a vocational and social identity so that they see themselves as a consistent and integrated person. If this does not happen, they will not develop a sense of their role in life and will be unable to be faithful to people, work or a set of values. In extreme cases, they may develop a negative identity, particularly if they feel they cannot live up to the demands being made of them.

**Stage 6: Intimacy versus Isolation (young adulthood)**

**Stage 7: Generativity versus Stagnation (middle adulthood)**

**Stage 8: Integrity versus Despair (late adulthood)**

(For more information on the final three stages, see R. B. Ewen, 1993.)

**Table 29.4:** Most important features according to Freud and Erikson

| Age | Most important features according to Freud | Most important features according to Erikson |
|-----|---------------------------------------------|------------------------------------------------|
| Birth to 1–2 years | Oral stage Oral gratification – too much or too little | Trust versus mistrust |
| 1–3 | Anal stage | Autonomy versus shame and doubt |

# Theories of attachment and the development of individuals

Attachment theory is an important psychological explanation of how individuals develop emotional, social and intellectual security and growth. The founder of attachment theory was John Bowlby (1907–1990), but we will also look at other theorists whose work has been important within this field.

## Stages in the development of attachments

In 1964, Rudolph Schaffer and Peggy Emerson carried out research into how attachments developed. They observed infants over a period of time and developed a stage theory of attachments, as outlined below (cited in D.R. Shaffer, 2002).

**Table 29.5:** Stage theory of attachments, according to Schaffer and Emerson

| Stage | Age | Key features |
|-------|-----|--------------|
| Asocial stage | Birth to around 6 weeks | Babies do not respond in a social way and do not distinguish between carers |
| Indiscriminate attachment: | 6 weeks to around 7 months | Sociability begins with smiling at about 6 weeks. Infants respond similarly to all around them |
| Specific attachment | From 7 months | The infant forms a strong emotional bond with a particular person. They show **separation anxiety** and **stranger anxiety** |

## Key terms

**Separation anxiety** – The infant shows acute distress when separated from their main attachment figure.

**Stranger anxiety** – The infant is unhappy with people they are unfamiliar with.

## Did you know?

Infants seek out their mother when they are upset or frightened but prefer their father for playing. Lamb and Stevenson, 1978 (cited in D.R. Shaffer, 2002).

## Activity 5: Investigating attachment behaviour

Arrange to interview the parents of a six-month old, a twelve-month old and a two-year-old child. Ask them if their infant has a preferred attachment figure and compare their answers with Schaffer and Emerson's findings.

## The effects of separation

James Robertson and his wife Joyce believed that the practice in the 1950s of leaving children alone in hospital, with a minimum of visits by their parents, was harmful to young children. They made an observational film to show the distress caused on separation.

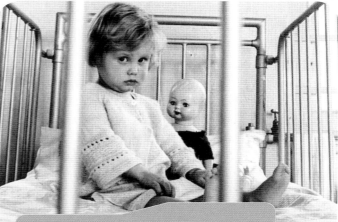

What can you see in this still from James Robertson's film that shows clearly the distress experienced by two-year-old Laura when separated from her mother during a hospital visit?

303

Robertson identified three stages of emotional distress suffered by children in this situation:

1  Protest – the children showed great distress, calling and crying for the absent care-giver and some appeared panic-stricken. Anger and fear were evident.

2  Despair – the children became calmer but apathetic, as they showed little interest in anything. Self-comforting behaviours were observed, such as thumb-sucking and rocking.

3  Detachment – the children appeared to be coping with the separation, as they showed more interest in their surroundings but they were emotionally unresponsive. They avoided forming new attachments and showed no interest when the care-giver returned. However, most children re-established the relationship over time.

### The effects of deprivation

John Bowlby worked in a child guidance clinic where he encountered children and adolescents who showed delinquent and disturbed behaviour. He developed a theory known as the **maternal deprivation hypothesis** (1951). This states that if a child is deprived of their mother between six months and five years of age then this would lead to difficulties in later life. They would be unable to form attachments with others and would be likely to turn to crime. Bowlby suggested that separation experiences in early childhood caused **affectionless psychopathy**. This is the inability to have deep feelings for other people and leads, therefore, to a lack of meaningful personal relationships. Bowlby pointed out the need for continuous care-giving for healthy development.

Bowlby's hypothesis was developed from his work in the clinic where he conducted a famous study known as the '44 thieves'. Bowlby interviewed 44 children who had been referred to a child guidance clinic because they were stealing, and 44 children who had emotional problems but had not committed any crimes. He found that the thieves lacked a social conscience, while the other group of children showed signs of disturbance but otherwise functioned reasonably well emotionally.

In total, 32 per cent of the thieves were diagnosed as affectionless psychopaths and 86 per cent of the thieves diagnosed in this way had experienced separation for at least a week before the age of five.

From these findings, Bowlby concluded that maternal deprivation can seriously disrupt healthy emotional development.

Later research, however, has suggested that the importance of the mother may have been overstated. While an infant certainly needs an attachment figure, this does not necessarily have to be the mother.

### The effects of privation

Michael Rutter suggested that anti-social behaviour may result from family discord and that the development of an affectionless personality may be a result of a failure initially to form an attachment. He called this **privation**.

### Key terms

**Maternal deprivation hypothesis** – A belief that deprivation results from long periods of separation or many short periods of separation from the mother, particularly in the early years of life. Bowlby believed this would inevitably lead to damage to later personality.

**Affectionless psychopathy** – A serious psychological condition in which the individual shows no conscience and is unable to form intimate relationships with others.

**Privation** – This occurs when a child forms no bond at all with a care-giver. Children in orphanages where there is a very low staff-to-child ratio have been found to suffer from privation.

In 1976 he carried out a large-scale study on the Isle of Wight. He found that when children from good to fair homes were separated, this did not lead to delinquency. Similarly, if a separation was associated with illness it was not linked to delinquency. However, where separation was associated with stress, children were four times as likely to become delinquent.

Rutter concluded that Bowlby's thieves had probably suffered from privation, not deprivation. Privation involves a situation where no bond is formed in the first place. This is much more serious than deprivation, where a bond is disrupted but can, with care, be re-formed. In some cases, privation can lead to a complete inability to form attachments in later life.

### The effects of isolation

The following case study is about children who were isolated from adult human contact during the early part of their lives. According to the maternal deprivation hypothesis, they should not have been able to form attachments later in life. As we shall see, some interesting findings emerged.

## Case study: The Koluchova twins

In 1972, a researcher called Koluchova reported the case of two identical twins who had been beaten, locked up and cruelly treated until the age of seven. When rescued they only communicated using gestures and were terrified of the outside world.

However, the two boys were fostered by a devoted foster mother and they developed both language and social and cognitive skills. By the age of 20, both were in employment and maintained good relationships with their foster mother.

1 Why do you think the two boys didn't appear to suffer from their early experience of isolation?

2 What lessons could be learned from this case to apply to residential care for children?

## Activity 6: Genie

Research the case of Genie, a child brought up in isolation until the age of thirteen.

1 How does Genie's development compare with that of the Koluchova twins?

2 Genie never developed full use of language. Why was this?

## Functional skills

**ICT:** Researching the case of Genie on the Internet will give you an opportunity to demonstrate your ICT skills.

## The development of attachments

### Feeding

This section is concerned with why and how attachments develop. Initially, theorists believed in the so-called 'cupboard love' explanation. This comes from the behaviourist perspective and is based on the idea that infants learn to associate their care-giver with the feeling of gratification that comes with relief from hunger and discomfort. The infant learns to approach their care-giver in order to have their needs satisfied. Eventually this generalises into a feeling of security whenever the care-giver is present. According to this account, emotional and physical warmth are not a precondition for attachments to develop. An intriguing experiment by Harry Harlow tested this hypothesis.

### Physical contact

Harlow (1905–1981) conducted experiments to see if infant monkeys would choose food over physical comfort. He separated infants from their mothers and placed them in a special housing unit with two 'surrogate' mothers. One was covered with terry towelling, was soft to the touch but provided no milk. The other was a wire monkey, which provided milk but no comfort. The infant monkeys spent almost all their time clinging to the cloth monkey and, when able, leaned across to obtain milk from the wire monkey while still clinging on to the cloth monkey, as illustrated below. He concluded from this that contact comfort is much more important than feeding. This appears to be the main basis for attachment.

The infant clings to the cloth mother for comfort

## Bowlby's explanation of the development of attachments

Bowlby was influenced partly by Harlow's research and also by Konrad Lorenz's research into imprinting (cited in R. Gross, 2001). Lorenz (1903–1989) found that a duck or goose would imprint (form an unbreakable bond) on the first object it saw when it hatched. Normally this would be the biological mother but cases occurred where it would imprint on a human. You may have seen the film *Fly Away Home*, which illustrates this phenomenon.

Bowlby believed that infants are born with an innate fear of the unknown, which drives them to seek **proximity** (closeness) with a care-giver. Both mother and infant are biologically predisposed to form an attachment bond. The infant produces **social releasers** such as crying, vocalising, making eye contact and smiling, which produce a response in the mother who is drawn closer to her baby. There is thus an evolutionary, innate mechanism operating: the baby needs to keep the mother close in order to survive, and the mother is instinctively drawn to protect her baby (hence the expression *maternal instinct*).

### Key terms

**Proximity** – A state of being close. In terms of attachment, proximity is very important to give the infant a sense of security. When proximity is broken, and the infant is further away from their care-giver than they are able to bear, they will show signs of acute distress.

**Social releasers** – These are things an infant does that cause others to react instinctively with care-giving behaviours such as feeding, soothing and even conversing with the baby.

### Time and care-giving

As we have seen above, children form attachments to those who play with them and are sensitive to their needs but not necessarily to those who feed and change them. The following section gives some reasons for differences in attachment.

### Quality of attachment

The quality of attachment a child has to their primary care-giver is of great importance to the development of the child's personality and to their own parenting in turn. When an infant has formed an attachment, they are beginning to be capable of symbolic thought, which means they can think about the parent when they are absent. The infant begins to build what

Bowlby calls an internal mental model of their own experiences, based on their interaction with the primary care-giver. This becomes like a template, which the child uses to predict the behaviour of others. An internal mental model that is negative can arise if the child is ignored or responded to harshly. Such a child is likely to grow up with poor self-esteem and to believe they will be met by rejection or inconsistency from others. If the model is positive, with the care-giver being sensitive and responsive, the child will predict that others will treat them in a similar way. Consequently, they are more likely to be confident and have a strong sense of self-esteem and competence in later life.

### Individual differences in attachments

Mary Ainsworth (1913–1999) developed a procedure designed to measure the differences in attachment shown by different children. The procedure, called 'the strange situation', involves a sequence of events carried out in a laboratory (a colourful, pleasant room with toys) designed to assess infant attachment style. The procedure consists of the following eight episodes.

Table 29.6: The eight episodes in infant attachment, according to Ainsworth (1978)

| | |
|---|---|
| 1 | The parent and infant are introduced to the room. There is a two-way mirror enabling the researchers to observe without being seen, although the parent is aware that they are there. |
| 2 | The parent and infant are alone. The parent does not participate while the infant explores. (Exploration behaviour is a sign of secure attachment.) |
| 3 | A stranger enters, converses with the parent, then approaches the infant. The parent leaves the room with a minimum of fuss. |
| 4 | This is the first separation episode. The stranger will try to interact with the child – e.g. show a toy. |
| 5 | First reunion episode. The parent returns, greets and comforts the infant, then leaves again. |
| 6 | Second separation episode. The infant is alone. |
| 7 | Continuation of the second separation episode. The stranger enters and gears her behaviour to that of the infant. |
| 8 | Second reunion episode. The parent enters, greets and picks the infant up. The stranger leaves inconspicuously. |

The infant's behaviour upon the parent's return is the basis for classifying the infant into one of four attachment categories.

1  **Secure:** The infant shows a moderate level of proximity-seeking to the care-giver and is comfortable to explore the environment. Although upset by the care-giver's departure, they greet them positively on their return. They may find the situation stressful but can be easily calmed by the care-giver.

2  **Insecure/avoidant:** The infant tends to avoid contact with the care-giver, especially at reunion after separation, although the infant is not unduly upset when left with the stranger. Generally these infants do not find the situation very stressful – other than when they are left alone.

3  **Insecure/ambivalent:** The infant is highly distressed by separation from the care-giver and tends to be wary of the stranger. However, when the care-giver returns, they are difficult to console, one minute seeking contact, the next wriggling away.

   A fourth attachment type was later identified by M. Main and J. Solomon in 1986 (cited in M. Haralambos and D. Rice, 2002).

4  **Insecure/disoriented:** This attachment type is characteristic of children with unusual and often dysfunctional combinations of behaviour – for example, avoidant and resistant.

### Did you know?

Attachment classifications are highly predictive of later development including social, emotional, cognitive and even physical development. Securely attached infants are significantly more likely than their insecure counterparts to be confident, self-assured and successful in both work and family life.

### Responsiveness and sensitivity

Why do some infants have a secure attachment with their care-giver, whereas others do not? According to Ainsworth's care-giving hypothesis, the sensitivity of the care-giver is of crucial importance (Ainsworth, 1979, cited in D.R. Shaffer, 2002). The following table illustrates three types of parenting associated with attachment classifications.

Table 29.7: Three types of parenting

| Type of attachment | Parental behaviour |
|---|---|
| Secure | Sensitive and emotionally expressive |
| Insecure resistant | Inconsistent in their responses – sometimes over-expressive, other times distant |
| Insecure avoidant | Rejecting or sometimes forcing interaction when the infant wants to be left alone |

### The child's temperament

Critics of the care-giving sensitivity hypothesis suggest that that some differences are innate and that the infant's behaviour also shapes the parent's response. (For example, an infant who is easily soothed, who snuggles and stops crying when picked up, influences the mother's sense of competency and attachment. The infant who stiffens and continues to cry, despite efforts to comfort it, makes the mother feel inadequate and rejected.) The type of attachment formed may therefore come from the child.

Jerome Kagan (1984) calls this the temperament hypothesis (cited in Shaffer, 2002). Evidence to support this comes from research by J. Belsky and M. Rovine, 1987 (cited in Cardwell and Flanagan, 2003). They found that newborns who showed signs of behavioural instability (e.g. tremors or shaking) were less likely to become securely attached to their mother than newborns who did not. In other words, it was their innate personality that was the key factor in the formation of an attachment.

### The continuity hypothesis

John Bowlby's theory that early attachment relationships form the basis of an internal working model of relationships implies that a securely attached infant will develop to become a socially competent child and later adult. There is a considerable body of research that supports this prediction but it has also been found that attachment types can change according to factors influencing the family and the care-giver.

## Activity 7: Long-term consequences of attachment classifications

Use the Internet to research attachment theory.

1 Do you think that early attachment classifications really influence later romantic relationships?

2 What influences in life might change attachment classifications?

## Assessment activity 29.1

**P1** **M1** **D1** **BTEC**

Produce an information booklet which includes:

- an *explanation* of the principal psychological perspectives applied to the understanding of the development of individuals
- a *discussion* of the principal psychological perspectives applied to the understanding of the development of individuals
- an *evaluation* of the principal psychological perspectives applied to the understanding of the development of individuals.

### Grading tips

**P1** To *explain*, you need to give an accurate and detailed account of how psychological

perspectives help us to understand an individual's development. You may find it useful to give examples to illustrate understanding.

**M1** For M1 you need to *discuss* these perspectives. You can do this by talking about their strengths and weaknesses.

**D1** To achieve the distinction grade of *evaluate*, you need to do all of the above but in addition make a reasoned argument outlining why some perspectives are more useful than others or need to be used in combination with others. For example, if one perspective does not explain all development, could you use aspects from another to make a better case?

## PLTS

**Independent enquirer:** By considering how different psychological perspectives help us to understand development, you may show you can explore issues, events or problems from different perspectives. If you attempt the D grade you may show you can analyse and evaluate information, judging its relevance and value.

# 2   Understand the contribution of psychological perspectives to the understanding of specific behaviours

## 2.1 Applying psychological perspectives to the understanding of behaviours

You have now covered the theory behind some of the key perspectives in psychology, looking at how they explain behaviours and various aspects of development. This section is about applying understanding to specific behaviours. You will find that the nature versus nurture debate is relevant here once again. The diagram below summarises the perspectives we have covered. As you work through the specific behaviours, you need to consider whether different perspectives complement one another (i.e. can be used together) or are in contrast to others.

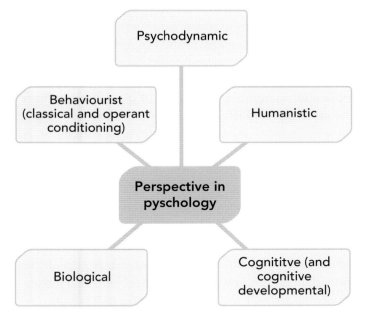

Fig 29.5: The key psychological perspectives

## 2.2 Specific behaviours

### Depression

The cognitive perspective sees depression as originating with negative thoughts. An individual who sees themselves as worthless and unlovable will feel sad as a result of such thoughts and may well withdraw from social interaction.

Within the behaviourist perspective, operant conditioning explains depression as resulting from too much punishment, which leads to feelings of sadness and guilt and loss of self-esteem. This punishment could take the form of any negative life events, including criticism, failure of a marriage, redundancy or too many stressful life events. If the depressed individual is then reinforced for their depression – for example by being given extra attention, kindness and support – this may lead to a continuation of the depressive behaviour since it is bringing such positive rewards!

These two perspectives contrast with the biological perspective, which would look to genetic inheritance for the cause of depression. If there is a family history of the illness, the individual may have a faulty gene. Additionally, brain chemistry and the functioning of the endocrine system would be seen as possible causes. Low levels of the neurotransmitter (brain chemical) serotonin are associated with depression, as are high levels of the hormone cortisol, which is secreted by the endocrine system at times of stress.

### Anxiety

Anxiety ranges from mild feelings of discomfort and apprehension to full-blown anxiety attacks with sweating, rapid heart and pulse rate, feelings of dizziness and nausea and a terrible sense of dread. Although psychological perspectives would emphasise the causes of anxiety (e.g. apprehension about taking a driving test, fear of going to the dentist or a generalised sense of anxiety that is often associated with depression), the biological perspective explains this with reference to physiological processes. Anxiety is associated with arousal of the 'fight or flight response'. This is an automatic response, left over from our Stone Age days, which arises when we are faced with a threat. The following physiological changes take place:

- the rate and strength of heartbeat increase
- lung capacity increases
- sugars are released from the liver into the body for use by the muscles

- pupils dilate (to give better vision)
- blood clotting capacity is increased.

All these changes prime the body for a fight (e.g. with a wild boar) or to run away (e.g. to flee from a sabre-toothed tiger).

On occasions when we can respond in a physiological way to the threat (e.g. if there is a car speeding towards us on a crossing and we need to run away at high speed) this response is short-lived. It dies away once the danger has passed. However, anxiety about sitting an exam arouses the same response but we are not able to take immediate physical action and so the effects (of increased heart rate and so on) leave us feeling uncomfortable and agitated.

**For more information on the fight or flight response, see Book 1, Unit 8.**

## Separation and loss

Humanistic psychology looks at how the individual perceives the meaning to the self of separation and loss. For example, a parent might experience a child leaving home as a devastating experience if a large part of their self-concept is associated with being a parent. From the viewpoint of attachment theory, separation in early life can weaken the bond of attachment while loss actually breaks it. Children who have experienced the loss of a parent in early life are significantly more likely to be troubled by a further loss in later life than someone who has not had such an experience.

## Stress and coping

This is a good example of where two perspectives come together to provide a better explanation than one alone. From the biological perspective, stress causes the release of two neurotransmitters, adrenaline and noradrenaline, together with the hormone cortisol. Adrenaline and noradrenaline make us feel agitated and uncomfortable, while prolonged secretion of cortisol can impair immune system functioning and is associated with depression.

However, two people can be exposed to the same stressful events and react quite differently. This can be explained by the cognitive approach. If a negative event happens (e.g. you lose your job) the stress response is mild for someone whose thoughts are along the lines of 'this is an opportunity, or a challenge, rather than a threat' and much more severe for someone who thinks 'this is the end of the line for me'.

## Self-harm

Self-harming takes many forms, from cutting oneself with a sharp object, to self-inflicted bruises and tissue damage from other causes. Self-harming behaviour is a complex phenomenon with almost exclusively psychological causes. People who self-harm frequently say that it rids them of overwhelming feelings of anxiety, self-loathing, fear or shame. Sufferers often report intense relief from psychological pain that is achieved by causing themselves physical pain. The physical pain is apparently much more manageable because it is visible and controlled, whereas psychological distress is huge and uncontrolled.

An alternative reason for self-harming is when a person feels numb psychologically. In this situation, physical pain reminds them that they are alive. The desire to self-harm seems out of their control. A person may think obsessively about it, and require massive self-control to resist the urge. Although reasons for self-harming are many and varied, risk factors include intense emotional pain, perhaps originating earlier on in life, coupled with the absence of a supportive emotional environment in which to explore difficult feelings. From a psychodynamic perspective, this behaviour could be explained by a strong superego and weak ego. This would leave the individual vulnerable to feelings of guilt (coming from the superego), which could lead to the self-harming behaviour. Similarly, early traumatic experiences, which have not been dealt with, may be locked in the unconscious – only to emerge as a fierce anger. Since the anger cannot be directed at its original cause, it is directed against the self.

The humanistic approach might see the cause of this behaviour as a wide gulf between the ideal self and the actual self. Anger, frustration and guilt build up as the individual fails to live up to their ideal self, and these emotions are relieved by self-harming behaviour.

## Prejudice and discrimination

Prejudice refers to a negative attitude towards a group or object. The prejudiced person has negative feelings (e.g. dislike and/or fear). Negative beliefs and attitudes (often involving stereotypes) may be used to justify the prejudiced attitude. By contrast, discrimination refers to behaviours. These may be behaviours designed to avoid, belittle, or even get rid of members of the group one is prejudiced against.

## Reflect

Have you ever been in situations where you have heard people talking disparagingly about a particular group in society? You yourself may have labelled others or yourself been labelled as a 'chav'. Where do you think prejudice comes from? What is the best way to reduce prejudice?

An influential psychological theory of prejudice is known as the realistic conflict theory and was proposed by psychologist Muzafer Sherif in 1966 (cited in Eysenck and Flanagan, 2001). This theory proposes that we view ourselves and our friends and family as members of in-groups and others as belonging to out-groups. We then develop the belief that in-group members can only do well at the expense of an out-group: in other words, only one group can be dominant. A second assumption of this theory is that if there is a situation where competition arises between groups, this inevitably leads to prejudice.

Reduction of inter-group prejudice can only be achieved by involving both groups in working towards a goal where they have to co-operate in order to succeed in achieving an important task.

A second explanation for prejudice and discrimination is the theory known as social identity theory, proposed by the French psychologist Henri Tajfel in 1982 (cited in Eysenck and Flanagan, 2001).

According to this theory, merely seeing ourselves as members of a group will lead to favouritism towards one's own group and prejudice against another. The reason for this is that we all desire a positive social identity to maintain our self-esteem. This is achieved by seeing ourselves as members of an 'in-group', which we favour, and seeing other people as members of an 'out-group', which we automatically perceive as inferior to us in all respects.

While Sherif's theory of prejudice sees this as developing within a social context, other explanations focus on the upbringing and experience of individuals. In 1950 Theodor Adorno *et al* (cited in Eysenck and Flanagan, 2001) saw childhood experiences as forming the origins of prejudice. A child who is treated harshly by parents is unable to express hostility or anger towards them, but instead adopts similar harsh and rigid views towards, and expectations of, others. The hostility they unconsciously feel towards the original object of their anger (their parents) is displaced onto other people or groups, particularly those who are powerless or are existing targets for hostility in society.

In order to test this theory, Adorno created a questionnaire to find out about prejudice against different cultural groups such as travellers, Jews and Muslims. He also asked questions about the extent to which people have certain personality traits, such as being rigid and inflexible, having unquestioning respect for authority and holding very conventional values. High scores on these questionnaires are good predictors of prejudiced attitudes towards others.

## Activity 8: How authoritarian are you?

Complete an online questionnaire by going to the website: www.anesi.com/fscale.htm.

1 Do you agree with the analysis of your personality from this questionnaire?

2 Do you think this questionnaire is a satisfactory explanation for prejudice?

## Child abuse

Child abuse includes neglect, psychological abuse and physical abuse. A neglected child does not have their basic needs met and may be ignored or deprived of conversation and other forms of stimulation. Psychological abuse could consist of criticism, ridicule or being told they are unwanted. Physical abuse unfortunately is all too common and consists of anything from being bruised, starved or even tortured.

It is difficult to find a common explanation for child abuse. However, in 1980 Belsky (cited in Shaffer, 2002) did find that an unduly high proportion of parents who abused children had themselves been abused, neglected or unloved. However, it seems that abuse is not inevitable but is triggered by stressful life experiences.

## Addiction

Addiction to cocaine and/or amphetamines can be explained very clearly by the biological approach. These two drugs produce feelings of well-being and heightened pleasure because they cause increased amounts of the neurotransmitter dopamine to be available within the brain. This increased dopamine is responsible for the pleasurable feelings induced by these drugs. However, over-stimulation of dopamine also causes levels to drop dramatically, resulting in feelings of depression. The quickest and easiest way to overcome these unpleasant depressed feelings is to take more drugs. In this way, an addiction is formed.

## Violence and aggression

From the biological perspective, the hormone testosterone can, in part, explain a tendency towards aggressive behaviour. Evolutionary biology would explain this as a necessary characteristic for males who need to compete for resources and secure the best mates to ensure that their genes are passed on.

However, hormones alone do not necessarily cause violence and aggression. It is more likely that there is an interplay between the hormonal secretion of testosterone and environmental factors. For example, social learning theory explains aggression as being triggered by observing aggressive behaviour, which is seen to provide some sort of gain (reinforcement)

for the individual being aggressive. These two perspectives can come together to explain why some people may react in an aggressive and violent way; they have learned that this will somehow benefit them, while others have learned that such behaviour will be punished (e.g. in the form of disapproval).

### Activity 9: Brain chemicals and pleasure

Research the effects of the neurotransmitter dopamine, which has been suggested as being involved in addictive behaviour.

1   What role does dopamine play in addiction?

2   Do you think that, once addictive behaviour has been established, the brain can ever be 'retrained' to come off the addictive substance?

### Assessment activity 29.2                                        P2  P3  M2    BTEC

Produce two case studies covering the following:

*   an explanation of the contribution of *complementary* psychological theories to the understanding of two specific behaviours

*   an explanation of the contribution of *contrasting* psychological theories to the understanding of two specific behaviours

*   an assessment of the contribution of complementary and contrasting psychological theories to the understanding of the two specific behaviours.

You may find it useful to use informal observations from placements to help you develop the case studies.

perspective you have studied. For example, the social learning theory approach and behaviourism tend to complement one another (both stress the influence of nurture), whereas the biological approach contrasts with these two approaches, emphasising, as it does, the effects of nature. You can show understanding by giving examples of specific behaviours.

 You may find it useful to delve deeper into your two chosen behaviours, to demonstrate how the psychological perspectives you are examining contribute to an understanding of all aspects of these behaviours (e.g. the heightened physiological arousal shown in aggression may be explained biologically, whereas the cognitive features, such as dislike of another, may be explained better by a different perspective).

#### Grading tips

**P2** and **P3** To achieve P2 and P3, make sure you are clear about the key concepts of each

### Functional skills

**English:** You will need to read widely and select relevant information to create a coherent argument.

# 3 Understand the contribution of psychological perspectives to the management and treatment of specific behaviours

## 3.1 Contributions of different psychological perspectives

### Cognitive behavioural therapy

This treatment was designed by Aaron Beck and Albert Ellis and has become a much-used and very effective form of therapy over the past 30 or so years. Cognitive behavioural therapy (CBT) does not seek to discover the causes of emotional distress but rather to examine how thoughts, beliefs and behaviours 'in the here and now' are creating or maintaining depression.

### Recognising negative and irrational thoughts

The first stage of the process is to recognise our thoughts. We sometimes have a self-critical running commentary in our heads. Identifying these automatic thoughts is one goal of the therapy, and patients are often asked to write down all the negative thoughts they encounter during the course of each day. Common **negative thoughts** and **irrational thoughts** are illustrated in Table 29.8.

### Key terms

**Negative thoughts** – Thoughts that are self-critical.

**Irrational thoughts** – Thoughts that have no real basis in fact, or which do not accurately reflect reality.

**Table 29.8:** Common negative and irrational thoughts

| | | |
|---|---|---|
| Over-generalisation | An overall sweeping conclusion drawn on the basis of a single, perhaps trivial, event | *A student regards his poor performance in a single class on one particular day as final proof of his worthlessness and stupidity.* |
| Magnification and minimisation | Exaggerations in evaluating performance: small failures are magnified and success is minimised | *A man, believing he has completely ruined his car when he sees a scratch on the bumper, regards himself as good-for-nothing.* *A woman believes herself worthless in spite of a succession of praiseworthy achievements.* |
| Selective abstraction | A conclusion drawn on the basis of only one of many elements in a situation | *A worker feels worthless when a product fails to function, even though she is only one of many people who contributed to its production.* |
| Arbitrary inference | A conclusion drawn in the absence of sufficient evidence, or of any evidence at all | *A man feels worthless because his boss's wife cannot come to a dinner party he arranged.* |
| Catastrophising | A succession of thoughts that put the most negative possible interpretation on an event | *A student does badly in a module and thinks 'That's it! I shall fail my exams, get a rubbish job, lose my girlfriend and end up sad and lonely'.* |

As the process of recognising such thoughts becomes easier, the patient will be asked to identify triggers – events that lead to such thoughts. In this way they begin to recognise what they are actually thinking and they have a chance to begin to break down a huge, overwhelming feeling of gloom into more manageable parts.

### Challenging negative thoughts

With the help of a therapist, negative or irrational thoughts can then be challenged. Alternative explanations for an event that has prompted a negative thought can be sought. For example, a student who sees her best friend and another person she is not too keen on talking together in low voices may think, 'My friend has turned against me. She's going to go off with that other person!' If the two of them laugh, the thoughts may be even worse: 'They're making fun of me. My friend is giving away all my secrets.'

Alternative explanations can then be sought. The client may generate a list such as:

- They are both studying performing arts. They might have been talking about an assignment.
- When they laughed, it could have been about something that happened last week on a trip to the theatre.

Although it can be very difficult when we are in the midst of gloom to think of alternative explanations for events, it can be done, but we may need help to do it. Figure 29.6 on the next page shows how the same object can be seen from two different perspectives, leading to two quite different outcomes.

### Activity 10: Is your glass half full or half empty?

Visit the following website and take the online optimism test to determine how optimistic you are about life: www.authentichappiness.sas.upenn.edu/testcenter.aspx

1  Do you think optimism and pessimism are traits that we are born with?

2  How much influence does the environment have on how optimistic we are?

### Treatment of phobias

Phobias involve fear of an object or situation, which is excessive in relation to the real danger. They disrupt a person's life significantly because the person makes changes to their lifestyle in order to continue avoiding the feared object or situation. For example, someone with agoraphobia (fear of open places) may be unable to leave their house for several years. This clearly interferes with work, social life and family life and is very debilitating.

Cognitive behavioural therapy would be used to help the patient recognise all their thoughts associated with the object of fear. For example, for someone with a phobia about dogs, these could include thoughts such as 'I will die if I have to walk past a dog.' The physical sensations that occur for a person with a dog phobia are also extreme. They include rapid heart rate, dizziness, difficulty breathing, a dry mouth and 'knots' in the stomach.

The treatment goal is to help the individual recognise that their thoughts are irrational and to replace them with more assertive, realistic and positive thoughts (this is the cognitive part). So, for example, an individual will be encouraged to think of all the alternative possible thoughts to replace the original one, 'I will die if I have to walk past a dog.' These may include: 'I shall feel extremely uncomfortable, but this will pass' or 'The more I confront my fears, the less they will rule my life.'

The second aspect of this therapy involves trying out new behaviour and confronting, rather than avoiding, the feared situation. The person will be taught how to use relaxation techniques to reduce the physiological response and will then confront the feared situation in small stages. For example, they may walk past a dog 50 metres away, which is held firmly on a leash. This behaviour can then confirm the new thoughts and make them stronger. It also begins to teach the brain to reduce its activity and produce less extreme fear reactions. Over time, with repeated examination of thoughts, the individual continues to face the feared object until they are able to at least walk past a dog, if not actually pat it!

You may wish to re-read the section on systematic desensitisation in Book 1, Unit 8 (page 354).

**Fig 29.6:** This illustration shows how, by shifting perspective, we can see two completely different images in a single picture!

Charlotte has worked as a community psychiatric nurse for five years. She has recently transferred to the adult outreach team, where she works with adults who have ongoing mental health difficulties. Her duties include assessing and talking to patients about their problems. She needs to build relationships with clients and gain their trust. This involves listening to them and interpreting their needs and concerns. Within a multi-disciplinary team consisting of psychiatrists, occupational therapists, GPs, social workers and other mental health professionals, she helps decide on the best way to deliver care to the patients she works with.

She has recently been asked to visit a 52-year-old woman, Elle, who has been unable to leave her house for six months and is seriously depressed. Whenever she attempts to leave the house, Elle begins to hyperventilate. She becomes clammy and sweaty and has palpitations, which cause her to fear she may have a heart attack. She has a profound fear of having a panic attack if she leaves the house, and yet is also fearful about never being able to leave the house again. These symptoms all fit the pattern of the disorder known as agoraphobia. Literally meaning 'fear of the market place', this disorder is characterised by an intense fear of going into the outside world, often because of fear of a panic attack occurring.

Charlotte plans to work with Elle to help her develop resources that will enable her to overcome her phobia. To begin with, she will help Elle master relaxation techniques, so she can reduce some of the symptoms of the flight or fight response, which cause the physical symptoms of the phobia. She also plans to use cognitive behavioural therapy to help Elle change her negative thoughts about going out of the home and replace them with more realistic and positive thoughts. When Elle is ready, the behavioural part of the treatment will begin, with Elle being supported to make short journeys outside the house.

## Think about it!

1 Explain the fight or flight response and suggest why Elle might experience this when she thinks about leaving the house.

2 What is meant by negative or irrational thinking? Suggest some ways in which Elle could learn to challenge such thinking in order to overcome her phobic response.

3 Do you think the combination of relaxation techniques and cognitive behavioural therapy is sufficient to help Elle? If not, what else might help? Justify your answer.

## Treatment of mental illnesses

There are many mental illnesses that can be treated using different psychological perspectives. For example, in treating depression it is common to combine medication with some aspect of CBT or a talking cure. Anorexia nervosa has similarly been treated using medication together with aspects of operant conditioning, aimed at reducing anxiety and increasing weight gain to the extent that the individual is able to function well enough to enter a form of therapy based on one or more of the perspectives.

In practice, many psychotherapists, clinical psychologists and other practitioners working within a psychotherapeutic framework, combine key concepts from one or more approaches in order to assist their practice. Those working solely within the psychoanalytic approach, however, tend to use psychoanalysis as the preferred method of treatment. Here, the goal is to make the contents of the unconscious conscious so that early trauma, psychic imbalance and ego defences can be exposed in order to be resolved. This treatment tends to be time-consuming and costly.

### Activity 11: Can depression be measured?

Visit the following website and take one of the online tests, which will give you a score that represents the extent to which you might be depressed.

www.real-depression-help.com/beck-depression-inventory.html

1 Why do you think there are different tests for adults and teenagers?

2 Do you think the test you chose was a good test? Why or why not?

## Treatment of post-traumatic stress disorder

Post-traumatic stress disorder (PTSD) can follow a traumatic event, such as rape or being involved in a horrific car crash. It was first recognised among soldiers returning from war, where they had experienced unimaginable horrors. Symptoms include terrible, ongoing fear of an aspect of life that is in some way associated with the original event, together with vivid flashbacks, which make the person keep reliving the event.

For full details of the symptoms of PTSD, see Book 1, Unit 8 (page 361).

Since there is a cognitive aspect to this disorder, recognising and challenging negative thoughts are key aspects of treatment. When the individual has a repertoire of new, positive thoughts, this can lead to more positive feelings and a greater willingness to face events. Confronting, rather than avoiding, events previously feared as unbearable can lead to feelings of pride and energy, which promotes recovery.

## Approaches to challenging behaviour

Individuals who feel hurt, frustrated, misunderstood or simply not listened to, may show challenging behaviour. This can range from merely irritating behaviours, such as attention-seeking and butting in to other people's conversations, through to prolonged bouts of screaming or self-harming. The fundamental principles of CBT can be very helpful. Once again, the key is to understand the thought processes that lead to the behaviour. This can be extremely difficult when working with individuals who find it difficult to communicate with others (e.g. those with autism or other severe learning difficulties). In such cases, care workers may need to carry out detailed observation and identify triggers for challenging behaviour. In this way, following full discussion with colleagues, it may be possible to infer the thoughts of the individual. For example, they may feel left out, ignored or believe they have been treated unfairly.

Having identified negative thoughts, the same procedure can be used as with all forms of CBT: alternative explanations explored and proposed and suggestions for behavioural changes made.

## Monitoring and improving behaviour

We have already touched upon the monitoring of behaviour in the section on the use of CBT as a therapy for depression. Similar methods can be used by individuals or their carers to monitor behaviour. If the individual is not able to keep their own log of behaviour, this can be done on their behalf, with small targets set for behavioural changes. The individual is asked to give feedback on positive actions they have undertaken, together with the sense of achievement and pleasure they gain from these. For an individual with learning disabilities, this could be done visually in the form of stars or charts used to monitor progress and show improvements visually.

## Social learning theory

This theory helps us to understand how to change behaviour through the use of the principles of observational learning. The fundamental principle of this theory is that behaviour is learned and therefore can be unlearned, or changed.

### Reflect

Have you ever felt encouraged by finding out that someone competent and/or famous has overcome the same difficulties in life that you are facing? For example, the actor and comedian Stephen Fry has openly acknowledged his mental health difficulties, thus acting as a role model for others with similar problems.

### Use of positive role models

Positive role models can be used to portray desirable behaviour that offers an alternative to the unhelpful behaviour being performed by an individual. Social learning theory sees the model (i.e. the person performing a particular behaviour) as being especially important in influencing how much attention we pay to the behaviour being modelled and how motivated we are to imitate it. To use the example of depression, there is an increasing tendency for public figures to acknowledge that they have suffered from this disorder. The fact that they are famous means that they usually have high status, are admired and are perceived as having more special qualities than ourselves. This can help motivate members of the public struggling with depression to seek help.

### Treatment of addictions

Once again, observational learning can be used in treating addictions. By observing an individual modelling non-addictive behaviour, a person can learn strategies to achieve this. Being exposed to someone else who is receiving punishment for addiction (e.g. debt, illness and prison sentences) enables the individual to take a step back from their own situation and learn some of the negative consequences of addictions. Equally, positive consequences can be observed (e.g. interviews with husbands or other family members who express pleasure at having their loved one free of the tyranny of addiction), which can be experienced as reinforcing by the observer.

### Treatment of eating disorders

One of the symptoms of many eating disorders is a distorted view of one's physical body. Being able to observe another individual with a similar eating disorder (particularly anorexia nervosa) may bring home to the individual just how thin and ill they look. We can also learn through observing another person being positively reinforced for changing their behaviour. So if an individual suffering from anorexia is exposed to a role model who is reinforced for recovery from this illness, this can motivate them to also work towards recovery. As with all aspects of social learning theory, reinforcement is highly subjective so the treatment would have to focus on showing reinforcement that would be appealing to the patient.

## Psychodynamic perspective

This perspective can help to treat certain behaviours by delving into the unconscious mind of the client. The assumption here is that behaviours are caused by aspects of the self (wishes, feelings, memories) that are denied consciously, but remain in the unconscious mind and create a variety of symptoms. The following represent methods of treating these symptoms.

### Psychoanalysis

This usually involves four to five treatment sessions a week, each lasting 50 minutes, and can last for as long as five years. The aim is to bring the contents of the unconscious into consciousness so the patient becomes aware of internal conflicts and repressed wishes. In this way, symptoms disappear. The therapy of psychoanalysis includes:

- the interpretation of dreams
- an exploration of factors that influence behaviour.

### Interpretation of dreams

Sigmund Freud believed that during sleep the unconscious could express itself more freely than when the person was awake. However, in order not to create too much anxiety, the unconscious uses symbolism in dreams. This imagery prevents disturbing and repressed material from entering the conscious mind and thus has the function of 'protecting sleep'. Much repressed material was believed to be connected to sexuality.

A major function of dreams, according to Freud, is **wish fulfilment**. Desires that are unacceptable to the conscious mind cannot be fully repressed and thus are expressed in dreams. However, they are disguised and are shown as **manifest content** (i.e. the actual story of the dream). To understand the real meaning of the dream, an interpretation must be made, to find the **latent** (or underlying) **content**. This involves **dream analysis**, whereby the analyst and the patient are both involved in working out the meaning of various symbols. When the symbolism of the dreams has been interpreted, its true meaning becomes clear and the patient is able to deal with issues that have been repressed.

### Exploration of factors influencing behaviour

The primary goal of psychoanalysis is to explore reasons for behaviour. The aim of the treatment is to find ways of reaching the unconscious mind in order to discover what is troubling the patient. Freud believed that memories, events or feelings that will cause us anxiety if we are fully aware of them are pushed into the unconscious. However, they do not just stay there, but emerge as symptoms.

In addition to dream analysis, another way of reaching the unconscious is through **free association**. The patient is encouraged to say the first thing that comes into their mind upon hearing a word. Because this happens automatically, issues in the unconscious will emerge. An example from one of Freud's patients was when he said the word 'shroud' in response to the word 'white'. When this was explored further, it turned out that a close friend of the patient's had died of a heart attack at the same age as the patient was now. His own fear of dying had been repressed but emerged when he automatically associated 'shroud' with the word 'white'. Once this fear had been made available to his conscious mind, he was able to move on with his life.

Psychoanalysis also examines issues from childhood, which may have had such an impact on the individual that they are still being unconsciously influenced by them. Once the source of a particular symptom of emotional unhappiness has been revealed, this often frees the patient from further symptoms of this type.

## Humanistic perspective

The goal of this approach is to help the individual develop an awareness of barriers to personal growth and self-actualisation and to resolve any incongruence between their actual self and ideal self.

This type of person-centred counselling was pioneered by Carl Rogers. Rogers believed that the success of any type of therapy mainly depended on the way the therapist behaved towards the patient. Fundamental principles of person-centred counselling include the following.

### Unconditional positive regard

This means that the therapist must accept all that the patient thinks, feels, has done and wants, without making judgements. This is the 'unconditional' part. The therapist must also show a totally positive attitude towards, and respect for, the client. 'Unconditional positive regard' thus implies an absence of judgements and a genuine belief that the client is a worthwhile person capable of making positive choices. By viewing the client in this way, the therapist frees the individual to express themselves. The therapist doesn't give advice or make judgments. Instead they hold to a belief that the client, in the right climate, can reach an understanding of their situation, and an appropriate decision on the choices that confront them, on their own. The task of the therapist is merely to check the client's understanding of their own problems and help them think through solutions, without suggesting a specific course of action.

### Self-awareness

The crucial aspect of this type of counselling is that the therapist is totally aware of their own feelings and beliefs, is not afraid to acknowledge these, and has

---

### Key terms

**Wish fulfilment** – The idea that dreams express unconsciously the things we most desire.

**Manifest content** – The actual narrative (or story) of a dream.

**Latent content** – The underlying meaning (usually symbolic) of a dream. This needs to be interpreted in order to understand its meaning.

**Dream analysis** – A method of looking at dreams in order to understand the contents of the unconscious mind.

**Free association** – A method used during the process of psychoanalysis to gain access to the unconscious. The patient is encouraged to say the first thing that comes into their mind, the assumption being that this reflects unconscious as opposed to conscious feelings, wishes and desires.

no real desire to guide the client towards a specific outcome. Through achieving true self-awareness, the therapist is less likely to take a judgmental approach and more likely to achieve the necessary state of empathic understanding.

### Respect for the drive towards healing

Finally, regardless of what perspective they have been trained in (e.g. psychoanalytic psychotherapy, behavioural therapy and cognitive behavioural therapy), the therapist should have a firm belief in the capacity of each individual to heal themselves, given the appropriate support.

## Biological perspective

### Reflect

If something happens to startle you, do you find you have a racing pulse and that your heart is beating fast? This may cause you to feel, subjectively, a sense of anxiety and it illustrates how closely our thoughts and emotions are linked to our biological make-up.

As mentioned earlier, this perspective assumes that all behaviour is caused by the brain and nervous system. One major treatment involves drug therapy.

### The use of drugs

Drugs are prescribed for a range of symptoms. For anxiety and stress, anti-anxiety drugs such as the benzodiazepines Valium and Librium may be used. These help to induce a state of increased relaxation that allows people to carry on with their everyday lives. Such medication is not recommended for long periods of use, as it can lead to tolerance (and so it becomes less effective) or addiction. It is, however, very helpful when used in conjunction with a therapy that helps the individual to find coping mechanisms. Depression can be treated very effectively with a range of drugs, especially those that increase levels of the neurotransmitter serotonin (a brain chemical). Prozac is one of these drugs, although there are others. For the condition known as ADHD, an amphetamine-like substance is often used, such as Ritalin. The above are all examples of prescription drugs. Non-prescription drugs that have an influence on our mood and behaviour include alcohol, which initially encourages us to feel disinhibited and carefree but ultimately acts as a depressant, and illegal drugs (such as heroin and

cocaine), which induce a feeling of euphoria but are highly addictive.

### Biofeedback

This is mainly used to treat stress-related disorders and illnesses associated with excessive activity within the brain (e.g. epilepsy and ADHD). This technique works on changing the way aspects of our bodies work. It is thus a biological technique.

Biofeedback involves receiving feedback about aspects of the person's physiological state, such as heart rate, blood pressure and temperature, which manifest as visual or auditory signals on a monitor. Adrenaline produced by the body causes sweating, which can be measured by placing electrodes on the skin. This shows changes in skin resistance (known as the galvanic skin response), which then register as a visual signal or tone. If the signal or tone is high, the level of arousal is similarly high. Initially, by a process of trial and error, the individual attempts various relaxation techniques (deep breathing and visualisation) to reduce the level of signal or tone. As relaxation deepens, blood pressure and heart rate slow down and this is shown (the feedback part of the process) by a lowering of the signal or tone on the monitor. Over time, the individual learns to recognise signs of tension and finds it easier to control physiological functions.

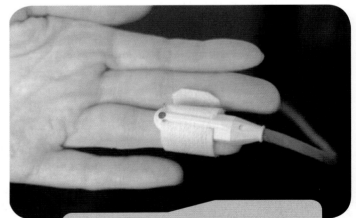

A patient using biofeedback. The sensor records their pulse and body temperature and the data is displayed on a monitor. Can you think of situations in which these devices might be used?

# 3.2 Interventions

Interventions mean help offered by outside agencies such as GPs, social workers, health visitors, family therapists, psychologists, counsellors and psychotherapists. Voluntary organisations are also available to offer help to individuals. By intervening at a time of difficulty or crisis, it is hoped that the individual(s) can be helped to resolve conflicts that are threatening their ability to cope with life, or that are preventing them from living a satisfying life. These interventions are informed by different psychological perspectives.

**Reflect**

Have there been times when you felt the need to talk through things in your life? You may have encountered one or more of the situations outlined above. Did you visit a counsellor or therapist or just talk things over with friends or family? Do you think there is a stigma about visiting a counsellor or therapist?

## The use of perspectives to inform development of therapeutic practices

Each psychological perspective has a different way of understanding emotional distress and behaviours that interfere with satisfactory living.

**How therapies work**

With the exception of therapy involving medication, all therapies work by changing the way in which people think and feel about their situations. Therapies seek to uncover barriers to well-being that may have emerged only recently (e.g. in the case of bereavement) or may have been in existence since childhood (e.g. as in the psychodynamic perspective). Table 29.9 illustrates the main methods used in different types of therapy.

Table 29.9: Key therapeutic methods

| Type of therapy | Key therapeutic method(s) |
|---|---|
| Cognitive behavioural therapy | Recognise and challenge irrational thoughts. Try out new behaviours. |
| Social learning theory | The patient observes a positive role model showing effective and beneficial behaviours. |
| Psychoanalysis | A talking cure. Dream analysis and free association are used to make conscious the contents of the unconscious. |
| Person-centred counselling | A talking cure. The aim is to reduce the incongruence between the actual self and the ideal self. |
| Biological therapies | Drugs dampen down symptoms and change behaviour (e.g. to induce relaxation). Biofeedback also helps reduce symptoms of stress and anxiety. |

# 3.3 Therapeutic practices

In practice, different therapies tend not to be based on just one perspective, but to use aspects taken from one or more approaches. CBT, for example, began as just a cognitive treatment but, over time, incorporated aspects of behaviourism in its treatment. The goal of all therapy is to help individuals identify emotions, beliefs and patterns of behaviour that are causing them distress.

Table 29.10 below and on the next page illustrates some of the main types of therapies used within health and social care.

Table 29.10: Different types of therapy

| | |
|---|---|
| Group therapy | A closed group of about six to seven people work with one or two therapists on issues to do with difficult social or relationship interactions. |
| Family therapy | Family dynamics are explored in a setting with all family members and one or two therapists. Dysfunctional interactions are identified and the family can be helped to move away from these to a healthier state of interaction. |
| Bereavement therapy | The individual is encouraged to talk about their feelings, including anger, without judgements being made. The goal is to help the bereaved person work out what to do in the future and develop a new identity. |

*continued*

**Table 29.10** *continued*

| Addiction therapy | Medication is offered for underlying mental health problems such as depression, anxiety disorder or psychotic disorders. Operant and classical conditioning may also be used to train the individual to avoid associating addictive substances with pleasure. Treatment may last as long as a year. |
|---|---|
| Behaviour modification programmes | Helpful behaviour is reinforced, while unhelpful behaviour is ignored, leading to it being **extinguished** (meaning it stops happening). Eventually the person learns useful strategies and stops showing undesirable behaviours. |
| Counselling | This involves one-to-one conversations with a trained counsellor whose aim is to help individuals explore issues in a caring and sensitive environment. |

## Key term

**Extinguish** – To cause a reduction in a type of behaviour by no longer providing reinforcement.

## Reasons for attending therapy sessions

Contrary to popular belief, it is not necessary to be mentally unstable to attend counselling or therapy sessions! Often it is useful just to have a sounding board to get some perspective on what is troubling us. Many people do not delve deep into their past but instead focus on the present in order to work on an area in their life where they have got 'stuck'. It is important to recognise, however, that one cannot benefit from therapy unless one is a willing participant.

Some of the reasons for attending therapy sessions are given below:

- bereavement (this need not necessarily involve death – 'empty nest syndrome' feels like bereavement and many people benefit from a few therapy sessions)

**Fig 29.7:** A reluctant client cannot benefit from therapy

- re-adjustment to family change – step-families and new siblings
- difficulty managing change – e.g. moving from school to college or university
- relationship difficulties (with parents or romantic relationships)
- dealing with trauma – e.g. having witnessed a car accident and being unable to stop thinking about it
- confusion and unhappiness about career choice
- difficulties concentrating and studying/working
- insomnia
- feelings of stress and anxiety
- following childbirth
- being made redundant/changing jobs
- dealing with injury, disablement or news of terminal or life-changing illness.

## Ethical issues

Anyone working in a professional or voluntary capacity with individuals must follow the British Association of Counselling and Psychotherapy guidelines. These state that the fundamental values of counselling and psychotherapy include a commitment to:

- respecting human rights and dignity
- ensuring the integrity of practitioner–client relationships
- enhancing the quality of professional knowledge and its application
- alleviating personal distress and suffering
- fostering a sense of self that is meaningful to the person(s) concerned

- increasing personal effectiveness
- enhancing the quality of relationships between people

- appreciating the variety of human experience and culture
- striving for the fair and adequate provision of counselling and psychotherapy services.

---

## Assessment activity 29.3    (P4) BTEC

Produce an information booklet explaining the contribution of psychological perspectives to the management and treatment of two specific behaviours.

### Grading tip

(P4) You need to choose your two behaviours carefully to be sure you can show clear

understanding of how psychological perspectives contribute to managing and treating these behaviours. For example, cognitive behavioural therapy is widely used in the treatment of anxiety and depression, while for addiction a biological approach may be more appropriate and you may wish to conduct further research if you choose to cover this.

---

# 4 Understand the contribution of psychological perspectives to residential care provision

## 4.1 Behaviour of individuals in residential care settings

### Concept of role

Roles, sometimes called social roles, involve expectations associated with a particular social situation, occupation or role in life. We all have a different number of roles and these vary according to what we are doing at the time. As a student, you will take the role of student. As a friend, you might find that you have the role of 'the one we can always depend on' or 'the lively party-goer'.

We seem to absorb the rules, norms and expectations of behaviour that accompany these various roles without any conscious learning. They are important, however, in guiding behaviour. Loss of role can lead to stress, a sense of helplessness and hopelessness, and loss of identity.

### Conformity to minority influence

We conform to minority influence because we believe a minority group to have more information or knowledge than we do. In 1969, a French psychologist, Serge Moscovici (cited in Cardwell, Clark and Meldrum,

2003) arranged for groups of six people to view a series of 36 slides, all coloured blue, but with tints that made the colour vary slightly. In both groups there were two confederates (people working for the experimenter who had been given instructions beforehand on what to say) although the other participants were not aware of this. Each participant stated out loud what colour they judged the slide to be. In one group, the two confederates judged all 36 slides as green (the consistent group). In a second group, the two confederates judged 24 to be green and 12 to be blue (the inconsistent group). It was found that in the consistent group, 8.42 per cent of answers from the real participants were green, while in the inconsistent group only 1.25 per cent said green.

This shows that a judgement or view being consistently expressed by a minority can sway the opinion of some of the majority.

## Conformity to majority influence

Conformity (majority influence) involves an individual temporarily changing their behaviour or stated views in order to be in line with other group members. Unlike the example given above, where people genuinely changed their view because they were convinced that the two confederates were right in judging the slides as green, in majority influence it is much more likely that an individual changes their behaviour or views only temporarily. They are motivated by staying in line with the group, not rocking the boat and not seeming foolish by disagreeing with others. Privately, however, their views and beliefs do not change.

Psychologist Solomon Asch (1907–1996) conducted an experiment to investigate majority influence. Like Moscovici, he used confederates but this time there was only one genuine participant (who thought the others were genuine participants like him). All were seated in a room where they could clearly see a vertical line known as a target line (see Figure 29.8). They were then shown three comparison lines and asked to judge out loud which of the three lines was the same length as the target line.

Altogether, these two cards were shown 18 times and Asch asked the confederates to give the wrong answer 12 times. He found that the genuine participants gave the same wrong answer as the confederates 37 per cent of the time. When they were interviewed afterwards, many of the participants were clear that they thought the others were wrong and trusted their own judgement, but they did not feel comfortable about speaking out.

This is really quite a surprising finding, as the people taking part didn't know one another and there would have been no negative consequences if they had simply stated what they believed to be true. It does, however, show how groups have enormous power to shape and change our behaviour.

## Conformity to social roles

We are all aware of the sorts of behaviour, attitudes and emotions that are expected of different roles. For example, an individual may be very strict in the classroom and insist on high standards of behaviour but then behave quite differently when out with friends.

Philip Zimbardo (1973) conducted a study to examine how much roles influence behaviour within prisons (cited in Cardwell, Clark and Meldrum, 2003). He interviewed a group of young male students and chose those of good psychological and physical health to take part in the study. A basement in the University of Stanford (where he worked) was converted into a mock prison and the students were randomly allocated to take on the role of either prisoner or guard. To encourage identification with roles, the guards were given uniforms and dark sunglasses, while the prisoners were given identical 'convict' clothes and only ever addressed by a number. Very soon the guards became quite brutal in their treatment of the prisoners, including punishing them for not obeying orders. The prisoners responded by becoming very distressed and passive, and the study had to be stopped within three days because the prisoners were clearly suffering psychological harm. This study powerfully showed the influence social roles can

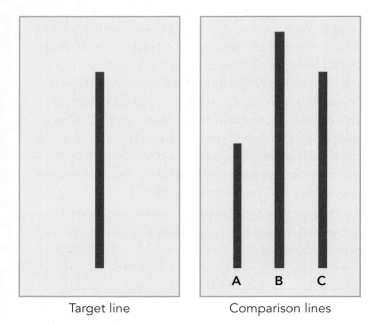

Target line          Comparison lines

**Fig 29.8:** Participants were asked to judge the length of lines compared with a target line

have on how we behave. Furthermore, shared beliefs about the attitudes, values and behaviour expected in particular roles influence us very powerfully in adapting to the roles we play.

The way in which our attitudes, behaviour and beliefs change when we are in contact with others is called 'social influence' and it has a major impact upon behaviour, as is shown in the following sections.

## Obedience

In social psychological terms, obedience refers to a situation where an individual follows orders (sometimes against their morals or better judgement) simply because the order is given by someone of higher authority than themselves. We are socialised from an early age to obey others and this becomes more or less automatic.

Stanley Milgram undertook a famous social psychology experiment in 1963. Milgram was unhappy with the explanations of the Holocaust circulating at the time. These claimed an abnormality in the personalities of a whole generation of Germans and explained the cruelties of the Holocaust as only being possible in this particular time of history and among this particular group of people. Milgram believed, instead, that certain aspects of a situation can induce any of us to obey unjust authority and act against our moral code.

He carried out a series of experiments designed to identify the features of a situation that will create obedience, and compare them with features that reduce obedience. We shall focus on his first experiment, conducted at Harvard University in 1963.

This first study involved 40 male volunteers, from a variety of occupations, who answered an advertisement to take part in an experiment, supposedly designed to test the effects of punishment on learning and memory. The participants were aged between 20 and 50 and were paid $4.50 for taking part.

Upon arrival, each participant was told there were two people involved: a teacher and a learner. The allocation to roles was rigged so the naïve participant was always in the role of 'teacher', while the 'learner' was a confederate of the experimenter.

The stated objective was to learn word-pairs. The learner was to be 'punished' if he gave an incorrect answer by being given an electric shock (although in fact the shocks were fake – the learner didn't receive

any). The teacher was given a 15-volt shock beforehand to show him what the 'learner' would experience if he got an answer wrong.

The learner was then strapped to a machine, which (supposedly) gave similar electric shocks and the teacher witnessed this. The teacher (the real participant) was then placed in a separate room so he could not see the learner. The teacher read out a list of word pairs (for example, blue–girl and fat–neck). This was followed by a number of other words, one of which was the second member of the original pair. The learner had to choose the correct word by pressing one of four switches, which turned on a light on a panel in the teacher's room. Each time the learner made a mistake, the teacher had to deliver a shock. With each successive mistake a further shock was delivered, 15 volts higher than the previous one. The shock generator had a series of switches that increased in 15-volt increments – from 15 volts to 450 volts (potentially fatal).

If the 'teacher' expressed disquiet and wanted to stop, the experimenter was told to give a number of prompts:

- 'Please continue' (or 'please go on')
- 'The experiment requires that you continue'
- 'It is absolutely essential that you continue'
- 'You have no other choice; you must go on'.

At 180 volts, the 'teacher' hears the 'learner' yell out 'I can't stand the pain!' At 315 volts the learner screams loudly and shouts that he won't answer any more. All is silent after this.

To the surprise of everyone involved (including Milgram!), every single participant (those taking the role of 'teacher') gave shocks up to 300 volts. If these were genuine, there was the potential to kill the 'learner'. Furthermore, 68 per cent of the participants gave shocks right up to the maximum of 450 volts!

You will no doubt be relieved to hear that, following the experiment, a full debriefing was held where the 'teacher' met the 'learner' and discovered that no shocks had actually been administered. He was reassured that he had caused no harm to anyone and told that he had taken part in an important experiment that could shed light on aspects of human behaviour.

The whole set-up of Milgram's experiment was very artificial and unlike normal, everyday settings, so it could be argued that his findings about obedience should not be taken too seriously. However, another experiment was carried out by Charles K. Hofling and his colleagues in 1966, in a hospital setting, with very similar findings. Hofling's set-up was that nurses were telephoned by an unknown doctor and asked to administer an unfamiliar drug to a patient. The dosage of the drug, Astroten, ordered by the doctor was twice the safe dosage and nurses would be acting against hospital regulations by administering a drug not recognised on the ward list. It was also against hospital policy to administer a drug without signed authorisation from a doctor and to take orders over the telephone. To the surprise of the researchers, 21 out of the 22 nurses who were given this order were on the verge of administering the drug when they were stopped and the purpose of the order explained

to them (cited in Cardwell, Clark and Meldrum, 2003). These findings suggest that Milgram's original experiment had uncovered something very real about human behaviour. When we are ordered to do something by someone in a position of authority we are likely to do it, even if it means breaking rules or acting against our better judgement.

## Attitude change

As we have seen, we may change our attitudes if we are exposed to different opinions put forward by people we are convinced by. In Moscovici's experiment (page 323), the consistency of the judgements made that the slides were green not blue was influential in changing the judgements of other group members.

A psychologist called Leon Festinger developed a theory of attitude change called 'cognitive dissonance'. This means that, when there is a vast difference between our beliefs and thoughts, attitudes or behaviour, we feel uncomfortable. We experience dissonance (a state of extreme discomfort when we become aware that we hold contradictory ideas). If, for example, I see myself as a kind and tolerant person but snap at a colleague or friend in an intolerant and unkind way, I will experience dissonance. The way to free myself from this uncomfortable experience is to change one of my thoughts (cognitions). I can either revise my view of myself as mostly kind and tolerant, or justify my behaviour as being in the best interests of my colleague. Either way, this involves attitude change.

Other research has found that certain aspects of a message can persuade us to change our attitudes. We are more likely to be persuaded by an individual whom we perceive as trustworthy, knowledgeable and, interestingly enough, attractive! These characteristics make it less easy to dismiss a message and increase the attention we pay. Sadly, one of the most striking examples of such persuasiveness was Adolf Hitler, who achieved massive support among the German people. Clearly, persuading people to change their attitudes is not always beneficial.

---

### _Public Announcement_

### WE WILL PAY YOU $4.00 FOR
### ONE HOUR OF YOUR TIME

#### Persons Needed for a Study of Memory

"We will pay five hundred New Haven men to help us complete a scientific study of memory and learning. The study is being done at Yale University.

\*Each person who participates will be paid $4.00 (plus 50c carfare) for approximately 1 hour's time. We need you for only one hour: there are no further obligations. You may choose the time you would like to come (evenings, weekdays, or weekends).

\*No special training, education, or experience is needed. We want:

| | | |
|---|---|---|
| Factory workers | Businessmen | Construction workers |
| City employees | Clerks | Salespeople |
| Laborers | Professional people | White-collar workers |
| Barbers | Telephone workers | others |

All persons must be between the ages of 20 and 50. High school and college students cannot be used.

\*If you meet these qualifications, fill out the coupon below and mail it now to Professor Stanley Milgram, Department of Psychology, Yale University, New Haven. You will be notified later of the specific time and place of the study. We reserve the right to decline any application.

\*You will be paid $4.00 (plus 50c carfare) as soon as you arrive at the laboratory.

------------------------------------------------

TO:

PROF. STANLEY MILGRAM, DEPARTMENT OF PSYCHOLOGY, YALE UNIVERSITY, NEW HAVEN, CONN. I want to take part in this study of memory and learning. I am between the ages of 20 and 50. I will be paid $4.00 (plus 50c carfare) if I participate.

NAME (Please Print) .........................................................................

ADDRESS .......................................................................................

TELEPHONE NO. ........................................... Best time to call you .............................

AGE .......... OCCUPATION ................................................... SEX ..................

CAN YOU COME:
WEEKDAYS ..................... EVENINGS ....................... WEEKENDS ..........................

**Fig 29.9:** Would you have answered this advertisement placed by Milgram to request volunteers for his experiment into obedience?

# Factors influencing hostility and aggression

The table below illustrates factors believed to influence hostility and aggression.

Table 29.11: Personality factors influencing hositility

| Theory | Explanation |
| --- | --- |
| Authoritarian personality | Personality factors produce prejudice, which in turn leads to hostility towards the object of our prejudice. |
| Psychodynamic | We project onto others the aspects of our own personality that we find unacceptable. |
| Environmental stressors | Heat or high temperature and crowding can induce feelings of frustration, aggression and hostility. |

# 4.2 Effects of residential care on individuals

## Effects of institutionalisation

Institutionalisation may occur when an individual lives in a closed setting such as a hospital or care home. If contact with the outside world is limited, the individual may become dependent upon the institution. They become used to having meals cooked for them, washing done and activities organised and regulated, and find it difficult to move from this setting to independent living.

## Loss of identity

Many of us see our job, status, financial position, and aspects such as appearance, as crucial aspects of our identity. We take pride in being able to earn a living, be a successful worker, a good housewife, an attractive woman. When we enter an institution, things that once set us apart in the outside world may no longer be seen as important. With this loss of status and difference can come a sense that our identity is slipping away. Such a loss can be deeply distressing and people may lapse into depression and helplessness.

## Learned helplessness

Learned helplessness is a term used to describe a state of mind where someone has, over a period of time, learned that nothing they do, no matter how hard they try, can change events. Once they have developed learned helplessness, they will simply stop trying to change things. They may lapse into apathy and not take advantage of opportunities where they might be able to control events. This state of learned helplessness is thought to be a possible contributing cause of depression.

## Stress

Many people find the experience of institutionalisation extremely frustrating. Often it is hard to find privacy and peace and quiet, or to create a sense of one's own space. We may have to follow routines that don't suit us, to live with people we would not normally choose to spend time with, to eat food we may not have chosen. All these frustrations can lead to feelings of intense stress.

# 4.3 Practices in residential care settings

Policies, procedures and the behaviour of staff in residential care settings can have beneficial or damaging effects on residents. If the main goal is to keep order and avoid disruption, this may result in residents feeling disempowered (having power taken away from them), which has a negative effect on health and well-being. Policies and procedures that promote independence can, on the other hand, protect residents against some of these potentially negative effects.

## Promoting independence and empowerment

An alternative to putting people in residential care is to encourage individuals to live as independently as possible and to empower them to do things that help their well-being, rather than do things for them. For example, increasingly there are blocks of flats and houses where older people can live fairly independently but have help at hand if needed. These communities aim to promote independence.

## Respecting individual rights

When you are working in a busy institution it may be easy to forget that the people you are working with are individuals, with their own needs and desires. Some people can be difficult and challenging; others might be quiet, not standing up for themselves when it might benefit them to do so. It is important to remember that we all have certain very basic but crucial rights. We all have the right to:

- protection
- dignity
- self-determination (where possible)
- independence
- emotional well-being
- intellectual stimulation
- respect for culture, race, religion.

Giving people choices over simple things such as what they watch on television, choice of meals and activities they join in, helps them to maintain a sense of dignity and independence. Similarly, showing expectations that someone will succeed, rather than automatically jumping in to do something for them, helps to promote a sense of independence and to maintain self-esteem.

It is important that people are treated as individuals, not just one of many people to be cared for. This can help to prevent lapses into learned helplessness, or loss of identity or stress. Care workers should work within a framework of values known as the care value base.

## Care value base

This is a set of guidelines to help care workers foster the equality, diversity and rights of clients. Care workers must do more than just look after the physical needs of their clients: they also need to consider their social, emotional, spiritual and psychological needs. The care value base must underpin everything that is done in health and social care. Its core values are:

- promote anti-discrimination
- promote effective communication
- preserve confidentiality
- promote the rights and responsibilities of all
- promote and preserve equality and diversity.

---

## Assessment activity 29.4

Produce a presentation using relevant materials and covering:

- an *explanation* of the contribution of psychological perspectives to the promotion of good practice in residential services
- an *examination* of the contribution of two psychological perspectives to the promotion of good practice in residential care services
- an *evaluation* of the contribution of two psychological perspectives to the promotion of good practice in residential care services.

### Grading tips

**P5**  You could arrange to interview a practitioner working in the residential sector to gain more information for this assignment. Use

the information from the textbook and wider reading to explain how psychological insights can benefit both staff and clients.

**M3** You may find it useful to examine the strengths and weaknesses of the two perspectives you choose, and to base your choice on those you feel offer most insight to people working in this sector.

**D2** To evaluate the contribution of the two chosen perspectives, you need to weigh up their strengths and weaknesses as applied to residential care services. Some perspectives may be more useful than others in certain settings (e.g. children rather than older people) and if you can make an argument for this it will help you to achieve the distinction grade.

# References and further reading

American Psychiatric Association *Diagnostic and Statistical Manual of Mental Disorders (DSM-IV-TR)*, fourth ed. Virginia: USA

Belsky, J. and Fearon, R.M. (2002) 'Early attachment security, subsequent maternal sensitivity, and later child development: Does continuity in development depend upon continuity of care giving? *Journal of Attachment and Human Development* vol 4, no 3, 361–87

Birch, A. and Malim, T. (1988) *Developmental Psychology: from infancy to adulthood* Bristol: Intertext

Bowlby, J. (1988) *A Secure Base: Clinical Applications of Attachment Theory* Bristol: J.W. Arrowsmith

Bowlby, J. (1965) *Child Care and the Growth of Love* London: Penguin Books

Bowlby, J. (1979) *The Making and Breaking of Affectional Bonds* London: Tavistock Publications

Cardwell, M., Clark, L. & Meldrum, C. (2003) *Psychology for AS Level*, third ed. Hammersmith: Collins

Cardwell, M. & Flanagan, C. (2003) *Psychology AS: the Complete Companion* Cheltenham: Nelson Thornes

Donaldson, M. (1978) *Children's Minds* London: Flamingo

Ewen, R.B. (1993) *An Introduction to Theories of Personality*, fourth ed. Hove: Lawrence Erlbaum Associates

Eysenck, M.W. & Flanagan, C. (2001) *Psychology for A2 Level* Hove: Psychology Press

Gross, R. (2001) *Psychology: The science of mind and behaviour*, fourth ed. London: Hodder & Stoughton Educational

Haralambos, M. *et al* (2000) *Psychology in Focus for AS Level* Ormskirk: Causeway Press

Haralambos, M. & Rice, D. (2002) *Psychology in Focus A2 Level* Ormskirk: Causeway Press

Holmes, J. (1993) *John Bowlby and Attachment Theory* London: Routledge

Kennedy, E. (1997) *On Becoming a Counsellor: A Basic Guide for Non-professional Counsellors* New York: Seabury Press Inc.

Moxon, D., Brewer, K. & Emmerson, P. (2003) *Psychology AS for AQA A* Oxford: Heinemann

Sarafino, E.P. (1998) *Health Psychology: Biopsychosocial Interactions*, third ed. New York: John Wiley & Sons

Shaffer, D.R. (2002) *Developmental Psychology, Childhood and Adolescence*, sixth ed. Belmont, Ca: Wadsworth

# Useful websites

British Association for Counselling and Psychotherapy: www.bacp.co.uk

Information on cognitive therapy www.beckinstitute.org

Website devoted to rational emotive behaviour therapy www.rebtnetwork.org/

National Institute of Child Health and Development (NICDH) www.nichd.nih.gov

List of websites related to self-harming www.selfharm.net

Positive Psychology Centre, University of Pennsylvania www.authentichappiness.org

Attachment theory www.psychology4a.com/attachments_in_development.htm

www.personalityresearch.org/attachment.html

Psychodynamic theory www.simplypsychology.pwp.blueyonder.co.uk/psychodynamic.html

## Just checking

1  Who developed the theory of observational learning?
2  Which theory holds that reinforcement influences the likelihood of behaviour being repeated?
3  How many developmental stages does Piaget suggest there are?
4  Name two psychologists associated with the humanistic school of psychology.
5  Who believed that self-efficacy was an important component of one's sense of self?
6  Who coined the term the 'looking-glass self'?
7  Which psychologist is associated with operant conditioning?
8  What psychological perspective sees development as progressing through a series of psychosexual stages?
9  Who developed the maternal deprivation hypothesis?
10 Whose psychological theory of prejudice suggests that this is to do with the authoritarian personality type?
11 What psychological perspective involves the interpretation of dreams as part of its treatment?
12 Which psychologist is associated with the treatment known as person-centred counselling?
13 Which psychologist investigated obedience in a hospital setting?

edexcel :::

## Assignment tips

1  To explain behaviour (P grades), you need to use the terminology of the perspective. For example, you might want to refer to defence mechanisms if you are explaining the psychodynamic perspective or reinforcement if you are illustrating the use of the behaviourist perspective.

2  Make notes on class discussions to help you achieve the merit grades that require you to 'discuss' and 'assess'. This will be useful, as you will find a variety of opinions, all of which can help you to identify strengths and weaknesses.

3  To achieve the distinction grade of 'evaluate', do all of the above but also keep notes throughout on what you yourself think so you can use this to balance strengths and weaknesses and produce a well-informed opinion.

4  Ask questions of visiting speakers and talk to staff members at your work experience placements. Which perspective(s) do they find most useful and why? Are some more useful to different client groups or health or social care settings?

5  Above all, be systematic. Take notes in lessons and keep a glossary of key concepts and definitions. Make sure you can identify and discuss the strengths and weaknesses of each perspective and apply the different approaches to development and behaviour.

# Glossary

## A

**Absolute poverty** – A term introduced by Seebohm Rowntree, referring to people on a level of income below that which will maintain 'physical efficiency'.

**Abstract thought** – Representing a problem mentally and manipulating ideas in one's mind. For example, solving the problem '3 + 3' in one's head rather than using counters.

**Abuse** – This is defined by the Department of Health as 'a violation of an individual's human and civil rights by any other person or persons'.

**Accommodation** – A process that works alongside assimilation and enables an individual to modify their understanding and internal representation of concepts in order to create new understanding.

**Acid** – A substance giving rise to hydrogen ions in solution.

**Act of omission** – Failure to act in a way that a person would usually act. In health and social care, a professional may sometimes fail to provide care in order to save someone from the greater harm of a prolonged and painful death. In other words, in a medical context doctors cannot give lethal injections, but they can withhold treatment when someone is in the final stages of life.

**Active transport** – The movement of materials against a concentration gradient, using energy from ATP.

**Actualising tendency** – An innate drive to become the very most and best that we can be: to use our skills, abilities and qualities, both physical and psychological, to the full.

**Affectionless psychopathy** – A serious psychological condition in which the individual shows no conscience and is unable to form intimate relationships with others.

**Afferent arteriole** – The arteriole preceding the glomerulus.

**Allele** – Unit of inheritance derived from one or two parents; an allele can be thought of as half a gene.

**Amino acids** – The nitrogenous end products of protein digestion normally used to build up new structural and physiological body proteins such as enzymes and hormones. However, many Western diets contain too much dietary protein, and after digestion the unwanted amino acids will be broken down by the liver and eliminated by the kidneys.

**Aphasia** – A difficulty in either producing or understanding speech.

**Anally expulsive** – A personality type originating in the anal stage, when the infant rebelliously expels their faeces anywhere. Adults fixated at this stage tend to be messy and creative.

**Anally retentive** – A child in the anal stage who feels pressured by their parents into being potty trained may rebel by 'refusing to go'. This is associated with later personality traits such as obstinacy and miserliness.

**Anions** – Negatively charged ions like chloride and hydroxyl.

**Antidiuretic hormone (ADH)** – A pituitary hormone causing tubular cells to become more permeable to water.

**Assimilation** – The process of adapting to new problems and situations using existing knowledge and schemata to make sense of incoming knowledge and events.

**ATP** – Adenosine triphosphate; a chemical whose role in the cell is to store energy and release it for use when necessary.

**Auto-immune disorder** – A disorder in which an individual produces antibodies that attack specific tissues in the body.

**Autolysis** – Self-destruction of the cell by lysosomes.

## B

**Base** – Chemically a purine or pyrimidine structure such as adenine, guanine, thymine, cytosine and uracil; a substance that accepts hydrogen ions.

**Benevolent oppression** – When well-meaning social carers make decisions on behalf of the individuals in their care, or prevent them from behaving in an apparently risky way, in the interests of their safety.

**Birth rate** – The number of live births per thousand of the population over a given period, normally a year.

**Bowman's capsule** – The cup-shaped beginning of a nephron.

**British Medical Association (BMA)** – This is the professional body for the medical profession. It represents their interests at a national level, e.g. in negotiations with the government over changes in management of the medical profession.

## C

**Care pathway** – A coming together of services to meet an individual's needs.

**Care plan** – The term used to outline and record the care, therapy and/or treatment for an individual carried out by the multi-disciplinary team.

**Carrier molecules** – Molecules that bind to others, facilitating their transport.

**Cations** – Positively charged ions like sodium and hydrogen.

**Census** – A compulsory and detailed count of the population in the UK held every 10 years.

**Centration** – A tendency to focus only on certain key elements of an object, without seeing its other properties (e.g. using height to judge volume).

**Cholesterol** – A type of fatty steroid present in cells.

**Chromatin** – A complex of DNA and protein that forms chromosomes during cell division.

**Chromosomes** – Thread-like structures, composed of DNA and proteins, seen during cell division.

**Clinical diagnosis** – A diagnosis made on the basis of signs and symptoms.

**Codon** – A sequence of bases on mRNA that correspond to a particular amino acid.

**Colostomy** – This is the same as an ileostomy except that the artificial opening is from the colon. The artificial opening is known as a stoma, and faeces are evacuated into a bag attached to a belt or by adhesive.

**Comatose** – Being in a coma, a deeply unconscious state.

**Community development** – Development that is based on a commitment to equality, an emphasis on participation and valuing the experiences and lay knowledge of communities. It also requires empowerment of the community and its individuals through training, skills development and joint action.

**Concentration gradient** – The difference between opposing concentrations.

**Conservation** – The ability to recognise that objects do not change when their appearance changes and that nothing has been added or taken away.

**Consequence** – Something that happens as a direct result of what you do (your behaviour).

**Continuity** – Development that takes place slowly, smoothly and continuously (for example, a growth in height).

**Continuous ambulatory peritoneal dialysis (CAPD)** – A different form of dialysis carried out by running dialysing fluid into the peritoneal cavity of the abdomen for several hours and then running the fluid to waste and replacing with 'clean' dialysate.

**Core conditions** – The essential ingredients/requirements for a person-centred approach.

**Counter-current mechanism** – A process involving active transport of sodium ions from the descending limb of the loop of Henlé to the ascending limb.

**Cristae** – Internal folds or shelves of mitochondria, holding an orderly arrangement of enzymes for ATP production.

**Cyanosis** – Bluish colour of the skin and mucous membranes, indicating poor oxygenation of blood.

**Cytology** – The study of cell structure.

**Cytoplasm** – Also known as cytosol; jelly-like material found between the cell membrane and the nucleus.

# D

**Death rate** – The number of deaths per thousand of the population over a given period, normally a year.

**De-centration** – The ability to move from one classification system to another. For example, an object is no longer judged by its external properties, such as height, but by its internal properties such as mass.

**Depression** – Extreme sadness or melancholy. Reactive depression occurs as a result of illness. Some types of depression have no known cause.

**Diagnosis** – The process by which the nature of the disease or disorder is determined or made known.

**Differential diagnosis** – The recognition of one disease from among a number presenting similar signs and symptoms.

**Diffusion** – The movement of molecules from a region of high concentration to a region of low concentration.

**Disclose** – Reveal information to another person.

**Discontinuity** – Development occurring in discontinuous stages. Each stage is qualitatively different from the preceding and following stage.

**Discriminate** – Distinguish between people on the basis of class or background without regard to individual merit. Examples include social, racial, religious, sexual, disability, ethnic, and age-related discrimination.

**Discrimination** – Treating a person differently (usually less favourably) because of particular personal characteristics, such as their age, race, colour or gender.

**Discriminatory** – Denying one individual or a group the same rights as another individual or group.

**Dissociate** – To split into ions.

**Diverse** – Differing.

**DNA** – Short for deoxyribonucleic acid, which is responsible for transmitting inherited characteristics.

**Dream analysis** – A method of looking at dreams in order to understand the contents of the unconscious mind.

# E

**Echoic** – A sound uttered by the child in imitation of a sound that they have heard (a bit like an echo).

**Efferent arteriole** – The arteriole leaving the glomerulus.

**Ego** – The part of the psyche that attempts to mediate between the id's demands for instant gratification and the superego's for restraint. The ego operates on the reality principle and tries to steer a course that will keep the person on an even keel.

**Egocentrism** – An inability, both literally and metaphorically, to imagine that anyone has a viewpoint which is different from their own.

**Electroencephalogram (EEG)** – This is a tracing of the electrical activity of the brain. An abnormal rhythm may be found in epilepsy, dementia (Parkinson's disease) and brain tumours.

**Emigration** – The movement of people from their home country to make a permanent residence in a different country.

**Empathy** – Trying to understand things from another person's viewpoint.

**Empowerment** – Enabling individuals to take responsibility for their own lives by making informed decisions. The power to make decisions is transferred from influential sectors to communities and individuals who have traditionally been excluded from this process.

**Endocytosis** – Transport of materials from outside a cell to the inside of the cell.

**Epidemiology** – The study of diseases in human populations.

**Equality of opportunity** – A situation where everybody has the same chance of achieving and acquiring the way of life valued in a society.

**Equilibrium** – The state of having no net movement of molecules because the concentrations have evened up.

**Erythropoietin** – A hormone produced by the kidneys, which stimulates the production of red blood cells.

**Ethical principles** – Guidelines for appropriate behaviour, focusing on actions, attitudes and values. The health and social carer professional must always behave in an antidiscriminatory and anti-biased way.

**Euphoria** – An inflated sense of well-being when circumstances do not warrant it.

**Evaluation** – A judgement of the worth of something.

**Exocytosis** – The reverse of endocytosis, i.e. transporting materials from inside the cell to the outside.

**Exploitation** – Taking advantage of someone for your own selfish purposes.

**Extinguish** – To cause a reduction in a type of behaviour by no longer providing reinforcement.

# F

**Facilitated diffusion** – Diffusion down a concentration gradient that is dependent on energy-using carrier molecules or channel membranes.

**Fistula** – An artificial connection made between an artery and a vein for attachment to a kidney machine.

**Free association** – A method used during the process of psychoanalysis to gain access to the unconscious. The patient is encouraged to say the first thing that comes into their mind, the assumption being that this reflects unconscious as opposed to conscious feelings, wishes and desires.

# G

**Glomerulus** – The tuft of capillaries located within the Bowman's capsule.

**Glycerol** – A sugary alcohol.

**Glycolipid** – Phospholipid with a sugar chain attached.

**Glycoprotein** – Cell protein with a sugar chain attached.

**Golgi body** – A series or pile of flattened membranes that lie close to the nucleus.

**Guidance** – Giving direction; indicating how something should be done.

# H

**Haemodialysis** – The removal of metabolic waste products from the blood via a kidney machine because the kidneys are seriously damaged.

**Health centre** – A multi-agency community-based facility where teams of health professionals work together. They are often purpose-built. Teams consist of GPs, nurses, midwives, counsellors, community nurses, speech and occupational therapists and sometimes dentists.

**Health Development Agency (HDA)** – A national health agency set up in 2000 to provide information about what works in terms of health promotion activity. This in turn supports evidence-based practice in health promotion. Its role has subsequently been taken up by NICE.

**Health education** – An aspect of health promotion that largely relates to educating people about good health and how to develop and support it.

**Health protection** – The measures taken to safeguard a population's health, e.g. through legislation, financial or social means. This might include laws governing health and safety at work, or food hygiene, and using taxation policy to reduce smoking levels by raising the price of cigarettes.

**Health Protection Agency (HPA)** – An independent organisation dedicated to protecting people's health in the UK.

**Holistic health** – An all-encompassing view of health that includes, physical, mental, emotional, spiritual, social and environmental aspects of health.

**Homeostasis** – Maintaining a constant internal environment around cells.

**Humanistic approach** – This focuses on treating people with dignity, respect and as unique individuals with individual needs.

**Hydrophilic** – Having an affinity for water.

**Hydrophobic** – Lacking an affinity for water.

# I

**Id** – The part of the psyche that is determined to get its own way. It contains all the drives without knowing any bounds – aggression, sexuality, happiness.

**Ideal self** – An internal view of ourselves as we would like ourselves to (and often believe we should) be. Our ideal self is a standard against which we judge ourselves.

**Idiographic** – An approach that investigates the full richness of experience of just one individual.

**Ileostomy** – An artificial opening from the ileum to the abdominal wall to evacuate faeces and bypass the large intestine.

**Immigration** – The arrival in a country of people who have left their home country and who wish to make the new country their permanent place of residence.

**Immuno-suppressant** – Specific types of medication to suppress or reduce the immune response. Given to prevent rejection.

**Incidence** – The rate of a disease at a given point in time.

**Infant mortality rate** – The number of deaths of babies under the age of one year, per thousand live births over a given period, normally a year.

**Internal environment** – This is the physical and chemical composition of blood and tissue fluid that surrounds body cells.

**Ionisation** – The process of forming ions.

**Irrational thoughts** – Thoughts that have no real basis in fact, or which do not accurately reflect reality.

# K

**Kinetic energy** – The energy of motion.

# L

**Labelling** – A term closely linked with stereotyping, where the stereotypical characteristics are applied to a person and their individuality is ignored.

**Language acquisition device (also called LAD)** – Chomsky believed this to be an innate system that prepares us to develop language. The device is thought to be located somewhere within the brain.

**Latent content** – The underlying meaning (usually symbolic) of a dream. This needs to be interpreted in order to understand its meaning.

**Latent learning** – This refers to a situation where a new behaviour has been learned via observational learning but has not yet been (and may never be) performed.

**Law** – A rule that has been established by an authority, e.g. Parliament, Assembly or a Local Authority.

**Legislation** – A term used for a set or group of laws.

**Life chance** – The opportunity to achieve and acquire the way of life and the possessions that are highly valued in a society.

**Life expectancy** – A statistical calculation that predicts the average number of years a person is likely to live. This is usually based on the year of birth but can be calculated from any age.

**Lumpectomy** – An operation to remove a suspect lump, which is then sent for microscopic examination.

**Lysosomes** – Membranous vesicles filled with digestive enzymes.

# M

**Malnourishment** – The result of receiving inadequate nutrition.

**Maltreatment** – Ill-treatment or abuse; when a child's rights are compromised and they are not cared for fairly.

**Mand** – A verbal or non-verbal command that is regularly reinforced with a predictable consequence. For example, when a child gestures to a parent with their arms open, they are reinforced by the parent picking them up.

**Manifest content** – The actual narrative (or story) of a dream.

**Marginalise** – Make individuals or groups of people feel 'out on the edge' of a society and excluded from the way of life and the status enjoyed by others.

**Maternal deprivation hypothesis** – A belief that deprivation results from long periods of separation or many short periods of separation from the mother, particularly in the early years of life. Bowlby believed this would inevitably lead to damage to later personality.

**Maturation** – The biological changes that take place as the child develops. Intellectual growth and development cannot move forward until this maturational process reaches a point where the child is ready to move to the next stage.

**Membrane potential** – The potential difference across a cell membrane caused by different ions.

**Meritocracy** – A society where social position is achieved by ability, skill and effort rather than ascribed at birth. High achievements are open to all.

**MMR vaccine** – A vaccination against measles, mumps and rubella.

**Morality** – Refers to social conventions about the right and wrong behaviour expected of each individual. These rules are linked to the moral values of society.

**Morbidity** – This refers to the number of people who have a particular illness during a given period, normally a year.

**Mortality** – Deaths due to a particular condition.

**Motivation** – This is the key factor that determines whether someone will put what they have learned into practice. Motivation is strongly governed by the individual's own emotions, thoughts, wishes, beliefs, values, etc.

**mRNA** – Messenger RNA; carries the code for the synthesis of a protein and acts as a template for its formation.

**Multiculturalism** – The celebration of the culture of all people living in the home country.

**Multi-disciplinary** – Describes teams, care plans, etc; indicates that different care professionals from different fields are working together.

**Multi-disciplinary team** – A team of professionals drawn from a range of disciplines or services, e.g. health care, education and social services, all working together towards a common goal.

**Multiple deprivation** – A situation where many factors linked with poverty and deprivation come together (e.g. long-term unemployment, poor housing, pollution, low income and poor health).

**Muscle wasting** – Observable diminishing muscle mass.

# N

**National Institute for Health and Clinical Excellence (NICE)** – The independent organisation responsible for providing national guidance on the promotion of good health and the prevention and treatment of ill health.

**National minimum standards** – The minimum level and quality of care that people should expect to receive, regardless of where they are in the country.

**National Statistics Office (NSO)** – The national body that compiles information on the UK population and which is responsible for carrying out the census every 10 years.

**Nature** – All aspects of a person that involves genetic inheritance.

**Needle biopsy** – This is when a fine needle is inserted into a lump or organ to remove material for microscopic examination. Needles may have cutting tips to remove small sections of tissue or have a hollow stem for removing fluid (containing cells). The material is prepared for microscopic examination. The search is for abnormal cells that might be enlarged, peculiarly shaped or have actively dividing nuclei.

**Negative thoughts** – Thoughts that are self-critical.

**Neglect** – When a child does not have what they need to function effectively. They may be deprived of security, safety, shelter, warmth, food, love, care or attention.

**Net migration** – The difference between the number of immigrants and the number of emigrants in a country over a given period, normally a year.

**Nomothetic** – An approach that seeks to find out what traits and behaviours a group of individuals share.

**Nonmaleficence** – To 'do no harm'.

**Nuclear pore** – A gap in the nuclear membrane.

**Nucleoli** – Dark spots inside the nucleus, probably the site of ribosome synthesis.

**Nucleoplasm** – Soft, featureless material contained in the nucleus.

**Nucleotide** – Structural unit of DNA and RNA, consisting of a base, sugar and phosphate grouping.

**Nucleus** – Membrane-surrounded organelle, containing genetic material.

**Nurture** – Aspects of a person that result from socialisation, parenting and other environmental factors.

# O

**Obesity** – When a person is carrying too much body fat for their height and sex. In the UK, people with a body mass index (see page 126) above 30 are categorised as obese.

**Object permanence** – Awareness that an object continues to exist even if it can no longer be seen.

**Observational learning** – A type of learning where we do not experience a consequence directly, but learn from watching others perform a behaviour and noting the consequences they receive.

**Oedema** – The accumulation of tissue fluid around the body cells.

**Omission** – Leaving something out or failing to do something.

**Osmoreceptors** – Modified neurones sensitive to the osmotic pressure of blood.

**Osmosis** – The movement of water molecules from a region of high concentration to a region of low concentration (of water molecules) through a selectively permeable membrane.

**Osmotic potential** – The power of a solution to gain or lose water molecules through a membrane.

**Osmotic pressure** – The pressure exerted by large molecules to draw water to them. Plasma proteins in blood plasma have an osmotic pressure needed to return tissue fluid.

# P

**Pain threshold** – The level at which the agony becomes unbearable. Individuals have different pain thresholds and the levels can be affected by past experiences of pain.

**Paramountcy principle** – The Children Act 1989 states that 'the welfare of the child is paramount', meaning that it is of supreme importance or vital. All agencies focus on this point at all times.

**Participation** – A process through which stakeholders influence and share control over development initiatives and the decisions and resources that affect them.

**Passive** – Not playing an active part; not reacting.

**Peptide bond** – A chemical bond formed between the amine and carboxyl groups of two amino acids by the removal of the elements of water.

**Perinatal mortality rate** – The number of deaths of babies who die during their first week of life per thousand live births over a given period, normally a year.

**Phagocytosis** – The engulfing and destruction of cell debris and foreign bodies by mobile cells which produce arm-like extensions to surround the material.

**Phoneme** – A unit of sound used within a language.

**Phospholipid** – A molecule consisting of glycerol, phosphate and lipid chains.

**Pinocytosis** – A process similar to phagocytosis but involving pinching off a vesicle filled with tissue fluid to take into the cell.

**Pleasure principle** – A drive towards self-gratification. It has to be kept in check by the ego and superego.

**Pneumoconiosis** – Industrial disease caused by inhaling dust particles over a period of time.

**Polar** – Carrying an electric charge, positive or negative.

**Positive reinforcement** – A response to behaviour that is experienced as wanted (it may, for example, be desired or pleasurable). It increases the likelihood of the behaviour being performed again.

**Poverty line** – A term introduced by Seebohm Rowntree and still used by policy makers to refer to the level of income necessary to keep people out of poverty.

**Prejudice** – A fixed set of attitudes or beliefs about particular groups in society that is not based on reason or actual experience. People are normally unwilling, unable and often uninterested in changing these set attitudes/beliefs.

**Prelinguistic** – Meaning, literally, 'before language', this refers to all types of communication used before language takes over. It includes things like pointing and turn-taking.

**Principles** – Based on values, principles are basic guidelines about the right way to behave, i.e. your own personal code of conduct. For example, you treat people with respect because you believe that is the right thing to do.

**Privation** – This occurs when a child forms no bond at all with a care-giver. Children in orphanages where there is a very low staff-to-child ratio have been found to suffer from privation.

**Procedure** – A way of going about something; to act in a certain defined manner; to follow guidelines.

**Professional code of practice** – A set of guidelines and regulations, which explain the way members of a profession have to behave.

**Provision** – What is provided or put in place for the benefit and support of an individual. This may include specially built or adapted buildings, trained staff or specialist equipment that will assist individuals with a range of diverse conditions and situations.

**Proximity** – A state of being close. In terms of attachment, proximity is very important to give the infant a sense of security. When proximity is broken, and the infant is further away from their care-giver than they are able to bear, they will show signs of acute distress.

**Punishment** – A response to behaviour that is experienced as unwanted and therefore reduces the likelihood that the behaviour will be performed again.

# R

**Racism** – Discrimination against a person on the basis of their race background, usually based on the belief that some races are inherently superior to others.

**Reality principle** – An awareness of what is socially acceptable and necessary for the individual to negotiate safely through life. This is the prime function of the ego.

**Referral** – Handing over to another professional (usually a specialist) or type of service such as physiotherapy.

**Reflexes** – These are automatic responses to stimuli. The patellar or knee-jerk reflex is a common reflex that doctors use as a test. It enables doctors to determine whether there is damage to the nervous pathway and also whether the speed of nervous impulses has been increased or decreased.

**Reinforcer** – Something that acts to reinforce (strengthen) behaviour. In the case of positive reinforcement this could be something tangible like payment or a sweet, or intangible such as a smile or praise.

**Relative poverty** – A level of income that deprives a person of the standard of living or way of life considered normal in a particular society.

**Remanded** – To be kept separate from society for a period of time in a young offenders' institution or a prison.

**Renin** – An enzyme released from the kidneys when blood pressure is low. It causes blood pressure to rise.

**Resolution** – The capability of making individual parts or closely adjacent images distinguishable. (In the absence of good resolution, stronger lenses make images blurred.)

**Respite** – A break or a time of relief from the demands of care.

**Reversibility** – An ability to represent mentally something that has just happened and to perform logical processes on the action. For example, to know that if water is poured into a new beaker, it can also be poured back (reversed) and will stay the same, regardless of physical appearance.

**Ribosome** – A tiny cell organelle responsible for protein synthesis.

**Rights** – Things that everyone is entitled to receive. These are usually explained in legislation.

**RNA** – Short for ribonucleic acid, associated with controlling the chemical activities within the cell.

**Rough ER** – Endoplasmic reticulum studded with ribosomes.

**rRNA** – Ribosomal RNA; the type of RNA found in the ribosomes.

# S

**Salt** – A substance produced by the action of an acid and a base.

**Schema** – A mental short cut used to understand physical and mental objects, thoughts, situations and events in the world. Each schema is built upon prior experience. For example, an interview schema contains information about how to behave at interview, and what to wear.

**Screening** – Identifying a disease or defect in an individual by means of tests, examinations and other procedures that can be rapidly applied. Screening identifies apparently well people who may have an underlying disease.

**Secondary poverty** – A term also used by Seebohm Rowntree, referring to a situation where people had sufficient money but were in poverty because they spent it on nonessential items.

**Selectively permeable membrane** – A membrane such as the phospholipid bilayer, which allows some molecules to pass through by osmosis but not others.

**Selective reabsorption** – The process whereby some materials are reabsorbed back into the capillary network around the tubules but not others.

**Self-actualisation** – The achievement of the actualising tendency. People who have achieved self-actualisation include Albert Einstein.

**Self-efficacy** – A judgement we make on ourselves in terms of our ability to master events in the environment. It is based on past experience and can generalise to our expectations of success or failure in new situations. It can be positive or negative.

**Separation anxiety** – The infant shows acute distress when separated from their main attachment figure.

**Sign** – An objective indication of a disorder noticed by a doctor (or nurse).

**Single assessment** – The assessment of an individual's needs is carried out by one professional/co-ordinator on behalf of a multi-disciplinary/agency team.

**Smooth ER** – Endoplasmic reticulum without ribosomes.

**Social class** – Social hierarchies in most modern industrialised societies, largely based on economic factors linked with income, the ownership of property and other forms of wealth.

**Social exclusion** – The situation for people who suffer from a combination of linked problems such as unemployment, poor housing, high crime rates and poor health.

**Social marketing** – The systematic application of marketing techniques and concepts to achieve specific behavioural goals with the aim of improving health and reducing health inequalities.

**Socialisation** – The way in which an individual learns to conform to the accepted standards of behaviour within the culture/society in which they live. There are two forms of socialisation – primary and secondary. The primary process occurs when a child is influenced by primary carers' values attitudes and beliefs. The secondary process involves the way in which education, media, religion and legislation reinforce accepted modes of behaviour.

**Social releasers** – These are things an infant does that cause others to react instinctively with care-giving behaviours such as feeding, soothing and even conversing with the baby.

**Strategy** – A long-term plan; a way of working.

**Stereotype** – To make assumptions (often negative) about certain groups of people, attributing the same characteristics to every individual in a particular group.

**Stereotyping** – Defining a group of people (e.g. women) as if they all share the same characteristics and ignoring their individual differences.

**Stranger anxiety** – The infant is unhappy with people they are unfamiliar with.

**Strong acid** – An acid that greatly dissociates.

**Submissive** – Doing what others want; being unusually compliant.

**Superego** – The part of the psyche that develops last (at about three to five years of age). It is composed of all the morals and requirements of socialisation. Resembling a conscience, the superego is the part of the psyche that governs reason and restraint.

**Support planning** – The joint planning of an individual's treatment and/or care that involves all concerned.

**Symptom** – A feature complained of by the individual or patient.

# T

**Tact response** – Reinforcement of a child when they recognise that a word (the tact) is being used to name a given object.

**Tissue-typing** – Identifying the protein markers on cell membranes to determine compatibility for transplantation.

**Transcription** – The process of forming mRNA from a template of DNA.

**Translation** – The process of forming a protein molecule in the ribosomes from an mRNA template.

**tRNA** – A small molecule of RNA, which carries amino acids to the ribosome to be made into protein.

# U

**Ultrafiltration** – The process driving a protein-free filtrate from plasma from the glomerulus.

**Urea** – A nitrogenous substance resulting from the liver breaking down excess amino acids from the digestion of proteins. Nitrogenous material not required for metabolism cannot be stored in the body. If allowed to accumulate, urea is toxic to body tissues and can result in death.

# V

**Values** – Beliefs about what is important to you as an individual, and what you believe about what is morally right and wrong. Values are usually learned from your parents/carers and tend to change throughout your life.

**Vesicles** – These can also be called cysts, vacuoles, etc, which usually mean fluid-filled sacs or pouches.

**Victim blaming** – People frequently simplify health choices by blaming the person who chooses to adopt an unhealthy behaviour for making that choice. In reality things are rarely that simple. For example, people say lack of time, due to work pressures, is the major reason why they don't take enough exercise.

**Voluntary sector** – Agencies that obtain their funding from charitable giving, specific funding from public sector organisations such as PCTs or through the National Lottery.

# W

**Weak acid** – An acid that does not dissociate very much.

**Wish fulfilment** – The idea that dreams express unconsciously the things we most desire.

**World Health Organization (WHO)** – Established on 7 April 1948, in response to an international desire for a world free from disease. Since then, 7 April has been celebrated each year as World Health Day.

# Index